RELIGION, THEOLOGY AND THE HUMAN SCIENCES

Religion, Theology and the Human Sciences explores the religious consequences of the so-called 'End of History' and 'triumph of capitalism' as they have impinged upon key institutions of social reproduction in recent times. The book explores the imposition of managerial modernity upon successive sectors of society and shows why many people today feel themselves to be oppressed by systems of management that seem to leave them no option but to conform. This culture has spread through education, health and social services and has been welcomed by the churches. Richard Roberts seeks to challenge and outflank such seamless, oppressive modernity through reconfiguration of the religious and spiritual field.

This volume will be of use to a range of students in the humanities and social sciences (particularly theology and the sociology of religion) and should become standard reading for those concerned with the practical application of contemporary theology in a postmodern world.

RICHARD H. ROBERTS is Professor of Religious Studies at Lancaster University. He has not shrunk from controversy and is known among senior British academic figures for his pursuit of a consistently critical line against the managerialisation and bureaucratisation of both universities and churches. His publications include *Hope and its Hieroglyph: A Critical Decipherment of Ernst Bloch's 'Principle of Hope'* (1990), *A Theology on its Way?: Essays on Karl Barth* (1992), *The Recovery of Rhetoric: Persuasive Discourse and Disciplinarity in the Human Sciences* (co-edited with J. M. M. Good, 1993), *Religion and the Transformations of Capitalism: Comparative Approaches* (editor, 1995), *Nature Religion Today: Paganism in the Modern World* (co-edited with Joanne Pearson and Geoffrey Samuel, 1998) and *Time and Value* (co-edited with Scott Lash and Andrew Quick, 1998).

RELIGION, THEOLOGY AND THE HUMAN SCIENCES

RICHARD H. ROBERTS

Lancaster University

CAMBRIDGE
UNIVERSITY PRESS

PUBLISHED BY THE PRESS SYNDICATE OF THE UNIVERSITY OF CAMBRIDGE
The Pitt Building, Trumpington Street, Cambridge, United Kingdom

CAMBRIDGE UNIVERSITY PRESS
The Edinburgh Building, Cambridge CB2 2RU, UK
40 West 20th Street, New York, NY 10011-4211, USA
477 Williamstown Road, Port Melbourne, VIC 3207, Australia
Ruiz de Alarcón 13, 28014 Madrid, Spain
Dock House, The Waterfront, Cape Town 8001, South Africa

http://www.cambridge.org

First published 2002

Printed in the United Kingdom at the University Press, Cambridge

Typeface Baskerville Monotype 11 /12.5 pt.   *System* LaTeX 2ε   [TB]

A catalogue record for this book is available from the British Library

Library of Congress cataloguing in publication data
Roberts, Richard H., 1946–
Religion, theology, and the human sciences / Richard H. Roberts.
p.   cm.
Includes bibliographical references and indexes.
ISBN 0 521 79151 0 (hardback) – ISBN 0 521 79508 7 (paperback)
1. Religion and sociology – History – 20th century.   2. Management – Religious aspects –
History – 20th century.   3. Capitalism – Religious aspects – History – 20th century.   4. Religion
and sociology – Great Britain – History – 20th century.   5. Management – Social aspects – Great
Britain – History – 20th century.   6. Capitalism – Social aspects – Great Britain – History –
20th century.   I. Title.
BL60.R585 2001
291.1'75 – dc21   2001025948

ISBN 0 521 79151 0 hardback
ISBN 0 521 79508 7 paperback

For Audrey and Anthony,
with heartfelt thanks and love

Contents

Preface

The essays brought together in this collection originate from the period 1989–99, a decade marked at its outset by the momentous events of 1989–90 when Marxist socialist societies collapsed and the Berlin Wall was breached, accompanied by the proclamation of the much-vaunted 'End of History', which then turned out to be a chaotic and unpredictable 'New World Order' characterised both by much disorder and by the banality of globalisation. Until the summer of 1989 I had been a lecturer in theology at the University of Durham, but I became M. B. Reckitt Research Fellow at Lancaster University in the autumn of that year and embarked upon the project Religion and the Resurgence of Capitalism, a move which rerooted me in the interdisciplinary ambience of religious studies. This new location also allowed me to begin to respond to social and cultural change in what I would regard, in the final analysis, as a form of contextual theology. In 1991, I moved again, this time to the Chair of Divinity at the University of St Andrews.

As it happened, and as is critically outlined in chapter 4 of this book, the beginning of the decade 1989–99 also marked the onset of the greatest revolution in the history of British university education. A whole life-world in which theological, religious, gender and intellectual identities co-inhered in a setting supported by a liberal, critical, individualistic ethos (that had been relatively generously funded during the Keynesian expansion of the Robbins era) was to end, and to be replaced by an industrialised model of mass-production higher education. Having set out to become an individual agent of the critical and reflexive transmission of theological and intellectual traditions, and with the personal goal of helping to create within students a similar relative autonomy, I began to find myself an isolated dissident at odds with a new social reality. This process of 'reform' began under the then Prime Minister, Mrs Margaret Thatcher, and later continued as 'modernisation', or more accurately 'managerialism', under the New Labour government of Mr Tony Blair.

These non-consensual changes encountered the acquiescence and the active (albeit reluctant) cooperation of the overwhelming majority of British academic staff. They accepted the reconstitution of their existence and identity along Neo-Fordist lines without serious questioning or resistance. Readers of this book will soon realise that I regard this as a fundamental *trahison des clercs* for reasons made abundantly clear in what follows.

During four years as Professor of Divinity at the University of St Andrews from 1991 to 1995 I encountered at first hand some of the most acute tensions in contemporary educational, cultural and political life in their distinctively Scottish context and found myself in a senior academic position at odds with the policies of 'reform' then enacted. I returned to Lancaster University in the late summer of 1995, just in time to witness once again the slow, inexorable process of managerial 'normalisation' taking place. The mass higher education regime envisaged in the Dearing Report was imposed upon a university that had until then preserved its own distinctive practice more successfully than most such organisations. From 1995 onwards I concentrated upon trying to probe the roots of global issues in relation to which, I believe, the religious and spiritual 'capital' of humankind still has a critical and creative role to play. Whilst the essays collected in this volume are driven by a growing awareness of systemic crisis on many levels, the contents are so organised as to provide a coherent pattern of concerns.

As a continuing student of the traditions I have taught for twenty-five years, I do not regard the sense of crisis that pervades this book as merely the product of the personal aberration of an individual. In it, I provide a focused account of key religious aspects of processes in the managerialisation of a de-traditionalised society existing under the conditions of advanced modernity. As such, this collection is certainly transitional, but I have done my utmost to develop a narrative in which critique is balanced with a sense of hope. There is, I believe, the possibility of developing a new paradigm for the committed study of religion(s) and spiritualities that recognises and facilitates their emancipatory potential in a post-traditional world. Whether, however, this paradigm can be adequately exemplified, never mind fully realised, within the present systems of human production in either universities or areas of mainstream religion where most operatives have ceded their cultural agency, relative autonomy and ethical responsibility remains an outstanding question. Effective commitment to truth-seeking in higher education requires the recognition that the form of knowledge production and the content of knowledge cannot be divorced without damaging consequences, and that to enforce pre-determined human outcomes in the 'delivery' of the human and social sciences is to reduce real education to mere training. Given present conditions, I believe that the future survival of fundamental truth-seeking, the production of knowledge and genuinely 'owned' university teaching, together understood as part and parcel of the total way of life, may well only be assured through cultural migration, and the creation of new, subversive and marginal institutional embodiments.

Acknowledgements

At the outset, I wish to express my thanks to many friends and colleagues. First of all, the social psychologist James Good, the late and inimitable Irving Velody and others who were much-valued friends and co-conspirators in the Group (later the Centre) for the History of the Human Sciences, which provided a forum for critical interdisciplinary discussion in the University of Durham in the 1980s. I am indebted to the sociologist James Beckford, who was my intellectual mentor in Durham as I worked my way deeper into the socio-scientific study of religion. I acknowledge with grateful thanks his long-standing encouragement and positive criticism, as I do the stimulation and support of my friend and former colleague at Lancaster, the anthropologist Geoffrey Samuel.

Second, I should like to register my gratitude to the Christendom Trust, which funded the M. B. Reckitt Research Fellowship that I held in the Department of Religious Studies at Lancaster University from 1989 to 1991. Many discussions with colleagues at Lancaster in the course of the project Religion and the Resurgence of Capitalism made this a very fruitful experience. Particular thanks are due to John Clayton, Sarah Coakley, Adrian Cunningham, Angela Cunningham, Paul Heelas, John Milbank and Paul Morris, who all contributed in different ways to academic conviviality of a high order. In recent years Deborah Sawyer has been a stalwart and supportive Head of Department.

During the period 1989–99 my friends and colleagues Julia Davies and Jonathan Gosling of the Lancaster University Management School granted me *entrée* to the fascinating and sometimes rather surprising world of management training, where I have been able to engage in both teaching and action research on two key programmes, the M.Phil. in Critical Management and the International Masters in Practising Management (IMPM). My warm thanks are due to them both.

Since the conference Nature Religion Today held at Ambleside in 1996, I have enjoyed a growing involvement with environmental activists and have been drawn into an ever deeper questioning of both ancestral Western Latin theology and social constructionism of late modernity, and then impelled into the area denoted by the term 'human ecology'. In making this transition, my friend the ecologist and activist Alastair McIntosh has provided relentless creative provocation, as have other friends and colleagues in the Centre for Human Ecology, Edinburgh. We have discovered much common ground and found mutual encouragement in the realisation that the creative loci of critical thought are often enough being driven out of the institutional academy into the margins, the true 'borderlands' of our time.

My thanks are also due to Brendan Hill and Kathleen Sullivan, who, with members of the Findhorn Foundation and Deep Ecology UK, planned and facilitated the international conference For the Love of Nature?, which took place in May/June 1999. Participation in this event and then later in the conference Forgiveness, also held at Findhorn in October 1999, proved to be very important events for me. I continue, with Phyllida Anamaire and David Burbidge, work begun with Robert Greenway and John Seed: my heartfelt thanks are due to them all.

I am indebted to outstanding students at St Mary's College, University of St Andrews, among them Philip Pascalides, James Taylor, Victoria Taylor and Darren Zamora (there were many others), who, both during and after my time as holder of the Chair of Divinity, remained loyal to the ideals and practice of what I would venture to call 'real' university education. Patricia Esler, Philip Esler, Miss Susan Millar and Mrs Vera Prunty have been significant friends and colleagues in St Andrews: thank you once more. My research students (past and present) at Lancaster, Sana Mmolai, Joanne Pearson, Alexandra Ryan and Bülent Senay are amongst those whose presence has made my time at Lancaster rich and fruitful. I thank them all. The same thanks are also due to Lynsey Foster of the Department of Philosophy at Lancaster University, who undertook some vital and careful work in transcribing texts into word-processed format.

The preparation of this book has been ably supported by Kevin Taylor, my editor at the Cambridge University Press. Thanks and acknowledgement are also due to four anonymous readers who provided rigorous and helpful reports to which I have done my utmost to respond, and to Pauline Marsh for her careful copy-editing.

I am grateful for permission to republish all or parts of the following papers and chapters: to Blackwells Publishers for 'Theology and Social Science', in David Ford (ed.), *The Modern Theologians* (Oxford:

Blackwell, 1996), pp. 700–19; 'The Construals of "Europe": Religion, Theology and the Problematics of Modernity', in Paul Heelas (ed.), *Religion and Modernity* (Oxford: Blackwell, 1998), pp. 186–217; and 'Time, Virtuality and the Goddess', in Scott Lash, Andrew Quick and Richard Roberts (eds.), *Time and Value* (Oxford: Blackwell, 1998), pp. 112–29; Sage Publishers for 'Religion and the "Enterprise Culture": The British Experience in the Thatcher Era (1979–1990)', *Social Compass*, 39/1 (1992), pp. 15–33; Scottish Academic Press for 'Transcendental Sociology? – Review Article of A. J. Milbank's *Theology and Social Theory*', *Scottish Journal of Theology*, 46/4 (1993), 527–35; Edinburgh University Press for 'The Chthonic Imperative: Gender, Religion and the Battle for the Earth', in Joanne Pearson, Richard H. Roberts and Geoffrey Samuel (eds.), *Nature Religion Today: Paganism in the Modern World* (Edinburgh: Edinburgh University Press, 1998), pp. 57–73; Routledge Publications for 'Power and Empowerment: New Age Managers and the Dialectics of Modernity/Postmodernity', in R. H. Roberts (ed.), *Religion and the Transformations of Capitalism: Comparative Approaches* (London: Routledge, 1995), pp. 180–98; T. & T. Clark for 'Lord, Bondsman and Churchman: Integrity, Identity and Power in Anglicanism', in C. E. Gunton and D. E. Hardy (eds.), *On Being the Church* (Edinburgh: T. & T. Clark, 1989), pp. 156–224 and 'A Postmodern Church: Some Reflections on Ecclesiology and Social Theory', in D. F. Ford and D. L. Stamps (eds.), *Essentials of Christian Community* (Edinburgh: T. & T. Clark, 1996), pp. 179–95; Taylor & Francis for 'Globalized Religion? The Parliament of the World's Religions (Chicago, 1993) in Theoretical Perspective', *Journal of Contemporary Religion*, 10 (1995), 121–37.

Introduction

During the final decade of the twentieth century, I was able to make a series of contributions to what has now become a developing dialogue between the study of theology and the practice of religious studies on the one hand, and the social and human sciences (*les sciences humaines/ die Geisteswissenschaften*) on the other.[1] This book draws together widely distributed papers in journals and chapters in books which were associated with that continuing dialogue. Taken as a whole, what follows embodies a journey of religious, theological and intellectual exploration of the cultural impact of the 'triumph of capitalism', and then an engagement with the shifts in consciousness and changes in cultural practice associated with globalisation, the contested matrix of the modern/postmodern condition, and the ongoing crisis and dissolution of main-line religious traditions which were all characteristic concerns of religious reflection in the late twentieth century. *Religion, Theology and the Human Sciences* affords a wide-ranging interdisciplinary commentary upon aspects of the past decade, and it looks into a future in which religion(s), spiritualities and a migrating 'sacred' may well continue to undergo transmutation and recomposition.

This book seeks an inner coherence that flows, not least, out of the author's continuing quest to locate, investigate and critique the legitimacy of roles for religion and theology in the creation and sustenance of sustainable human identities – and the 'future of the human' – in a globalised, commodified and managerialised late modern world. Beyond such a basic interlinkage, the contents are arranged so as to enhance and justify the sense that there is an underlying logic that informs what might seem, at first sight, to be the extended chaos of fragmentation of the postmodern – and increasingly post-human – condition. Whilst such

[1] See introduction to R. H. Roberts and J. M. M. Good (eds.), *The Recovery of Rhetoric: Persuasive Discourse and Disciplinarity in the Human Sciences* (Charlottesville, VA: University of Virginia Press, 1993).

developments may seem to be haphazard networks, a rhizomic pattern lacking any obvious rational ordering or hierarchy, it is nonetheless possible through the combination of narrative diachronicity and the fullest possible conspectus of interdisciplinary synchronic analysis to discern the invasive patterns that both threaten – and seduce – humankind. On reflection, what has driven me forward is a quest to locate the transcendental conditions of what it is to be, and to become, fully human.

Thus understood, *Religion, Theology and the Human Sciences* traces a path from the immediate post-Second World War reassertion of comprehensive 'metanarratives' to be found in both systematic theology and in sociological 'grand theory', respectively, through their dissolution as aspects of what Daniel Bell called the end of the 'age of ideology', and into a new and fragmented era of reflexive postmodernisation. The latter 'condition' is characterised by an apparent loss of shared human universals, the proliferation of 'culture wars' and confrontation with the 'ends' of 'history', 'nature' and 'the human'. In such an overall setting, where the threat of chaos is normative, religion, quasi-religion and ambiguous new religiosities have gained an increased yet undoubtedly problematic social and cultural salience. Critical exploration of this zone of intermediacy is the central concern of this collection.

The contents of this collection are organised under three major headings. First, in part 1, 'Spirits of capitalism and the commodification of the soul', the collapse of Marxist socialism and the so-called 'End of History' are examined in relation to processes of near unrestrained expansion of invasive commodification and the global proliferation of managerialism that together generate new 'spirits' of triumphant capitalism, and threaten and stultify humankind. In part 2, 'Theology and power in the matrix of modernity/postmodernity', the impact of the managerial revolution from above imposed by resurgent capitalism upon theology, church polity and governance is reviewed in terms of categories drawn from Hegel's ambiguous conception of power, the modernity/postmodernity debate, and the contemporary fragmentation under postmodernising conditions of much 'grand theory' in the human and social sciences. This part concludes with a consideration of the internal responses of Christian theology to emergent social science. In part 3, 'Religion and social science: identity, globalisation, and the transmutations of the religious field', three distinct themes – the identity of 'Europe'; religion and globalisation; and the contemporary transmutations of the religious field – are explored as instances that will require the restructuring of relationships between theology and the study of religion on the one hand, and the social and human sciences on the other. In part 4, 'Conclusion', the first three parts of the book are drawn together in the last chapter, 'Identity as vocation: the prospect for religion'.

In the remainder of this introduction the contents are developed more fully with a view to giving emphasis to the integrative themes that embody the decline and renewal of paradigms. The title of part 1, 'Spirits of Capitalism and the Commodification of the Soul', reflects the interface of declining traditions, both Christian and Marxist, with a modernity driven by economic forces now seemingly freed from any fundamental critique. In the first chapter Francis Fukuyama's forceful promulgation of the idea of the 'End of History' is taken up and represented, despite its contentious character and acknowledged weaknesses, as a bid to create an ideology of global management fit for a new world order in which both religion and socialism have been superseded. Fukuyama's assertion that capitalist liberal democracy constitutes the ultimate political system, beyond which there is no conceivable alternative capable of providing such a broad range of benefits, both economic and societal, contains within it the implication that social evolution has reached its terminus. Thus all that is now required is the regularisation, the 'normalisation' of the world in ways which incorporate and express this finality. However ill founded Fukuyama's historical predictions concerning a peaceful transition to post-communism may have proved, there are elements of validity in his scheme: this is a coded, quasi-mythologised vision for a fully managerialised world. Liberal democracy is thus understood as a unilinear, progressive and comprehensive view of history; but it furnishes a deficient polity in ways which require correction and supplementation. There are, according to Fukuyama, deeper, largely suppressed human needs which were lost in both socialism and Christianity. For Fukuyama, it is Hegel and Nietzsche who best articulate these neglected requirements. At an analogous point of transition in the 'first postmodernity' of Weimar culture,[2] Spengler reverted to these ancestral dialectics in a spirit of pessimism, setting them within the framework of a cyclical evolutionary 'morphology' of world history that could function as a post-Christian surrogate for theodicy in explanation of the defeat of Germany. In 1990, Fukuyama once again attempted both to close and to close off the circle of Christianity and socialism, by subsuming each under the category of slave morality. In this first chapter Hegel's dialectic of Lord and Bondsman (*Herr und Knecht*) emerges for the first of a number of times in this book

[2] See 'Barth and the Eschatology of Weimar', in R. H. Roberts, *A Theology on its Way?: Essays on Karl Barth* (Edinburgh: T. & T. Clark, 1992), ch. 6.

as the subliminal logic, the cultural unconscious, of a triumphant and globalised capitalist culture.[3]

Having begun with the 'End of History', chapter 2 contains a socio-rhetorical examination of the rise and fall of 'enterprise culture' in Britain, taking the twenty-year period since the election of the Conservative government of 1979 as an exemplary episode which exerted an influence that extended far beyond the confines of the United Kingdom. Within this setting, 'hard' and 'soft' regimes for the social order were increasingly apparent, boundaries between different spheres of society were blurred and the initially strident hegemonic discourse of the New Right passed into a pervasive managerialism now advocated indiscriminately by both the political Left and the political Right. A 'routinisation of charisma' on the level of economic culture has been increasingly and ever more intimately bound up with religious change as new 'spirits' of capitalist renewal have emerged. The resultant cultural contradictions in which religion(s), spiritualities and religiosities all feature are traced through the ethnography that informs this book. Since 1997, the Blairite 'Third Way' has combined the endorsement of religious values seen in the revival of a version of religious socialism with yet further attempts to return to a contemporary equivalent of 'Victorian values', and the extension of an internalised factory discipline across society. This process is associated with the relentless destruction of what Harold Perkin once called 'professional society'.[4] Central to the visions of the Conservative 'New Britain' and the New Labour 'Cool Britannia' has been the gradual ascendency of a managerial *dirigiste* elite, and thus the implementation of the 'triumph of capitalism' by means of the largely silent managerialist bureaucratisation of society. A managerialist modernity is then explored as it has impacted way beyond the confines of business and commerce.

Consistent with this theme, chapter 3 contains a contextualised ethnographic study of a pioneering international conference in which, at the very apogee of Conservative Thatcherite self-confidence, the spiritual and quasi-religious ambitions of a large group of elite management consultants were expressed and enacted as transformative myth and ritual. Given 'hard' and 'soft' styles of management corresponding to the Thatcherite dichotomy between the disciplinary 'law' and an enterprise 'gospel' of freedom, these change-master consultants were acting out the

---

[3] For a brief survey in support of this contention, see R. H. Roberts, 'The Reception of Hegel's Parable of the Lord and Bondsman', *New Comparison*, 5 (1988), 23–9. See also Fredric Jameson, *The Political Unconscious: Narrative as Socially Symbolic Act* (London: Methuen, 1981).

[4] Harold Perkin, *The Rise of Professional Society: England since 1880* (London: Routledge, 1989).

role of 'organisational shamans' in that they deployed psycho-spiritual techniques with a view to reaching and changing those parts of individuals and organisations that other human resource methods fail to reach, thereby effecting deep-seated individual and corporate identity-change. First-hand involvement in management training and continuing field research in the borderlands of psychotherapy and spirituality make it apparent that this is not uncontroversial territory. Whenever the core identity of an individual (or group of individuals) is to be regarded as a fluid resource adaptable to the demands of culture change within organisations, then important ethical issues arise for those who still believe in an individual's 'right to identity'. Such a 'right' as regards the individual has been neglected at a time when the 'right to manage' has come to comprise what Lady Thatcher once described as the task of changing the 'soul' of a nation. Whilst reflection upon 'communitarian rights' has received much attention, the defence of the 'rights' of the neglected individual has become increasingly exposed to the expert application of the power of social construction in human resources management.

In the first three chapters of this book, three different locations of the 'triumph' of resurgent capitalism are touched upon in cumulative succession: the putative 'End of History', the British 'enterprise culture', and the ambition of the transformatory management consultants who facilitate the psycho-spiritual transmutation of organisational dinosaurs in need of rapid evolution. Building on this foundation, chapter 4 contains a long and detailed analysis of the imposition of managerialism upon British universities, which, paradoxically, appear to have lacked any distinctive leadership 'charisma' and therefore provide a remarkable example of consistent bureaucratic 'routinisation'. In terms rendered classic by Braverman, the 'degradation' of academic labour has proved an essential step in a subtle and all-embracing imposition of the neo-Fordist 'ownership' of non-consensual change, a veritable *Gleichschaltung*. This has been achieved through the internal regulation of the self and the introduction and instrumental imposition of approved (as opposed to contested) discourses, a process prefigured with prescience by George Orwell. The staged and progressive aggregation of the university sector into perceived national requirements has involved the virtual elimination of any traditional 'idea of the university' and its replacement by 'mass higher education'. These developments corroborate the analysis of religious change and signal a forcible 'end' of both tradition-bearing and sustained creative dissension as valued societal tasks: a banal societal unison displaces a spontaneous yet appropriately facilitated cultural polyphony. Again, the implications for human identity are such as to demand a theological and religious response; indeed, no other forms of discourse would appear to have sufficient purchase upon the dimensions of ultimacy that arise once 'capitalism has triumphed' – and become ineluctably entrenched.

In part 2, 'Theology and power in the matrix of modernity/ postmodernity', the locus of the argument shifts from a contextualised examination of the renewed capitalist revolution to recent Christian theology, and, more specifically, to ecclesiology as a key area of controversy. Whereas twenty years ago 'ecclesiology' was a relatively neglected area of theological concern, it has now moved from the periphery to the core as religious organisations like churches have become increasingly self-aware embodiments of alternative resolutions of the modernity/postmodernity matrix. The opening chapter of part 2 contains a long and controversial critique (inspired by Hegel, George Steiner and Leonardo Boff) of post-Second World War Anglican theology, and by wider implication, of main-line Western Latin theology as a whole. Central to the chapter is a deconstructive critique of the English Anglican theology that has in recent years prepared the ground for and facilitated the rapid and largely uncritical managerialisation of main-line established Christianity. Through the deployment of the resources drawn from liberation theology, these Anglican preoccupations with 'authority' and its translation into the exercise of 'real power' are represented as an ecclesial strategy in which archaic patterns of master–slave relationships are reproduced. A decade ago, this chapter controversially predicted a theological 'celebration of power': this is now seen in the 'executive church' and the extension within the Body of Christ of a managerialist 'performance culture'. The reimported managerial 'mission' of the Church of England is seen in its dedication to the efficient delivery of a religious 'product' and the 'moulding' of the people through the rendering of 'Quality' liturgical 'services'.

Throughout part 2, these and other developments are questioned as to their capacity for sustaining and enhancing basic religious functions in a late modern and ever more thoroughly commodified society, in which there are diminishing opportunities for encounters with any sense of a transcendent 'other' that might challenge the prescribed limits of experience. Chapter 6 builds upon the historical and theological foundations laid in part 1 and contains a critique of the 'executive', 'Quality' and 'performance culture' characteristic of the ecclesiological managerialism that is currently being implemented in largely unreflective ways within main-line English Anglican Christianity. Looked at from the standpoint of organisation and ritual theory, these top-down 'reforms' fundamentally endanger humane and emancipatory religious functions, and will, without appropriate constraints, subvert the fragile integrity of 'vocation' (personal, professional and religious) in an increasingly atomised surveillance society. The discourse of 'accountability' as justification of managerial change and de-professionalisation is interrogated. This is so not least because the human right to an identity grounded in transcendence is once more under threat. The remainder of this chapter reviews the range of strategies open to committed reflection on the part of a church, in this latter instance the Church of Scotland, that might take seriously the implications of the modern–postmodern debate, the resurgence of religion and the contemporary proliferation of alternative religiosities. At the centre of attention is the reality of a religious 'market-place' in which instrumental spiritualities and religiosities compete to provide spiritual services for a de-traditionalised and insecure population. Popular culture ingests and commodifies religious symbols and quasi-shamanic practices. The dilemmas and possibilities confronting main-line religion are outlined and evaluated. These dilemmas are not unique to Christian traditions, and can be seen as shared to a qualified extent by other non-Christian traditions in advanced industrial societies in which complex interactions between de- and retraditionalisation may be detected.

Part 2 is brought to a close with chapter 7, which contains a selective consideration of internal Christian theological responses to the rise of social science. This chapter turns to the formal theological tradition in order to discover how it has handled the impact of the growth of the human and social sciences. The disjunction between theology and the social sciences is outlined and on this foundation there then follow analyses of five representative strategies of encounter exemplified in the work of leading twentieth-century Christian theologians. The dangers and limitations of such encounters are explored and related to the increased salience of religion in the world system and to the twofold 'deaths' of 'God' and of 'man' propounded by Nietzsche. These are treated as the prelude to re-engagement with the 'enigma of identity', in which a reflexive striving for 'transcendence' is not an obsolete, but a central concern.

Chapter 7 also includes a critical response to the work of John Milbank, whose *Theology and Social Theory* has provided the intellectual basis for the renewal movement within Christian theology known as 'radical orthodoxy'. This school asserts the necessity of a systemic disjunction between 'theology' (the cultural-linguistic practice of a neo-Augustinian Church) and a 'heretical' and deviant 'social theory' that comprises the social and human sciences in their entirety. In this scenario, individuals are faced with what amounts to an unmediated, criterionless choice between a so-phisticated 'radical orthodox' quasi-fundamentalism – and the 'heretical' project of modernity itself. The 'radical orthodox' strategy relaunches the contents of theological tradition in a way similar to that undertaken by Karl Barth in the mid twentieth century. Understood as response to the erosive and invasive late modernity outlined in this book, Milbank's magisterial project brings with it a number of extremely problematic consequences: not least it repeats in a repristinated Anglo-Catholic form a quasi-Barthian recapitulation of tradition-in-isolation, but does so as a dialectical nihilism lacking even the residual and surrogate temporal ontology of Barth.[5] In an even more questionable way, when Milbank depicts the human and social sciences as 'heretical' and spurns the use of those socio-theoretical tools, he risks blinding the eyes and cutting off the hands without which it is impossible responsibly to make the con-dition of humankind visible – and thus to change it. Theological and ecclesial 'practice' thereby loses its exploratory and healing touch with regard to the much-threatened ecologies of 'nature', human community and 'the human' itself. This chapter marks a turning-point from explo-ration and critique towards epistemic reconstruction precipitated, not least, by the drastic reappraisal of identity.[6] All in all, the second part of *Religion, Theology and the Human Sciences* consists in an extended critique of contemporary abuses of theological power.

In part 3, 'Religion and social science: globalisation, identity and the transmutation of the religious field', there are three chapters which deal with identity and the shifting epistemic base of ideas of 'Europe', globalisation and religion, and the contemporary recomposition of the religious field, respectively. In chapter 8, I draw indirectly upon my expe-rience as holder of the Chair of Divinity in an ancient university set within a Scotland heading towards devolution. Awareness of the consolidation of Europe as political entity, and of the continuing and controversial in-tegration of Britain in 1992 and later, impelled an examination in some depth and detail of the kinds of image of 'Europe' that might serve as

[5] See Roberts, *A Theology on its Way?*, ch. 1.

[6] I am acutely aware of the importance of the issues raised by gender in relation to identity and intend to address this in future work. Meanwhile, see R. H. Roberts, 'The Chthonic Imperative: Gender, Religion and the Battle for the Earth', in Joanne Pearson, Richard Roberts and Geoffrey Samuel (eds.), *Nature Religion Today: Paganism in the Modern World* (Edinburgh: Edinburgh University Press, 1998), pp. 57–73.

symbolic and ideological points of integration at a time of renewed national consciousness. This chapter tackles these questions in such a way as to make them the framework for consideration of the reconstrual of 'divinity' within the Scottish and wider context, where 'Europe' presents itself as an alternative to 'Britain' or the United Kingdom as point of political attachment and identity. Originally presented as an inaugural lecture, the chapter is historical in orientation and affords a Foucaultian archaeology and comparative typology of the 'souls of Europe'. Understood as a quest for a viable new *episteme* for theology or 'divinity', this project was essentially optimistic, but for me it proved (as was the case with regard to chapter 6) to be an approach informed with insufficient awareness of the powers of social construction operative in a decaying tradition.

Whereas chapter 8 looked outwards into the limited universality of 'Europe' from the standpoint of the local identities of a renascent Scotland, chapter 9 develops the hypothesis that contemporary global and globalised religion as exemplified in the Chicago Parliament of the World's Religions of 1993 may be regarded as a resource which is central rather than marginal to current human concerns in a threatened world. Continuing my move from disembedded theological reflection to contextualised ethnography, a short personal narrative first gives some sense of what happened at the Parliament, and how this appeared to affect those present. Then, as a means of conveying the vast scale of the meeting, a brief content analysis and interpretation of the programme shows how (within certain limits) practical collaboration between highly diverse participants was made possible. On this basis three insights are drawn from contemporary sociology that facilitate an assessment and evaluation of the Parliament as emancipatory event. These are world system and globalisation theory, socio-cultural differentiation in an 'economy of signs and space', and the search for 'meta-theory' in the 'condition of postmodernity', which taken together allow for a positive evaluation of the salience of religion(s) and of spiritual-body practices. The implications of this analysis and interpretation are then drawn out in ways which support the proposal that religion can be understood as a differentiated global resource, an ambiguous yet dynamic form of 'cultural capital' of vital import in an era of postmaterialist value-formation. Consequently, the globalised religion represented by the 1993 Parliament of the World's Religions may have considerable implications for the study of contemporary religion and forms of religiosity. In this scenario, religion returns from the theoretical and cultural periphery (a marginalisation promoted by traditional secularisation theory) and comes closer to the core issues of the present. This interpretation reinforces Immanuel Wallerstein's 'Kairos' theme in world system theory: globalisation may embody threats but it also affords unrivalled positive opportunities.

The cumulative effect of this book is intended to promote the well-grounded impression that the intimate interface between religion, culture and society is best explored not by the measurement of declining religiosity but by fresh investigation of key zones of affinity and interconnection. Whilst much of the material educed in order to justify what distinguished sociologists of religion regard (with varying degrees of pessimism) as the inevitable decline of religion relies upon stratigraphic and statistical analysis of mainline religious observance, this provides an incomplete and misleading account of the present situation.[7] In the penultimate and concluding chapters the argument moves decisively beyond the confines of the now markedly traditional orthodoxies of the secularisation model towards a remapping of the religious field.

In chapter 10 the reconfiguration of the religious field is mapped on the basis of a consideration of time, virtual and cyborg cultures and gender. New axes have appeared that extend from super-biological female cyborg supremacism, in which prosthetic enhancement would appear to free women from both biological determination and social construction, to the near essentialist 'chthonic imperative' and 'the return of the Goddess' in some variants of gendered spirituality. Correspondingly, male corporeality becomes problematic when it wanders apparently lost in a new world of female empowerment. In his cybernovel *Neuromancer* William Gibson represents the attainment of full embodiment as a salvific event, and his hero Case may even be understood in quasi-Christological terms: this a version of the '*kenosis* of masculinity' that contrasts with the '*plerosis* of womankind'. The dialectics of embodiment (initiated in second- and third-wave feminism) provide a source on the basis of which it is possible to outline a gendered typology of contemporary religiosities within the overall paradigm of a post-secular 'return of religion'. Here the creative manipulation of virtual reality and outright primordial regression coexist as extreme alternatives open to adepts active in different sectors of the field.

In a modern/postmodern world dis/order the quest for identity becomes a predominant concern. In pre-modernity the impact of humankind upon nature was relatively moderate, and whilst it would be

---

[7] See Roy Wallis and Steve Bruce, 'Secularization: The Orthodox Model', in Steve Bruce (ed.), *Religion and Modernization* (Oxford: Clarendon Press, 1992), pp. 8–30.

misleading to romanticise the ecologically sensitive complementarities of hunter-gatherer and later agrarian communities, it is nonetheless a relevant truism that religion was integral to cultures, which might, in turn, function in relatively synergistic ecological relationships with the natural world.[8] Under the pressures of modernisation, mastery of nature through the application of instrumental rationality turned dialectics of thought into dichotomies of practice. The extension of causal explanation banished inherited mythological and symbolic systems into marginality, and transcendence retreated into interstitial status, glimpsed through the *Brüche* in the yellow brick road of universal rationality that is modernity itself. The Enlightenment project, modernity and the managerial imperative are now called into question because they fail to engage in a critical and positive way with the demands of a sustainable and fully human ecology.

When confronted with the multiple pressures upon identity outlined and explored in this book, humankind may respond as aspirant 'pilgrims' and articulate a new, post-socialist, human ecological balance between capitalistic growth and the chthonic imperative, or defer to the atomised and tribal 'vagabonds' whose multiple alienations threaten all tolerable human communities. In this setting religion(s) and spiritualities are capable of providing resources through which cultural practices that unite head, heart and hand can be (re-)developed which may prove capable of regrounding humankind, albeit in an exemplary way, outside and beyond the endlessly proliferating economies of simulacra that shield us from the contingencies of existence and the demands of conviviality. Identity as vocation has a future in a world order in which very little is left to chance by globalised capitalism; obedience to such a calling will entail the difficult and demanding consequences experienced by all those who seek, as Vaclav Havel has written, to live in truth – and to be rooted in being. Even more adventurously, such identity as vocation, the falling to earth and into the body, and the new democracy in the Spirit burdens each individual with responsibility and opens him or her to the possibilities that come with the call. This may be the true meaning of incarnation for our time – it is at odds with the nihilistic, passionless, commodified, managerialised world that sucks in and absorbs the human, and spews forth a derogate post-humanity.

This book attempts to comprise the particular and the universal in ways which may both provoke and irritate some readers. Many issues

---

[8] This is, of course, a complex and disputed issue; I shall return to it in due course in future research.

within it merit further investigation; some questions of detail have been accorded provisional answers and have been put, as it were, on hold. My aim is that readers might be helped to glimpse life beyond the seamlessness of the life-worlds that preclude rather than facilitate the fully human emergence, the delight in life and affirmation of the 'other' that it is the vocation of religion to realise, and of theology to seek to understand.

PART I

Spirits of capitalism and the commodification of the soul

CHAPTER I

The closed circle: Marxism, Christianity and the 'End of History'

This book begins with the image of a closed circle, that is with the idea that the separated strands of Western, and increasingly world history, have converged and that a sense of closure is widespread. The phenomena of globalisation and environmental degradation now serve to compound this impression; yet, simultaneously, as the drive towards uniformity takes place so differences, economic, social and cultural, increase and intensify, and these phenomena are often exacerbated by what Theodor Hanf has depicted as the 'sacred markers' that provide focal points for the assertion of identity in the face of homogenisation.[1] The decade from 1989 to 1999 is marked by a progressive realisation that the apparent optimism of the earliest years of the decade has been undercut by events, of which the wars in the former Yugoslavia have proved to be but one of the best-publicised instances of political and societal disfunctionality. The tension between the rather facile hopes of ideologues who saw a New World Order freeing itself from the sterile polarities of the Cold War and the onset of renewed forms of chaos and disintegration, all overshadowed by an ever more apparent global environmental degradation amounting to an 'ecological eschaton',[2] serves as a natural point of departure for these reflections on the changing configuration of the relationships between religion, theology and the human sciences.

The Japanese-American political theorist Francis Fukuyama represented the transition marked by the events of 1989–90 as the inauguration of the 'End of History', and the interrogation of this assertion serves as a point of departure for a long journey into the confused and changing cultural field that is the central concern of this book. The 'closed circle'

---

[1] See Theodor Hanf, 'The Sacred Marker: Religion, Communalism and Nationalism', *Social Compass*, 41/1 (1994), 9–20.

[2] This was a term that I coined in 1989 when preparing the conference Religion and the Resurgence of Capitalism, which took place at Lancaster University in 1990. This notion has gained salience during the intervening years and is directly responded to in part 3 below.

in the title of this chapter thus refers to the generalisations that underlie Fukuyama's claim that the collapse of ideological polarities presages a united world in which all that remains to be undertaken is the safe management of a progressive adjustment to the reality principle of 'liberal democratic capitalism'. In such managerial terms, the issues of history are resolved, and all that stands out is the task of presentation and thus a perceptual problem of reality acceptance on the part of an expanding and increasingly globalised world bourgeoisie. For the influential ideologue Francis Fukuyama, we inhabit both a post-Christian and a post-socialist world in which the ancestral struggle between the strong and the weak becomes a matter of managed cultural adjustment. Fully unfettered, the strong will tend to destroy the weak and provoke their discontent; but if the strong are not permitted a measure of freedom, then the weak and mediocre will paralyse the now universal liberal capitalist world order. Fukuyama seeks to reconcile these contrasting impulses on the basis that a pre-Christian and pre-socialist answer is required.

Given the scenario outlined above, the notion of the 'End of History' is outlined critically as it becomes the context in which to examine and evaluate Fukuyama's rehabilitation and synergistic juxtaposition of Hegel's parable of Lord and Bondsman and Plato's deployment of the archaic term *thymos*. According to Fukuyama this conjunction provides the remedy for the present and likely future ills of triumphant capitalism. The recovery of Hegel and Plato forms the core of a concerted attempt to fill the ideological and mythic vacuum left after the decay and implosion of the slave ideologies represented by Marxism, Christianity and their socio-cultural adjuncts. Fukuyama argues that,

Christianity and communism were both slave ideologies (the latter unanticipated by Hegel) that captured part of the truth. But in the course of time the irrationalities and self-contradictions of both were revealed: Communist societies, in particular, despite their commitment to principles of freedom and equality, were exposed as modern variants of slave-holding ones, in which the dignity of the great mass of the people went unrecognised. The collapse of Marxist ideology in the late 1980s reflected in a sense, the achievement of a higher level of rationality on the part of those who lived in such societies, and of their realization that rational universal recognition could be had only in a liberal social order.[3]

Fukuyama attempted to outflank and supersede these defective alternatives by exposing their real similarities within the single context

---

[3] Francis Fukuyama, *The End of History and the Last Man* (London: Hamish Hamilton, 1992), p. 205.

represented by the termination of the era of antithesis between traditions and ideologies and thus of their capacity for the enslavement of humanity. I maintain, on the other hand, that the post-Hegelian histories of socialism and religion actually possess a dialectical potency that escapes Fukuyama's repressive interpretation, once this is more fully unearthed. But, significantly, the very notion of the 'End of History' involves a suppression of contradiction, and it is this that is most troubling. Fukuyama's closing of the circle, a gambit that consists in the joint condemnation of Marxist socialism and Christianity and a rather superficial return to Hegel in the context of universal supersession by 'liberal democratic capitalism', may indeed be represented as closure and as an 'End'. But at a more fundamental level the Hegelian dialectic of power resists all such attempts at closure. Whilst Fukuyama's 'End of History' thesis sanctions a limited reopening of a more banal history in the contained revival of a domesticated 'warrior' and Promethean ethos of *thymos*, his domestication of the dialectic of the real and its recasting within the bounds of capitalist 'normalisation' obscure what I shall represent as the truth-seeking and 'living in truth' central to the creation of fully human identities. I therefore argue that Fukuyama's 'closure' is in reality a *fore-closure*, a suppression of dimensions of reality that not only disguises the full significance of contemporary cultural change, but also disarms and disempowers a fully human and humane response to a nihilistic culture.

In a globalised and, above all, in a *managed* world,[4] the expert suppression of real contradiction and its relocation in a sealed and repressed cultural unconscious becomes feasible. Given the weakening or even the demise of both religious and socialist alternatives, ethically and culturally responsible access to that repressed unconscious becomes more difficult for both individuals and communities, not least when other gateways, such as main-line education and religion, are aggregated into the managerial paradigm. The repression or marginalisation of these dimensions of human existence (as is proposed in a limited way by the traditional secularisation thesis) is, however, moderated precisely because, as we shall later see, the tapping of the unconscious and the facilitation of 'spirituality' have themselves been assimilated into the managerial prerogative, in a process facilitated by 'soft capitalism'.[5] Moreover, indeed, the true ambitions of managerial governance shift from material and economic

---

4 Our reliance upon a managerial paradigm of 'modernity' is supported by Willard F. Enteman's *Managerialism: The Emergence of a New Ideology* (Madison: University of Wisconsin Press, 1993).

5 Nigel Thrift, 'Soft Capitalism', unpublished lecture delivered at the Centre for the Study of Cultural Values, Lancaster University, June 1996.

goals to the politics of culture, and even to exercising conscious control over the construction of the human 'soul' itself. These are all features of the remarkable migration and mutual exchange of attributes that has taken place following the events of 1989–90. In brief terms, the bureaucratic 'democratic centralism' epitomised by Stalinism headed west to extend and reinforce the managerial prerogative, and radical marketisation and socio-economic atomisation moved east, where it has had, when unmitigated, highly destructive consequences, not least in Russia. As we shall see, this interchange took place in an environment in which the struggle for ultimacy and the guardianship of the sacred also migrated from their traditional strongholds in main-line religion. The latter has sometimes uncritically adapted itself to, and, on occasion, even ingested commodification and managerialism in its desire to act as handmaid to a largely unchallenged managerialised Mammonism. A degraded sacrality has become but a shifting and ambiguous set of experiential opportunities and disembedded values open to both benign capture and malign manipulation. The attendant and contrasting religious and ethical implications of these migrations are important features of the recomposition of the religious field in late modernity that are to be analysed in the course of the ensuing argument.

It is important to acknowledge that Francis Fukuyama's now famous article 'The End of History', published in the summer of 1989,[6] and his subsequent book, *The End of History and the Last Man*, did indeed mark the end of one epoch and the beginning of another. The theses presented in *The End of History* were heavily criticised, but in daring to articulate a transition, Fukuyama took a worthwhile risk. In *The End of History*, he at least recognised a historical watershed and expressed optimism about the future of the human condition, and the capacity of 'liberal democratic capitalism', rightly understood, to deliver a tolerable, humane historical inevitability after the final collapse of Marxist socialism. Like Oswald Spengler, to whom he refers at length, Fukuyama tried to give meaning to contemporary history. In *The Decline of the West*,[7] Spengler addressed the apparent failure of German culture and civilisation following the Armistice and defeat of Germany in the First World War in a 'morphology of world history', in what amounted to the secular analogue to theodicy. Meaning was given to defeat through a pattern of repetition, the inevitable cycle of the rise and fall of civilisations: Germany could rise

[6] Francis Fukuyama, 'The End of History', *The National Interest*, 16/2 (1989), 3–18.
[7] Oswald Spengler, *The Decline of the West: Form and Actuality* (London: George Allen & Unwin, 1926).

again. In his turn, Fukuyama addressed the failure of Christianity and the collapse and defeat of Marxist socialism: neither is adequate to the requirements of the new epoch after, as he would have it, the end of the age of ideology. In the events of the *Wende* of 1989–90, Fukuyama argues that capitalism had shown itself to be the only viable way of organising the world; but the triumph of capitalism does not, however, in and of itself solve the problem of ideological and mythic exhaustion.

According to Fukuyama, the legitimacy of liberal democracy has so grown through its economic conquest of the rival ideologies of hereditary monarchy, fascism, and now communism, that it may now be regarded as the 'end point of man's ideological evolution', and the 'final form of human government'.[8] An immediate implication of this assertion of the ideological finality of liberal democracy is that, 'while earlier forms of government were characterised by grave defects and irrationalities that led to their eventual collapse, liberal democracy was free from such fundamental internal contradictions'.[9] As will become apparent in the following chapter, it has indeed been a core trope of the public discourse of resurgent and triumphant capitalism as rendered by its apologists to represent 'reality' as plain, indisputable facts subsisting beyond ideology, in what amounts to a comprehensive 'reality principle'. Within this framework it will also become clear that whilst some contradictions are deemed essential to socio-economic dynamism, others that do not serve this goal have to be suppressed. Fukuyama acknowledges this problem when he suggests that even after the vanquishing of fascism and communism, liberal democracy may still leave us fundamentally unsatisfied. He poses the question: 'Are there contradictions that will remain at the heart of liberal order, even after the last fascist dictator, swaggering colonel, or Communist party boss has been driven from the face of the earth?'[10] My response is in the affirmative, but I would also assert that these contradictions are not simply or primarily those associated with Fukuyama's reintroduction of a domesticated Prometheanism, but run far deeper and subsist at the level of the expropriation and alienation of the sources

---

[8] The term 'liberal democracy' is not, of course, value-free. I prefer Ralph Milliband's designation 'capitalist democracy'. See Milliband's 'The Socialist Alternative', in Larry Diamond and Marc F. Plattner (eds.), *Capitalism, Socialism and Democracy Revisited* (Baltimore: The Johns Hopkins University Press, 1993), p. 112. More representative and less misleading in this connection for English readers is Michael Novak's preferred term 'democratic capitalism'. See R. H. Roberts, 'The Spirit of Democratic Capitalism: A Critique of Michael Novak', in Jon Davies and David Green (eds.), *God and the Marketplace: Essays on the Morality of Wealth Creation* (London: Institute of Economic Affairs, 1993), pp. 64–81.

[9] Fukuyama, *End of History and the Last Man*, p. xi.

[10] *Ibid.*, p. 284.

of socio-cultural and psychological identity-formation, the very springs of humanity itself.

Thus whereas this opening chapter concerns itself with Fukuyama's representation of the human condition after the implosion of communism and the 'triumph of capitalism',[11] it also seeks to explore and subvert the discursive seamlessness of the post-socialist condition and its instrumental imposition through global managerialism. Rather in the way that the assertion 'Communism was the riddle of history solved' could become an ideology of non-contradiction in which 'socialist reality' was forced to follow ideology into a fantasy of suppressed contradiction in the former Soviet bloc, so triumphant capitalism can be seen arrogating finality to itself through Fukuyama's assertions. Mockery of the ideologue is relatively easy where physical terror is absent. When, however, seamless capitalism proliferates and differentiates itself in the form of managerialism and the universal imposition of performativity, then the 'terror' of which Jean-François Lyotard wrote in *La Condition postmoderne* becomes a pervasive, internalised *habitus* of fear, which, as I shall show in this book, grips ever more sectors of human endeavour. The absence of a plausible 'other', a point of leverage outside the seemingly infinite elasticity of the all-enveloping 'cage' that now represents itself as co-terminous with reality as a whole, presents a great challenge to any mind and heart unsatisfied with the limits of the cage. All critical knowledge becomes deviance at the moment it raises the question of foundations and ventures to suggest that a full human identity that understands itself as 'vocation' or 'call' must seek a grounding beyond the bounds of an all-embracing capitalistic and managerial prerogative. Naturally enough, a major goal of globalised and managerialised capitalism is to suppress or eliminate such deviance by whatever means permissible under any given set of circumstances.

The claims made above do, it should be conceded, pre-empt the fuller argument of this book, and so in this chapter the reader's attention is directed primarily towards grasping the significance of Fukuyama's depiction of the transition from the world of living antitheses and real alternatives to a closure, or 'End', of history. This 'End' is not marked, as Fukuyama would have it, by the advent of universal liberalism, but by

---

[11] The word 'triumph' as used by present-day apologists for contemporary capitalism and the adjective 'triumphalist' are applicable. See my analysis of this form of discourse in R. H. Roberts, 'Rhetoric and the Resurgence of Capitalism', in R. H. Roberts and J. M. M. Good (eds.), *The Recovery of Rhetoric: Persuasive Discourse and Disciplinarity in the Human Sciences* (Charlottesville, VA: University of Virginia Press, 1993), and chapter 2 below.

an internal colonisation so complete as to eliminate all positive reference to critical counterfactuals and countervalues. Here, however, I provide a broad historical perspective, a context within which both the managerial revolution from above and the re-emergent salience of the religious factor can be more fully understood. Then, in turn, attention may be drawn to both the difficulties and the rewards that flow from the exploration and reconfiguring of the contemporary recomposition of the religious field.

At the heart of Fukuyama's argument there is what may be called a New Hegelian metanarrative. The latter is based upon a construal of post-socialist, mature liberal democracy as the part calculated, part spontaneous resolution of *thymos*. For Fukuyama, thymic drives are the defining feature of humankind. They are manifested in an insatiable lust for 'recognition', the prestige-seeking impulse that constantly subverts and transcends the mere needs, wants, preferences and desires associated with biological subsistence and the consumerist settlement of 'post-history'. According to Fukuyama, human identity ultimately consists in an ambiguous and risk-fraught tendency to seek recognition and prestige. Given the historic failure and contemporary anachronisms of the slave moralities of Christianity and Marxism, the rehabilitation of *thymos*, a manly 'spiritedness', is the core value of Fukuyama's vision.

In the most general terms Fukuyama (in a way similar to Michael Novak) appropriates and inverts Marx: the *spiritual* ultimacy of liberal democracy is to be substituted for the *material* (pseudo-) finality of communism. In order to effect this substitution, Fukuyama reverts to Hegel; and in attempting such a recovery he draws down two descending arms of history into the sides of a circle. Post-Enlightenment Christian theology and Marxist socialism stem in large degree from Hegel, and when we return to the latter the inadequacies of both are exposed. Yet, it does not require profound historical knowledge to become aware that both traditions have already engaged in this apparently regressive, yet in reality emancipatory, dialogue with Hegel. Fukuyama's argument ranges far and wide, and it includes, not least in his account of Hegel (largely derived from Alexandre Kojève[12]), much which could well be contested in detail. Such a deconstructive scholastic exercise would be pointless at this juncture, and it is of more value for present purposes to construe *The End of History* as a cultural artifact in need of interpretation that should be read as an aspirant mythopoeic symbol of its time. What Fukuyama

---

[12] Alexandre Kojève, *Introduction to the Reading of Hegel* (New York: Basic Books, 1969); see also Barry Cooper, *The End of History: An Essay on Modern Hegelianism* (Toronto: University of Toronto Press, 1984); and Michael S. Roth, *Knowing and History* (Ithaca, NY: Cornell University Press, 1988).

would intend is thus a new paradigm in the Kuhnian sense,[13] a statement of the transcendental principles of the total context of construal and interpretation, and so it is in these terms that the truth and utility of his efforts may also be assessed.

As already noted, central to Fukuyama's vision is a re-Hegelianisation of cultural principles; in particular this is achieved through a refunctioning of the parable of Lord and Bondsman taken from Hegel's *Phenomenology of Mind* of 1807 and its representation as the contemporary analogue of Platonic *thymos*, the lost warrior spirit. It is the grandiloquent and capitalised 'History' of Hegel, that is 'history understood as a single, coherent, evolutionary process, when taking into account the experience of all peoples in all times',[14] that really interests Fukuyama. The 'posthistory' which now appears to succeed its hypostatised and capitalised form is a form of fallenness, a lessening of the grandeur that is the human prerogative. What many of those who first heard of Fukuyama's ideas at second or third hand not infrequently imagined is that he endorsed such a de-Historicisation. In reality, the contrary is the case, for he purports to give an affirmative answer to the question 'Whether, at the end of the twentieth century, it makes sense for us once again to speak of a coherent and directional History of mankind that will eventually lead the greater part of humanity to liberal democracy?'[15] There are, he asserts, two reasons for such a progression, the first economic, the second concerning the 'struggle for recognition' and the pursuit of prestige as the main components of human identity.

The former ground for a coherent and directional view of history is not in fact expanded on a basis of purely *economic* progress as such, but in terms of the 'Mechanism', that is the reified 'logic of modern natural science [which] would seem to dictate a universal evolution in the direction of capitalism'.[16] Fukuyama recognises, however, that overall coherence in history (and society) is guaranteed by instrumental, applied scientific reason. Fukuyama's notion of the 'Mechanism' is interestingly reminiscent of the *demiurge* of Plato's *Timaeus* and a de-organicised version of the 'hidden hand' of a residual and vestigial Providence preserved in Adam Smith's *Wealth of Nations*. Eschewing, however, both the quasi-providential 'hidden hand' and the ruthless excision of sentimentality

---

[13] Thomas Kuhn, *The Structure of Scientific Revolutions*, 2nd edn (Chicago: University of Chicago Press, 1970).

[14] Fukuyama, *End of History and the Last Man*, p. xii.

[15] *Ibid.*, pp. xxii–xxiii.

[16] *Ibid.*, p. xv.

characteristic of Thatcherism, Fukuyama lays the foundation for qualified mythopoeisis. The modernisation associated with technology increases wealth and maximises human satisfaction and leads to ever
greater homogenisation of human societies. Centralisation of the state,
urbanisation and the displacement of traditional forms of social organisation by economic rationality are not simply to be reported, but to be celebrated. Global markets and a consumer culture will become universal.[17]
There is nothing particularly remarkable about Fukuyama's general
characterisation of modernisation[18] and of globalisation processes.[19]
Unlike, however, the prominent Roman Catholic apologist for 'democratic capitalism', Michael Novak of the American Enterprise Institute,
Fukuyama concedes that there is no 'economically necessary reason
why advanced industrialization should produce political liberty'.[20] He
acknowledges that authoritarian capitalism (like that of the 'four little
dragons' of South Korea, Taiwan, Hong Kong and Singapore and other
countries on the Pacific Rim) may well be the most efficient form of
economic organisation. A little ironically, perhaps, the Asian economic
crisis was not foreseen by the author of *The End of History*. The mere
existence of the Mechanism is not enough to explain the emergence

---

[17] *Ibid.*, pp. xiv–xv.

[18] Perry Anderson, 'Marshall Berman: Modernity and Revolution', in *A Zone of Engagement* (London: Verso, 1992), ch. 2; R. N. Bellah, 'Meaning and Modernization', *Beyond Belief* (Berkeley: California University Press, 1970), pp. 64–73; R. N. Bellah, 'New Religious Consciousness and the Crisis in Modernity', in Charles Y. Glock and Robert N. Bellah (eds.), *The New Religious Consciousness* (Berkeley: California University Press, 1976), pp. 333–52; Peter L. Berger, *Facing up to Modernity: Excursions in Society, Politics, and Religion* (New York: Basic Books, 1977); Marshall Berman, *All that is Solid melts into Air: The Experience of Modernity* (London: Verso, 1982); Anthony Giddens, *The Consequences of Modernity* (Cambridge: Polity, 1990); Jürgen Habermas, *The Philosophical Discourse of Modernity: Twelve Lectures* (Cambridge: Polity, 1987); David Harvey, *The Condition of Postmodernity: An Enquiry into the Origins of Cultural Change* (Oxford: Blackwell, 1989); Max Horkheimer and T. W. Adorno, 'The Concept of Enlightenment', in *Dialectic of Enlightenment* (London: Allen Lane, 1972), pp. 3–80; Agnes Heller, *Can Modernity Survive?* (Cambridge: Polity, 1990); Scott Lash, *Another Modernity: A Different Rationality* (Oxford: Blackwell, 2000); Bryan S. Turner (ed.), *Theories of Modernity and Postmodernism* (London: Sage, 1990); Zygmunt Bauman, *Modernity and the Holocaust* (Cambridge: Polity, 1989); Gianni Vattimo, *The End of Modernity: Nihilism and Hermeneutics in Post-modern Culture* (Cambridge: Polity, 1988); Sam Whimster and Scott Lash (eds.), *Max Weber, Rationality and Modernity* (London: Allen & Unwin, 1987).

[19] Roland Robertson, 'The Globalization Paradigm: Thinking Globally', *Religion and Social Order*, 1 (1991), 207–24; Mike Featherstone (ed.), *Global Culture: Nationalism, Globalization and Modernity* (London: Sage, 1990); S. Gill and D. Law (eds.), *The Global Political Economy: Perspectives, Problems and Policies* (London: Harvester, 1988); Anthony King, *Culture, Globalization and the World System* (Binghampton, NY: SUNY, 1989); R. Peet, *Global Capitalism: Theories of Societal Development* (London: Routledge, 1991); L. Sklair, *Sociology of the Global System: Social Changes in Global Perspective* (London: Harvester, 1991); W. H. Swatos, Jr (ed.), *Religious Politics in Global and Comparative Perspective* (New York: Greenwood Press, 1989).

[20] Fukuyama, *End of History and the Last Man*, p. xv.

and the growing universality of liberal democracy; for that something further is required, an adequate doctrine of human nature, for, he asserts, 'economic interpretations of history are incomplete and unsatisfying, because man is not simply an economic animal'.[21] Fukuyama's response to this deficit implies the relativisation and supercession of 'the Mechanism', for, he argues, 'Hegel's understanding of the Mechanism that underlies the historical process is incomparably deeper than that of Marx or of any contemporary social scientist. For Hegel the primary motor of human history is not natural science or the ever expanding horizon of desire that powers it, but rather a totally non-economic drive, the *struggle for recognition*.'[22] We may agree with this ascription of depth to Hegel, but we have to inquire whether Fukuyama has dug deep enough.

If we concede a measure of plausibility to *The End of History*, then what is humankind likely to be? It is in answer to this question that Fukuyama turns to Hegel's early philosophical anthropology and the parable of Lord (*Herr*) and Bondsman (*Knecht*), and here his spade turns as it strikes bedrock: modernity contains no 'Beyond', beyond Hegel. Yet informing Hegel's thought there are the societally contextualised partitions of the soul to be found in Plato's *Republic*. Here Fukuyama locates the lost treasure of *thymos*, the 'spiritedness' of the warrior or guardian class who stand between the philosopher kings and the plebeian producers. Whereas all animals seek food, drink, shelter and self-preservation, the utter distinctiveness of the human consists in the fact that:

> Man differs fundamentally from the animals, however, because in addition he desires the desire of other men, that is, he wants to be 'recognised'. In particular, he wants to be recognised as a *human being*, that is a being with a certain worth or dignity. This worth in the first instance is related to his willingness to risk his life in struggle over pure prestige.[23]

The struggle for self-transcendence, the attainment of higher, abstract principles and goals, lifts man above basic animal instincts. It is worth noting that feminism and feminist theory have a minimal presence in Fukuyama's argument, and it is scarcely necessary to be a convinced feminist to be aware that his line of argument would seem masculinist in the extreme when he traces the doctrine of a generic human nature to conflict and resists any form of holistic resolution. Fukuyama's identification

21 *Ibid.*, p. xvi.
22 *Ibid.*
23 *Ibid.*

of the human concern with identity with a search for 'pure prestige' is somewhat constricted when the desire for recognition is contained within the closure of history, and his reading of Hegel is both mythologising and curiously literal:

According to Hegel, the desire for recognition initially drives two primordial combatants to seek to make the other 'recognize' their humanness by staking their lives in a mortal battle. When the natural fear of death leads one combatant to submit, the relationship of master and slave is born. The stakes in this bloody battle at the beginning of history are not food, shelter, or security, but pure prestige. And precisely because the goal of the battle is not determined by biology, Hegel sees in it the first glimmer of human freedom.[24]

This reading of Hegel in terms of 'self-esteem' – and its *denial* precipitating *anger, individual failure* leading to *shame*, and *correct evaluation* issuing in *pride* – assumes the emergence of an initial differentiation of the human race in terms of those, the masters, who were willing to risk their lives, and those others, the class of slaves, who gave in to their fear of death. In a literal, but ironically paradoxical transition from *ancien régime* to modernity (supremely enacted in the French Revolution) this antithesis is overcome. According to Fukuyama, in modernity, slaves have become their own masters through the principle of popular sovereignty and the rule of law.[25] Thereby universal and reciprocal recognition through *rights* supersedes the unequal recognition of masters and slaves. Likewise on the international plane, Fukuyama argues that liberal democracy lessens the likelihood of wars based on the pursuit of pure prestige. Hegel's parable is in this way absorbed and partially domesticated into a renewed metanarrative of modernity. The question of the durability of narrative is a subject to which we later return in considering the 'hypernarrative' or transcendental principles of societal constitution as successor to failed and fragmented metanarrative. Almost needless to say, Fukuyama's argument once more tends to present the reader with a rather facile dissolution of Marx's conception of the proletariat, the class outside all classes as the hammerhead of historical inevitability – and the 'negation of the negation'. In the new, post-socialist situation, rendered by Fukuyama (echoing Nietzsche) as the 'End of History', there emerges the 'last man', a hollow-chested non-entity produced by liberal democracy, the appearance of which provokes the urgency in Fukuyama's question as to what *is*? – what *will be* the human? The universal domestication of

---

[24] *Ibid.*

[25] Ironically, what this book shows is that what slaves become is their own slave-masters.

primal struggle into a regularised global bourgeoisie and the resolution of transcendence does not preclude the need for the contemporary equivalent of the 'Lord', a theme to which we return later.

Yet, contrary to Fukuyama, it would be plausible to argue that Hegel's representation of Lord and Bondsman in the *Phenomenology of Mind* can and should resist ready reduction and resolution into any fixed or sequential historical transition.[26] The loci of lordship (*Herrschaft*) and bondage or slavery (*Knechtschaft*) are 'moments' (*Momente*) in a dialectical *coincidentia oppositorum*, a coincidence of opposites, the outcome of which is not pre-determined or assured as Marx in the *Communist Manifesto*, or indeed, as Fukuyama would have us believe, resolved in the emergence of global 'liberal democracy'. To imagine otherwise of Hegel would be to risk regarding liberal democracy, the bourgeois condition, as amounting to *Aufhebung*, the transition that itself constitutes ultimate supercession – even the onset of transcendence. If, of course, Fukuyama's interpretation of Hegel were to be conceded, then it would naturally follow that the extension of the liberal capitalist triumph into all aspects of the human condition, including the domain of the spirit, would be real, rational and legitimate. In more aggressive terms, does not Fukuyama's interpretation of Hegel achieved through the appropriation of Alexandre Kojève's reading of the parable of Lord and Bondsman (that of a future European Community bureaucrat) amount to the *embourgeoisement* and domestication of a thinker whose radicality even now outruns the limits set by those who acknowledge his authority as mentor?[27] In effect, Fukuyama

---

[26] George Steiner, *In Bluebeard's Castle: Some Notes Towards the Re-definition of Culture*, T. S. Eliot Memorial Lectures (London: Faber, 1971); L. S. Stepelevich, *The Young Hegelians: An Anthology* (Cambridge: Cambridge University Press, 1983); K. Barth, 'Hegel', *Protestant Theology in the Nineteenth Century* (London: SCM, 1972), pp. 384–421; G. W. F. Hegel, *Early Theological Writings*, tr. T. M. Knox (Philadelphia: University of Philadelphia Press, 1971); G. W. F. Hegel, *The Phenomenology of Mind*, tr. J. B. Baillie (London: Macmillan, 1910); G. W. F. Hegel, *Phenomenology of Spirit*, tr. A. V. Miller (Oxford: Clarendon Press, 1977); P. C. Hodgson, 'Hegel', in N. Smart et al. (eds.), *Nineteenth-Century Religious Thought in the West* (Cambridge: Cambridge University Press, 1986), vol. I, pp. 17–40; Q. Lauer, *Hegel's Concept of God* (Albany: State University of New York Press, 1982); Alasdair MacIntyre, *Hegel: A Collection of Critical Essays* (Notre Dame: University of Notre Dame Press, 1976); Charles Taylor, *Hegel* (Cambridge: Cambridge University Press, 1975); Mark C. Taylor, *Journeys to Selfhood, Hegel and Kierkegaard* (Berkeley: University of California Press, 1980); J. E. Toews, *Hegelianism: The Path toward Dialectical Humanism* (Cambridge: Cambridge University Press, 1980); Rowan Williams, 'Hegel and the Gods of Postmodernity', in Philippa Berry and Andrew Wernick (eds.), *Shadow of Spirit: Postmodernism and Religion* (London: Routledge, 1992), pp. 72–80.

[27] This radicalism has not been lost on second- and third-wave feminist theorists who, following Simone de Beauvoir's assimilation of the *Phenomenology of Mind* through Jean-Paul Sartre's *Being and Nothingness*, repeatedly return to the parable in their representation of the condition of womankind under conditions of patriarchy. Male humankind has much to learn from feminist theory. See

is a right wing but non-theistic Hegelian who extends and transposes the latter's equation of the real and the rational in the *Philosophie des Rechts* from the Prussian state to the global totality.

Fukuyama reinforces the legitimacy of his reading of Hegel by the inclusion of *thymos*, a word which originates in Homeric epic,[28] where it had a semantic range that extended from 'soul' to 'anger'. These meanings do not, as it happens, adequately express what was intended by the Greek term,[29] and contextual analysis of its use is important. Studies by Erwin Rohde,[30] Joachim Bohme,[31] Bruno Snell[32] and R. B. Onians[33] carry the investigation of *thymos* into the most distant Greek antiquity. The possible meanings of *thymos* – 'soul', 'spirit', the 'principle of life', 'feeling' and 'thought', especially of strong feeling and passion,[34] and such more concise expressions as 'life-soul' and 'life-breath' – clearly surface in Fukuyama's understanding of both the *Republic* and the *Phenomenology of Mind*. E. D. Francis' articulation of *thymos* as 'that which animates and endows the human being with consciousness, air blown into the lungs by the winds',[35] suggests that 'life-soul' might be an appropriate translation. Yet as Caroline Caswell observes at the conclusion of her synchronic formulaic analysis, 'Modern English can supply no better than crude approximation, either linguistically or conceptually.'[36] Such rich, wide-ranging resonance makes *thymos* an ideal vehicle for Fukuyama's venture into mythopoeisis.

In the specific setting of Plato's thought the tripartite division of the psyche in terms of desire (*to epithumetikon*), spiritedness (*to thumoeides*) and reasonableness and practical skill (*to logistikon*) appears in the

---

R. H. Roberts, 'The Reception of Hegel's Parable of Lord and Bondsman', *New Comparison*, 5 (1988), 23–9 and Roberts, 'The Chthonic Imperative: Gender, Religion and the Battle for the Earth', in Joanne Pearson, Richard Roberts and Geoffrey Samuel (eds.), *Nature Religion Today: Paganism in the Modern World* (Edinburgh: Edinburgh University Press, 1998), pp. 57–73.

[28] See the brief monograph by Caroline P. Caswell, *A Study of Thumos in Early Greek Epic*, Supplements to *MNEMOSYNE* (Leiden: E. J. Brill, 1990).

[29] *Ibid.*, p. 1.

[30] Erwin Rohde, *Psyche: The Cult of Souls and Belief in Immortality among the Greeks* (London: Kegan Paul, 1925).

[31] Joachim Bohme, *Das Seele und das Ich im homerischen Epos mit einem Anhang: Vergleich mit dem Glauben der Primitiven* (Leipzig, 1929).

[32] Bruno Snell, *The Discovery of the Mind: The Greek Origins of European Thought* (Cambridge, MA: Harvard University Press, 1953).

[33] R. B. Onians, *The Origins of European Thought: About the Body, the Mind, the Soul, the World, Time and Fate* (Cambridge: Cambridge University Press, 1951).

[34] Caswell, *Thumos*, p. 11.

[35] E. D. Francis, 'Virtue, Folly, and Greek Etymology', in C. A. Rubino and C. W. Shelmerdine (eds.), *Approaches to Homer* (Austin, 1983), pp. 89–103.

[36] Caswell, *Thumos*, p. 62.

Phaedrus-myth (*Phaedr.* 246 ff.) and the *Republic* (*Rep.* II.275b; IV.435 ff.; IX.580 ff.).[37] In the *Timaeus*, *thymos* is associated with *philotimon*, the love of honour (*Tim.* 70). The abstract noun *to thumoeides* and the cognate adjective *thumoeides* apply to the 'virtue' (*andreia*) of the Guardians.[38] This provides one source of that conception of manly *vertu* that is later re-cast in the proto-realpolitik of Machiavelli's *The Prince*,[39] and eventually in the self-realisation of the Hegelian Lord in the *Phenomenology of Mind* and the fateful Nietzschian 'Will-to-power' (*Die Wille zur Macht*) itself.[40] Whilst Fukuyama endorses the necessity of *thymos* as the condition of so-cial and economic vitality, he also attempts to address the ethical failure associated with the de-contextualisation of the will to live and to secure recognition. Without a supportive framework, human identity assertion slips into the abyss of rampant nihilism.[41] There is an interesting paral-lel here between Fukuyama's line of argument and that pursued by the anthropologist Charles Lindholm with regard to 'charisma' and its role in identity-formation to which we shall return later.[42]

A further preliminary conclusion can be drawn from this that affects the direction of the argument to be pursued in this book. A funda-mental dilemma has begun to emerge: if, on the one hand, society is de-traditionalised and main-line religions cease to operate effectively in facilitating basic processes of socialisation, and if, on the other, all charis-matic action or shamanistic experience is perceived as malign in its con-sequences, then societal renewal through the ritual function[43] dies away and humankind is condemned to what Stjepan Mestrovic represents as 'post-emotional society' in which basic human needs for communion will never be adequately met other than through the inadequate means (as I here argue) of control and consumption.[44] This, however, is to leap forward into concerns to be unfolded later in the course of this book. For

---

37 '[Plato] is looking for just those factors in the soul that will explain the three kinds of character (*tria gene phuseon*) which will enable different men to fill successfully the three vocations necessary for the efficient working of the state', N. R. Murphy, *The Interpretation of Plato's Republic* (Oxford: Clarendon Press, 1951), p. 30.

38 See *Plato's Republic: The Greek Text*, tr. B. Jowett (Oxford: Clarendon Press, 1894), pp. 328–9.

39 See Machiavelli, *The Prince and Other Writings* (London: Dent, 1995).

40 Fukuyama, *End of History and the Last Man*, p. 314.

41 See Charles Lindholm, *Charisma* (Oxford: Blackwell, 1993). Lindholm provides an excellent interdisciplinary account of the study of 'charisma', but his evaluation of the phenomenon is unfailingly negative.

42 See chapter 11 below.

43 Roy Rappaport, *Ritual and Religion in the Making of Humanity* (Cambridge: Cambridge University Press, 1999).

44 Stjepan G. Mestrovic, 'The Disappearance of the Sacred', *Postemotional Society* (London: Sage, 1997), ch. 5.

the present it is important to note how Fukuyama attempts to resolve the tension between the moribund societal banality of liberal capitalist democracy and the risk-fraught, but stimulant intoxication of *thymos*, the ancestral will-to-power. But any fuller assessment of this depends in turn upon an alternative reading of the parallel post-Hegelian traditions of Marxist socialism and Christianity, both of which are, in Fukuyama's estimation, outmoded slave moralities unsuited to the requirements of post-history.

Marxism[45] and Christianity, and above all, the successive stages in the evolution of both Marxist theory and Protestant Christian theology, have exhibited an interesting and often catastrophic mutual alienation since the death of Hegel. Christianity and Marxism are often conceived as polar opposites; in fact they not only share common roots in the Western Jewish and Christian traditions but are also constitutively influenced by the Enlightenment, and, above all, they share the context of the final flowering and subsequent disintegration of German philosophical idealism. The theoretical enlargement of both traditions flows out of the end of classical German philosophy as it was explored by left- and right-wing Hegelians following the sudden death of Hegel in 1831. This mutuality could be explored in a number of ways, but that most salient to present purposes is to construe the complex and differentiated developments of both Marxism and Christian Protestant theology as affording different resolutions of the Hegelian dialectic of lordship and bondage which is a central feature of Fukuyama's vision of the 'End of History'.

It is neither feasible nor necessary at this juncture to trace the complex Western dialectics of knowledge, power and being to their origins with, not least, Augustine of Hippo's *De Civitate Dei*.[46] Taking up a hint

---

[45] Eve Tavor Bannet, 'Marx, God and Praxis', in Philippa Berry and Andrew Wernick (eds.), *Shadow of Spirit: Postmodernism and Religion* (London: Routledge, 1992), pp. 122–34; E. Kamenka, *The Portable Karl Marx* (Harmondsworth: Penguin, 1983); Leszek Kolakowski, *Main Currents of Marxism* (3 vols., Oxford: Clarendon Press, 1978), vols. 1–3; N. L. A. Lash, *A Matter of Hope: A Theological Reflection on the Thought of Karl Marx* (London: Darton, Longman & Todd, 1981); G. Lichtheim, *Marxism: An Historical and Critical Introduction* (London: Routledge & Kegan Paul, 1964); D. McLellan, *Karl Marx: An Introduction to his Life and Thought* (London: Macmillan, 1975); D. McLellan, *Marxism and Religion: A Description and Assessment of the Marxist Critique of Religion* (London: Macmillan, 1987); D. McLellan, *The Thought of Karl Marx: An Introduction* (London: Macmillan, 1971); Karl Marx, *On Religion* (Moscow: Progress Publishers, 1957); Karl Marx, *Capital* (London: Swan & Sonnenschein, 1903); Karl Marx, *Early Writings*, tr. Rodney Livingstone and Gregor Benton (Harmondsworth: Penguin, 1974); Istvan Meszáros, *Marx's Theory of Alienation* (London: Merlin Press, 1975); B. Ollman, *Alienation: Marx's Concept of Man in Capitalist Society* (Cambridge: Cambridge University Press, 1971); R. Tucker, *Philosophy and Myth in Karl Marx* (Cambridge: Cambridge University Press, 1961; 2nd edn, 1972); P. Worsley, *Marx and Marxism* (Chichester: Ellis Harwood, 1981).

[46] See Karl Andresen (ed.), *Handbuch der Dogmen- und Theologiegeschichte* (Berlin: de Gruyter, 1985ff.).

from Herbert Marcuse, Luther's *Urtext* of German and Reformation consciousness, *The Freedom of a Christian Man* (*Die Freiheit eines Christenmenschens*)
of 1521 can be taken as a milestone in the evolution of consciousness:
here a theologian and the father of the German early modern *mentalité*
articulated the agonistic and ambiguous consciousness that is free, yet
simultaneously enslaved.[47] Both subsequent German philosophy and
Christian theology may thus be understood as working themselves out
within the possible resolutions of the dialectic of Master and Slave. One
of the few cultural critics to have grasped something close to the full and
dire implications of this dialectic of power is George Steiner, who writes
of the Hegelian (and Western) 'dialectic of aggrandisement' that characterises the mode of self-identity formation quintessentially expressed
in the parable of Lord and Bondsman.[48] This is a theme which will,
in various guises, return throughout this book in relation to theology,
religion and societal power. Rather than, as is the case with Fukuyama,
the parable of Lord and Bondsman being resolved within the narrative
of triumphant capitalism, it is this narrative that has to be reinterpreted
within the trans-historical parable.

In broad terms, processes of secularisation that were both inaugurated and accelerated by the Reformation were to consolidate the progressive marginalisation and privatisation of religious consciousness in
ways which increasingly cut the latter off from the wider human realm,
and eventually banished theology into both institutional and intellectual
isolation.[49] In Feuerbach's reductive critique of Lutheran Christianity
and Hegelian thought, Marx found the key by which he could, as he
thought, free the mind from the incubus of religion and its attendant fantasy and deception and thus allow it to unlock the causal processes and
interconnection in the fabric of human social reality. Indeed, as Leszek
Kolakowski reminds us, Karl Marx was first and foremost a German
philosopher[50] whose materialism grew out of dissatisfaction with and
rejection of the speculative philosophy which interpreted, but failed to
change, the world. As regards the dialectic of lordship and bondage,
Marx's inversion of Hegel comprised the relocation of the focus of causality in material relations. A revolution in consciousness could only take

---

[47] H. Marcuse, *Studies in Critical Philosophy*.
[48] Steiner, *In Bluebeard's Castle*.
[49] A process that culminates in the theology of the great Swiss German Reformed theologian Karl
      Barth. See Hans Urs von Balthasar, *Karl Barth: Darstellung und Deutung seiner Theologie*, 4th edn
      (Einsiedeln: Johannes Verlag, 1976). See chapter 7 below and also R. H. Roberts, *A Theology on
      its Way?: Essays on Karl Barth* (Edinburgh: T. & T. Clark, 1992).
[50] Kolakowski, *Main Currents of Marxism*, vol. I, p. 1.

place as a consequence of revolution in material relations of production. As Protestant theology became aware of the problematic nature of power as it painfully detached itself from Catholic Europe in the setting of early modernity and then the Enlightenment, so it also became conscious of the discrepancies within the Christological discourse of the God-Man Jesus Christ that lay at the very heart of the theology incarnated in the structures of the hierarchical church.

Hegel's parable comprises all these dynamics, and he confronted in a most remarkable way the power-play etched into the indelibly theological essence of ancestral European identity. In the aftermath of Hegel's death, therefore, a remarkable exchange took place: the theological essence expressed in the redemptive 'negation of the negation' effected by the infinite God who negates himself in order to permit finite consciousness to experience its true nature migrates from the ambiguous intellectual and spiritual realm of *Geist* to that of material relations. Thus Marx's depicts the apotheosis of the proleteriat as agent and bearer of the 'negation of the negation', and the location of the revolutionary transformation of history in the narrative of the class that is no class (the societal *Unding*). This excluded class will rise up and overwhelm a 'Lord' now represented by the owners of private property and capital, and thereby overcome and 'sublate' history. Correspondingly, and to a marked degree paradoxically, Protestant theology found itself embarrassed by the Promethean Christology of the superhuman God-Man that was its questionable inheritance. Thus the apotheosis of the proletariat can be juxtaposed, even correlated, with the increasingly secularised and downgraded representation of the Christ figure, who in losing his divine attributes of the Lord (*Herr*), becomes the self-emptied servant Christ (*Knecht*) of Lutheran kenotic Christology, the One who takes upon himself the form of the slave.[51] To pretend, as Fukuyama appears to do, that this dramatic inheritance is somehow obsolete, a reality leached out of European culture by the advent of liberal capitalism, is as spurious and implausible as were the former claims made on behalf of Marxist socialism that communism was a fulfilled existence free of contradiction, to which socialist reality had to conform. This book is directed, not least, at the exposure and decipherment of claims that Fukuyama presents in strident, vivid, yet rather superficial terms. The tools that Fukuyama provides for his own analysis are, it must be said, rather limited in scope; the manufacture

---

[51] In an extended exposition of Philippians 2. This theme is treated at length in theological and sociological terms in chapter 5 below.

and manipulation of reality in a globalised, managerial and commodified world is, by contrast, subtle and comprehensive. Fukuyama recalls Socrates' words:

What is to be done then? I said; how shall we find a gentle nature which also has great spirit, for the one is the contradiction of the other?[52]

Fukuyama opts for the 'great spirit', the active, value-creating existence of the exceptional human being, the man possessed of *megalothymia*. Such individuals

will deliberately seek discomfort and sacrifice, because the pain will be the only way they have of proving definitively that they can *think well of themselves*, that they remain *human beings*.[53]

The creation of a New Hegelian metanarrative and thus the recovery of a 'totally non-materialist historical dialectic'[54] requires careful refunctioning of thymotic man.[55] In fact such a refunctioning is already taking place, often, perhaps, at a more popular level than all theorists like to admit. Thus, for example, in the power feminism of Naomi Wolf,[56] in the more radical management training programmes of the enterprise culture, in Robert Bly's mythic recovery of the Wild Man,[57] and in countless New Age rituals (often using First Nation or Native American practices) the 'Warrior' is making many a return. How this may be correlated with the 'gentle nature' of which Socrates speaks is less than obvious. Moreover, there is much more that can and ought to be said about the nature and formations of human identity, not least, it might be added, when the ritual function of embedded cultures is more fully understood.

Fukuyama is most of all concerned with the revitalization of *thymos* as the means capable of inhibiting the inner rot to which liberal democracy is prone. Decadence becomes apparent in the mass production of the effete, weak 'Last Man' who calculates all and ventures nothing in a risk-aversion society. The contradiction that exists between *megalothymia* and *isothymia* is one between those who are willing to endorse and exemplify the seeking of legitimate human grandeur through risk

---

[52] Glaucon replies to Socrates in Republic II, 375: Plato, *The Dialogues of Plato*, tr. B. Jowett (2 vols, Oxford: Oxford University Press, 1871), vol. II, p. 57.

[53] Fukuyama, *End of History and the Last Man*, p. 329.

[54] *Ibid.*, p. 144.

[55] *Ibid.*, p. 180.

[56] See Naomi Wolf, 'The Feminine Fear of Power', *Fire with Fire: The New Female Power and How it Will Change the 21st Century* (London: Chatto & Windus, 1993), ch. 17.

[57] See Robert Bly, *Iron John: A Book About Men* (Shaftesbury, Dorset: Element Books, 1990).

and sacrifice and those who seek equality at all costs, the covert collectivists, who whilst enjoying liberal democracy undermine its dynamism by subverting difference. Fukuyama seeks out a new path in the renewal of 'History' that takes the form of an outlet for legitimate human aggression between what J. A. Schumpeter called the 'utopian emotionalism' of the intellectuals and the 'unromantic and unheroic civilization' of capitalist time-servers.[58] In this scenario other contradictions like that between wealth and poverty scarcely feature; they are secondary to the cultural contradiction between the strong (and effective) and the weak (and burdensome).[59]

Rather than resort to what Fukuyama regards as the 'perfectly contentless formal arts of Japan'[60] or other creative risk-laden diversions we (that is those with thymotic drive) need once more to live dangerously as free and unequal human beings:

> For as Hegel teaches us, modern liberalism is not based on the abolition of the desire for recognition so much as on its transformation into a more rational form. If *thymos* is not entirely preserved in its earlier manifestations, neither is it entirely negated. Moreover, no existing society is based exclusively on *isothymia*; all must permit some degree of safe and domesticated *megalothymia*, even if this runs contrary to the principles they profess to believe in.[61]

After the 'End of History', licensed *megalothymia* will become the new *via media*, realisable in a future value-creating humanity existing in the New Hegelian order. As a matter of simple realism Fukuyama argues for a similar domestication of the past risks of religion and nationalism:

> If nationalism is to fade away as a political force, it must be made tolerant like religion before it. National groups can retain their separate languages and sense of identity, but that identity would be expressed primarily in the realm of culture rather than politics. The French can continue to savor their wines and the Germans their sausages, but this will be done within the sphere of private life alone.[62]

Humanity must recognise that although all humankind is on the same 'wagon train'[63] of post-history and heading west towards a common goal;

---

[58] J. A. Schumpeter, *Capitalism, Socialism and Democracy*, 3rd edn (New York: Harper & Row, 1950), p. 160.

[59] See Daniel Bell, *The Cultural Contradictions of Capitalism* (New York: Basic Books, 1976) and Fredric Jameson, *The Political Unconscious: Narrative as Socially Symbolic Art* (London: Methuen, 1981).

[60] Fukuyama, *End of History and the Last Man*, p. 320. This is a rather puzzling observation, not least, perhaps, for those with first-hand experience of Japanese martial arts.

[61] Fukuyama, *End of History and the Last Man*, p. 337.

[62] *Ibid.*, p. 271.

[63] *Ibid.*, pp. 338–9.

some will crawl slowly whereas others will struggle with pride towards it. In effect, let us, Fukuyama urges, reward those who struggle and sacrifice – even as we may have to tolerate the calculating crawlers. Thus Fukuyama (and, he would have us believe, Hegel and Plato) requires us to rehabilitate *thymos*, the basis of the virtues, but let it be ruled by reason and made an ally of desire. Rather in the way the chairman or chief executive of a corporation might seek to promote a 'company culture', so in *The End of History* Fukuyama translates corporate image-making onto the global level. This book is thus a true cultural artifact of its age, a presentational exercise intended to capture the more exploratory minds of the generation that sets out in 'post-history', and which needs to have its energies safely channelled into the pursuit of pure prestige. In such a brave new world order the function of democracy is not so much political as anthropological:

> it would seem natural that liberal democracy, which seeks to abolish the distinction between masters and slaves by making men masters of themselves, should have different foreign policy objectives altogether. What will produce peace in the post-historical world will not be the fact that major states share a common principle of legitimacy. This state of affairs existed at times in the past, for example when all the nations of Europe were monarchies or empires. Peace will arise instead out of the specific nature of democratic legitimacy, and its ability to satisfy the desire for recognition.[64]

Whilst Fukuyama may have successfully, but in part, crystallised a moment of historical transition, his interpretation of such a passage as the above is misleading. A mythologised recoding of the human condition represses and obscures the dialectical core of human self and societal experience as it is focused in the task of identity-formation in the modern/postmodern condition. It is not too difficult to dispute the adequacy of both Fukuyama's reading of the meaning of Hegel's resonant image of lordship and bondage (*Herrschaft und Knechtschaft*) and of the Hegelian history of Marxist socialism and Christian theology in the nineteenth and twentieth centuries. More significantly, *The End of History* does, however, confront the reader with more profound issues that relate to the representation of the triumph of 'liberal democratic capitalism' as a state of existence subsisting beyond real contradiction.

The assertion made by the Right, and represented in mythopoeic terms by Francis Fukuyama, that the true sublation of history and of the human condition is enacted in the triumph of capitalism is now no matter

---

[64] *Ibid.*, p. 279.

of assent or dissent, but an untruth incorporated in a myriad of cultural practices and suffused through reality in a differentiated and managerially enforced *habitus* and societal transcendental which continues to invade and replicate itself across all areas of civil society. In what follows we investigate some of the manifestations of the 'triumph of capitalism' that underpins the assertion of the 'End of History'. When understood in this setting, the present state of the interface between religion, theology and the human sciences opens up areas of intense concern for closer inspection: the future of the human is at stake.

CHAPTER 2

Religion and the 'enterprise culture': the British experience from Thatcher to Blair (1979–2000)

The events of 1989–90 marked a historic transition which was represented by Francis Fukuyama in mythopoeic terms both as the 'End of History' and as a contingency requiring in response a global shift in consciousness.[1] Fukuyama's macroscopic vision implied an outflanking of the out-worn ideologies of Christianity and socialism by the inevitable victory of 'liberal democratic capitalism', which, in turn, demands universal global acceptance. This new order supersedes all alternatives, thus 'ending' history as a conflictual narrative comprising any fundamental disagreement about alternative resolutions. In the ensuing decade the brutal actualities of human conflict have proved that the assertion of the 'End' was nugatory not least as regards nationalism, which has proved to be far more resilient and vigorous than the harmless cultural atavisms of French wine and the German sausage envisaged by Fukuyama. Where, however, a sense of ending is genuinely detectable is the point at which the 'triumph' of capitalism inaugurates increasingly managed – and managerialised – forms of governance legitimated periodically by 'liberal democracy'. The global discourse of the 'End of History' did indeed suggest a loss of dangerous human grandeur and pretension, but when attention is directed away from the level of world-historical discourse and to the investigation of key individual examples of societal evolution, it would appear that important changes have taken place. A multiplex closure or ending is apparent as management and surveillance displace agency and dissolve residual trust.[2] Seen thus, the 'End of History' is a specific encoding of the 'end of the human' as regards both

---

[1] I am indebted to James Beckford's comments upon an early draft of this chapter, which was first presented as a plenary paper at the biennial Conference of the Société Internationale de Sociologie des Religions at Maynooth, Ireland, 19–23 August 1991. This chapter is a substantial revision of the published paper 'Religion and the "Enterprise Culture": The British Experience in the Thatcher Era (1979–1990)', *Social Compass*, 39/1 (1992), 15–33.

[2] Francis Fukuyama, *Trust: The Social Values and the Creation of Prosperity* (London: Hamish Hamilton, 1995).

the individual and the collective. Under such ever-extending conditions of aggregation and control the more extreme forms of identity-formation are liable to survive – and even thrive – albeit in displaced and transmogrified forms.

Following the election of Mrs (later Lady) Margaret Thatcher in 1979, Britain became an exemplary focal point for a societal transition which began with the rediscovery and redistribution of the 'culture' of individual 'enterprise' and then laid the foundations for a new configuration of cultural tensions. At the heart of these uneasy juxtapositions was the promotion of a fateful symbiotic but oppositional relationship between an ever more emancipated enterprising managerial elite and the seemingly inexorable expansion of a managed mass humanity. Britain provides a key 'local' example that may allow the grandiose discourse of putative universals, be they, for example, those of Francis Fukuyama, Mrs Thatcher or Mikhail Gorbachev, to be anchored in the contingencies of national and institutional change. Under these conditions the 'return', 'resurgence' or 'revival' of 'religion' or the 'sacred' has in transmuted forms emerged as a dynamic but inherently ambiguous arena of possibilities. As the limits of control and influence expand, so the remaining traces of unmastered alternatives become the hard-fought frontiers, some of which are examined in this book. In this chapter the broad context and content of these changes are outlined; in the following chapter the inner dynamics of the consciousness of the new elite are explored. In ensuing chapters we shall see how other sectors of identity – and culture-forming sectors have been absorbed, either through conscious volition or unwittingly, into a new cultural configuration.

Global ideologues, and not least such a figure as Francis Fukuyama, who was significantly dependent upon Nietzsche, may well have shared tacit assumptions about the decline of the religious dimension shared by proponents of the standard secularisation model which was central to the post-Second World War sociological study of religion.[3] Yet, as will become apparent, when the passage from the relatively loose forms of social control associated in Britain with the post-war Keynesian consensus of 'Butskellism', the 'rise of professional society' – and with national economic decline – to a more obviously polarised and fully managed society with a new set of cultural contradictions is explored and understood, then 'religion', 'religiosities' and 'spirituality' can be seen to

---

[3] See, for example, Steven Bruce (ed.), *Religion and Modernisation: Sociologists and Historians Debate the Secularisation Thesis* (Oxford: Clarendon Press, 1992). See also Mikhail Gorbachev's construal of the greater Europe in chapter 8 below.

have gained a renewed if not unproblematic salience. This, then, is the transformatory matrix to be first addressed in this chapter and then pursued through other contexts in the course of this book.

As the ideological self-confidence of the New Right grew following the election of Mrs Thatcher in 1979, so the ultimate goal of her successive administrations became nothing less than the rehabilitation of a nation, the re-creation of a 'Britain strong and free'.[4] During the 'Thatcher era', a socio-economic 'British experiment'[5] took place with a view to creating a 'New Britain'.[6] In global terms this is an extraordinary and exemplary episode which merits generous contextual presentation. Furthermore, for present purposes this is an essential aspect of the setting within which the recomposition of the religious field has to be understood. Thus whilst it might at first sight seem disadvantageous to examine the Thatcher era and the 'enterprise culture' from the uneasy borderland between religion, the economy and politics, it will become evident that the contrary is in fact the case.[7] The growing socio-economic and ideological hegemony of Thatcherism and the 'enterprise culture' projected itself through an uncompromising ruling discourse before which all alternatives seemed impotent. Given the relative weakness and disarray of the opposition parties, on a superficial level, 'religion' initially gained an unexpected prominence in the period 1979–90 as it temporally became one of the increasingly limited societal niches for an alternative public discourse. There is therefore some plausibility in regarding religio-political controversy in the Thatcher era as a displacement phenomenon ironically similar in some respects to the role of the churches in the pre-1989–90 Poland, in the then German Democratic Republic, and later in Romania.[8] The systemic ambiguity of the evidence concerning the changing societal role of religion that began during the period under examination is such as to require preliminary qualification of the terms 'religious' and 'religion'.

---

4 Conservative Party Conference Speech, 14 October 1978 in A. B. Cooke (ed.), *Margaret Thatcher: The Revival of Britain. Speeches on Home and European Affairs 1975–1988* (London: Aurum, 1989), p. 167.

5 Taken from the title of the then Chancellor of the Exchequer Nigel Lawson's Fifth Mais Lecture 'The British Experiment', delivered at the City University Business School, 18 June 1984.

6 As was again Nigel Lawson's ambition in his speech 'The New Britain: The Tide of Ideas from Atlee to Thatcher', delivered on behalf of the Centre for Policy Studies at the Carlton Club, 19 January 1988.

7 Evidence relating to mutual 'resurgences' of religion and capitalism in the British or world contexts is ambiguous and fragmented. See the introduction to R. H. Roberts (ed.), *Religion and the Transformations of Capitalism: Comparative Approaches* (London: Routledge, 1995). This collection contains an extensive bibliography.

8 See Sabrina Petra Ramet (ed.), *Catholicism and Politics in Communist Societies* (Durham, NC: Duke University Press, 1990) and her *Protestantism and Politics in Eastern Europe and Russia: The Communist and Post-Communist Eras* (Durham, NC: Duke University Press, 1992).

In this chapter the term 'religion' and cognate expressions operate at three levels. First, during the Thatcher era it is possible to recognise a significant readmission of explicit religious factors into political life and public controversy, regardless of what may have been the declining level of belief in the population at large. As David Martin observed: 'Anyone observing the media at the beginning of 1989 would have been struck by the increased salience of news about religion in Britain as contrasted with the decreased salience of religion in the beliefs and practices of ordinary people.'[9] This observation primarily pertains to main-line religion. Second, as introduced above, there are those aspects of the Thatcher era and the 'enterprise culture' which invite analysis employing religious and theological concepts and categories as metaphors. This definition of 'religion' may allow us to understand the strange but often-repeated passage from the metaphorical to the real which characterises the capture of consciousness of each new sector of society as it fell (and sectors continue to fall) under the thrall of managerial modernisation. I designate these the quasi-religious aspects of Thatcherism, the 'enterprise culture', Conservative 'reform', and the 'modernisation' associated with New Labour.[10] In James Beckford's terms, this aspect of the present argument has to do with the 'religious dimensions of social conflict', and in particular the linguistic consequences of such a shift. Third, I argue that there is a distinctive core of ideas and social phenomena, an individualised charismatic religiosity which may be designated an 'enterprise religion'. Whilst the latter is facilitated by the developments outlined in this chapter, this entrepreneurial and increasingly marketised spirituality has to be understood as a sector within the changing and evolving religious field as a whole. This form of religiosity is shared by overlapping networks of individuals and groups who operate as adjuncts to the leading edge of the enterprise culture, but it still remains largely outside the institutional structures of the main Christian denominations and other major religious groupings in Britain.[11] As we progress towards an account of the comprehensive recomposition of the religious field it becomes apparent that a new 'main line' has emerged, in the form of a variegated alternative

---

[9] 'The Churches: Pink Bishops and the Iron Lady', in D. Kavanagh and A. Seldon (eds.), *The Thatcher Effect* (Oxford: Clarendon Press, 1989), p. 330, n. 5. The ambiguous aspects of any apparent 'resurgence' of religion in the British context in the Thatcher era are compounded in the light of the evidence envinced by Peter Brierley in the MARC Europe English Church Survey; see '*Christian' England: What the English Church Survey Reveals* (London: MARC Europe, 1991).

[10] See J. Beckford, 'The Sociology of Religion 1945–1989', *Social Compass*, 37/1 (1990), 57.

[11] For a comprehensive account see Paul Heelas' notable study of contemporary religious change, *The New Age Movement: The Celebration of the Self and the Sacralization of Modernity* (Oxford: Blackwell, 1996).

religiosity persisting outside the major main-line Christian denominations and other religious groupings. In late 2000 it is tempting to liken
the present state of some main-line Christian denominations in Britain
to that of religious 'outlets' sharing the fate of well-established multiple
stores (like Marks and Spencer) which suddenly found themselves with a
range of products which did not relate to a rapidly changing 'designer'
market. Confronted with a changing situation and its implications for
the sociological study of religion, James Beckford has argued that it is
debatable whether 'the nostalgia for old theories' on the part of sociologists of religion is 'any more helpful than is nostalgia for the old gods
and goddesses'.[12] His remarks were prescient and apposite, as it seems
that the insights of the founding fathers of the sociology of religion may
be less useful than they were before. In brief, 'religion' understood in the
threefold differentiation outlined above ceases only to denote a shrinking marginal reality closed to all but fossilised adherent-groupings and to
ethnic minorities and is better understood as a function of socio-cultural
change as a whole.

In the first instance early Thatcherism found strident expression in the
distinct, but at first eccentric and marginal discourse of the New Right
devotees; later Thatcherism carried itself forward on the basis of the revival of a dominative public rhetorical style not experienced for many
decades in Britain. The disputatious character of Thatcherite rhetoric[13]
was intended in the first instance to divide and polarise, rather than to
integrate society or indeed to legitimate Thatcherism as an ideology. The
price of transformation was seen to be in re-energising division – and
not in achieving consensus. Thus the retrospective definition and contextual analysis of the key concepts of 'Thatcherism' and the 'enterprise
culture' require us to recollect their visionary and rhetorical excess, and
their use as a means for the communication of policy which uninten-
tionally helped create social space for a short-lived 'resurgence' of public
or main-line religion. The media career of such figures as the Bishop
of Durham, David Jenkins, was nourished by a culture of public confrontation so very obviously relished by Mrs Thatcher and her immediate supporters. The abandonment of this style and its supplanting by the

---

[12] Beckford, 'The Sociology of Religion 1945–1989', 45–64.
[13] Here the recent discussion of rhetoric in relation to the human and social sciences is presupposed.
For an introduction and exhaustive bibliography see R. H. Roberts and J. M. M. Good (eds.),
The Recovery of Rhetoric: Persuasive Discourse and Disciplinarity in the Human Sciences (Charlottesville, VA:
University of Virginia Press, 1993).

regulatory and managerial approach to governance characteristic of Mrs Thatcher's successor, the Conservative Prime Minister John Major, and then of the New Labour Prime Minister Tony Blair – and even of mainline religion itself – amounted to a routinisation of fateful significance: the bang of triumphant capitalism ends in the whimper of pervasive banality of managerialism.

The ambitions of the New Right knew no bounds and implied, indeed demanded, the reworking of the human condition, for as Margaret Thatcher famously observed: 'Economics are the method. The object is to change the soul.'[14] Mrs Thatcher's resonant words captured in a characteristically stark way the relationship between the dominant ideology that came to be known as 'Thatcherism' and an often reluctant populace increasingly subject to an imposed inner conversion process, and on an organisational level to the enforced teleology of societal 'reform'. Thus the apparently piecemeal series of measures introduced after the Conservative election victory of May 1979 came to assume the form of a fully consistent programme that embodied ever bolder ideological and cultural ambitions, pretensions which came to include the transformation of the 'souls' of individuals.[15] The ever-extending remit allocated to and appropriated by the enforcers and facilitators of change in the innermost identity of individuals and groups is one of our major concerns: as we shall see, the enlargement of the manager's right to manage amounts to a transgression of boundaries already weakened by secularisation, modernisation and a postmodernising culture. The set of tensions between two contrasting but complementary tendencies of Thatcherite reform and enterprise culture provides a secular analogue of the contrast between 'law' and 'gospel', a dichotomy which has progressively dissolved and redefined class and status boundaries in terms of 'hard' and 'soft' cultural regimes. 'Thatcherism' as such (understood as an ideologically driven array of economic and social policy measures) and the so-called 'enterprise culture' (an inspirational

---

[14] Margaret Thatcher, *The Sunday Times*, 7 May 1988.
[15] Accounts of the changes in economic policy, the precondition of the Thatcher social reforms, include: Samuel Brittain, 'The Thatcher Government's Economic Policy', in Kavanagh and Seldon, *The Thatcher Effect*, pp. 1–37; and P. Munford, 'Mrs Thatcher's Economic Reform Programme – Past, Present and Future', in R. Skidelsky (ed.), *Thatcherism* (London: Chatto & Windus, 1988), pp. 93–106. For an excellent overview, see Peter Jenkins, *Mrs Thatcher's Revolution: The Ending of the Socialist Era* (London: Pan, 1987), and further to this Dennis Kavanagh, *Thatcherism and British Politics: The End of Consensus* (Oxford: Oxford University Press, 1987). The standard political biography is Hugo Young, *One of Us: A Biography of Margaret Thatcher* (London: Macmillan, 1989).

goal, an ideal and transformed future state) have informed a capitalist revolution from above enacted in the British experiment.

'Thatcherism' and the 'enterprise culture' were intimately related, but they were not identical. Thatcherism may be understood as the economic and public policy foundation of the ideal, future socio-cultural goal of an 'enterprise culture'; both, however, subsisted together as related aspects of a process of societal transformation. The former was a package of measures designed to expand the free market and thereby enhance the 'freedom' and 'choice' of the universal consumer, banish the 'culture of dependency', and thus emancipate the entrepreneurial activity of the 'sovereign individuals' of capitalism.[16] The role of such discourse was *fundamental* to the enactment of the Thatcherite enterprise culture: thus rail users were addressed as 'customers', students 'consume' education, hospital patients likewise 'consume' health-care services, and so on. The population had to learn to use new commonplaces so as to facilitate its ownership of cultural reidentification. Resistance to such reidentification on the part of both 'providers' and 'receivers' has remained a function of the composite strength of the inherent identities of each sector; it has, for example, proved difficult to recategorise mental patients as 'customers' engaged in voluntary consumption. Thatcherism construed thus can be understood as the necessary condition of the enterprise culture, the outward and visible programme that precedes and accompanies the inner transformation of the enterprising 'soul'. On its more abstract and 'inner' level, the enterprise culture aimed to secure permanent changes in the self-perception, attitudes and behaviour of the whole populace; it implied as its foundation socio-cultural engineering conceived on a national, an international and ultimately a global scale.

The definition of Thatcherism is problematic, for, as Dennis Kavanagh noted, it could have applied equally to Margaret Thatcher's personal beliefs and goals, to a set of social policies, or indeed to the international application of policies legitimated by their original use in Britain. To a degree unprecedented in post-war British political history the

---

[16] This allusion presupposes familiarity with recent literature on capitalism and the market economy. See, for example, Peter L. Berger, *The Capitalist Revolution: Fifty Propositions about Prosperity, Equality, and Liberty* (Aldershot: Wildwood House, 1987); Anthony Giddens, *Capitalism and Modern Social Theory: An Analysis of the Writings of Marx, Durkheim and Max Weber* (Cambridge: Cambridge University Press, 1971); Michael Novak, *The Spirit of Democratic Capitalism* (London: Institute of Economic Affairs, 1982); and R. H. Roberts (ed.), *Religion and the Transformations of Capitalism* provides extensive bibliographical information.

personal convictions of one individual came to dominate a government and its policies. Mrs Thatcher herself could put it in very simple terms:

And I say to them [foreigners applying her views], Thatcherism is much older than me. It's based on fundamental common sense, the limitations of the powers of government and handing more and more powers and the fruits of their work to people. And it works.[17]

Looked at more broadly, Thatcherism has of course its own history and development, which have been well documented from a variety of political standpoints.[18] Its sources lay within a complex conversion process within British Conservatism, through which it withdrew from Keynesian consensus politics as it came under the influence of the thought of the New Right. A seminal text in the breaking of the egalitarian consensus inherited from R. H. Tawney was Keith Joseph and Jonathan Sumption's *Equality*, with its Orwellian slogan 'Poverty is not Unfreedom.'[19] The enactment of Thatcherism involved a remarkable process of transmission, as yet not fully documented, whereby a series of social policies derived from privately funded New Right 'think-tanks'[20] were passed into legislative draft by the Civil Service. Bills were then subjected to a limited measure of critical appraisal by Parliament in a procedure, which, given something close to 'parliamentary dictatorship', amounted to little more than ritualised abuse and subsequent enactment in law. The outcome has been mixed: some 'reforms' became widely acknowledged successes, while in other instances there have been dire long-term consequences. Thus the early history of rail privatisation has only just emerged in the setting of the catastrophic transport and environmental crisis of late 2000.[21]

[17] Television interview with Brian Walden, 29 October 1989, in David Cox (ed.), *The Walden Interviews* (London: LWT Boxtree, 1990), p. 41.

[18] See Kavanagh, *Thatcherism and British Politics*, pp. 9ff., n. 5. From the Left: Stuart Hall and Martin Jacques, *The Politics of Thatcherism* (London: Lawrence & Wishart, 1983); and R. Jessop, K. Bonnett, S. Bromley and T. Ling, *Thatcherism: A Tale of Two Nations* (London: Polity, 1988). From the emergent Liberal Democrat centre: David Marquand, *The Unprincipled Society: New Demands and Old Politics* (London: Cape, 1988).

[19] 'The New Right' is the title of chapter 3 of Keith Joseph and Jonathan Sumption, *Equality* (London: John Murray, 1979). For a useful introduction to the ideas of the New Right see David G. Green, *The New Right: The Counter-Revolution in Political, Economic and Social Thought* (Brighton: Harvester, 1987).

[20] Information concerning these organisations was usefully provided in Arthur Seldon, *Capitalism* (Oxford: Blackwell, 1990), pp. 404–6.

[21] In early 2001 it would therefore appear that the systemic crises relating to bovine spongiform encephalopathy (BSE) and foot and mouth disease (FMD) in agriculture, the failure of Railtrack, acute teacher and health-worker shortages, and so on all share the same dynamic of 'top-down' managerialist regulation having confronted and destroyed economically 'irrational' 'bottom-up' local cultures in ways congruent with the pattern of 'modern management' outlined in this chapter.

Thatcherism understood as a consistent economic and political creed may be summarised in terms of the following. Government possesses limited capacity to do lasting good, but a great capacity to do harm. Heavy stress is to be laid upon individual responsibility and the existence of an objective morality of clearly defined right and wrong. There should, however, be a strong state capable of performing the limited 'primary tasks' of ensuring adequate defence of the realm and preserving internal law and order.[22] The solution of an individual's own problems lies primarily with him or herself or in the context of the family (expanded, if necessary, by an appeal to neighbours), rather than in calling upon government, either central or local. Strict monetary discipline is required which recognises that increases in public expenditure without corresponding economic growth and efficiency result in more taxation and thereby lessen the 'choice' expressed in spending power, which is regarded as the real basis of 'freedom'. The market is regarded as the best, indeed the only fully satisfactory means of promoting economic growth and free choice, and of thereby safeguarding personal liberty. More expenditure on one service usually means less investment in another, unless resort is to be made to borrowing or inflation. Government intervention on behalf of the weak, the sick and the unemployed may be positively harmful in terms of slowing down society's ability to adapt in a changing world.[23] The ever-extending 'privatisation' of industry and public utilities is an imperative, and the marketisation (and, it may be added, the consequent commodification) of virtually *all* areas of human life are also highly valued imperatives. At the time of the introduction of these ideas as policy measures in the decade following 1979 their impact was revolutionary. As individual characteristics of socio-economic change each would ideally require the full and close analysis that cannot be undertaken here, but what is remarkable at the outset of the twenty-first century is how many of these ideas remained integral to the Third Way consensus that has informed the social and economic policies of Britain and the United States during the prime ministership of Tony Blair and the presidency of Bill Clinton.

Thatcherism, as seen in the foregoing cluster of economic and socio-political policies and practices, gained confidence and clarity during the

---

[22] Mrs Thatcher clarified her views on the role of the state in her speech to the Bow Group, 6 May 1978, in Cooke, *Revival of Britain*, p. 76, n. 6.

[23] The defeat by complexity argument was most provocatively expressed in Christian terms by Digby Anderson (ed.), *The Kindness that Kills: The Churches' Simplistic Response to Complex Social Issues* (London: SPCK, 1984). See also B. Griffith, *Morality and the Market Place* (London, Hodder & Stoughton, 1982); and B. Griffith, *The Creation of Wealth* (London: Hodder & Stoughton, 1984). Professor Griffith was the leading ideologist of Christian Thatcherism.

period under consideration. The ideal and proleptic goal of Thatcherism was represented by the 'enterprise culture', properly so-called. At the core of the latter resided a distinctive vision of personal and social renewal achieved on the basis of the morally unencumbered practice and celebration of wealth creation. Such a conviction, which entails freedom from guilt about greed, proved for some unattainable without a fundamental *metanoia*, a conversion experience which could not be generated on the basis of mere inductive rationality. Indeed, as Jonathan Raban wrote of Thatcherism (the husk surrounding the kernel of the enterprise culture): 'To be a "Thatcherite" is, in Margaret Thatcher's own terms, to experience an epiphany, to undergo a religious transfiguration.'[24] The *quasi-religious* character of Thatcherism, its demand for 'conversion', was part and parcel of the rhetoric of conviction that eschewed conventional modes of persuasion embodied in the consensual mainstream of post-war British politics. It was an ideology that demanded of its proponents sufficient conviction to allow them to break with a long-standing post-war *sensus communis* and the politics of 'Butskellism',[25] and to press for the imposition of policies in the name of a higher, distant goal. The conflictual mismatch between the policies imposed and the actual state of any given social context was incidental. Indeed, the distress caused by marketisation was an unfortunate but wholly necessary 'egg-breaking' that would have to take place on the preparatory path to the great banquet of the enterprise culture. In terms of international comparison the consequences of such policies inevitably varied: Britain, Russia and (say) the Czech Republic provide ample evidence of such contrasts. For any morally aware individual to remain convinced of the rightness of the Thatcherite conception of the enterprise culture required an enduring will to believe. There had to exist in the individual an adamantine acceptance that the ultimate end of creating an enterprise culture justified the grossly unequal interim outcomes, and the means employed. For others, indeed perhaps the majority, straightforward greed and personal gain were their own justification, and the attendant legitimation of the hardening and loss of conscience provided welcome emancipation from the last vestiges of constraint lingering on in the religious afterglow of a post-Christian culture. The remarks of newspaper editor and tycoon Jocelyn Stevens, who was appointed chairman of English Heritage in 1991,

---

[24] Jonathan Raban, *God, Man and Mrs Thatcher* (London: Chatto & Windus, 1989), p. 27, n. 17.

[25] The loose combination of policies drawn from the Conservative R. A. Butler, the architect of the 1944 Education Act, and Hugh Gaitskell, who between them marked out the middle ground in British politics in the 1950s and 1960s, territory from which Labour and then the Conservatives were to depart in the course of the 1970s.

crystallised this change in national sensibility: 'If I have a reputation for being a cold-blooded sacker . . . it is because I believe people who are not fully employed or are past their best should go if the rest are going to survive . . . There is no room for charity today.'[26]

Perhaps the most fundamental point of distinction between the pre- and post-Thatcher eras was the rejection of the belief in the desirability of full employment and the *explicit* acceptance not only of a pool of unemployed, and thus in principle mobile, available labour, but also the *implicit* acceptance of a new configuration in social stratification: the emergence of a national 'underclass', first publicly stigmatised by Mrs Thatcher as the 'enemy within' in the course of the 1984–5 Miners' Strike.[27] The likely consequences of creating by default inner-city or peripheral 'reservations' to contain what amounted to a willed, but unplanned, demographic surplus that lacked the skills required by the European and global labour market were largely ignored. These people become a problem to be contained by a (so far as possible privatised) internal management system. In consequence, it was the inner-city problem and the urban priority areas (UPAs) that focused much church attention during the tense decade of the 1980s.

By contrast with the rigour, the *lex* of Thatcherism, the *kerygma* of the 'enterprise culture' can be best understood as a cluster of loosely related inspirational values endowed with teleological intent. In a keynote speech of September 1989, Lord Young, one of the chief architects of the new political order, spoke of 'the virtues of responsibility, initiative, competitiveness and risk taking, and industrious effort' that best encapsulated the culture of enterprise.[28] Prior to the appearance of Lord Young those present were publicly cautioned by a pro-vice-chancellor, who intimated that there should be no hostile questioning of Lord Young as this might be interpreted as an infringement of the academic freedom of the speaker, and the University could well be fined. Lord Young's moralising conception

---

[26] Reported in the *Independent*, 10 August 1991. Stevens' retirement from this post nine years later allowed for a change in policy on (for example) the use of Stonehenge as a place of pagan celebration of the Summer Solstice in 2000. Stevens' successor values negotiation above confrontation. Socio-scientific evidence for basic attitude change is less easy to come by. See M. Abrams, D. Gerard and N. Timms (eds.), *Values and Social Change in Britain* (London: Macmillan, 1985); and S. D. Harding and D. Phillips, *Values in Europe: A Cross National Survey* (London: Macmillan, 1985). See also the *Observer*/Harris poll of December 1989 reported in the *Observer*, 31 December 1989, and the BBC/MORI poll reported in the *Independent*, 3 May 1989, the so-called 'Thatcher's children' survey. Both surveys revealed mixed responses to different aspects of the emergent enterprise culture.

[27] See Frank Field, *Losing Out: The Emergence of Britain's Underclass* (Oxford: Blackwell, 1989).

[28] 'Enterprise Regained', speech at The Values of the Enterprise Culture Conference in September 1989 delivered at Lancaster University, in Russell Keat and Nicholas Abercrombie (eds.), *Enterprise Culture* (London: Routledge, 1991), p. 6, n. 16.

of the enterprise culture was superficially markedly at variance with the infamous popular archetypes of Thatcherism: the ruthless amoral up-wardly mobile 'yuppy' and the oafish working-class 'Loadsamoney' who stalked the British media (and the streets) in the 1980s. Young's paradigm lay close to the virtues of Samuel Smiles' *Self Help*,[29] that is to indepen-dence, self-reliance, autonomy and individualism, and to self-realisation combined with a certain self-righteous moral unctuousness; the former lacked, however, the overt religious tenor of the latter.[30]

Despite the heavy-footed presentational rhetoric of Thatcherism and the invasive metaphors of its propagandists, the 'enterprise culture' as such proved to be a paradoxical and ironically *fragile* commodity: in soci-ety and business 'enterprise' and its 'culture' are as delicate as they are in religion. Such is the seemingly inevitable fate of 'charisma'. The enter-prise culture involved processes that were easily inhibited by contextual constraints; for its practitioners it involved risk, stress, marginalisation, cognitive dissonance and the unfailing expression of energy. Individual personal performance became the supreme virtue in what amounted to a neo-vitalist celebration of the individual's capacity to effect change. The enterprise culture therefore implied a whole ethos of performance, a new aesthetic of the body, and modes of activity which were in conflict with the consensual *pathos* and passivity of recalcitrant, bureaucratised insti-tutions, be they in business and industry, in government, or in the sectors of health, education and social welfare, not to mention the equally rou-tinised organisational structures of indigenous British religious traditions and their cycles of enactment. 'Enterprise culture' was the vital antithe-sis of 'dependency culture': its very success depended upon the public recognition of a contrast between two alternative and, in the minds of some, mutually exclusive ways of being human. What is most obviously experienced is, as with Fukuyama, a societal contrast between an active minority of *megalothymics* and a passive majority of *isothymics*.

The ethos of the enterprise culture was largely self-referential, and, de-spite the much-vaunted 'trickle-down' theory of wealth redistribution,[31] it and Thatcherism proved incapable of generating a compelling moral

---

[29] In Samuel Smiles, *Self Help, with Illustrations of Character and Conduct* (London: Murray, 1863), we find one of the chief contributors to the development of the ethos of Nonconformist self-improvement.
[30] See the autobiographical apologia by Lord Young of Grafham, *The Enterprise Years: A Businessman in the Cabinet* (London: Headline, 1990).
[31] See A. Eyre, 'Faith, Charity and the Market', in Peter Gee and John Fulton (eds.), *Religion and Power, Decline and Growth: Sociological Analyses of Religion in Britain, Poland and the Americas* (London: British Sociological Association, 1991), pp. 42–51; and Frank Field, 'How Have Britain's Poor Fared?', in M. Allison and D. L. Edwards (eds.), *Christianity and Conservatism: Are Christianity and Conservativism Compatible?* (London: Hodder & Stoughton, 1990), pp. 242–62.

vision. The 'enterprising self' searched for forms of expressive realisation that might soften individual isolation and rehumanise an increasingly harsh and atomised social reality. In Britain, above all in England,
for millions the final traces of organic, land-based community were already extinct, and the Thatcherite uprooting of many of the surrogate
intermediate organisations associated with the post-war Welfare State
made for an even deeper sense of deracination. The early urbanisation
of the Industrial Revolution, massive post-Second World War rehousing
programmes, and then the progressive dismantling of the Welfare State
and the weakening of residual associative structures led to a combination
of factors which had negative implications for the sustenance of community. Indeed, one key factor in the accelerating cultural decoupling
of Scotland from England during the period 1989–99 was an enduring
Scottish respect for the idea and reality of the 'common good'. Under
Thatcherism a sudden and marked increase in the demand for a welfare role implicitly devolved upon the churches, and above all upon the
Church of England as sole remaining quasi-official agency present in 'no-
go' areas of acute urban decay; this was another important factor that
promoted the controversial prominence of religion in the public sphere.

In reality, the 'enterprise culture' tended to be narrowly moralistic
and affective, rather than ethical or seriously reflective. The resurgent
problems of crime, violence, pornography and sexual excess, and so on
appeared to lie largely outside its intrinsic concerns.[32] A pervasive educational crisis was, however, to be tackled by managerial, neo-Fordist
measures which were to become the true inheritance of Thatcherism.
The potentially unstable ethos of the 'enterprise culture' was to play no
central part in comprehensive 'reform': it was to become the prerogative of an elite. In ideological terms the imposition of 'enterprise' upon the
British public sectors of health, education and the social services as the
policy measures to be taken to in order to achieve a full enterprise culture
concealed an illusion. What emerged has been very different: for example, the 1988 Education Reform Act contained an array of essentially
managerial measures which were to have enormous implications for all
those involved in the 'education industry', which are to be investigated
later.[33] Socio-ethical issues in the public domain were progressively subsumed under a centralised style of government and privatised commercial means of social control and cultural commodification. The so-called

[32] The Home Office figures of April 1991 recorded an astounding 24 per cent increase in the rate
of crime over the preceding year.
[33] As regards the universities see chapter 4 below.

'active citizen' faced a long march in an anomic social desert hemmed in by external restraints enforced by an ever-growing private 'security industry' committed to the defence of private property rights. Public space, the public and the common good shrivelled away. With hindsight, all of this can be seen as the realisation, through a range of means, of the conviction that lay behind Mrs Thatcher's notorious remark: 'There is no such thing as society; there are individual men and women and there are families' ventured in an interview in the journal *Woman's Own*. It is important to note that as an 'authoritarian populist' Mrs Thatcher made some of her most telling communications in the popular mass media (the BBC Radio 2 *Jimmy Young Show* being a favourite outlet).

There are therefore paradoxical points of connection between religion and the 'enterprise culture', given that the latter ultimately functioned as a sugared coating for what was to prove to be the invasive managerialism that Thatcherism in its routinised form was to become. In effect, both Thatcherism and the enterprise culture were ethically undercommitted, yet, given British constitutional arrangements, they were overempowered: there has proved to be no separation of powers capable of resisting the amazing growth of centralisation that proceeded apace in the years following the collapse of Marxist 'democratic centralism' in the East.[34] An ever-extending disciplinary regime for the many and self-realisation for the few confronted traditional churches in a post-traditional society that were, and remain, rhetorically overcommitted, but simultaneously drained of effective social influence, and thus often unable to deliver. During the post-Second World War period, British religion was largely represented sociologically by means of the theoretical and empirical appraisal of processes of secularisation.[35] British (and in particular English) religion has become increasingly differentiated along ethnic lines following waves of immigration,[36] but for the moment Christianity nevertheless remains through the two main churches of England and Scotland, and increasingly the Roman Catholic Church, an important means of expressing symbolically the

[34] Thus from late December 2000 the abolition of Community Health Councils and their replacement by officers employed by each Area Health Authority has brought patient (customer) complaints under rational managerial control freed from the perceived inefficiency of any residual separation of powers.

[35] An extended discussion of secularisation dominated British sociology of religion for a quarter-century. The bibliography is very extensive: see again Bruce, *Religion and Modernization*.

[36] Accounts of the configuration of British religion are to be found in P. Badham (ed.), *Religion, State and Modern Society in Britain* (Lampeter: Edward Mellen Press, 1989), Grace Davie, 'Believing Without Belonging: Is This the Future of Religion in Britain?', CISR paper, Helsinki, 1989, and Grace Davie, *Religion in Britain since 1945: Believing Without Belonging* (Oxford: Blackwell, 1994).

integration of the nations of the United Kingdom, and of orchestrating 'folk' and 'implicit' religion. Interestingly, however, the enterprise culture understood in a broader sense not only used quasi-religion in its promotion, but also came to express its own distinct forms of religiosity which, as has become apparent, ill suited traditional British religion.

A key factor in future developments may well lie in the disproportionately high religiosity of ethnic groups of immigrant origin in comparison with the relative indifference of the host population to organised religion, as Grace Davie has demonstrated.[37] Hence 2 million Muslims constitute one of the largest single bodies of active religious believers in Britain, and increasing efforts are now being made to attract their political support. In this context new religious movements (NRMs) are perhaps more significant in media perception than in real demographic terms. Recent surveys indicate growth in the neo-charismatic house church movement against the background of a general decline in the main Christian denominations, most marked in the case of the Roman Catholic Church. The as-yet relatively apolitical role of new religious movements and the extra-ecclesial Christian renewal groups puts them outside immediate concern in this chapter. However, in the cultural exhaustion of a *post-postmodern* condition and in the context of the societal neo-Fordism imposed by central government, the experience of the often religiously informed drive towards national devolution within the United Kingdom now suggests that those with *any* convictions have a powerful advantage over those with none.

The New Right's intended role of the churches in reinforcing personal and family morality as sacred duties had already been weakened not only by 'collectivist' tendencies, made most visible for some in the social teaching of the *curia* of the Church of England Board for Social Responsibility, but also, paradoxically, by the radical dehistoricisation of Christianity as a world religion advocated by Edward Norman in his much-publicised Reith Lectures of 1978. Norman, a mentor of the New Right religious agenda, proposed a return on the part of the Christian faith to its foundational 'eternal truths' and to the cultivation of the spiritual growth of the individual. Norman had directed the churches and Christians away from *all* temporal concerns and contributed to an increasingly marked polarisation of views concerning the nature and

---

37 See Grace Davie's development of her 1989 paper in *Religion in Britain since 1945: Believing Without Belonging* (Oxford: Blackwell, 1994).

purpose of Christianity and religion in society.[38] According to Norman, 'the teachings of the saviour clearly describe a personal rather than a social morality' and contemporary Christianity had reduced 'what were once the unique revelations of eternity to a desiccating and secularised blueprint for moral concern' and 'an insistence on the priority of social change over the cultivation of personal spirituality'.[39] Later, Digby Anderson carried forward this line of argument in decrying the naivety of the 'kindness that kills'.[40] Repeated attempts to stage a return to 'Victorian values' failed to precipitate a recovery of, for example, the traditional marriage ethic and the nuclear family.

There are, however, four clear instances in which explicit main-line religion gained public prominence during the Thatcher era, and each can be related to continuing societal change. The first of these was the acrimonious clash between Mrs Thatcher and the Conservative government and Anglican Archbishop of Canterbury, Robert Runcie, over the content of the Falklands War memorial service in 1982. The reluctance of the Church of England authorities to organise an unambiguously triumphalist service of thanksgiving occasioned serious public disagreement between the established church and the state. The form of service was in fact very similar to that used in 1945 at the end of the Second World War.[41] A second conflict took place with the publication of the Church of England *Faith in the City* report in 1985,[42] which was denounced immediately prior to its publication as 'Marxist theology' by detractors in the so-called 'right-wing press'. In third place, the political role of the prominent, even notorious Bishop of Durham, Dr David Jenkins, helped polarise opinion both within and outside the churches. As yet there is no adequate critical account available of this notable bishop's activities. Bishop Jenkins occasioned violent controversy by using his office as the ex officio bearer of *authority* in the church as a means of promoting the exploration of the *truth* of theological propositions comprised in the Creeds.[43] The sociological implications of

[38] See E. R. Norman, *Church and Society in England 1770–1970: A Historical Study* (Oxford: Oxford University Press, 1976), especially the concluding summary, pp. 473–4.

[39] E. R. Norman, *Christianity and the World Order* (Oxford: Oxford University Press, 1979), p. 80.

[40] Anderson, *The Kindness that Kills*.

[41] Edward Bailey pointed this out to me in a personal communication.

[42] The Report of the Archbishop of Canterbury's Commission on Urban Priority Areas, *Faith in the City: A Call for Action by Church and Nation* (London: Church House Publishing, 1985).

[43] More circumspect approaches adopted by other Anglican church leaders are explored in chapters 5 and 6 below.

this episode await proper exploration. On the 'collectivist' side, Bishop David Sheppard's *Bias to the Poor* of 1983 and the *Faith in the City* report of 1985 widened the gulf between what Mrs Thatcher's Conservative Party saw as true and individualistic Christianity and a crypto-socialist (even 'Marxist') and 'collectivist' clerical meddling in politics. In terms of political expectations, the blatant public contrast between the Conservative stress upon the gospel of individual moral autonomy before God and the 'social gospel' of the theological collectivists exposed all too clearly the reluctance of the main denominations, Anglican, Roman Catholic and Methodist, to throw themselves wholeheartedly into the area of legitimate activity allocated to them by Thatcherism and the enterprise culture.

Finally, in the summer of 1988 Mrs Thatcher delivered a fateful speech to the General Assembly of the Church of Scotland in Edinburgh, the so-called 'Sermon on the Mound' (1988). The personal importance of the issues for the Prime Minister herself was demonstrated when she addressed the Assembly on 21 May 1988.[44] Not within living memory had a British political leader of equivalent seniority taken with such seriousness the religious destiny of the 'soul', indeed the *individual soul*, and spoken 'personally as a Christian, as well as a politician'.[45] This text is fundamental for a full understanding of both the religious and moral dynamics of Thatcherism and the role of religion in an enterprise culture. Also, it should be added, Mrs Thatcher's exploitation of this privileged position in Scottish society, the pre-devolutionary parliamentary surrogate embodied in the General Assembly, had the catalytic effect of introducing what was perceived as a particularly objectionable form of Englishness into the very heart of one of the central institutional bearers of pre-devolutionary Scottish identity.[46]

All these episodes took place within a broadly Christian ambit, and they failed at the outset to command the attention or interest of the English liberal intelligentsia, which had encountered their own problems as they were increasingly threatened and marginalised by Thatcherism. Repeatedly devalued by media pronouncements depicting them as the superannuated 'salariat' and the 'chattering classes', they felt marginalised and impotent. Some efforts were made to counter these attacks, notably by the London-based signatories of Charter 88. The implied parallel with the Czech Charter 77 was deliberate: Thatcherism

---

44 This text is conveniently available in Raban, *God, Man and Mrs Thatcher*, pp. 7–20.
45 *Ibid.* p. 9.
46 The others being the Scottish educational and legal systems, which were left outwith the control of Westminster under the terms of the Union of the Parliaments of 1707.

was perceived as a totalitarian ideology in the face of which human rights had to be reasserted. Religious indifference suddenly vanished with the disturbances surrounding the publication of Salman Rushdie's novel *The Satanic Verses* in 1988, and the subsequent proclamation of the Iranian *fatwa* against its author. Suddenly, the size and potential power of the Islamic minority in Britain became apparent for the first time and endangered the liberal values of the vocal middle-class supporters of immigrants and their interests. Religion forced its way back onto the political and social agenda despite wide acceptance of the broad theses of secularisation. The relative compliance of the Jewish community with the new socio-economic agenda and Mrs Thatcher's personal respect for Judaism was returned in full by the then chief Rabbi, Sir Immanuel Jakobovits, who endorsed the individual and familial mores of Thatcherism. Elites within the Islamic and Hindu minorities also responded positively to the economic dictates of Thatcherism, an eventuality which also became apparent just as their relative political invisibility diminished.[47]

None of these episodes does adequate justice to the more fundamental issues raised by the encounter of religion and the enterprise culture as such, understood as a transformatory process energised by a vision of total economic and social renewal. The onset and development of Thatcherism were in effect confronted by the main-line denominations on the level of social ethics; the *religious* dimensions of the enterprise culture as such were, and remain, scarcely addressed.[48] The atomising and anomic tendencies of Thatcherism, effectively bringing about a severing of the 'species bonds' embodied in a corporate Welfare State, redefined the relation between the public and private spheres. As we have seen, the churches and other religious bodies temporarily took on a more important public role. In the aftermath of these developments and with hindsight, it is possible to generalise and articulate two contrasting modes of assimilation of religion and enterprise culture in the established Church of England and the business and commercial spheres, respectively. It is here that a distinction can be drawn between the socio-ethical protest of established Christian religious traditions directed against the policies of the Thatcher era, on the one hand, and, on the other, phenomena which

---

[47] Much public play is made of the economic success of Asian entrepreneurs, some of whom have played a leading role in the 'Thatcherisation' of commercial practice. See K. Knott, 'Hindu Communities in Britain', and J. S. Neilson, 'Islamic Communities in Britain', in Paul Badham, *Religion, State, and Society in Modern Britain* (Lampeter: Edwin Meller Press, 1989) and M. S. Raza, *Islam in Britain: Past, Present and Future* (Leicester: Volcano Press, 1991).

[48] See, however, relevant sections of Paul Heelas and Paul Morris (eds.), *The Values of the Enterprise Culture* (London: HarperCollins Academic, 1992).

suggest a response (in some instances certainly an instrumental one) to the religious needs of those involved in the realisation of the enterprise culture.

In the Thatcher era the Church of England largely followed rather than defined social change. Thus during the imposition of the 'enterprise culture' the established church, itself an organisation dependent upon particularly pure forms of *rentier* and market capitalism, was depicted by the New Right as a body wedded to an anachronistic love of dependency and collectivism. The church correspondingly resisted the imposition of a reconceived Thatcherite role as guardian of the autonomy of individual choice and legitimator of family values. Mrs Thatcher's own views were typically straightforward:

> For a nation to be noted for its industry, honesty and responsibility and justice, its people need a purpose and an ethic. The State cannot provide these – they can only come from the teachings of a Faith. And the church must be the instrument of that work.[49]

A direct appeal to the General Synod of the Church of England along these lines was made by the then Home Secretary, Douglas Hurd, in February 1988. Durkheim himself could scarcely have put the issues more clearly when Mr Hurd argued that 'We need to work together to rebuild the moral standards which should form the sure foundations of a cohesive and united nation.'[50] The newly appointed Archbishop of Canterbury, Dr George Carey, who succeeded the less than compliant Dr Robert Runcie in 1991, prominently advocated the implementation of managerial practices and schemes of appraisal that would enhance ministerial 'performance' and incidentally secure closer control of clerical ideology in what amounted to an ecclesiastical 'neo-Fordism'. The English Anglican appropriation of these aspects of Thatcherism occurred precisely at the historic juncture where Thatcherism as a political creed faltered and lost its overall hegemony. In this context, the 'enterprise culture' properly understood (as opposed to a Thatcherite version of line management) has remained largely alien to the established churches.

The remythologisation of the *effective* and *affective* self in the religiosity of the enterprise culture is conducted around the quest for ever greater energy and efficiency. A pragmatic *and* immanentist ethos of the maximisation of self-awareness and performance would appear to sit ill with the traditional Christian cultivation of sacrifice, dependence and

---

[49] Address in St Lawrence Jewry, 30 March 1978, Cooke, *Revival of Britain*, p. 68, n. 6.
[50] Report in the *Independent*, 11 February 1988.

passivity in the face of transcendence. A self-conscious search for the charismatic *persona*, the super-performer, is to be found at the very core of the enterprise culture. This is a type reminiscent of the Weberian charismatic personality, the creative deviant, who may threaten established and bureaucratic power structures. The enterprise culture is in part an attempt to *de-routinise* the obsolescent rationality of late or advanced capitalist society and to rediscover *charisma*. The British societal situation is one in which pre-modern cultural relics (commodified as 'heritage'), modernising tendencies (an information-technology driven welfare/surveillance bureaucracy), and postmodern factors (an active market in consumable identities) co-exist uneasily. British religio-cultural survival such as the established churches has proved largely resistant to relating positively either to the Thatcher era or to the New Age ethos and its attendant forms of religiosity as they emerge in a 'post-Christianity'. In the 'after-life' of religion,[51] new forms of religiosity grow fungi-like on the rotting trunks of the fallen trees of past identities – or so it may seem to beleaguered traditionalists faced with the rampant chaos of post-modernity. As will become apparent, these traditionalists have found the emergence of the managerial society a far more attractive proposition.

Paradoxically and ironically, the de-routinisation implicit in the enterprise culture required the imposition of a new *order* in the name of 'choice' and 'freedom'.[52] The British enterprise culture was a proleptic vision bearing within it the ironies of a secularised, antinomian Montanism that required for its realisation the imposition of the Roman *lex* of Thatcherite economic and societal discipline. It is arguable that enterprise culture is not intrinsically bound to a particular political or party-political commitment; it may have far more to do with the charismatic function of the innovator, and as such, be politically value-free. The realisation of enterprise culture is, however, closely related to the social distribution of competence. The art of *making things happen* is a rare human characteristic valued in many contexts.[53] A *religious* refunctioning of 'enterprise culture' within *traditional* religion is a possible but highly unlikely outcome.

[51] This image is suggested by George Steiner, 'In a Post-Culture' and 'Tomorrow', *In Bluebeard's Castle: Some Notes Towards the Re-definition of Culture*, T. S. Eliot Memorial Lectures (London: Faber, 1971), chs. 3 and 4.

[52] The manifest limitations of this conception of freedom are explored in K. D. Ewing and C. A. Gearty (eds.), *Freedom Under Thatcher: Civil Liberties in Modern Britain* (Oxford: Clarendon Press, 1990).

[53] The former managing director of ICI, Sir John Harvey-Jones, enjoyed a huge and unexpected popular success with his book *Making it Happen* (London: Guild Publishing, 1987; London: Collins, 1988). The creative flowering and massive societal empowerment of the management paradigm in Britain since 1979 is considered in chapter 3 below.

Towards the end of the Thatcher era the leading proponents of Thatcherism and the enterprise culture began to harbour far-reaching national, and even world-historical, ambitions which were expressed in a triumphalist discourse that attained its most strident expression shortly after the revolutionary events of late 1989. Ironically, this form of discourse attained its apogee precisely at a national turning-point where the intended and unintended consequences of the far-reaching social, economic and political policy measures taken in Britain over the previous decade suddenly began to subvert the plausibility of the vision that had inspired and driven them forward. For example, on 27 February 1990, Peter Morgan, the then Director General of the Institute of Directors, addressed the annual meeting of the Institute and exclaimed: 'Since this convention [of the IOD] was planned, Eastern Europe has had its revolution. The market economy has triumphed.'[54] Morgan asserted without caution or hesitance the universal claims of the market economy and its 'enterprise culture', and attacked all those members of society who still dared to resist their enactment. Morgan continued: 'An enterprise culture is one in which every individual understands that the world does not owe him or her a living, and so we act together accordingly, all working for the success of UK PLC.'[55] According to Morgan, the enterprise culture had its 'flagships' (successful companies); its 'heroes' (the directors who lead); and its 'pride' (the products). The whole nation was conceived as locked in global economic war in which there were to be no non-combatants. The education of the population as 'economic warriors' was, however, an imperative impeded by three obstacles: 'Establishment attitudes' (epitomised by bishops who denigrated wealth creation and praised wealth distribution); the 'middle-class salariat' (the educated but errant sector of the population that parroted the 'liberal Establishment' in the classroom, the pulpit and the media); and the 'lumpenproletariat' (the last 40 per cent of the population, which had nothing and had no stake in society other than parasitic dependency). Morgan's speech was one small instance in the renewal and reordering of society on the scale implied by the German word *Gleichschaltung*, a term first used in the public domain by the distinguished Roman Catholic academic Nicholas Boyle. *Gleichschaltung* is a word with strong Nationalist Socialist overtones and denotes an enforced regime of 'political co-ordination, bringing into line, elimination

---

[54] Text of press release, 27 February 1990, p. 1.
[55] *Ibid*, n. 12.

of opposites'.[56] No one suggests that Mrs Thatcher employed the physical means of National Socialism, but her ambitions were not free from totalitarian implications: according to the perspective that has emerged from Thatcherism the very need for an Opposition (and principled conflict) fades away in a successfully managed society. Morgan's speech well represents the phenomenon of 'metaphorical invasion' which was characteristic of the totalitarian cultural tendencies of the period in question. The resignation of Chris Woodhead in November 2000 may mark the end of an era. Woodhead's role at the head of the Office for Standards in Education (OFSTED) was exercised according to the buccaneering style of classic Thatcherite managerial brutalism. His depiction by a senior Westminster MP as 'witch-finder general' is indicative of the controversial nature of his role as a societal overseer.

Whilst Morgan's scheme may well have included some imperfect and highly biased sociology, it nonetheless well illustrates the conspiratorial suspicions of a new and heroic *classe dirigeante* that perceived itself to be confronted by the inertia and apathy of vested interests at all levels of society. Consequently, Morgan did not attempt to persuade – he proclaimed; he did not appeal through cumulative argument or induction – he propounded a new, virile commonplace, a societal *topos* that offered an alternative to a discredited past of effete dependence. All that remained was to take the final steps in enforcing the imposition of the new order upon the whole of society – and, indeed, the world. Morgan's speech now appears as a rhetorical extravagance,[57] a hubristic declaration replete with irony and thus similar to the high-flown claims of Francis Fukuyama. Yet their style is fully representative of the era. Jonathan Raban's perceptive comment upon Mrs Thatcher's famous address to the General Assembly of the Church of Scotland applies no less to Morgan's style of communication: 'This is the language of power, of parliamentary majority translated into unimpeded action and unimpeded words; a language bereft of concessions, as it is bereft of all the usual strategies of persuasive argument.'[58] It is again not without irony that Morgan's speech

---

[56] 'Understanding Thatcherism', *New Blackfriars*, 70 (1988), 309.

[57] See Paul Morris, 'Freeing the Spirit of Enterprise: The Genesis and Development of the Concept of Enterprise Culture', and Raman Seldon, 'The Rhetoric of Enterprise', both in Keat and Abercrombie, *Enterprise Culture*. Both rely largely upon unpublished sources.

[58] Raban, *God, Man, and Mrs Thatcher*. Raban's classic deconstruction of the General Assembly speech is an important text and an essential aid in the sociological interpretation of the religiosity of Mrs Thatcher and its place in the evolution of Thatcherism.

was followed by an astonishing and rapid loss of confidence on the part of a government which, despite its overwhelming (even if unrepresentative) majority,[59] slid into the train of events that was to lead to the resignation of Mrs Thatcher in November 1990. As Dennis Kavanagh has observed: 'Politicians live by rhetoric'; so also, we can add, they may die by it.[60]

However, following Mrs Thatcher's resignation in 1990 there were multiple political and economic crises; first and foremost of these was the Community Charge or Poll Tax, which came to symbolise the abuse of power and had serious unintended consequences in promoting the likelihood of the break-up of the United Kingdom. Both the Prime Minister, John Major, and the Archbishop of Canterbury, George Carey, had to cultivate gentler images and identify themselves as 'prolier than thou',[61] that is as self-made men from humble origins who had made good by dint of their own unaided efforts. The difficulties were accompanied by chaotic attempts on the part of John Major to redefine foreign (especially European) and social policy on a number of fronts simultaneously.[62] In late 1990 and early 1991 the 'economic miracle' of the Thatcher era withered as widespread recession struck not only classic examples of the enterprise economy and the much-vaunted small businesses, but also the financial sector; and a manufacturing base, much diminished in the early Thatcher years of 'shakeout' in 'overmanned' industries, fell victim to soaring interest rates followed by stagnation.

This continuing crisis re-exposed the long-term British economic decline temporarily obscured during the Thatcher years.[63] The less strident (but more complex) political legitimation of 'Majorism', embodied in the so-called *Citizens' Charter*, translated 'human rights' and 'workers' rights' into *consumer* rights.[64] The consolidation of market-centredness,

59 Secured on the basis of a simple majority electoral system now unique in Europe; this is held to ensure strong (albeit unrepresentative) government.

60 Kavanagh, *Thatcherism and British Politics*, p. 281, n. 5. The last chapter, 'The Reordering of British Politics', provides useful background.

61 Leader in the *Independent*, 26 November 1990. For non-British readers, this was an amusing play on the phrase 'holier than thou'.

62 Notably in a first departure from the previous party line on European integration in his Bonn Speech of 11 March 1991.

63 Accounts of British economic decline include the classic (but disputed) study by M. Wiener, *English Culture and the Decline of the Industrial Spirit 1850–1980* (Cambridge: Cambridge University Press, 1981) and A. Gamble, *Britain in Decline: Economic Policy, Political Strategy and the British State* (London: Macmillan, 1981). For the wider context, see Henk Overbeck, *Global Capitalism and National Decline: The Thatcher Decade in Perspective* (London: Unwin Hyman, 1990).

64 In specific terms, consumers of public services. See John Major, *The Citizens' Charter: Raising the Standard* (London: HMSO, 1991). The foreword merits careful study.

privatisation and commodification proceeded under a growing managerial style of government. Under such conditions, the world-historical, universalistic and totalitarian discourse of Thatcherism and the enterprise culture receded in significance. The decline of the British Conservative Party was accelerated by deep internal divisions over European integration and episodic corruption. Yet the non-arrival of the 'enterprise culture' as such, like the failure of the Parousia in the early Christian church, nonetheless left important traces. These are political in the sense that much drawn from the economic-reality principles of Thatcherism became a fundamental element in the politics of the so-called 'Third Way'[65] which marked the last decade of the twentieth century. As regards socio-cultural change, what took place has been a routinisation: the quasi-apocalyptic temporality of the Thatcherite messianic goal of the 'enterprise culture' was aggregated into a modification of pre-existent social structure. In essence, an implied future presented as a challenge to the whole of society remained a motivational agent for the risk-taking small entrepreneur (the minor sectarians of the quasi-religion of economic renewal), but the new home of the discourse was as a resource for a newly consolidated elite, the managers. Given the decline of effective social mediation and the disappearance of associative structures (a significant if questionable achievement of the Thatcher era), an enormous burden passed into the sphere of influence of 'management'. What emerges is a primal antithesis not between property owners and the propertyless, but between managers and the managed, and a complex tension between the cultural practice of reward, including spiritual and personal development benefits for 'enterprise' within management, and an ever-extending regime of compliance for the managed. It is this new complex that is addressed in the following chapter.

The eclipse of the strident public rhetoric of Thatcherism and the enterprise culture removed the societal lever offered to the traditional denominations. In effect, as the sphere of highly generalised, transformatory public discourse in which government and religious individuals and groups could confront each other was shut down, so the political visibility of religion correspondingly declined. The former anti-theoretical Thatcherite rhetoric of facticity (all counter-argument was at one stage met with the seemingly unanswerable: 'the plain fact of the matter is . . .') gave way to an economic and political presentational complexity ill suited to the earlier polar moralism of political and religious protagonists.

---

[65] See Anthony Giddens, *The Third Way* (Cambridge: Polity, 1998).

As argued above, the enterprise culture, like Thatcherism, failed to achieve the status of universal commonplace or *topos* in British society; this being so, it was reaggregated into the pre-existent but changing patterns of social stratification and their attendant sub-cultures. The culture of enterprise at present occupies a restricted niche in British society from which a large proportion of the population remains excluded by virtue of scarce and inequitably distributed intellectual and 'cultural capital'. 'Religion' and the more vital forms of contemporary religiosity remain largely the preserve of social micro-strata and ethnic subgroups. A substantial proportion of the population is experiencing deculturation (a 'dumbing-down'), social atomisation, increasing criminality, the breakdown of traditional family structures, growth of child abuse, and the loss of communicative ability between the sexes and the social classes amidst a general failure of socialisation. This is a crisis which tends to resist spontaneous public articulation, not least because of a line-managerial style of government, the purpose of which is to secure *conformity* rather than to generate and affirm *consensus*. With the 'death of socialism' there now remains no adequate ideology available for the systematic articulation of the legitimate claims of majorities who remain politically invisible in a new era of cultural politics. Strident pressure groups (ethnic, national, gender, religious, sexual and ecological) tend to capture the main channels of social communication, and this helps distance civil society from the suppressed frustration and the latent (and actual) violence of an increasingly alienated underclass. The challenge to religion is complex and acute, but as yet largely unvoiced.

With immediate historical hindsight the Thatcher era and its religion exude a certain pathos, akin to that of a failed secular eschatology. Real 'enterprise culture' remained a marginal conception. Moreover, 'enterprise' is stressful and a deviation from the norm and normality. Its exponents are an elite exception in both religion and society at large. The enterprise culture demands resources which traditional religion can only rarely provide for good sociological reasons. In the contemporary world it also requires educational and cultural resources far beyond what Thatcherism and Majorism were prepared to concede to a subject population.

Traditional, established English religion is to be understood as recovery space, a haven of dependency; and it is fraught with inconsistencies that it defends with the deadly weapons of inertia and resistance to change. It is thus ill suited to adaptation to the demands of either contemporary British society as a whole or the 'enterprise culture' in particular. Yet the latter, rightly understood, might furnish the possibility of the creative and radical *tertium quid* of innovation, as opposed to the apparently exclusive alternatives of recrudescent fundamentalism or outright secularisation. 'Enterprise' in religion could then perhaps be the basis of a 'searching for God outside the religious club, so that godliness may be saved from being the hobby of the few'.[66] Here the tasks of the sociologist and of the religious professional may be seen to converge, for it is at this juncture that a fuller exploration of the religious aspects of the new spirits of capitalism might well begin.

In the period following the British General Election of May 1997, the New Labour government has remained remarkably consistent in its advocacy of the managerial paradigm. As with the Conservative regimes of Margaret Thatcher and then John Major, policy advisors and 'think-tanks' of an appropriate political hue have continued to exercise significant influence.[67] Central to the programme of 'Third Way' politics in Britain has been a continuation of the radical bureaucratisation of the social domain and civil society through the continued imposition of the managerial paradigm. In the following chapters we shall explore this process of implementation as a routinisation not only of 'charisma' in the polyvalent sense used in this chapter, but of the root sources of the social production of human beings as well. Religion, religiosities and spiritualities have all developed new affinities under these conditions, and it is the exploration of the origins and present reconfiguration of these which will remain a linking thread of analysis through what follows.

---

[66] Robert Towler, *The Fate of the Anglican Clergy* (London: Macmillan, 1979), pp. 204–5.
[67] See Richard Cockett, *Thinking the Unthinkable: Think-Tanks and the Economic Counter-Revolution, 1931–1983* (London: HarperCollins, 1995) and James A. Smith, *The Idea Brokers: Think Tanks and the Rise of the New Policy Elite* (New York: Free Press, 1991).

Power and empowerment: New Age managers and the dialectics of modernity/postmodernity

In succeeding chapters[1] we have moved from the global, grandiose world-historical discourse of Francis Fukuyama through the routinisation of the enterprise culture and the evolution of Thatcherism, and the emergence of the so-called Third Way in the exemplary local culture of Britain to the insider–outsider microculture of management and, more precisely, to the kernel of the latter in the small but highly empowered world of the management consultant. Thus in chapter 3 the argument focuses upon the dynamics of the new managerial imperative and upon the clarification of the psycho-spiritual hermeneutics deployed in the interpretation and control of the subtle interface between discipline and rewards, between 'hard' and 'soft' cultures, and between controlling and being controlled that falls to the consultant. Given the ever-extending remit of the managerialism that succeeds J. A. Schumpeter's triad of capitalism, socialism and democracy,[2] this new hegemony is not confined to the workplace, for the frontiers between public and private spheres have been weakened, especially for those whose training, skills and expertise once accorded them professional or quasi-professional status. The 'degradation of work' now extends beyond the realm of the craft or skilled worker to include a wide range of human services: the headworker salariat is now undergoing incorporation into neo-proletarian status. In attaining this ingestion the new spirit of capitalism does not, however, leave untouched the realm of spiritual intimacy: the prerogative of informed human resources management now extends to the 'love', the 'heart' and even the 'soul' of everyone and everything it touches.

---

[1] This chapter originated as a paper prepared in the context of the project Religion and the Resurgence of Capitalism which I coordinated in the Department of Religious Studies at the University of Lancaster (1989–91). The paper was first published as 'Power and Empowerment: New Age Managers and the Dialectics of Modernity/Postmodernity', *Religion Today*, 9/3 (1994), 3–13.

[2] See W. F. Enteman, *Managerialism: The Emergence of a New Ideology* (Madison: University of Wisconsin Press, 1993).

Under these conditions Stephen Pattison has maintained that management 'becomes religion', that is a closed cultic mode of self-serving empowerment and meaning-creation. Thus according to Pattison,

Management is a collection of beliefs, symbols, myths, rituals, understandings and practices that together make up a total worldview within which individuals can situate themselves and act meaningfully. There is a strong case for evaluating it directly as, at least in some respects, a religious movement.[3]

Whilst the quasi-religious features of managerial power may merit its depiction as 'religion' in this 'real' sense, we are not here in the business of construing management as cultic community, but are concerned with the placement and analysis of the exploitation of the human experience of ultimacy and identity-creation in 'spirituality' as a resource for and tool to be used in promoting organisational change. In other words, what concerns us is the deployment and manipulation of psycho-spiritual power in organisations, not the self-development of a socially isolated elite. Whilst the exploitation of metaphor is part of the task of accessing the emotional and spiritual logic of organisational life, the 'power' deployed in 'empowerment' is real, not least because it may constitute or reconstitute 'reality' itself. Managers are 'mediators' with a latent and implicit cultural meaning well beyond what most practitioners might be fully aware of, or consciously own as individuals. It is, perhaps, only on the wilder shores of management which we are about to explore that locations become momentarily visible where this implicit task of mediation appears in the exalted discourse of visionary empowerment. Both 'mediation' and 'hegemony' float in a multi-dimensional and 'disorganised' matrix with complex diachronic and synchronic features underlaid by the modern/postmodern problematic. This complex situation is being explored sequentially in this book as we seek to relate the core and peripheries of social change.

In the setting outlined above, 'spirituality' is recovered from the apparent periphery of religious decline and marginalisation and refunctioned at the core. Spirituality affords human renewal, peak experiences and an enhanced sense of reality: thus why should not management be improved – and improve others – by entering into a new relationship with a willing partner, and offer intense forms of self-realisation as both an inducement to and reward for higher performance – and ever greater degrees of cultural integration within organisations? Weber's

---

[3] S. Pattison, *The Faith of the Managers: When Management Becomes Religion* (London: Cassell, 1997).

Protestant Ethic thesis asserted affinities between the growth of capitalism and this-worldly asceticism which were informed by displacement
of the disinterested single-minded pursuit of God, but it is not our object to explore here the parallels between past and present experience.[4]
So, then, what greater reward could there be for those who are, in
effect, to be given their 'souls' at work? What could possibly be lost
by such a development? These are not, as will become apparent, idle
questions – they take us directly into what Michael Novak has represented in mythopoeic terms as the 'empty shrine' at the epicentre of
'democratic capitalism'.[5] Novak assumes that this mythicised space of
necessary alienation and identity-formation is the focal point of freedom where the vacant self seeks spiritual empowerment so to re-enter
the battle for economic survival and success armed with religion. It is
my contention that the assumed neutrality of such alienation is naive.
In effect, Novak inverts Marx's doctrine of alienation as it is found in
the posthumously published *Economic and Philosophical Manuscripts of 1844*.
Far from being a disaster, capitalist alienation is what we might depict
as the surrogate 'primal religion' of advanced modernity, the equivalent
of a rite of passage performed entirely within the parameters of 'democratic capitalism'. For Novak this is 'wilderness', the 'dark night of the
soul', which embraces alienation from nature. 'Spirituality', in effect the
residuum of religion under conditions of late or advanced capitalism, can
become a synergetic partner; but used as a resource to be exploited by an
imprudently empowered elite it is at best ambivalent and at worst problematic and even dangerous. As will become more fully apparent in later
chapters, global change is now driven forward by those whose 'right to
manage' increasingly escapes any meaningful and effective democratic
and social control. In a globalised and commodified world order, little if
anything escapes continual redefinition within a totality in which ever-
changing core–periphery designations respect no intrinsic or embedded
cultural frontiers.

Changes of government in Britain since 1979, in particular the New
Labour victory under the leadership of Tony Blair in the British General
Election of 1997, modulated but did not radically divert the socio-cultural
changes associated with managerialism which, in turn, facilitate the

---

4 For a brief account see R. H. Roberts, 'Religion and Economic Life', in Neil J. Smelser and Paul
   M. Baltes (Editors-in-Chief), *International Encyclopedia of the Social and Behavioural Sciences* (Oxford:
   Elsevier, 2001).
5 See also R. H. Roberts, 'The Spirit of Capitalism: A Critique of Michael Novak', in Jon Davies
   and David Green (eds.), *God and the Marketplace: Essays on the Morality of Wealth Creation* (London:
   Institute of Economic Affairs, 1993), pp. 64–81.

return of the religio-spiritual dimension from societal margins to the centre. In summary, it was argued earlier that these basic features of change comprised a general pattern of a 'hard' Thatcherite *lex*, a disciplinary and quasi-punitive view of society crystallised in the doctrine of 'rational expectations', a kind of 'reality principle' characteristic of the early years of the Thatcher era which has subsequently evolved into various forms of managerial control for the many. This 'hard' doctrine initially co-existed ideologically with a 'soft' understanding of the enterprise culture as the visionary goal of a new dynamic business-driven, enterprise-orientated society of free-ranging entrepreneurs, so thoroughly emancipated from dependency corruption that they could be motivated by reward rather than by the threat of punishment. The crucial difference between the early 'Thatcher era' and subsequent 'Majorism' and 'Blairism' consists in the extension and imposition of specifically managerial control to many areas of societal space, and to the virtual abandonment of high-profile, rhetorical public discourse in favour of context-related presentational and enforcement policies. Thus in his lecture 'Economics and Business' delivered at the inauguration of the Centre for Research into Industry, Enterprise, Finance and the Firm (CRIEFF), University of St Andrews, in 1992, Professor John Kay of the London Business School argued for a helpful three-stage account of the evolution of microeconomics: corporate planning (1960s–1970s), vision and mission (1970s–1980s) and implementation (1980s–1990s). On the one hand, the privatisation of many potentially profitable state monopolies has taken place; on the other, the residual areas of state welfare, notably health and education, have been subjected to drastic reform, or 'implementation', in which managers and managerialism have resulted in rapid, non-consensual revolutionary socio-cultural change from above and systemic crises in the indigenous cultures of the professions affected. Prime Minister Tony Blair as the putative inheritor of Mrs Thatcher's radical vision has repeated the cycle: exalted discourse promoting the vision of 'New Labour' in a 'New Britain' globally branded as 'Cool Britannia' and projected with the image of the Millennium Dome at Greenwich as a global, but unintendedly ambiguous icon of British national renewal which has likewise undergone crisis and routinisation.[6] Thatcherite and Majorite 'reform' has become Blairite 'modernisation': the real shift within this paradigmatic assertion of the managerial prerogative has been from the expansion of 'external'

---

[6] For fuller comment on the Dome as cultural icon see the introduction to Scott Lash, Andrew Quick and Richard Roberts (eds.), *Time and Value* (Oxford: Blackwell, 1998), pp. 1–3.

and 'internal' markets and cost-efficiency to the securing of ever greater control of the production or service delivery processes in all sectors.

The 'hard' side of the culture that has emerged is designated as the equivalent of the Roman *lex*. This is a structured, delimited form of existence in which obediential conformity to laws 'presented', transmitted and received through visible (and apparently universal) line-management structures is required. 'Structure' is a potentially misleading term. What is involved is not usually a visible and rigid system, unless the mode of visibility chosen for strategic managerial purposes requires this. Thus, for example, in organisational studies, the key terms are 'formations of power' and 'circuits of power', which recognize the dynamic, recirculatory character of effective systems which maintain their stability through the constant incorporation or exclusion of real or threatened deviance.[7] These lines of command have gradually been extended as far as politically possible though the public sphere – so as to become effectively co-terminous with civil society itself. Within this matrix of differentiated enforcement there are degrees of severity and a few exceptions: it is the highly significant rise and rise of the manager as member of an elite and the marked decline of other professionals which constitute a key factor.[8] In contradistinction to Harold Perkin's depiction of the 'rise' of professional society, we may now observe its 'decline' and displacement by managed and *managerial* society. The role of this new managerial elite as key mediators, as a societal *Vermittlung*, is an important issue (not least for religious professionals) that has yet fully to be evaluated, not least in relation to the traditional forms of association provided by main-line religions which we investigate in later chapters.

Apparently opposed to the first 'hard' type of British enterprise culture there is a second broad tendency focused in the charismatic managerial elite of so-called 'core-workers', potentially antinomian in character, which in terms of the parallel, can be understood as the 'quasi-Montanist' or 'neo-gnostic' microcosm of those who are permitted and encouraged to maximise their performance and accumulation of economic and cultural capital through dynamic self-realisation, rather than conformist

---

[7] See Stewart R. Clegg, *Frameworks of Power* (London: Sage, 1989); *Modern Organization: Organization Studies in the Postmodern World* (London: Sage, 1990); and Stewart R. Clegg and C. Dunkerley, *Organization, Class and Control* (London: Routledge & Kegan Paul, 1980); and R. H. Roberts, art. 'Power', in Andrew Linzzey (ed.), *The Routledge Encyclopaedia of Theology and Society* (London: Routledge, 1996), pp. 673–78.

[8] See Harold Perkin, *The Rise of Professional Society: England since 1880* (London: Routledge, 1989) and H. Braverman, *Labor and Monopoly Capital: The Degradation of Work in the Twentieth Century* (New York: Monthly Review Press, 1974).

rule-governed behaviour. On the theoretical level this juxtaposition of ideal types corresponds to a marked degree with a well-established, although much-disputed and repeatedly defined and redefined distinction between 'modernity'[9] and the 'postmodern condition'.[10] This juxtaposition of concepts is incapable of any dogmatic or doctrinaire representation which does not mislead: all definitions should, in the final analysis, have an empirical point of reference. We therefore return repeatedly to the same theoretical core which is rediscovered in the contexts to be investigated in successive chapters. Given this wider remit, for present purposes we draw on Anthony Giddens' relatively straightforward articulation of the contrast between modernism and postmodernism before articulating correlative managerial styles. Modernism can be defined as:

[C]ultural or aesthetic styles, visible in various realms such as architecture, the plastic and visual arts, poetry and literature . . . developed in conscious opposition to classicism; it emphasises experimentation and the aim of finding an inner truth behind surface appearances. Postmodernism, supposedly, is in some part a recovery of a classical romantic outlook. It is not a reversion to tradition, because tradition today is just as defunct as is the truth for which modernism strove. Postmodernism is decentred; there is a profusion of style and orientation. Stylistic changes no longer 'build on the past', or carry on a dialogue with it, but instead are autonomous and transient. Any attempt to penetrate to a 'deeper' reality is abandoned and mimesis loses all meaning.[11]

Much could be made of this passage, but it suffices here to note that both modernism as quest for inner truth beneath surface appearance and postmodernism as stylistic eclecticism ungrounded in either 'truth' or 'tradition' refer to artistic genres, which, when transposed, developed and applied in the socio-cultural theories of modernity/postmodernity, assume new but related characteristics. The broad distinction between the modern and the postmodern may, in turn, be applied to the fundamental

---

9 See chapter 1, n. 18 for references on 'modernity'.

10 On the 'postmodern condition, see: R. J. Bernstein, *The New Constellation: The Ethical-Political Horizons of Modernity/Postmodernity* (Cambridge: Polity, 1991); Hal Foster, *Postmodern Culture* (London: Pluto, 1985); Anthony Giddens, *Modernity and Self-Identity: Self and Society in the Late Modern Age* (Cambridge: Polity, 1991); David Ray Griffin, *God and Religion in the Postmodern World: Essays in Postmodern Theology* (New York: State University of New York Press, 1989); David Harvey, *The Condition of Postmodernity: An Enquiry into the Origins of Cultural Change* (Oxford: Blackwell, 1989); Charles Jencks, *What is Post-Modernism?*, 4th rev. edn (London: Academic Press, 1989); Arthur Kroker and David Cook, *The Postmodern Scene: Excremental Culture and Hyper-Aesthetics* (New York: St Martin's Press, 1986); Hilary Lawson, *Reflexivity: The Post-modern Predicament* (London: Hutchinson, 1985); Jean-François Lyotard, *The Postmodern Condition: A Report on Knowledge*, 2nd edn (Manchester: Manchester University Press, 1984).

11 A. Giddens, 'Uprooted Signposts at Century's End', *The Times Higher Education Supplement*, 17 January 1992, 21–2.

contrast that can be drawn for present purposes between what is designated as a 'hard' type-A 'modern' or 'scientific management' and a 'soft'
type-B 'postmodern management'. The former was classically expressed
by Frederick W. Taylor, who describes how the embedded knowledge of
pre-modern craft expertise is garnered in and reduced to 'truth' by modern managers, who then re-present this to the workers for their ingestion.

Under the old type of management, success depends almost entirely upon getting the 'initiative' of the workman, and it is indeed a rare case in which this
initiative is really attained. Under scientific management the 'initiative' of the
workmen (that is their hard work, their goodwill and their ingenuity) is obtained
with absolute uniformity and to a greater extent than is possible under the old
system; and in addition to this improvement on the part of the men, the managers assume new burdens, new duties and responsibilities never dreamed of in
the past. The managers assume, for instance, the burden of gathering together
of the traditional knowledge which in the past has been possessed by the workman and then of classifying, tabulating and reducing this knowledge to rules,
laws and formulae which are immensely helpful to the workmen in doing their
daily work.[12]

The point of absolutely critical importance that must be borne in mind
throughout the succeeding argument of this book is that this is 'Fordism',
that is 'modern management' as applied to skilled workers whose relative
autonomy is sacrificed in order to gain cost efficiency. What we encounter
is contemporary management not only as it exploits spirituality, but as
it features in the 'reform' imposed upon British universities and education and health services more widely, and in the *residua* of tradition in the
managed churches of main-line Christianity. This serves as a prelude to
explorations of the images and *episteme* of Europe, of the transformations
of gendered spirituality as God the Goddess evolves in consciousness,
and of virtual and cyborg religion, and the overall recomposition of
the religious field. All provide recurrent, interlinked, yet transmuted instances of the matrix of modernity/postmodernity. In each setting the
latter complex affords us an intricate texture of reflexive possibilities, and
thus offers a range of possible identity options which are real, although
both contended and contentious.

Broadly opposed to the ideal type-A 'modern management' is a type-B
'human resources management' which is open to far more flexible development, as is made evident in the rich range of alternatives apparent in

[12] First published 1911. See Frederick W. Taylor, 'The Principles of Scientific Management', in
Scientific Management (New York: Harper, 1947). Cited in Victor H. Vroom and Edward L. Deci,
Management and Motivation: Selected Readings, 2nd edn (Harmondsworth: Penguin, 1992), p. 357.

the relevant literature,[13] which will shortly be illustrated in ethnographic terms. This 'soft' form of management is focused upon the enhancement of reflexivity and 'management learning'[14] and joyfully exploits an array of 'postmodern' characteristics of anti-hierarchical fluidity, flat organisation, multi-tasking, fragmentation and mutability in identity construed as part of, rather than the enemy of, managerial effectiveness. Indispensable to type-B management is 'self-development', which implies the possibility of a constant renewal and expansion of the managing self. In the context of the death of metanarratives and the *disponibilité* of all cultural artifacts in a globalised market-place in which global economic capital is the controlling factor in the production, distribution and acquisition of all cultural goods (and thus 'cultural capital'), it is this 'self' which adopts a stance that may allow for the most intense maximisation. Precisely what form this maximisation might take is the zone in which financial and affective (that is to say human developmental) rewards are interfused.

[13] The bibliography is very extensive, and the following are examples of a distinct genre: John Adams (ed.), *Transforming Leadership* (Alexandria, VA: Miles River Press, 1986); James A. Belasco, *Teaching Elephants to Dance* (London: Hutchinson Business Books, 1990); Warren Bennis, *On Becoming Leader* (London: Hutchinson Business Books, 1989); R. Boyatzis, *The Competent Manager* (New York: John Wiley & Sons, 1982); D. L. Bradford and A. E. Cohen, *Managing for Excellence: The Guide to Developing High Performance in Contemporary Organizations* (New York: John Wiley & Sons, 1984); Mark Brown, *The Dinosaur Strain* (Shaftesbury, Dorset: Element Books, 1988); Andrew Campbell and Marion Devine, *A Sense of Mission* (London: Business Books, 1990); Sheena Carmichael and John Drummond, *Good Business* (London: Century Hutchinson, 1989); John Constable, *The Making of British Managers: A Report to the BIM and CBI into Management Training, Education, and Development* (Corby: British Institute of Management, 1987); T. Deal and A. Kennedy, *Corporate Cultures* (Harmondsworth: Penguin, 1988); Peter F. Drucker, *Innovation and Entrepreneurship* (London: William Heinemann, 1985); Roger Evans and Peter Russell, *The Creative Manager* (London: Unwin Paperbacks, 1989); Charles Handy, *The Age of Unreason* (London: Business Books, 1989); Charles Handy, *Gods of Management* (London: Pan, 1985); Charles Handy, *The Making of Managers* (London: HMSO, 1987); Charles Handy, *Understanding Organizations* (Harmondsworth: Penguin, 1987); John Harvey-Jones, *Making it Happen* (London: Guild Publishing, 1987; London: Collins, 1988); John Heider, *The Tao of Leadership* (London: Wildwood House, 1986); J. Kotter, *The General Managers* (New York: Free Press, 1982); Bob Messing, *The Tao of Management* (London: Wildwood House, 1989); Rosabeth Moss Kanter, *The Change Master* (London: Unwin Paperbacks, 1984); Richard Tanner Pascale and Anthony G. Athos, *The Art of Japanese Management* (London: Penguin, 1982); Tom Peters, *Thriving on Chaos* (London: Pan, 1989); Tom J. Peters and Nancy Austin, *A Passion for Excellence* (London: Fontana/Collins, 1986); Tom J. Peters and R. H. Waterman, Jr, *In Search of Excellence* (New York: Harper & Row, 1982); Alice G. Sargent, *The Androgynous Manager* (New York: American Management Organisation, 1983); Anne Wilson Schoef and Diane Fassel, *The Addictive Organisation* (New York: Harper & Row, 1988); Alvin Toffler, *The Third Wave* (London: Pan, 1989).

[14] I am of course aware that the term 'soft management' has been developed with much success by Henry Mintzberg of McGill University. Here the term 'soft' is employed as a generic cultural feature applicable across disciplinary and sphere boundaries. See Henry Mintzberg, *Mintzberg on Management: Inside Our Strange World of Organizations* (New York: Free Press, 1989).

The conceptual contrast between scientific type-A management and type-B human resources postmodern management can be expressed in a number of ways, but a distinction can be drawn of some utility for the present argument. Classical scientific or modern management was above all preoccupied with the transfer of reflexive agency from worker to management in order to obtain economically rational control over the total productive process. In formulating two contrasting 'hard' and 'soft' types of management an abstraction is made which has heuristic significance, but this should never obscure the fact that most real-world organisational settings are characterised by a complex interconnection of both 'hard' ('modern') and 'soft' ('postmodern') characteristics. This can be readily illustrated with reference to the ever-extending application of British Standard 5750, the so-called 'Quality Audit', to the many human service settings in which 'Quality' goals are the driving force of management. BS 5750 is defined as:

A systematic and independent examination to determine whether quality activities and related results comply with planned arrangements, are implemented effectively and are suitable to achieve objectives.

This definition of the 'Quality circle' may be both externally verified and as it were 'externally' managed by supervisory managers in a basically 'modern' setting. The greater the reflexive burden and distinctive contextual complexity of any given productive or service function, the less plausible it becomes that the manager can oversee each aspect of the process. The worker or 'provider' has to accept and own self-supervision, and thus reassume a portion of the reflexive burden in the context of the mission and goals set by management. In the way Marx spoke of the Reformation putting the external priest into the heart of the believer, so the managee learns to manage himself or herself. Whilst pure automatism is doubtless possible for some, the reflexive turn draws into consideration the so-called postmodern attributes of mutability and, for the successful manager, a serial ability to attain the *tabula rasa*, the empty inner slate upon which new identities may be written. Some find it difficult to achieve the requisite vacuity and may suffer in consequence. The readiness to receive and internalise new identities raises important but little-discussed ethical questions about the nature of social and cultural identity to which we return both in this and later chapters.

Human resources management as it has been defined here is concerned with understanding and with connecting individual motivation to corporate goals through active *transformation* and *synergesis*. Type-A management stresses overt power, obedience and conformity, in a low- or no-trust environment; type-B management seeks to devolve power and enhance reflexivity and agency through 'empowerment'. Any contrast drawn between type-A 'low-trust' 'power' and type-B 'high-trust' or 'empowerment' approaches to the management of human resources is, as noted above, an extreme simplification of complex real situations; nonetheless, it is representative enough to be employed for clarificatory and critical purposes in this investigation.

The viability and appropriateness of type-A and type-B management approaches in any given setting depend upon a number of factors, of which the following are important: (1) the historical 'culture' of any given organisation; (2) the type of task undertaken by the organisation; (3) the economic condition of the organisation; (4) the quality of the existing management. The crucial problem is the following: any given organisation may fall primarily under a type-A or type-B category of management; but if *either* type A decides to change into type B, *or* if an organisation wishes to combine *both* within a single (usually stratified) structure, then two problems occur with which the organisation is often ill-equipped to cope. If change is to take place, then a level of reflexivity is usually required beyond the capacity of the extant organisation; in other words a 'midwife', 'facilitator' or 'enabler' is needed. If, on the other hand, type A and type B are to co-exist, then the transition points and fault lines have to be understood and managed effectively if staff are to cross the boundary without unproductive psycho-personal dysfunction. 'Change masters' are required who (if we are to believe in the validity of their remit) deploy catalytic and alchemical powers of transmutation. Apart from sheer terror or physical intervention, the most powerful agents of individual and corporate cultural change are charismatic, hence the indispensable role of spirituality in organisational change.[15] What is now to be described in this chapter is not exceptional, as Stewart Clegg reports:

About one third of Japanese organisations give their employees 'spiritual training', akin to techniques of religious conversion, therapy and initiation rites. These emphasise social cooperation, responsibility, reality acceptance and perseverance in tasks. Such techniques apply particularly to members of the internal

---

[15] The literature on 'charisma' is very extensive. Given her subsequent career, Rosabeth Kanter's doctoral thesis is significant: *Communes: Creating and Managing the Collective Life* (New York: Harper & Row, 1973). See Charles Lindholm, *Charisma* (Oxford: Blackwell, 1993) for a highly informed but negative evaluation.

labour market, incorporated by the benefits they receive as well as the sanctions that quitting would produce. Anyone who wanted to leave would be seen as untrustworthy by other employers and hence unemployable. It is a system which works well in securing loyal commitment by virtue of low turnover and dissent in the highly competitive core. Core labour market skill-formation is enhanced, compared to situations of much greater reliance on the external market as the source of recruitment.[16]

When organisational change takes place it will usually precipitate crisis at the level of individual and corporate cultural identities and in the root paradigms of the organisational or company 'culture'. In a shrinking economy and global recession it may prove a short-term economy to discard staff whose cultural formation proves obsolescent, and in times of expansion new staff may require rapid inculturation and aggregation. If change is to be attempted with existing human resources, this may well require facilitation by individuals or teams of human resources specialists whose identities and agency are, as it were, unpolluted by the environment into which they are to enter. In short, humane change requires facilitation. It is interesting to note that type-A 'scientific' management would appear to be designed to safeguard a stable environment constructed for the implementation of settled policy, whereas the more flexible type-B human resources approach may equip a well-differentiated high-quality labour force with adaptive and innovatory skills, although not without cost.

Specialists in facilitating organisational change have a variety of designations: 'management consultant' and 'management trainer' are common terms in a large market in which a wide range of niches open and close as the business climate changes. It is this sector ('group' is a misnomer: a constantly reworked 'network' is more apt) which provides specialist human resources services to business, industry and the residual public sector. Their trade is, as it were, personality and behavioural modification, or to resort to the discourse employed, 'empowerment', 'transformation', 'realization', 'facilitation', 'enabling', and so on. The human services thus provided are, however, very different from those traditionally associated with 'scientific' (i.e. line-) management and its specialisms. This is not simply a matter of cognitive-behavioural technique involving a coherent scheme of punishments and rewards in the human equivalent of the maze – 'soft' changes involve self-willed transformations in consciousness and the opening up of the personality so

---

[16] 'Postmodern Management?', unpublished Inaugural Lecture, University of St Andrews, 11 March 1992, 16.

that selected employees will, through *self-discovery* and *self-development*,[17] uncover the sources of new dynamism in the context of the 'love'[18] that flows through the 'learning organisation'.[19]

These fairly complex issues may be illuminated through the ethnographic representation, grounded in participant observation, of a large international conference of New Age management consultants and trainers.[20] This one event brought into a possibly unrepeatable

[17] C. Argyris, *Personality and Organization* (New York: Harper & Row, 1957); P. D. Anthony, *The Ideology of Work* (London: Tavistock, 1977); M. Pedler and T. Boydell, *Managing Yourself* (London: Fontana, 1982); R. Holland, *Self and Social Context* (London: Macmillan, 1970); Aldous Huxley, *The Perennial Philosophy* (London: Chatto & Windus, 1946); Alfred Koestler, *The Ghost in the Machine* (London: Pan, 1975); G. Burrell, 'Post-modernism: Threat or Opportunity?', in M. C. Jackson, P. Keys and S. Cropper (eds.), *Operational Research and the Social Sciences* (New York: Plenum Press, 1989), pp. 59–64; T. H. Boydell, 'Transformations for Men?', in M. J. Pedler, J. G. Burgoyne and T. H. Boydell (eds.), *Applying Self-development in Organizations* (Hemel Hempstead: Prentice-Hall, 1988); J. G. Burgoyne et al. *Self-Development* (London: Association of Teachers of Management, 1978); R. Harrison, 'Strategies for a New Age', *Human Resource Management* 22/3 (Fall 1983), 209–35; M. J. Pedler, J. H. Burgoyne and T. H. Boydell, *A Manager's Guide to Self-Development*, 2nd edn (Maidenhead: McGraw-Hill, 1986); Mike Pedler, John Burgoyne, Tom Boydell and Gloria Welshman (eds.), *Self-Development in Organizations* (New York: McGraw-Hill, 1990); R. W. Revans, *The Origins and Growth of Action Learning* (Bromley: Chartwell Bratt, 1982); D. A. Schon, *Beyond the Stable State* (New York: Random House, 1871); Rosemary Stewart, *Choices for the Manager* (Maidenhead: McGraw-Hill, 1982); G. Lyons, *Constructive Criticism* (California: Wingbow Press, 1988).

[18] R. Harrison, *Organization Culture and the Quality of Service: A Strategy for Releasing Love in the Workplace* (London: Association for Management Education and Development, 1987).

[19] Once more the genre is prolific: G. Dearden, *Learning While Earning* (Oxford: Learning from Experience Trust, 1989); John Edmonstone, 'What Price the Learning Organization in the Public Sector?', in Mike Pedler, John Burgoyne, Tom Boydell and Gloria Welshman (eds.), *Self-Development in Organizations* (New York: McGraw-Hill, 1990), pp. 252–78; P. Honey and Alan Mumford, *The Manual of Learning Styles* (Maidenhead: Honey, 1986); M. Knowles, *Self-Directed Learning* (Chicago: Follett, 1975); D. Kolb, *The Learning Style Inventory*, Boston: McBernie & Co., 1976); D. Kolb, *Experiential Learning* (New York: Prentice-Hall, 1984); R. W. Revans, *Action Learning* (London: Blond & Briggs, 1980).

[20] Roberto Assagioli, *Psychosynthesis* (London: Turnstone Books, 1973); Richard Bandler and John Grinder, *Frogs into Princes: Neuro-Linguistic Programming* (Moab, UT: Real People Press, 1979); D. Bannister and Fay Fransella, *Inquiring Man* (Harmondsworth: Penguin, 1971); William Bloom (ed.), *The New Age: An Anthology of Essential Writings* (London: Rider, 1991); Jean Shinoda Bolen, *Goddesses in Everywoman: A New Psychology of Women* (London: Harper & Row, 1985); Ram Dass, *Journey of Awakening* (London: Bantam, 1985); Marilyn Ferguson, *The Aquarian Conspiracy: Personal and Social Transformation in the 1980s* (London: Paladin, 1989); Piero Ferruci, *What We May Be: The Vision and the Techniques of Psychosynthesis* (Wellingborough: Turnstone, 1982); Shakti Gawain, *Creative Visualization* (Mill Valley, CA: Whatever Publishing, 1978); Liz Greene, *Relating – An Astrological Guide to Living With Others* (London: Aquarian Press, 1986); Tad Guzie and Noreen Monroe Guzie, *About Men and Women: How Your 'Great Story' Shapes Your Destiny* (New York: Paulist Press, 1986); Lao Tzu, *Tao Te Ching*, tr. D. C. Lau (Harmondsworth: Penguin, 1963); Robert E. Ornstein, *The Psychology of Consciousness* (Harmondsworth: Penguin, 1975); Carol Riddell, *The Findhorn Community: Creating a Human Identity for the 21st Century* (Forres: Findhorn, 1992); Peter Russell, *The Brain Book* (London: Routledge & Kegan Paul, 1979); Ronald Shone, *Creative Visualization* (Wellingborough: Thorsons, 1984); Peter Spink, *A Christian in the New Age* (London: Darton, Longman & Todd, 1991); Starhawk, *Dreaming the Dark: Magic, Sex and Politics* (London: Unwin, 1990); Lowell D. Streiker, *New Age Comes to Main Street* (Nashville: Abingdon, 1990); Richard Wilhelm, *The I Ching* (London: Routledge & Kegan Paul, 1983).

conjunction a range of actors and factors. It took place in early 1990, when the second Thatcher government had reached a peak of self-confidence and the consumer boom had not yet faltered; there was a sense that the sky was the limit and that a new world order was breaking in which human resources management would play a leading role in the process of social enlightenment, and nothing less, indeed, than the evolution of a new cosmic and human order. Once more, as with Fukuyama, Thatcher and Blair, the exalted discourse of world transformation was present. Whilst this visionary excess might seem unrealistic, even self-deluded as regards its goals, the perception of power is an accurate one given the extension of the managerial paradigm. As it happens, by early 1991 and with characteristic responsive agility and resourcefulness respondents were rapidly shifting their activities into 'insolvency counselling'.[21] With the upturn in the economy that took place in the mid and late 1990s it has proved interesting to investigate new configurations in this flexible elite. Contrary, perhaps, to expectation, the routinisation of the enterprise culture and the imposition of the type-A managerial paradigm across many sectors has led to the implementation of disciplinary regimes in which the suppression of individual charisma is required in order to secure the reliable 'McDonaldisation' of behaviour.[22]

The event in question was co-organized by a team of management trainers based in the management school of a British university founded in the 1960s and a core team of independent consultants. It became apparent to me as an academic researcher working in the university that gaining entry to the event was not going to be as easy as I had initially anticipated. There was a definite psychic and intellectual security system in operation with which to filter out potentially disruptive attitudes. Thus it was that the only academic participants from the host university were a colleague (an anthropologist) and I, and it became clear that access would be possible only on the basis of *active* participation; this was indeed to be a bazaar in which *all* were to be both sellers and tasters. After a three-month period of intermittent negotiation the colleague (an archetypal 'fly on the wall' anthropological observer) was admitted in order to present and comment upon his audio-visual material; I was admitted as one of

---

[21] An assessment by a senior source who wishes to remain anonymous.

[22] It is extremely difficult to generate accurate figures, but it would seem that spiritual practitioners and adepts had in late 2000 extended their attention from implementing charismatic transformation within organisations to psycho-therapeutic work helping victims to cope with the human consequences of enforced managerialist routinisation.

a small team of 'narrators'. The narrators' role was to crystallise and reflect back to the conference the evolution of the event itself as it took place. This involved considerable initial culture shock, because far from observing from the margins it was necessary to take part in the plenary gatherings in a very exposed way as part of a small team of two women and two men (and two further part-timers). The team was under the direction of the women, both of whom were full-time partners in a leading independent consultancy specialising in the facilitation of transformatory techniques in 'learning organisations'. The initial briefing session made it apparent that the mode of control in the event was to be through a virtuoso juxtaposition of leadership/orchestration (with group improvisation) on the one hand, and the relative spontaneity of individuals on the other. This was no mean achievement in a highly diverse conference of some 150 participants, most of whom had a specific product to display, demonstrate and sell, and who were in immediate competition for market attention. Indeed the 'market' was not only the target of effort but also simultaneously the *context* of human self-realisation, interpersonal interaction and the arena of a variety of human relationships. The 'personal' market, as opposed to the so-called 'impersonality of the market-place', a conception often deployed for political purposes, remains an area worthy of further investigation.

The presentation and analysis of this event is structured in terms which reflect the cycle of the event itself. This was conceived as a totality, a large-scale initiatory and transformatory ritual enacted by the whole conference. The event involved a sequential pattern of entry, the creation of sacred performance space, psychic cleansing, illumination, transformation, collective reinforcement, bonding and a return to 'the world'. The diachronic structure was relatively simple; the pattern of a ritual journey from where each individual was at, as it were, into the unknown, was clearly understood by most of those present (individual exceptions became dysfunctional and underwent stress: they had to integrate or 'emigrate' very quickly). The synchronic structure was complex: outside the plenary occasions a myriad of activities was taking place in a pattern which might be best described as the ultimate postmodern spiritual bazaar in which all were both customers and sellers. The vast majority of those present were adepts; those who were not appeared to do their utmost to enter the flow as soon as possible. There was no detectable discord or overt dissent throughout.

The event proper began on two levels: the exoteric management of ritual and sacred space, and the esoteric sustaining of spiritual intent. First there was a briefing meeting on the opening morning of the event with the narrators, during which all were introduced to their collective role as narrators. The control of the group was pointedly non-hierarchical and woman-led, the emphasis being upon collective and affective planning along 'brain-storm' lines. The preparation consisted of the visual, oral and dramatic appraisal of the opening assembly and its location. From a visit of the performance site and some knowledge of rite and liturgy it was apparent that there was a considerable initial task to be faced that involved confronting and overcoming the grossly alien environment, a massive early 1980s lecture theatre built for mass higher education on a windswept, decaying brick-built campus. On the esoteric level the problem of repugnant modernity was tackled throughout by the publicly acknowledged deployment of two full-time women adepts/counsellors, who after an initial meditation over crystals with the narrators in a crowded university 'restaurant' provided spiritual support throughout the event through continual but discrete meditation.

The visual and affective deficiencies of the lecture theatre were confronted head-on in the first plenary session, once the spiritual power-base had as it were been set in motion in a series of introductions and announcements. It is not possible to reduce the opening 'ceremony' to a single dominant theme, but the ritual structure was obvious. The organising motif and ruling metaphor was the representation of the conference itself as an organic entity with a 'spiritual life' of its own that existed part-way between the source of the analogy, the 'spiritual life' and 'soul' of the individual, and the 'target' *analogans*, the organisations that were to be transformed. The often-alluded-to juxtaposition of spiritual narrative and real and imagined work contexts constituted a consistent pattern of 'inter-spirituality'. Thus, in this instance, the first questions posed in the opening plenary by one of the recognised leader-figures (an anthroposophist and follower of Rudolf Steiner) were: 'Does this Conference have a soul? And what is this soul like?' Extensive discussion of the nature of this 'soul' followed. Correspondingly, the explicit discourse of the conference specifically avoided (indeed excluded) all forms of traditional business or commercial language; thus such terms as 'money', 'finance management', even 'business', 'commerce' and their cognates, were conspicuous by their absence. The mediation of the transformatory process through discourses of spiritual enlightenment was rigorously (although apparently informally) enforced. This was an environment in which the refunctioned and relocated principle: 'Seek ye first the kingdom of heaven and all these things shall be added unto you' was thoroughly operationalised. Money and modernity did not transgress the perimeter of the exclusion zone in any discursively explicit form.[23]

The opening collective act of the conference proper involved the aural and visual sanctification of the stark and windowless lecture theatre. After an hour of intense expressive activity with paint and paper the room was transformed by covering all the walls with pictures, declarations, poetry and slogans embodying the hopes and fears of the participants. The bare room had become an internally differentiated sacred space with several focal points, including confessional, reflective and expressive wall spaces for the posting of spontaneous written utterances; the whole constituted a complete enclosure, a theatre of opportunity. There was, in addition, a specially arranged and dedicated computer network available for individual and interpersonal spiritual communication.[24] To venture into the lecture theatre was to depart from an instrumental and mechanical world and to enter into an affective realm of new possibilities made possible in the instantly created sacred space. For the relatively successful initiate, stomach-churning embarrassment could turn into achievement as 'risk-taking' built confidence and mutual trust in this theatre of risk and opportunity.

The team of narrators had conferred at length in preparatory meetings. It had become apparent that the only remotely organic image or artifact capable of functionalisation in the hostile environment of the lecture theatre was the skeleton of a small whale about five metres in length which had been washed up dead on a local headland, buried and then exhumed and suspended from the ceiling.[25] Thus it was that the narrators hit upon the key to resolving the problem set them, the instantaneous invention of a mythic narrative and particular ruling metaphor for the whole event. The following declamatory narrative was formulated and

---

[23] Ostentatious display was discouraged and 'casual power clothing' was in order.
[24] 'Networking' was not incidental: it was understood to have a specific 'spiritual' and developmental role. It was, perhaps, a way in which dissonance could be recognised and acknowledged, but removed from public gaze during the event. Some seemingly unlikely interfaces were operationalised, for example those between business interests and proponents of 'deep' ecology. After much intervening fieldwork reflected in the later chapters of this book, it is apparent to me that the recomposition of the religious and spiritual field requires corresponding effort in its remapping, a task attempted in chapters 10 and 11 below.
[25] The whale's remains had in fact been carried by strong-stomached university staff from a local headland to the campus, who buried, then cleaned and mounted then for the benefit of biology students (and, through fortuitous but fortunate synchronicity, made available for the enablers).

pronounced in antiphonic form in the opening plenary:

> Once upon a time there was a baby whale.
> That had the misfortune to float ashore not
> > > far from here.
>
> It's lost its mother
> > and lost its sense of direction.
>
> It ran aground
> > wriggled about
> > > tried to escape
> > > > But it died.
>
> And it began to smell – very bad
> > But some useful academics
> > > found it and they brought it back
> > > and buried it.
>
> And after two years they dug it up
> > and they thought
> > > their students could learn something
> > > > from it.
>
> And we may not be students of biology
> > But when we look at this
> > > dead baby whale.
>
> We know and
> > the students know it once lived.
>
> Its got a head, flippers, tail.
> > But its got no heart.
>
> It's dead – very dead.
>
> The question it poses
> > Is a universal one.
>
> Can these dry bones live?
>
> [The two teams alternating in unison]
>
> **No! No! No!**
> **Yes! Yes! Yes!**
>
> How can we get some flesh on it?
> How can we get it to move?
>
> Is this once living organism
>
> Like the organisation known to you?

In the classic manner of Van Gennep and Victor Turner ritual and myth were functionalised in active interlocution.[26] Through an instant rite of transition participants moved from the mundane into a timeless primal origin in the sea, passed through a vulnerable existence full of ecological pathos, and underwent the intervention of the critical instrumental intellect (and suffered its failure!) in order to experience the latencies of the present moment of re-enfleshment. Thus a ritual act began in pre-modern *arche* and the archaic passed into instrumental modernity and then melted and interflowed into postmodern mythopoesis – the event was launched, and sustained with great intensity over a three-day period.

The synchronic complexity of the event was apparent in the great diversity of the individual programmes offered. Closer examination of the descriptions put forward of each offering reveals a marked uniformity of discourse in which key commonplaces or *topoi* recur. It would be possible to draw a distinction between the discourse and form of the transformatory experiences on offer and the particular cultural and spiritual artifacts functionalised in the many individual rituals of transition. Thus through meditation (coloured or styled from a variety of sources), dance, explicit ritual acts of, say, Native American origin, psycho-drama, experiential paths of self-discovery, voice discernment and voice-therapy, and so on, the core terms took on flesh. Hence 'everyday spirituality', 'exploring the human spirit', 'connecting with your genius', the priority of the 'nourishment of the human spirit', 'spiritual common sense', seeking 'deeper Wisdom', 'resourcing the spirit', finding the 'soul of the business organisation', 'learning networks', attaining 'wholeness', 'guided visualisation', dealing with 'organisational angels and beasts', the 'organisational Dream', besides the whole panoply of what has now become a main-line alternative life-world of widely disseminated, so-called 'New Age' techniques.

Whilst there were many techniques of self-transformation on offer, one of the most striking 'disciplines' enacted was that of 'Warriors and Tyrants', which was demonstrated by a charismatic woman initiate of the Deer Tribe and Lowland Scotswoman originating from Glasgow, who

---

[26] For an introduction see Turner's wide-ranging article 'Ritual', in D. L. Sills (ed.), *International Encyclopaedia of the Social Sciences* (18 vols., New York: Macmillan, 1968–79), vol. XIII, pp. 520–6 and Richard Schechner, 'The Future of Ritual', in *The Future of Ritual: Writings on Culture and Performance* (London: Routledge, 1993), ch. 7.

outlined the cycle of conflict and resolution in the description circulated
in the following conference notes:

It is not actually that difficult to stay happy and centred whilst sitting on a
mountain top in India – commuting everyday to work in a large organisation,
or even living with your family or being with friends involves confrontation
with rather more tyrants. In this short session I will concentrate on sharing
some of the Deer Tribe teachings on how to be a Warrior. We will talk about
the tools of Reconnaissance, Tactics, Strategy, Forbearance, and timing to fight
the enemies of Fear, Anger, Stress and Anxiety, and learn to transform them
into the excitement of Stalking a Tyrant. The key to dealing with all tyrants is
knowledge. Firstly to have enough self awareness to know yourself, especially
your weak spots better than your tyrant. This knowledge will allow you to stay
centred within yourself whilst tyrants try to push you off balance.

Interviewed again in 1997, this practitioner had continued to offer her
services as a shamanic business consultant and had published a co-
written account of her work.[27] At this juncture it is relevant to record
that many of those present were advising senior management in a series
of reputable companies and on occasion given charge of complete co-
horts of managerial trainees in order to 'transform' and enhance their
personal human resources.[28] 'Right-brain' affective discourse predom-
inated in a collective willed suspension of belief in external prescriptive
modernity; this suspension was seemingly central to what then took
place. 'Seemingly', because as Tanya Luhrmann has argued, the
interrelation of instrumental rationality and affective 'irrationality' in
the 'play' involved in the refunctionalisation of the esoteric involves
systemic ambiguity.[29] In British terms, and as regards the host institution, this conference proved both controversial and effectively unrepeatable as the economic and institutional conditions that underlaid it
changed.

After an intense period of some three days of pure experiential involvement, the final plenary meeting was a congregational event which
involved the declamation of poetry, ecstatic utterance (including St Paul

[27] See David Firth and Heather Campbell, *Sacred Business Resurrecting the Spirit of Work* (Oxford:
Capstone Publishing, 1997).

[28] Substantial remuneration was involved for those successful in an ever more competitive market-
place. Given the cultural impropriety of money discourse it was not easy to elicit information
about fees and financial rewards. In 1989 £650 per diem plus VAT was the rate for individual
counselling of senior managers provided by one representative participant. In 1993, a respondent
who had been present at the conference contacted me to point out that his fee was £3000 per
diem plus expenses. No doubt the figures have grown in the interim .

[29] See Tania Luhrmann, 'Serious Play: The Fantasy of Truth', in *Persuasions of the Witch's Craft:
Ritual Magic in Contemporary England* (Oxford: Blackwell, 1989), ch. 22.

on love from 1 Corinthians), the recitation of personal myths and narratives, the recounting of individual sagas of self-development and the enhanced expression of a sense of intense fervour. A spoken yearning for the regeneration of the organisation – and of the cosmos itself – was expressed: the event had proved for some to be nothing less than a salvific locus of potentially world-historical significance. The narrators did their best to focus the event and prepare for collective reaggregation into the 'world' through the composition and declamation of the following. This also had the very useful purpose of isolating key terms used frequently throughout the conference.

A Deconstructive Prose Declamation (!)
(or)
Joining Forces – A Conference Alphabet

A is for avatar, aura, arrogant, act, for ally, angels . . .

and assertion

B is for beast, beauty, brute, baby, BMW, for birth . . .

and beginning

C is for colleagues and crystals, for calm, cause, for circles
and cycles, collision, collapse . . . and crisis!

D is for death, dance, delight, depths, decision, and the definition
(we're always resisting)

E is for empathy, enlightenment (where?)

Exegesis (what's that?)
eggs and eggheads,
ENERGY!!! . . . and emergence

F is for failure, fear, for freak-out . . . and FUTURE

G is for goddess, gold, goodness . . . for gripes? . . .

for your god (if you have one)

H is for hell-hole (the company office?) . . . hugging and healing

I is for injustice, impotence . . . and incarnation

J is for justice, 'judicious' (the bishop?), jealous and jinxed

K is for Kill! . . . kerygma (the company message!) and karma

L is for lucidity, lust . . . link-up and love

M is for money and mind, for magic, meditation . . .

and the company mission

N is for neutral (participant observer)

O is for organ, organism, orgy, orgasm . . . the ORGANISATION!

P is for peace-pipe, for persons, persuasion . . . and PERFORMANCE!

Q is for quaking and quelling disturbance

R is for reach-out, rebellion, rights, revolution/resolution

S is sincerity, sex, spirit, and SPIRITUALITY!

T is for terror and tyrants . . . and for telling the story

U is for ultimate . . . and for use and utility

V is for voice, victim, values . . . and victor!

W is for WOMEN, for whales, work, weeping, and WARRIORS . . .

and wimps

X is for exact, excitement . . . and X the Unknown

Y is for youth, for yodels and Yuppies

Z is for zany, for zoo . . . and it's over to you!

This quasi-bardic[30] declamation spoke back to the assembly the recurrent *topoi* or commonplaces of the conference, and each phrase encapsulates a fragment of what was in essence a coherent self-developmental shared ethos. Within the setting of the overall framework and orchestration of all the main plenaries, the opening and closing sessions may be understood as 'postmodern' in the pure sense of exploiting access to wide cultural capital resources unfettered by tradition, and the possession of sufficient social and economic power to engage in the eclectic refunctioning of psycho-cultural artifacts. Thus the spontaneous singing by a voice therapist of the hymn 'Amazing Grace' would follow a favourite poem, a dictum from Goethe, or a brief quasi-confessional narrative of a 'risk' taken. The general ocean of convergent feeling was filled as far as the eye could see with a myriad spiritual artifacts which gently rose and fell upon waves of emotion, although sometimes this liminality was disrupted and yet further reinforced when a primal scream would ring out as the raw unconscious rose like a Polaris missile from the psychic depths of a participant. In this oceanic consciousness anything seemed

---

[30] The rediscovery of the bardic gift is explored by the ecologist and environmental activist Alastair McIntosh in *Soil and Soul* (London: Aurum Press, 2001).

possible: this was visionary management at the threshold of the New Age and the approaching millennium.

As regards analysis, the discourse employed at this fascinating conference was highly distinctive, and always *reflected* speech. Everything was *constructive* and *complementary*; clearly one of the major reasons for excluding academics was to obviate any unrestrained critical and programmatic response to the play-led spontaneity and non-analytical, affective, goal-orientated style of all communications. No one who could not 'become as a little child' could enter this particular kingdom. Huizinga's description of play as 'a free activity standing quite consciously outside "ordinary life" as being "not serious", but at the same time absorbing the player intensely and utterly . . . It proceeds within its own proper boundaries of time and space according to fixed rules and in an orderly manner' is relevant at this juncture.[31] The recirculation of experience was constant and aided by the systematic practice of 'reporting back'. The overall mythic and narrative structure of the event was informed by the pervasive use of organic metaphors and the ascription of consciousness to the collective dimension: the conference itself had a 'soul' which became a palpable if transient reality by the end of the event.

It became apparent that the spiritual eclecticism was nevertheless informed by integrative themes. Central to the latter, and perhaps the most crucial, is the juxtaposition of 'being at cause' and 'being at effect'. The displacement of 'power' by 'empowerment' centred on the sustainability of social and network integration, and this is a field which remains in need of further exploration.[32] Observation of adepts in their capacity as management consultants and trainers indicated that a very close correlation between personal and work partnerships was sustained by 'switches' when one working relationship or partnership which had functioned well for a period of perhaps several years would be broken suddenly and apparently without the need for explanation other than a shared awareness of the individual impact of changes in market conditions. The ready acceptance of such ruptures would appear to be an

---

[31] Johann Huizinga, *Homo Ludens: A Study of the Play Element in Culture* (London: Routledge & Kegan Paul, 1949), p. 13.

[32] Paul Heelas' pioneering work on 'Self-religion' remains a key source: see, for example, Paul Heelas, 'Cults for Capitalism? Self Religions, Magic and the Empowerment of Business', in Peter Gee and John Fulton (eds.), *Religion and Power* (London: British Sociological Association, Sociology of Religion Study Group, 1991), pp. 27–41; Paul Heelas, 'The Sacralisation of the Self in New Age Capitalism', in N. Abercrombie and A. Ware (eds.), *Social Change in Contemporary Britain* (Cambridge: Polity, 1992), pp. 139–66.

integral part of an attitude and life-world commitment which then operated and still functions in terms of 'at-causality' and 'synchronicity'.
Wide-ranging contact with participants revealed little evidence of active
involvement with children or other dependants. Indeed, forms of 'dependency' were not a feature of the many 'programmes' and initiations on
offer. The 'performative absolute' requires the sacrifice of non-functional
aspects of the human condition.[33]

General goals were 'enhanced autonomy', increased self-awareness
and systematic 'accessing' of undiscovered or lost parts of the person.
The specific and prominent references made to the artist and visionary
William Blake by some participants were thoroughly representative of
the general belief frequently expressed that therapeutic and performance
striving could not be fully realised without the rediscovery and actualisation of a lost, primordial and empowering primal self. On the level of the
collective representations and 'metaphysics' of the event the discourse
revealed a relative lack of concern with the past. Thus there was very
little space given to regressive self-exploration: contact with the primal
self appeared to be an encounter with forces tending to *empowerment* and
not a judgemental *power* holding authority to bind or loose the past. Life
is *now* – and for *tomorrow*. The story begins where you want it to begin: the
metanarrative no longer commands – your individual story frees. The
informing motif of the event was a sense of discovering transcendental
power in and within the mundane. Each new encounter, each new decision, each task took on the character of an 'occasion of being', *my* being,
my self in greater fulfilment. The groundswell of the event involved 'connecting with your genius' and an 'everyday spirituality' which identified
self-realisation with the flow, an unwilled because willed-from-the-cause
identification which orchestrates reality and integrates self-fulfilment
with synchronicity and performance in the at-causality of primordial being. The ethical implications of these expressivist convictions are (despite
the affective benevolence) not risk-free.[34] The exploitation within innovative management training of highly diverse cultural artifacts ranging from
assimilations of witchcraft, astrology and 'organisational shamanism'
to the *Management Secrets of Attila the Hun*[35] raises intriguing questions.
How, not least, is it sociologically explicable that those best equipped to

33 This idea is expanded upon in chapter 6 in relation to Lyotard's *Postmodern Condition* and the
    managerialisation of priesthood.
34 As Paul Heelas has shown in 'God's Company: New Age Ethics and the Bank of Credit and
    Commerce International', *Religion Today*, 8/1 (1992), 1–4.
35 See Wess Roberts, *The Management Secrets of Attila the Hun* (London: Bantam Press, 1989).

exercise rational choice and to engage in economic maximisation seem equally well fitted to re-engage with spiritual practices and to live simultaneously in two worlds at a time when the plausibility structures of main-line religion are fading into societal insignificance?

In immediate and rather obvious terms the employment of so-called 'New Age' techniques in management training doubtless involves many as yet inadequately explored areas of theoretical, methodological and ethical concern. As regards the latter, three obvious and immediate areas arise. First, how far it is legitimate to oblige employees to submit themselves to training programmes which are (at the very least) mood-altering and may, if there is a predisposition, induce deep psychological disturbance or even health problems, both mental and physical? Second, should the distribution of 'spiritual' and behavioural training be organised in ways which entrench and reinforce structural differentiation in the labour force, on the assumption that such training may be understood as a reward or benefit paid in kind? Third, the *spiritual* development of human resources implies a problematic assimilation of religiosity as a human resource into a globalised capitalist world system. The latter thus might thereby assume control and management of *all* resources, material, economic, cultural – and now religious. Such an assimilation may well call into question basic convictions concerning the constitution and definition of 'the human' and lead us to inquire whether aspects of human rights need to be reconstrued in 'postmodernity'. Indeed, it is important to recognise and chart the constitutive role of the production, distribution and exchange of *religious* cultural capital in the micro- and macroeconomies of the local and global economic systems. Management training is now a drill square on which economic warriors, fully primed with spiritual awareness and techniques, are prepared for campaigns of endless conquest in fields far and wide, some of which we now turn to in earnest.

CHAPTER 4

The end of the university and the last academic?[1]

In memoriam:
Donald MacKenzie MacKinnon
(1913–1994)

It is through man's cruelty that the glory of God is revealed.[2]

We must compromise our principles, and do anything to raise money.[3]

British universities have for over fifteen years been subjected to some-thing approaching permanent revolution from above, and during this time higher education has been aggregated with primary and secondary education and reconceived as a mechanism capable of producing the numbers and kinds of skill-trained minds required by business and in-dustry at minimum cost, and with the highest degree of standardisa-tion possible. To this end, higher education has been subjected to three stages of reform. First, a gradual programme of greater financial account-ability was introduced with the budget-centre system, formula-funding and line-management (1982–6). Second, the 1987/8 Education Reform Act abolished academic tenure and introduced a series of measures, built around the imposition of 'teaching quality audit' (including the application of BS 5750 and ISO 9000), modularisation and semesterisa-tion, and the quinquennial Research Assessment Exercise. This period culminated in a doubling of the size of the tertiary sector and conse-quent dilution of the meaning of the term 'university'. Finally, in 1997,

---

[1] This chapter originated in an annual St Leonard's College (the postgraduate body of the University of St Andrews) Commemoration Address entitled 'The End of the University and the Last Academic', delivered before members on 8 November 1992. The long-term consequences of this expression of opinion for me were extremely serious. A succinct version of this address appeared as 'Our Graduate Factories', *The Tablet*, 11 October 1997, pp. 1295–7.

[2] Donald M. MacKinnon, *God the Living and the True* (Westminster: Dacre Press, 1940), p. 88.

[3] This is the self-fulfilling prophetic utterance of the Vice-Chancellor of a leading British university in his annual address to academic staff in the mid 1980s.

the Dearing Report envisaged the complete integration of the whole tertiary sector with further education in a flexible continuum, the reduction of state funding, a centralised academic audit mechanism monitored through a single, centrally approved external examining board for all degrees in each discipline, national curricula to assure uniform 'quality', and the implementation of 'benchmarking' and 'graduateness' (psycho-behavioural templates corresponding to each type of 'learning experience'). Now these measures are in the course of implementation: the 'life of the mind' now exists within the confines of national 'programme specifications' overseen by the Quality Assurance Agency (the QAA). The outcome is that in Britain we have created the equivalent of a national thought police. This amounts to the 'end of the university'. The above is in summary terms what has been imposed upon British higher education. What follows is an attack upon these measures, which are, in my judgement, a singular example of that forcible relocation of agency that takes place when the managerial prerogative 'reforms' – and destroys a culture.

I dedicate this chapter to the memory of Donald MacKinnon, formerly Norris-Hulse Professor of Divinity in the University of Cambridge, to whom I, like many others of my generation active in academic theology and religion, owe much. With his death ended an era; but by this I do not merely refer to the increased distance of the inter-war era, which MacKinnon could evoke with an intense vividness. No, there is now the sense that we have passed over a watershed pertaining to the very nature of the university and thus of the relation between teacher and taught, between intellectual leader and aspirant, that used to be central to the very fibre of authentic higher education. The major contention framing this chapter is that the free-ranging 'intellectual apostolate' of such a great but not flawless figure as Donald MacKinnon has become a functional impossibility in contemporary British higher education.[4] This I regret.

In advancing such a contention, I write on an issue so painfully close to my own experience that I can only with some difficulty maintain a critical distance.[5] Yet, for one who dares to invoke the name of Donald

---

[4] 'Theological Rhetoric and Moral Passion in the light of MacKinnon's "Barth"', in K. Surin (ed.), *Christ, Ethics and Tragedy: Pursuing the Thought of Donald MacKinnon* (Cambridge: Cambridge University Press, 1989), pp. 1–14.

[5] Yet I share with Pierre Bourdieu an irresistible 'need to gain rational control over the disappointment felt by an "oblate" faced with the annihilation of the truths and values to which he was destined rather than take refuge in feelings of self-destructive resentment', *Homo Academicus* (Cambridge: Polity, 1988), p. xxvi.

MacKinnon, the question here at issue, that of enforced change in the university and the creation of 'mass higher education', or what Professor Lord Conrad Russell has aptly termed 'battery higher education', is one from which the personal dimension cannot, indeed should not, be excluded. Donald MacKinnon taught those who came under his influence that the impact of morality and ethics upon the individual should never be ignored or overridden, and that, furthermore, there can be no easy marriage of – or divorce between – the 'moral' person and the 'immoral' organisation. The relationship between individual and institution is radically changed when alien managerial models non-consensually reconfigure universities into 'higher-education outlets' and a fundamental clash with the demands of a *real* university education is engendered. University education is like beer: it can be 'real' or a synthetic *Ersatz*, a concocted simulacrum, and we need to relearn the distinction between the two. This decipherment is, however, not an easy matter as it implies conflict with a massively empowered *Zeitgeist* – and with copious popular prejudice.

In seeking to articulate some of the present dilemmas in higher education in Britain, I call in question a range of further issues which cannot be tackled at this juncture; yet what has happened in the university is a microcosm of societal abuse characteristic of Britain as a whole since 1979. I refer deliberately to 'Britain', yet even the Scottish university in which I once held the tradition-bearing Chair of Divinity had departed from those ideals of the specifically *Scottish* university as the seat of the 'democratic intellect' (George Davie)[6] and 'community of contested discourses' (Alasdair MacIntyre).[7] What follows should, nevertheless, be understood as an exercise in contextual analysis in which any particularities serve only to illustrate and heighten emphasis upon the flawed and contradictory general principles that have been imposed upon higher education as a whole. As Professor Lord Conrad Russell has observed:

The current assault by the State on the Universities is thus in a long tradition. Yet within that tradition, it is an assault to which there are few parallels, because it is designed to change all the values by which Universities operate. Perhaps only a clergyman who had lived through the reign of Henry VIII would be capable of understanding how the Universities now feel.[8]

[6] See George Davie, *The Democratic Intellect: Scotland and her Universities in the Nineteenth Century* (Edinburgh: Edinburgh University Press, 1961); and *The Crisis of the Democratic Intellect: The Problems of Generalism and Specialisation in Twentieth-Century Scotland* (Edinburgh: Polygon, 1986).

[7] Alasdair MacIntyre, *Three Rival Versions of Moral Enquiry: Encyclopaedia, Genealogy, and Tradition* (London: Duckworth, 1990), p. 22.

[8] Lord Conrad Russell, *Academic Freedom* (London: Routledge, 1993), p. 3.

This engagement in contextual theology is undertaken in the spirit of Donald MacKinnon, who in 1972 wrote that 'the reality of apostleship is not proved by a quickly effective ministry of apologetic, but by a long and painful apprenticeship to which the individual knows himself constrained by that which will not let him escape'.[9] At the very core of what has been forcibly transmuted is a commitment to the integrity of the university as the realm of the critical mind, and this is underlaid by a compound principle no better expressed than by the theologian Dietrich Bonhoeffer, who wrote from his Nazi prison cell of the 'natural rights of the life of the mind'. In an incomplete fragment of the *Ethics*, Bonhoeffer asserted that

There are three fundamental attitudes which the life of the mind assumes with regard to reality: judgement, action and enjoyment (play and delight). In these attitudes man confronts in freedom the reality of which he himself forms part, and he thereby shows that he is a man.[10]

In this chapter we observe and analyse an imbalance: *judgement* has been expropriated by managerial *fiat*; *action* has been mechanicised into the policing of the meaningless circularities of 'Quality'; and *enjoyment* has become the casual pleasure of the 'receiver' or 'customer' who picks and chooses in the 'knowledge outlet'. That task integral to the 'natural rights of the life of the mind', the confronting in freedom of reality, and the proof thereby of one's humanity, has been, as will become apparent, largely elided from the educational task, or made so problematic in execution as to render the efforts of those who attempt it a counter-systemic aberration. No doubt there are some, now perhaps many, who view as a long overdue 'reform' the intellectual cleansing of higher education of powerful eccentricity and the exceptional confrontation with reality represented *par excellence* by a Donald MacKinnon. Such intellectual characteristics are incompatible with the 'mass higher education' criticised in this chapter, but the very existence of critically reflexive search for knowledge is under threat. The university should, to use Vaclav Havel's potent phrase, 'live in truth'.[11]

Recent changes imposed upon British university and tertiary education constitute part of the general reversal of what the historian Harold

---

[9] 'Theology as a Discipline in a Modern University', in Teodor Shanin (ed.), *The Rules of the Game: Cross-disciplinary Essays on Models in Scholarly Thought* (London: Tavistock Publications, 1972), p. 172.
[10] D. Bonhoeffer, *Ethics* (London: SCM, 1955), p. 186.
[11] Vaclav Havel, 'The Power of the Powerless', in Jan Vladislav (ed.), *Living in Truth* (London, Faber & Faber, 1987), pp. 36–122.

Perkin depicted as the 'rise of professional society'. Professionalism involves the occupational control of work and is distinct from bureaucratic and market-based forms of structuring work;[12] de-professionalisation involves the loss of a relative autonomy responsible to and for tradition. The contemporary manifestations of managerialism and the evolution of a planned, even a command economy in higher education have involved dramatic non-consensual alterations in the self-identity and practice of the academic profession. This is not only because of the latter's enlargement and consequent dilution through the sudden creation of many 'universities' out of a wide variety of pre-existing educational bodies, but also, and more significantly, because of an ineffectively contested bureaucratic revolution from above. In this setting, the socio-cultural identities of the 'university' and of the academic profession, already weak and ineptly (if ever) defined, have been reconstrued by political *force majeure* enacted through a series of administrative and managerial measures that have entailed a dramatic alteration of the largely implicit self-understandings of institutions and their life-worlds.[13] Academics have become mere 'factors of production': but are they – should they – be more than this?[14]

I shall argue that in the absence of effective constitutional safeguards the responsible autonomy and cultural agency (indeed the human rights) of academic staff, which were inexplicit and feeble, have in certain respects been eliminated. The 'natural rights of the life of the mind' have been overridden. Consequently, the pursuit of knowledge and a respect for truth have been subsumed under a system of customer-driven 'packaged learning' through a process of 'turning of diamonds into glass'. Academic resistance has been negligible: theirs is a *trahison des clercs* of the first order. The re-creation of critical reflexivity on the part of the academic profession will involve a collective response, the rebirth of the will-to-be, besides a willingness to engage in a careful analysis of the generation, nature and exchange of cultural capital in society as a whole.

---

[12] As is forcefully argued by Eliot Freidson, *Professionalism Reborn: Theory, Prophecy, and Policy* (Cambridge: Polity, 1994).

[13] A. H. Halsey, *The Decline of Donnish Dominion* (Oxford: Oxford University Press, 1988), has provided a comprehensive but morally vacuous account of developments in academia since the Second World War. Halsey is the kind of sociological realist who simply records without evaluation the inevitability of societal change in a way that an ethicist or theologian cannot.

[14] Academics are not of course alone in this. See Neil Millward, *The New Industrial Relations? Based on the ED/ESRC/PSI/ACAS Surveys* (London: Policy Studies Institute Publications, 1994), p. 133: 'On the basis of the patterns and trends that we have identified – and the continuing existence of a wide range of factors supporting or reinforcing these trends – British industry and commerce appear to be moving towards the situation in which non-managerial employees are treated as "factors of production".'

The retrospective abolition of academic tenure in the 1988 Education Reform Act was merely one factor in the complex disempowerment reviewed in this chapter. Present practice, with regard to the imposition of a crassly inapposite and old-fashioned system of line-management, the unilateral declaration of institutional possession of the intellectual property of employees, multiple systems of 'Quality Audit' and appraisal, the abolition of any meaningful separation of powers in the organisation, the unqualified subordination of academic staff to unaccountable student criticism, the reduction of Senates and faculty meetings from decision-making bodies to reception mechanisms, and pervasive fear, *all taken together*, amounts to a virtual enslavement, the creation of a class of intellectual 'living tools'. These are workers whose political and sociological naivety has permitted the unprotesting expropriation (in accordance with classic Taylorian line-management) of the exercise of their professional discretion, or cultural agency. As a result they are for the most part neutered, miserably complicit in the surgery that has been inflicted upon them. Thus deprived, as Nietzsche might have predicted, many academic practitioners now endorse the reduction of all their colleagues to a uniform self-policed mediocrity.[15]

To speak theologically, it is at this juncture that a distinction between the *penultimate* and the *ultimate* has been transgressed: the academic profession has been absorbed into the subtle and infinitely invasive web of a totalitarian managerialism, in the face of which many other social factors in a crisis-ridden society are trivial. For those who believe in the distinctive vocation of the university as a 'community of contested discourses', with a role both exploratory and critical in culture and society, and in its own special ways ultimate, this situation is an unnamed – even unnameable catastrophe. The consequence of disagreement with the new status quo is pervasive dissonance; the price of outright dissent may be total institutional and personal isolation – or worse. Yet, as Baroness Mary Warnock remarked with good intent, but to little practical effect:

In a democratic society, we cannot allow the universities to be despised, for it is from the universities that democratic freedom of thought will ultimately find its support.[16]

---

[15] I am able to confirm the truth of the following remark by Karl Kraus, cited by Piere Bourdieu: 'anyone who rejects the pleasure and easy profits of long distance criticism, in order to investigate his immediate neighbourhood, which everything bids him hold sacred, must expect the torments of 'subjective persecution'. Bourdieu, *Homo Academicus*, p. 5.

[16] Mary Warnock, *Universities: Knowing Our Minds. What the Government should do about Higher Education* (London: Chatto & Windus, 1989), p. 43.

This observation, although admirable in principle, has proved more an ironic expression of secular piety than a prediction of outcomes. It is, however, my intention in this chapter to help clear the ground for those with vision, hope – and will – sufficient to seek to reoccupy lost territory and to rebuild. This is therefore a response, if not a fully direct one, to Baroness Warnock, and also, furthermore, to the admirable Lord Conrad Russell, who observes towards the end of his study of academic freedom:

> The first question facing academics is whether battery higher education serves some useful purpose. Those who can answer 'yes' to this question may be able to continue to serve, in the hope that some day, the spark they keep alive may be brought out and burst into flame. Those who argue for this course must first explain what the useful purpose served by the expanded Universities will be, for it is only if an answer to this question can be offered that it is possible to engage in a debate with this approach. I will listen with interest to that debate when it begins, but so far, I have heard no justification.[17]

In seeking to resist a seemingly victorious enemy we have first to recognise that the purely formal recognition of academic freedom is inadequate inasmuch as it fails to relate the nature of knowledge to the conditions of its production. In the face of government opposition Lord Jenkins of Hillhead moved an Academic Freedom amendment to the Education Reform Bill on 19 May 1988, which was intended to ensure:

> The freedom within the law to question and test received wisdom, and to put forward new ideas and controversial or unpopular opinions without placing themselves in jeopardy of losing their jobs or privileges they may have at their institutions.

In some tertiary institutions this defence extends to criticism of the organisation of the conditions of the production and transmission of knowledge; in others such freedom is, *de facto*, non-existent. Thus, for example, the staff contract of one of the newest additions to the university sector specifically permits criticism of the management of the institution. Other (ancient and the more modern) universities offer no such freedom, and the clause governing 'dismissal for good cause' will no doubt exercise the ingenuity of academic managers for whom the generation of 'thematic redundancy' may become a fine art. In reality this managerial euphemism means that as course topics follow market fluctuations, so increasingly peripheral short-term-contract academic staff will become disposable items with an equally short shelf-life. My major point is that unless the

---

[17] Russell, *Academic Freedom*, p. 110.

definition of academic freedom includes certain rights to organise the production and distribution of knowledge in the setting of 'natural rights of the life of the mind', then that freedom is nominal and vacuous.

Universities have never, it may with some confidence be said, been popular. As F. M. Cornford pointed out many years ago in his *Micro-cosmographia Academica*, this distaste is traceable to antiquity. The politics of *ressentiment* are not new, as we see when Cornford recalled Plato's observations:

> 'Any one of us might say, that although in words he is not able to meet you at each step of the argument, he sees as a fact that academic persons, when they carry on study, not only in you as a part of education, but as the pursuit of their maturer years, most of them become decidedly queer, not to say rotten; and that those who may be considered the best of them are made useless to the world by the very study that you extol.'
> 'Well, do you think that those who say so are wrong?'
> 'I cannot tell', he replied; 'but I should like to know what is your opinion?'
> 'Hear my answer; I am of the opinion that they are quite right.'[18]

As regards the history of the 'idea of the university' there is, of course, no one single conception.[19] Medieval seats of learning were deeply in-fused with theological culture, and closely modelled upon monastic practice.[20] Even when and where the universities developed away from the monastic enclosure of learning, it was only with French absolutism and the Revolution of 1789 that for the first time universities slipped from the control of the church closer to that of an ever more ambitious and power-hungry state. It is interesting to note the ease with which some ancient educational institutions can move silently from the stone cell of pre-modernity to the iron cage of a Taylorised modernity. As C. F. Lamoignon, a member of the Paris Parlement, remarked as early as 1783:

> Education should be under the inspection of the public power, because it should be wholly directed toward public utility and the good of the State, and should not suffer from the variable views of private administration.[21]

[18] Plato, *Republic* VI as cited by F. M. Cornford, *Microcosmographia Academica: Being a Guide for the Young Academic Politician* (Cambridge: Bowes & Bowes, 1908), p. 9.

[19] The literature is considerable: see J. Pelikan, *The Idea of the University: A Reexamination* (New Haven/London: Yale University Press, 1992), for a wide-ranging survey and bibliographical guidance.

[20] The sociologist Stewart Clegg provides an excellent commentary upon the creative possibilities of *postmodern* organisation in his inaugural lecture, 'Postmodern Management', St Andrews, 1991.

[21] Cited by Elie Kedourie in *Perestroika in the Universities* (London: Institute of Economic Affairs, 1989), p. 17.

At the French Revolution, as in our own time, state power and popu-
lism may join forces.[22] Indeed, *dirigisme* might well have seemed improbable in Britain, say twenty-five years ago, but the government White
Paper of 1987, *Meeting the Challenge*, paved the way for a transformation,
the so-called 'reform' of the universities:

> Higher Education has a crucial role in helping the nation meet the economic
> challenges of the final decade of this century and beyond.[23]

The assimilation of higher education into national planning required,
ironically, the effective *nationalisation* of the universities, a revolution from
above, the full consequences of which have now been imposed and enacted. We thus stand at a historic juncture in the history of higher education, from where we can begin to discern the outline of the new
Panopticon. This may under certain conditions be legitimately depicted
as a *prison house of learning*, when, for example, university staff are subjected
to the increasingly intimate long-, medium- and short-term regimes of
mind control as the precondition of their being permitted to condition,
in turn, the student minds they win for processing. Fredric Jameson's
resonant argument in *The Prison House of Language* suggests this depiction
of the higher education as imprisonment in an imposed discourse, a pervasive *Newspeak* manipulated by a *nomenklatura* of managerial *apparatchiks*
whose selection and future prospects tend to depend upon one virtue
alone – unfailing compliance.

As regards the historical idea of the university, for present purposes two
conceptions are of importance: first, that of John Henry Newman, and
his ideas for a teaching body based on the Keble College of his youth, and
second, Wilhelm von Humboldt's University of Berlin, and the idea of a
research-driven institution built around extraordinary privileges for an
elite professorate and the principles of *Freiheit der Forschung; Freiheit der Lehre;
Einheit der Forschung und Lehre*. The newer English provincial universities
of the nineteenth century and those founded in the Robbins Report

---

[22] G. Flaubert, *Sentimental Education*, cited in Bourdieu, *Homo Academicus*, p. 159.

[23] *Higher Education: Meeting the Challenge*, Cmnd 114 (London: HMSO, April 1987), p. iv. Efforts at
educational *Gleichschaltung* tend to share a similar rhetorical tone. It is interesting in this regard to
record the words of Minister für Wissenschaft, Erziehung and Volksbildung Berhard Rust in his
declaration of the new Student Law of 6 May 1933: Wir blicken nunmehr in die Zukunft. Was
der Staat in diesem Augenblick tun kann, das tut er heute und wird er in der nächsten Zeit tun.
Er wird der deutschen Hochschule einen Lehrkörper reorganisieren, der dann gleichläufend
und gleichgerichtet mit dem Willen der Nation auch die Aufgabe erfüllen kann, die er in seiner
Zusammensetzung, wie ich sie am 30. januar vorfand, nicht zu erfüllen vermochte', cited in
Hans-Jochen Gamm, *Führung und Verführung Pädogogik des National-Sozialismus* (Munich: List
Bibliothek, 1990), p. 151.

expansion oscillated uneasily between two seemingly incompatible ideals, the collegial intimacy of Newman's vision and the German model of the research-driven university. It is only in the last ten years that this ambiguity has been resolved by the loosening-up of the meaning of the term 'university' so as to include any institution of sufficient size purveying higher education which can, in the current Newspeak, demonstrate sufficient 'Quality'. From the Orwellian standpoint, this chapter amounts to *crimethink* directed into the 'untranslatable' zones of human rights and referentiality.[24] Yet, I still labour under the seemingly perverse conviction that universities (and, not least, *Scottish* universities) have a number of distinctive functions; they may even have what Alasdair MacIntyre denotes a 'peculiar and essential function'. Let us, however, begin once more with Baroness Warnock, who is (by contemporary standards) refreshingly radical in her approach:

> The crucial difference between university and other forms of education lies simply in its necessary connection with research. For at school, sixth-form college or college of higher education, however good teachers may be, they are generally teaching the received wisdom in their subject. They may be critical of this wisdom; they may hold unorthodox or eccentric views. But it is very unlikely that they will themselves be engaged in discovering new things or publishing reasoned objections to orthodox thinking. They are unlikely to have either the time or the resources to enable them to enter new fields. More important, as teachers, their main task will be to help their students to get on to the next stage, and to pass examinations based on the 'received' view of the subject matter. If they do anything else, they fail in their duty. Thus the teacher, who is nothing but a teacher, is inevitably part of a conservative system, academically speaking.[25]

It is hardly surprising that Conservative adminstrations (and their New Labour successor) should seek to extend the teaching function so that it becomes an all-embracing effort. Baroness Warnock continues in terms which indicate the wider implications of the imposed change in all the values of the university. For, she argues,

> All of our knowledge must be filtered to us, and passed on by us, through the medium of language. It is essential that there should be those, philosophers, theologians, literary critics, linguists and linguisticians, who are trained to think critically about the relation between language and the world, and between one language and another. It is only through the use of language that we can think coherently and in general terms about either the past or the future.[26]

[24] See 'Appendix: The Principles of Newspeak', in G. Orwell, *Nineteen Eighty-Four* (Harmondsworth: Penguin, 1949), pp. 241–51. See especially p. 251.
[25] Warnock, *Knowing our Minds*, p. 21.
[26] *Ibid.*, p. 36.

Moreover, she concludes,

But with the universities it is different: they must be seen as the source of new knowledge, the origin of that critical, undogmatic, imaginative examination of received wisdom without which a country cannot be expected to have its voice heard, and from which ultimately all intellectual standards flow. It is this critical and imaginative function which is in danger, if civil servants and Ministers show themselves unable to accept the authority of the learned, the academic and the scholarly.[27]

Recent changes in universities imply precisely an abrogation of the absolute duty 'to think critically about the relation between language and the world, and between one language and another' and its displacement by an alien political and managerial prerogative that calls in question the identity and very continuance of the 'university' as opposed to the 'knowledge factory', the 'knowledge outlet' in a 'battery higher education' system. Given the nature of government policy and the unconstrained, ever-expanding remit of the new managerialism, the assumption must be that this critical, truth-seeking function is now perceived to be redundant. In such circumstances the dual allegiance of which MacKinnon wrote, that is to critical thought and to the 'opening up of the frontiers of the unknown that calls out one's energies' becomes a burden, indeed a positive disability in this new world of the top-down, intellectually managed, 'Quality'-encircled 'battery university' delivering 'mass higher education'.[28] It is this freedom that is foreclosed, as we shall see, through the imposition of self-administered and humiliating constraints.

By contrast, then, with Baroness Warnock's optimistic Eurocentric traditionalism, the following is but one example of the questionable and politically motivated (yet basically unchallenged) redefinition of the idea of the university. Lord Chilvers asserted in 1988 that

Every university in its charter is required to disseminate knowledge and, it's a very important point, that knowledge must be universally applicable. That's the meaning of the word university.[29]

What this actually meant is that the universal dissemination and application of knowledge is the test on the basis of which the retention or elimination of an institution from the category 'university' should be decided. This is a misleading, indeed a perverse, account of the role of

---

[27] *Ibid.*, p. 42.
[28] MacKinnon, 'Theology as a Discipline', p. 169.
[29] Lord Chilvers, *Times Higher Educational Supplement* 14 October, 1988.

knowledge in the university which fails to consider the conditions of its production. Once more we may draw a critical parallel. John Henry Newman was on solid ground when he characterised the university as a corporation, and speaking in front of a Catholic audience (keen, as is the present government, to extend its influence), he maintained that

As to the range of University teaching, certainly the very name of the University is inconsistent with restrictions of any kind. Whatever was the original reason of the adoption of that term, which is unknown, I am only putting on it its popular, its recognised sense, when I say that a University should teach universal knowledge. That there is a real necessity for this universal teaching in the highest schools of intellect, I will show by-and-by; here it is sufficient to say that such universality is considered by writers on the subject to be characteristic of a University, as contrasted with other seats of learning. Thus Johnson, in his Dictionary, defines it to be 'a school where all arts and faculties are taught'.[30]

The enclosure and constraint associated with mass higher education should not surprise us. The massification of higher education involves elaborate modular systems and functionaries who orchestrate their day-to-day operation. This fits all too well the Franco-American theorist Jean Baudrillard's depiction of the 'philosophy of lack of will' characteristic of mass-systems. The full implications of this understanding of the consequences of massification have yet to be successfully ingested by an academic profession that has largely accepted the new role of higher education as the processing of student bio-mass. Baudrillard describes this craven mentality as 'a sort of radical antimetaphysics whose secret is that the masses are deeply aware that they do not have to make a decision about themselves and the world; that they do not have to wish; that they do not have to know; that they do not have to desire'.[31] Baudrillard's epistemological critique fits the conception of the university as the knowledge outlet and of the academic as purveyor of modules to the 'customers' who browse through course catalogues. Responsibility to the 'natural rights of the mind' has been displaced by the extrinsically managed circulation of complex 'signs' in a controlled, closed system. Baudrillard argues as follows:

In this revolution, the two aspects of value [i.e. use and exchange] which sometimes used to be thought of as coherent and eternally linked, as if by natural law, are disarticulated; *referential value is nullified, giving the advantage to the structural*

---

[30] John Henry Newman, *The Idea of a University* (New York: Chelsea House, 1983), p. 19.
[31] 'The Masses: The Implosion of the Social in the Media', in Mark Poster (ed.), *Jean Baudrillard: Selected Writings* (Cambridge: Polity, 1988), p. 215.

play of value. The structural dimension, in other words, gains autonomy, to the exclusion of the referential dimension, establishing itself on the death of the latter. Gone are the referentials of production, signification, affect, substance, history, and the whole equation of 'real' contents that gave the sign weight by anchoring it with a kind of burden of utility – in short its form as representative equivalent. All this is surpassed by the other stage of value, that of total relativity, generalised commutative, combinatory simulation. This means that simulation in the sense that from now on signs will exchange among themselves exclusively, without interacting with the real (and this becomes the condition for their smooth operation). The emancipation of the sign: released from any 'archaic' obligation it might have had to designate something, the sign is at last free for a structural or combinatory play that succeeds the previous role of determinate equivalence.[32]

On first sight this may seem an obscure text, but its significance will become clearer when we explore the system of managerial control, Quality Audit and programme specification. For the moment, however, the reader is invited to substitute the word 'module' for 'sign' in the foregoing passage and to relate this back to Bonhoeffer's conception of the 'real' and its place in the coming into full humanity of the life of the mind. In fact, the success of the university as knowledge outlet requires the most complete uniformity and predictability of modules that can be attained; thus the modules become the equivalent, in Baudrillard's terms, of non-referential 'signs' circulating in a closed economy. In this system of exchange, 'permission' must be sought to alter modules and/or modify the political economy of the module in any respect. Thus, for example, academic staff have to show evidence of the *approval* of external examiners before any minor modification or updating of a course can be submitted for scrutiny by faculty committees, who then in turn may (or may not) allow a change (however small) to be made. This is not a system of consultation, but one of *control* based upon the pervasive but undeclared assumption of the universal incompetence and untrustworthiness of academic staff. This is the Panopticon reborn; an alien interest directs the production and distribution of knowledge.

Startling, perhaps, but congruent with this analysis, is the right-wing commentator Sir Douglas Hague, who outlined a vision of the 'knowledge industry' in a booklet that relishes venomous resentment and oozes a desire to humiliate an enemy long held in contempt:

We are approaching a new Hollywood era. Some UK academics are television mini-stars already. So, even more, are international (or US stars). This will

[32] J. Baudrillard, 'Symbolic Exchange and Death', in *Jean Baudrillard: Selected Writings*, p. 125.

become a very well-paid profession for those with internationally acceptable talent. There will, therefore, have to be programme producers as well as impresarios since knowledge is now being packaged. This really is 'show-biz' – and universities are hopeless at that![33]

Whereas Sir Douglas Hague's tone is often rumbustiously offensive, one may nevertheless have a little sympathy with his impatience at the shortcomings of some institutions and individuals. Hague's vision of the 'electronic cloning' of those designated as the best teachers and of the 'shamrock organisation' (a conception dependent upon the ideas of the management guru Sir Charles Handy[34]) is spelt out below in structural terms:

What will the university be? The short answer is that it will become a base for a diverse set of people and activities . . . the 'shamrock' organisation, which is now seen as typical of businesses in the 1990s, not least in the knowledge industries. The shamrock has three parts – hence its name: a professional core, a contractual fringe and a flexible labour force.[35]

In relation to this kind of attack upon the ethical and 'theological' dimension of their life-task, intellectuals and academics (those to whom Bertold Brecht might have referred to as *Kopf-Arbeiter*) are in a peculiarly difficult situation because of the comprehensively internalised nature of their socialisation and the self-willed abrogation of any simple or obvious public–private, work–home delimitation of spheres. This means that the removal of autonomy involves a profound invasion of selfhood, precisely because the opening and reconfiguration of the self has been the necessary condition of competence and effective professionalisation. One very considerable problem associated with academics unused to reflexive analysis is a tendency to divorce the activities involved in the creation and distribution of their knowledge from context, and to be paralysed by a fragile personal individualism which has proved utterly incapable of effective resistance. As it is now argued that individual rights have to be complemented by communitarian cultural rights, so correspondingly it is important to argue for the rights of trained, professional workers to participate in the constitution of the condition and character of their labour. Faced with this external assault a reader might have anticipated a ruthless self-appraisal, new forms of collective organisation and an aggressive

[33] Sir Douglas Hague, *Beyond Universities: A New Republic of the Intellect* (London: Institute of Economic Affairs, 1989), p. 59.
[34] See Charles Handy, 'The Shamrock Organisation', *The Age of Unreason* (London: Arrow, 1989), ch. 4.
[35] Hague, *Beyond Universities*, p. 57.

response on the part of those who are of a mind to offer themselves in this labour market; this response has not been forthcoming.

So far we have concentrated upon the context and history of the university revolution from above. In order to illustrate this we shall subject to content and rhetorical analysis a brief but wholly representative document. Thus the Principal's *Annual Report* of 1992–3 projected the image of the University of St Andrews into a global market-place. It was, as Professor Struther Arnott, an able and accomplished orator, implied in glossing his own text, a review of progress delivered 'not entirely tongue-in-cheek, to our new "shareholders" at the July 1993 Graduation':

I am the current Chief Executive of the St Andrews University enterprise, a company which must command respect since it has been trading continuously for 583 years. You will recollect that we started business in 1410 as a subsidiary of the Universal Church which had been a major business in St Andrews for more than 600 years before. A competing attraction, golf, had come to St Andrews just before we were set up. Whether we were installed to be an alternative or an additional attraction I am not sure.[36]

The Chief Executive goes on to speak of a 'major board room row' between 'our parent company over its Chief Executive, the Pope', of 'trading without a licence', the 'loss of an exclusive franchise', and of 'our market diminishing', 'restructuring', and 'restricting St Mary's College to special products' (as it happens, this was divinity), and so on. This document is extraordinary in that it does far more than risk a few oblique figurative allusions to 'raw material' (new students sourced from primary suppliers – the parents), 'value-adding' (what happens to the student at university) and the 'product' (the graduate) as is now fairly normal practice amongst principals and vice-chancellors in British higher education. Principal Arnott has the honest arrogance to unfold a comprehensive vision of the university as 'business', continuing in a similar vein with 'headquarters', 'special products', 'business recovery', 'up and down cycle', 'booming', 'drawing down prices', 'our company has a good designer label, a special market niche and good company policy summed up in two Greek words, which, when suitably translated, tell us "Always Strive for High Quality" (*Aien aristeuein*)'.

The Chief Executive's assimilation of the University's ancient motto into the discourse of 'Quality Audit' is absolutely crucial: it is here that the link between the business discourse and the realities of managerial control

---

[36] Principal Struther Arnott, 'Six Centuries of Service – The Principal's Report', *University of St Andrews Annual Report 1992–3*, p. 4.

is forged at the point at which the revolutionary transition has to be expressed. It is on the basis of the analysis of this public discourse that we may begin to unfold the practical consequences of the functionalisation of an invasive metaphor, the self-replicating virus that now infects the whole higher education system. Thus we shall begin to understand the formal structure that increasingly dictates the function. As prime articulator of a business culture, the Chief Executive would appear to straddle both worlds – but for how long? At this juncture, George Orwell's commentary on the problems of relating 'Oldspeak' to 'Newspeak' becomes relevant:

> When Oldspeak had been once for all superseded, the last link with the past would have been severed. History had already been rewritten, but fragments of the literature of the past survived here and there, imperfectly censored, and so long as one retained one's knowledge of Oldspeak it was possible to read them. In the future such fragments, even if they chanced to survive, would be unintelligible and untranslatable. It was impossible to translate any passage of Oldspeak into Newspeak unless it referred to some technical process or some very simple everyday action, or it was already orthodox (*goodthinkful* would be the Newspeak expression) in tendency . . . Pre-revolutionary literature could only be subjected to ideological translation – that is, alteration in sense as well as language. (pp. 250–1)

Orwell proceeds to argue that, for example, the sense of the opening passage of the Declaration of Human Rights, 'We hold these truths to be self-evident . . . ', would be untranslatable from Oldspeak to Newspeak without a fundamental change of meaning. The very notion of the existence of 'inalienable rights', amongst which are 'life, liberty, and the pursuit of happiness' would constitute an obstruction to enforced change, analogous I would submit, to the untranslatability of Bonhoeffer's 'natural rights of the life of the mind' into the contemporary 'reformed' university context at present under consideration.

　　It is interesting to note that whilst the Dean of Arts in his later contribution to the same St Andrews *Report* apparently sought to hold a balance, we nevertheless begin to become aware of the nature of the changes involved, and of the incommensurability of both discourses and practices:

> Resource management constitutes the canonical text of the policy-makers of higher Education, many say to the detriment of the humanistic values that should govern our attitudes to knowledge and learning. Nevertheless, let no one deny that good management is a prerequisite for effective teaching and research. To this end . . . [a whole series of structural changes originating with Executive *fiat* are then reported].[37]

[37] *Ibid.*, p. 11.

In rhetorical terms it is once again important to note the juxtaposition of the 'many say' (those muted voices who feebly protest the integrity of higher education?) with the assertive – even threatening – 'let no one deny'. We must remember that in a line-managed (but basically medieval) university the academic staff were in terms of their oath the *servi universitatis*, the servants or 'slaves' of the University, whose views did not need to be taken into account. In effect, even in the discourse employed to comprehend the motivation of all stake-holders a balance is not maintained: the managerial prerogative is dominant. Thus the Dean of Arts reported that departments have been combined into Schools in order to secure the 'good management' alluded to above, but the continued existence of disciplinary difference in these seven units was to be tolerated solely 'because it was felt that the humanist disciplines could not yield up their separateness without loss to [*sic*] their uniqueness and reputation'.[38] It is once more important to note the juxtaposition of the impersonal agency: an 'it' has decided; but the result, a 'yielding', is the language of an enforcement that lies beyond seduction – this is the verbal trace left by the institutional violation of academic and personal integrity.

In the representative institution under consideration *all* significant positions within the academic body (excepting the disempowered deans of faculties, who, far from exercising their traditional role of representing the interests of academic colleagues, were now to police controls on behalf of government-imposed schemes of oversight) have been emancipated from their elected status and reconstituted as appointed posts held strictly within the gift of the Chief Executive. This involved not only the abolition of the principle of the separation of powers essential to democratic practice, but also, most unfortunately, an endangering of the rule of law, because 'law' tended also to become a plastic creature of Executive prerogative. The inevitable result was the emergence of a *nomenklatura* who owed unquestioning allegiance to one individual. Traditional structures that assured a measure of dispersed power were modified so as to facilitate the efficiency of centralised decision-making. In that same Scottish university, for example, the Chief Executive confined all members of Senate to a single comment (duly recorded by the clerks for the future use of the Executive) on any one item of business. With the removal of the right to reply there was no need for debate; and without, in effect, the right to take decisions (Senate having become

---

[38] *Ibid.*

a mere opinion-gathering mechanism, a sounding-board on behalf of the all-powerful Executive) debate becomes pointless: meetings are usually completed in less than half an hour. In the absence of any meaningful separation of powers there could be no meaningful possibility of the publicly expressed disagreement that ought to be the *sine qua non* of intelligent decision-making in a university. The problem is yet again not simply one of discourses in collision: structural changes are required in order to secure the transition from historic university to standardised knowledge outlet.

The centrepiece of the new 'circuit of power'[39] imposed upon British universities and higher education is the so-called Quality Standard, the implementation of which has helped give rise to a highly invasive, self-propagating jargon that now inhabits many areas of academic discourse. The Quality Standard BS5750 speaks of

A systematic and independent examination to determine whether quality activities and related results comply with planned arrangements, are implemented effectively and are suitable to achieve objectives.[40]

We may summarise the associated circuit of power in the following terms.[41] The scheme consists of three main elements: (a) Quality Audit; (b) Quality Enhancement; (c) Credit and Accessibility. 'Standards' now in reality belong to a superseded life-world pertaining to academics and their assumed sphere of influence, but in terms of real power standards have been displaced by 'Quality'. Whereas 'Standards' are concerned with levels of achievement set against objective criteria, 'Quality' concerns fitness of purpose, in a context in which purpose is related to managerial prerogative. The result, as argued earlier, is the elision of referentiality.

In consequence, 'Quality control' as it effects university teaching and learning syllabuses is an operational function applied at all levels by an institution to its teaching activities, and is concerned in detail with the way these are organised, undertaken and evaluated. 'Quality assurance', by comparison, is concerned with the way in which a university exercises

---

[39] See Stewart R. Clegg, *Frameworks of Power* (London: Sage, 1989) for a sophisticated account of the nature of power in contemporary societies.

[40] There are several guides to the implementation of BS5750 and ISO9000: see for example, Lesley Munro-Fauré, Malcolm Munro-Fauré and Edward Bones, *Achieving Quality Standards: A Step-by-Step Guide to BS5750 and ISO9000* (London: Pitman, 1993).

[41] Here we rely upon an introductory talk to academic middle managers given in St Andrews by Peter Adam, then Chief Executive of National Academic Audit. The regulatory regimes and the attendent bodies continue to proliferate, but the basic intentions remain unchanged.

its corporate responsibility for its programmes, courses and qualifications. Through a systemic sleight of hand Quality Audit assumes the existence of the institution's own aims and objectives and is thus ostensibly value-free. Audit does not express views on the appropriateness of these institutional goals. Academic staff are, however, caught between a mechanism (one of an ever-increasing number of such mechanisms) designed to enforce uniformity and an authority that defines those aims and objectives that the Quality Audit seeks to enforce. In effect, the cultural agency and practices and the responsible academic freedom of the university researcher and teacher are conveniently elided between the mutual disavowals of the ruling partners: the jam in the sandwich is squeezed to the point of residual flavour!

The seven questions put by Quality Audit – : (1) What are you trying to do?; (2) Why are you trying to do it?; (3) How are you trying to do it? (4) Why are trying to do it that way?; (5) Why do you think that is the best way of doing it?; (6) How do you know it works?; (7) How do you approve it? – may seem reasonable enough taken on their own in a de-contextualised way, but in reality they run into two major sets of difficulties. On the one hand, the context of their enactment involves the corporate setting of aims and objectives by a collegially unaccountable 'management' or 'Executive' and a series of other controls which turn apparently useful questions into an oppressive and stultifying system of *self-policing*. On the other hand, this forms part of a comprehensive framework in which the preparation, validation and delivery mechanisms, together with the *subsequent* audit of delivery, are not only increasingly time-consuming but also tend inevitably to sever any remaining connections between research and teaching. The abrogation of the latter link weakens any remaining links with a European, in particular with the great Humboldtian, conception of the university built upon the principles of *Freiheit der Forschung; Freiheit der Lehre; Einheit der Forschung und Lehre.*[42]

An arbitrary check list of measures necessary to secure 'Quality' includes the following: the approval, validation and review of programmes of study and of the teaching, learning and communication processes; student assessment and classification procedures; staff development, training, appraisal and enhancement (with competence – perhaps *compliance* rewards might be a more accurate depiction); verification, 'feedback' and enhancement procedures; research assessment exercises, and so on,

---

[42] On German universities, see Karl Jaspers, *Die Idee der deutschen Universität: Die fünf Grundschriften aus der Zeit ihrer Neubegründung durch klassischen Idealismus und romantischen Realismus* (Darmstadt: H. Gentner, 1956).

all of which require evidential records in order to protect practitioners. As a result cultural agency does not expire through any single explicit prohibition but dies by a thousand administrative qualifications, each of which weakens the will of a given individual to exist as a critical and questioning intellect. The effect is *cumulative*, and escape comes only through privilege, sacrificial resistance – or departure.

In more general terms, we need to recall an idea of central importance in the last chapter, the assertion that modern line-management involves the ceding and loss of agency. As the management sage Peter Drucker informs us, now the time of 'modern management' has finally come as it is applied to the life of the mind.[43] Frederick W. Taylor argued the following, and this text is reproduced for a second time so that its contextual significance may be fully appreciated:

Under the old type of management, success depends almost entirely upon getting the 'initiative' of the workman, and it is indeed a rare case in which this initiative is really attained. Under scientific management the 'initiative' of the workmen (that is their hard work, their goodwill and their ingenuity) is obtained with absolute uniformity and to a greater extent than is possible under the old system; and in addition to this improvement on the part of the men, the managers assume new burdens, new duties and responsibilities never dreamed of in the past. The managers assume, for instance, the burden of gathering together of the traditional knowledge which in the past has been possessed by the workman and then of classifying, tabulating and reducing this knowledge to rules, laws and formulae which are immensely helpful to the workmen in doing their daily work.[44]

Most academics seem to have passed uncomprehending and silent to their intellectual slaughter; fatally they have neglected to investigate, in accordance with the canonical criteria of their own vocation, that is with critical and above all, *critically reflexive* thought, the weapons of the enemy. Taylor is explicit; his ideas have been transposed virtually without the need for meaningful translation into the context under consideration. Once more, it is salutary to think out the parallel between the following and the redefined 'task' of the esrtwhile academic:

Perhaps the most prominent single element in modern scientific management is the task idea. The work of every workman is fully planned out by the

---

[43] See Peter F. Drucker, 'From Capitalism to Knowledge Society', *Post-Capitalist Society* (London: Butterworth-Heinemann, 1993), ch. 1.

[44] Frederick W. Taylor, 'The Principles of Scientific Management', in Victor H. Vroom and Edward L. Deci (eds.), *Management and Motivation: Selected Readings* (Harmondsworth: Penguin, 1970; 2nd edn, 1992), p. 357.

management at least one day in advance, [but academic audit mechanisms require absolute predictability upto a *year* in advance!] and each man receives in most cases complete written instruction, describing in detail the task which he is to accomplish, as well as the means to be used in doing the work. And the work planned in advance in this way constitutes a task which is to be solved, as explained above, not by the workman alone, but in almost all cases by the joint effort of the workman and the management. This task specifies not only what is to be done but how it is to be done and the exact time for doing it.[45]

Where in this, we may ask, is there space for the 'democratic intellect'? In an era characterised in managerial terms by lack of honour and trust, total 'scientific' control and repeated 'reforms' and regular reviews designed to remove any surplus intellectual capacity that might be available for critical reflection on basic axioms, the old system cannot survive except as a dynamic (and penalised) archaism. Any alternative would require an institutional and systemic will to resist. The old system based on implicit trust, the stability necessary for long-term work, and relatively slow, reflected change has been extinguished without any effective protest. Articulation of a critical reflexivity capable of responding to the invasion and functionalisation of alien metaphors is not, however, without cost. Here we may draw some guidance from the French sociologist Pierre Bourdieu in his book *Homo Academicus*. Bourdieu exposes the resistance academics feel to the articulation of their condition:

To understand in this case is difficult only because we understand far too well, in a manner of speaking, and because we do not wish to see or know what it is we understand. Thus it is that the easiest thing can also be the most difficult because, as Wittgenstein says, 'The problem of understanding language is connected with the problem of the Will.' Sociology, which of all sciences is the best placed to know the limits of the 'intrinsic form of the true idea', knows that the force of the resistances which will be opposed to it will be very exactly commensurate with the 'problems of the will' which it has managed to overcome.[46]

The observations made in this chapter should not be construed as the repudiation of a proper place for *appropriate* modes of accountability. What is required is the restoration of a proper balance between a transferred managerial and commercial model on the one side and the proper aims and objectives and the corporate and individual goals of the university *qua* university with its attendant ethical implications on the other. What has been created in British higher education are closed

[45] *Ibid.*, p. 359.
[46] Bourdieu, *Homo Academicus*, p. 35.

'circuits of power' in which agency is concentrated and centralised, the division of powers and the preservation of proper spheres of competence abrogated, and the integrity and interests of academic staff not merely reduced, but forcibly reconfigured.

As we have seen, it is in the progressive and relentless accumulation of small things that the oppression of the new prison house of learning is most truly felt. In contrast with the trends of assimilation into the managerialised educational delivery mechanisms we may set a distinctively Scottish vision of the university drawn from the reflection of the philosopher Alasdair MacIntyre. I do not have the space in this chapter to spell out all the aspects and implications of this conception, but it is my contention that an institution which does not in general terms permit the positive application of the following principles to the critical examination of the conditions of the production of knowledge fails in its claim to be a university. MacIntyre argues that:

The beginning of any worthwhile answer to such questions, posed by an external critic, as 'What are universities for?' or 'What peculiar goods do universities serve?' should be, 'They are, when they are true to their own vocation, institutions within which questions of the form 'What are x's for?' and 'What peculiar goods do y's serve?' are formulated and answered in the best rationally defensible way.' That is to say, when it is demanded of a university community that it justify itself by specifying what its peculiar and essential function is, that function which, if it were not to exist, no other institution could discharge, the response of the community ought to be that universities are places where conceptions of and standards of rational justification are elaborated, put to work in the detailed practices of enquiry, and themselves rationally evaluated, so that only from the university can the wider society learn how to conduct its own debates, practical or theoretical, in a rationally defensible way. But that claim can be plausibly and justifiably advanced only when and insofar as the university is a place where rival and antagonistic views of rational justification, such as those of genealogists and Thomists (and, we might add, rival systems of human resources management – RHR), are afforded the opportunity both to develop their own enquiries, in practice and in the articulation of the theory of that practice, and to conduct their own intellectual and moral warfare.[47]

MacIntyre proceeds to conclude that: 'It is precisely because universities have not been such places and have in fact organized enquiry through institutions and genres well designed to prevent them and protect them from being such places that the official responses of both the appointed

[47] MacIntyre, *Three Rival Versions of Moral Enquiry*, p. 222.

leaders and the working members of university communities to their
recent critics have been so lamentable.' It is precisely the compound tendency of recent university 'reforms' to prevent precisely that evaluation
of rival and antagonistic modes of justification which nullifies the claim
of many proliferating higher education outlets to the cultural status of
the true university.

As in religion, so in the realm of the democratic intellect, there is a
hierarchy of truths and responsibilities: now is the moment to recover
our integral mission and service to an ideal, to the community, and
to the people whom we are privileged to serve through teaching and
supervision. To speak theologically, a distinction between the *penultimate*
and the *ultimate* has been breached. For those who believe in the distinctive
vocation of the university as a 'community of contested discourses', a role
which is exploratory and critical and in its own way ultimate, the present
situation is a grievous affront. The consequences of disagreement are
pervasive dissonance, and the price of dissent may (at the very least) be
total isolation or what amounts to constructive dismissal.

Fear is often widespread; there is an inner constraint reminiscent, in
my view, of the post-totalitarian condition as it is described by Vaclav
Havel in 'The Power of the Powerless'. Havel's argument concerns the
moral and personal consequences that await those who adopt and enact
ideologies in which they do not believe and which they *know to be wrong*.
Academics who enforce 'modern management' upon themselves and
their peers are the *greengrocers* of our society. In Havel's terms, they post
slogans in their shop windows in which they do not believe, and they
piously hope that there will be no problems as a result. Consequently, as
Milan Kundera puts it, they are purveyors of *kitsch*.[48] In reality, the loss is
not merely a loss of moral authority, but an evacuation of the personality
and character. Social evolution may go into reverse: sometime verte-
brates revert to empty crustaceans fighting blindly for their territory and
the perpetuation of their academic genes. Havel describes a situation
which I believe we now face in the era of triumphant capitalism and
managerial aggregation:

The profound crisis of human identity brought on by living within a lie, a crisis
which in turn makes such a life possible, certainly possesses a moral dimension
as well; it appears, among other things, as a deep moral crisis in society. A person
who has been seduced by the consumer value system, whose identity is dissolved

---

[48] See Andrew Shanks, *Hegel's Political Theology* (Cambridge: Cambridge University Press, 1991).
Shanks draws upon Kundera's conception of kitsch as 'the absolute denial of shit': kitsch is the
readiness to celebrate a revolution and dance on the day that good poets are hanged.

in an amalgam of the accoutrements of mass civilization, and who has no roots in the order of being, no sense of responsibility for anything higher than his or her own personal survival, is a *demoralized* person. The system depends on this demoralization, deepens it, is in fact a projection of it into society.[49]

As we have argued throughout, this is not merely a sociological or psychological problem; it is also ethical and even theological. The re-creation of critical reflexivity on the part of the academic profession will involve individual and collective responses and above all a willingness to engage in a comprehensive and careful analysis of the nature, transmission and exchange of cultural capital. In the final analysis three principles are at stake. First there is the *principle of enlightenment: sapere aude!* Dare to know! Have the courage, as Kant says, to use your own understanding: that is, in the present context, critical thought applied to the conditions of the production of knowledge. Second, there is the *principle of the authority of traditions*, that is the continuity of ideas and reflection that society and the thinker and teacher are responsible to. In the formulation, study and propagation of rival traditions (which may well and usually do conflict) there is a legitimate authority inherent in the individual and corporation that possesses and exercises the relevant competences. As Professor Lord Russell points out, the doctor should not expect a manager to dictate the time of discharge after an appendectomy.[50] Third, there is the *principle of responsible autonomy and critical reflexivity*, which is a contemporary way of referring our attention back to the responsibilities outlined by Bonhoeffer as they concern the 'natural rights of the life of the mind'.

Having started out in our sketch of a tenable idea of the university with a lengthy quotation from Alasdair MacIntyre, we conclude with a passage from T. S. Eliot, who, in arguing for an elitism that subsequently proved to be unpopular (for different reasons) with both the Right and the Left, nevertheless put his finger upon an important truth: too much power should never reside in too few hands. Indeed, at a time when the principle of the separation of powers is scarcely recognised in Britain, especially in higher education, Eliot argued for the indispensability of *friction*:

At this point I introduce a new notion: that of the vital importance for a society of *friction* between its parts . . . in any society which became permanently established in either a caste or a classless system, the culture would decay . . . an indefinite number of conflicts and jealousies which should be profitable to society. Indeed,

---

[49] Vaclav Havel, 'The Power of the Powerless', p. 62.
[50] Russell, *Academic Freedom*, p. 70.

the more the better: so that everyone should be an ally of everyone else in some respects, and an opponent in several others, and no one conflict, envy or fear will dominate.[51]

MacIntyre and Eliot are at one in recognising that it is not only the university but modern society as well which must exist as a community of contested discourses. The alternative to such discursive encounter is cultural cleansing with a view to creating a rational monoculture, whether secured by physical terror or by the pervasive fear that now infects many reaches of higher education (and other areas of society too). Bureaucratic, administrative and intellectual *Gleichschaltung* has subverted the critical intellect and has virtually paralysed the cultural agency of the universities and thus deprived a whole people of the fuller realisation of the active democratic intellect.

In short, each reader who aspires to be an active proponent of the university ideal defended in this chapter has to ask himself or herself the questions: how can I teach someone to think critically if I have uncritically submitted to a system in which I do not believe? Can a professor in an ancient university who is systematically stripped of her or his legitimate authority and subjected to the normalisation and forcibly organised mediocrity of a line-managed 'Quality'-controlled environment do other than respond to the inspiration of figures in the tradition worthy of respect, and denounce corruption? This is a rot that seeps from the top down which has then tragically mingled with the decay that has risen from atrophied and enfeebled roots. In such an environment a Donald MacKinnon would not merely be unwelcome – he would have become an impossibility.

---

[51] T. S. Eliot, *Notes Towards the Definition of Culture* (London: Faber, 1948).

PART 2

Theology and power in the matrix of modernity / postmodernity

CHAPTER 5

Lord, bondsman and churchman: integrity, identity and power in Anglicanism

INTRODUCTION

The pungent and abrasive title of this chapter indicates the main aspects of an investigation I propose into some of the contemporary dilemmas of English Anglicanism as represented prominently by a leading apologist for this tradition, then Professor Stephen W. Sykes, Van Mildert Professor, Regius Professor of Divinity in the University of Cambridge.[1] In two important and related, but perhaps not fully appreciated, works, *The Integrity of Anglicanism* and *The Identity of Christianity*,[2] Professor (later Bishop) Sykes sought first to rework Anglican theological method and self-understanding, and then to formulate and apply in the context of the church universal, and its task of defining the identity of Christianity, the contribution he believes it is the distinct vocation of the Anglican Communion to make. These are the positive proposals to be found in Sykes' project, but underlying them is a yet more fundamental theme, that of power, and it is the latter, I believe, which is of the greater theological significance in the long term. Indeed, I shall argue that the 'sub-plot' or 'sub-text' of the position developed in Sykes' two major works comprises the elaboration of a theory of theological power which is in effect the linking thread upon which hang glistening beads of historical and

---

[1] This chapter first appeared in C. E. Gunton and D. W. Hardy (eds.), *On Being the Church* (Edinburgh: T. & T. Clark, 1989), pp. 156–224. When first published, it largely escaped review. Thus, for example, in a review in the *Church Times*, 'Lord, Bondsman and Churchman' was not referred to, although all the other contributions were identified. The text appears here in its original form with revision confined to occasional necessary alterations to the verb tenses used and one or two small corrections. Whilst the chapter may in some respects be regarded as a period piece, it remains in my view a legitimate critique. Its basic predictive theses have proved accurate: we now have a managerial Church of England in which, as demonstrated in the following chapter, the unneurotic celebration of power ('real power') takes place. Bishop (then Professor) Stephen Sykes was struggling with the ancestral tension between 'authority' and 'power': managerialism decisively resolves that tension into the latter.

[2] *The Integrity of Anglicanism* (London: Mowbrays, 1978); *The Identity of Christianity* (London: SPCK, 1984). Henceforth referred to as *Integrity* and *Identity* respectively.

theological illustration. This interpretation may appear to run counter to certain aspects of explicit authorial intention, but what I develop below is a 'reading' of these texts that gives priority to the hermeneutic of power and accords relative status to the issue of 'identity'. I thus isolate a proposal with definite but questionable implications for the theory and practice of future Anglicanism.

In his two books Sykes has advanced a complex and sophisticated set of arguments which reflect his long-term engagement with German and North American theology, as well as with the intricacies of the English tradition. These arguments are promulgated at a time of almost unparalleled theological stress in which the positive formulation of the substance of the Christian faith (rather than its merely negative criticism) is a pressing necessity. Not only this, but the social and cultural aspects of the contemporary crisis, in particular secularisation in all its complexity, press in upon an ancestral English Anglican tradition burdened with multiple ambiguities. What Sykes in reality offers is in the first instance an internal reform, a reorganisation of the relationship in theology between the pursuit of truth as such and the responsible management of power on the part of the theologian, whose task it is, within certain limits, to define what Christianity should be for his or her tradition and generation. This dual task is initially articulated in relation to the policy of a particular tradition, but the impact of Sykes' proposals applies in the context of Christianity as a whole and is conceived through arguments which make frequent if not systematic allusion to materials lying outside strictly theological confines. It is my contention that whilst Sykes' proposals are of fundamental importance, engagement with substantial discussions of the relation of truth and power both within and outside Christian theology indicates that without revision his hypothesis would lead to the inhibition, even the prohibition, of that emancipation that ought in my view to accompany the grace and truth of the Gospel.

In order to justify these assertions I shall argue as follows: first, the historical context will be outlined in schematic terms indicating how theological developments are related to structural factors; second, a theoretical dimension will be opened up through reference to Hegel's ontological parable of the Lord and Bondsman, which provides important parallels with attempts to restate a theological position; third, the *Integrity* will be analysed; and then, fourth, the *Identity* will likewise be 'read' from the standpoint of the emergence of the sub-text which contains the key 'structure' that, we believe, informs and unites Sykes' endeavours;[3] fifth, the theory of power present in the sub-text is then expounded at length in relation to the theoretical insights provided by the Hegelian parallel; sixth, in conclusion, it is argued that my reading and interpretation of this renewal of Anglican theology in terms of an identity of authority with power contains possibilities which unchecked will lead to undesirable consequences.

My argument is, it must be emphasised, a *reading* of the texts of a contemporary theologian seen in their context. As such the approach taken to the work in question is *dialectical*; the latencies and potentialities present in the 'structure' of the texts are pressed to the limits and deliberately not resolved in a premature manner into compromise or *via media*. Thus the Hegelian model that overshadows much of modern critical epistemology likewise serves to draw out the implicit possibilities of an argument which might otherwise remain relatively unexplored. On this basis we reach conclusions which will have demanded the direction of 'resistance' to a number of features in traditional Anglican theological method and its attendant ethos. This, I believe, is justified by the importance of the issues involved.

THE HISTORICAL CONTEXT OF THE CONTEMPORARY ANGLICAN PROBLEM OF SELF-DEFINITION

There has as yet appeared no full-scale study of English theology in the nineteenth and twentieth centuries which respects both the historical and the sociological factors evident in an era of progressive secularisation. In the absence of such an adequate contextualisation the following outline takes the form of a hypothesis generated on the basis of an appraisal of the broadest features of the developments of the last century. To put

---

[3] The term 'structure' merits explanation. The way in which Sykes' books are here 'read' is 'structuralist' in the sense that I seek to present his texts as 'unified *structures*, through an examination of the interrelation of the different levels of each work'. Thus David Robey comments on Tzvetan Todorov's study of Henry James in the introduction to *Structuralism: An Introduction* (Oxford, Oxford University Press, 1973), p. 3. The close affinity between the approach taken up here and applied to contemporary theological texts and Todorov's treatment of the stories of James became obvious to me after the composition of the first draft of this chapter. Todorov's essay 'The Structural Analysis of Literature: The Tales of Henry James' contains the following comment, analogously applicable in the present theological context: 'The secret of James' tales is, therefore, precisely the existence of an essential secret, of something which is not named, of an absent, overwhelming force which puts the whole present machinery of the narrative into motion . . . on the one hand he deploys all his strength to reach the hidden essence, to unveil the secret object; on the other, he constantly moves it further and further away', p. 75.

it in the most succinct way, two fundamental tendencies are evident in Anglican theology, and these underlie the detailed discussion of any particular facets of the whole situation. First, since the magisterial defence of classical Chalcedonian orthodoxy by H. P. Liddon in his Bampton Lectures of 1867,[4] there has been a slow but inexorable decline of Christology 'from above' and a corresponding increase in interest in the themes of the humanity of Christ and in *kenosis*. Over the same period there has been a parallel and highly intransigent defence of a high doctrine of the ministry focused in the episcopate which extended from Charles Gore's attack[5] upon Edwin Hatch's Bampton Lectures *The Organisation of the Early Christian Churches*[6] through to K. E. Kirk's collective work *The Apostolic Ministry* of 1946.[7] The latter contains within it what may be justly termed a triumphalist *plerosis* of the episcopate which was conceived as embodying the *shaliach* or divine plenipotentiary of God. The historical conjunction of two such tendencies in the context of secularisation, that is the enforced retreat of the apparent reality of the sacred in society and the growth of pluralism, cannot but arouse the interest and ideological suspicion of anyone concerned for the integrity of the tradition. A struggle for and assertion of theological identity on the part of the ordained ministry would appear to have been contemporaneous with a loss of distinctive identity in the area of incarnational doctrine and the doctrine of the church. In contrasting these impulses, a progressive *kenosis* in the doctrine of the Incarnation and a corresponding *plerosis* in the doctrine of the ordained ministry, is it not plausible to assume some form of correlation if, as will become apparent, 'identity' is understood in the context of a competitive economy of meaning as one assertion made against others? Thus understood, the search for self-understanding on the part of the ordained ministry, the professional class within the church,

---

4 Henry Liddon, *The Divinity of Our Lord and Saviour Jesus Christ* (London: Longmans, Green & Co., 1867).

5 Charles Gore, *The Church and the Ministry* (London: Longmans, Green & Co., 1888); new edn, revised by C. H. Turner (London: SPCK, 1919).

6 Edwin Hatch, *The Organisation of the Early Christian Churches* (London: Longmans, Green & Co., 1881).

7 Kenneth E. Kirk, *The Apostolic Ministry: Essays on the History and Doctrine of Episcopacy* (London: Hodder & Stoughton, 1946). Kirk commented on the ultimate significance of the episcopate thus: 'But embedded in the system as we know it, is its foundation and justification, its only principle of continuity with apostolic times – the commission of the apostle or shaliach to act in our Lord's own Person. If it is this which we are offering to our separated brethren, and this which they desire to accept from us, all is well', p. 52. Acute controversy followed the publication of this work; my point is not based upon criticism of the historical basis of such a vision, but upon the ideological impulse implicit in its emergence and the essential – dependent – passive structure of theological priorities it embodies, to the acute detriment of a proper ecclesiology of the whole people of God.

could not merely be the assumption of an identity given through ancestral tradition; it had, by contrast, to be sustained through assertion and struggle. In the often intellectually isolated world of theological reflection the disjunction between explicit self-understanding and the actual social function of ideas is often extreme. It is crucial to understand that the assertion required to focus and establish an identity is not an act perpetrated in a vacuum. On the contrary, it is an act perpetrated against another. In re-establishing its threatened identity in the face of secularisation the Anglican (and here is meant the most theologically self-assertive catholic wing of Anglicanism) ordained hierarchy came to conceive of itself by means of an identity which, in asserting itself, correspondingly denied theological identity to the other, that is the laity. This process of definition through appropriation to the self and negation of the other is, I shall later argue, intrinsic to the human condition as understood in that most illuminating of traditions that extends in its modern form from Hegel through to, for example, the work of the French critic and historian Michel Foucault.

The more commonly raised issues concerning Anglican identity, in particular that of 'comprehensiveness', assume a conflict between alternatives within a framework originating in the Elizabethan Settlement and its initial rationalisation in Richard Hooker's *Laws of Ecclesiastical Polity*. It is one of the strengths of Professor Sykes' critique of contemporary Anglicanism that in it conflict is seen as inevitable. It is, however, my conviction that the notion of 'conflict' as conceived by Sykes is insufficiently developed and unnaturally restricted even when used in relation to the extended argument about 'power' within the church and Christian theology. It is, furthermore, my contention that theology understood as a field of competitive forces, a *struggle for power*, involves the definition of the very nature of power itself. The history of English Anglicanism in the past century would indicate *prima facie* that a largely silent struggle has taken place within the interrelated spheres of Christology and ecclesiology accompanied by the virtual absence of a theology of the laity, that is of the people of God as a whole. This is starkly apparent when the twentieth-century Anglican tradition is contrasted with the ecclesiology (albeit problematic) of Vatican II. Full engagement with these issues on the historical, theological and sociological levels lies outside the scope of this chapter. Less ambitiously, but no less pertinently, we confine ourselves to a critique of one significant attempt to confront these issues of integrity and power within Anglican theology and polity. Through a critical reading and analysis of the basic structure of Sykes' two important texts it will be apparent that the substantial and methodological issues and the putative answers afforded by Sykes are less than wholly satisfactory and indicate the need for a rather more ambitious conception of the role and nature of systematic theology itself as the primary tool to be used in the clarification of the task of the church in its contemporary context. Before turning to the exposition of a reading of these texts in context it is necessary to generate theoretical insight into the dynamics of power as provided in Hegel's mighty parable of the Lord and Bondsman. The ecclesiological struggle for identity, a conflict of polarities, of essential and dependent ministry within the church, parallels the ontological and epistemological 'moments' in Hegel's text. It is thus in the 'intertextuality' generated between the integrity and identity texts of Professor Sykes and the text of Hegel that some of the wider parameters of engagement will emerge. Above all, the question of social structure and hierarchy in relation to struggle *even within the Church* cannot be ignored without the possibility of ideological bewitchment and illusion.

LORDSHIP AND BONDAGE: HEGEL'S PREFIGUREMENT OF THE SOCIOLOGY OF KNOWLEDGE AND CRITICAL THEORY

The hermeneutics of power within Christian theology is underdeveloped, although pioneering work in this area is present in liberation theology.[8] Behind the development of Marxism, the sociology of knowledge and critical theory there lies the seminal text, Hegel's *Phenomenology of Mind* of 1807, which is of no lesser importance for contemporary Christian theology. This work, and in particular so far as this chapter is concerned, its second main section, concerned with 'self-consciousness' (*Selbstbewusstsein*), is an account of the emergence of consciousness from simple sense-certainty to absolute knowledge, which, whilst it reflects the basic division of Kant's first *Critique*, is dialectical in the sense that it recounts the contrasting 'moments' in a processual development rather than as the merely static conditions underlying and implied in the enactment of knowledge. In the second section of the *Phenomenology*, Hegel presents the construction of consciousness out of relation and division both within the subject and between subjects. The dynamic, conflictual pattern that emerges is represented in the parable of the Lord and Bondsman (*Herr und Knecht*), which is composed of resonant and

---

[8] Two obvious examples are J. L. Segundo's *The Liberation of Theology* (Dublin: Gill & Macmillan, 1977) and L. Boff's *Church, Charism and Power: Liberation Theology and the Institutional Church* (London: SCM, 1985).

suggestive images capable of multiple and complex interpretations. At root, however, the imagery is expressive of relations of independence and dependence and the concomitant forms of consciousness. Implicit in the parable and its resolution into the confrontation of stoicism and scepticism in the 'unhappy consciousness' (*unglückliches Bewusstsein*) is Hegel's final confrontation of the ancestral Christian, that is medieval, embodiment of a religious consciousness in the social antithesis of lordship and bondage with its dissolution in enlightened modernity. The juxtaposition of independent and essential and of dependent and inessential consciousness articulated by Hegel provides an exact formal parallel with the polarisation of pre-critical consciousness to be found in such anachronistic entities as the Anglican repristination of the theology of the episcopate (as essential ministry) and the presbyterate (the inessential ministry) that was implied in the previous section of this chapter. The question that arises is this: can we move beyond the crude, unreflective polarity of the ancestral juxtaposition of *ordo* and *plebs* – albeit decked out with the full panoply of biblical and patristic adornment in its mid-twentieth-century Anglican restatement – and, if so, how?

An answer to this question is not easy to find, but one plausible response is to set over against each other the dialectic of power as Hegel expounds it in the *Phenomenology* and as we see it in traditional Anglican ecclesiology and the renewed theory of theological power that is revealed in the crucial sub-text of the *Integrity* and the *Identity*. This, as we have already maintained, involves a 'reading' of both texts and a leap of intellectual imagination facilitated by the assumption that there is structure in both and that each writer is engaged with analogous confrontations of antiquity and modernity. For Hegel there are, in the simplest preliminary terms, three 'moments' in the emergence and completion of self-consciousness, a process analogous with the eruption of life itself:

(a) pure undifferentiated ego is its first immediate object. (b) This immediacy is itself, however, thoroughgoing mediation; it has its being only by cancelling the independent object, in other words it is Desire. The satisfaction of desire is indeed the reflexion of self-consciousness into itself, in the certainty which has passed into objective truth. But (c) the truth of this certainty is really twofold reflexion, the reduplication of self-consciousness.[9]

Whilst Hegel could write out of a riven personal experience 'I am not one of the fighters locked in battle, but both, and I am the struggle itself.

---

[9] Hegel, *The Phenomenology of Mind*, tr. J. B. Baillie (London: Macmillan, 1910), p. 226.

I am fire and water',[10] his concession to the reader comes in the imaged presentation of this conflict. Thus in the section entitled 'Independence and Dependence of Self-consciousness', self-consciousness is seen to exist 'in itself and for itself, in that, and by the fact that it exists for another self-consciousness; that is to say, it *is* only by being acknowledged or "recognised" '.[11] This first moment in the dialectic, the passage from unreflective unity into consciousness of existence 'for itself', can be put in parallel with the emergence of an epistemological and ontological elite in the church, by reference to whom those not so privileged define themselves. Thus, by analogy, an *ordo* invested with divine plenitude and existing for itself becomes the sociological reference point in which is located the Pneuma-Christ. An essential ministry serves as a source that must deny the other in order to affirm itself: knowledge of it comes only through acknowledgement of its ultimate distinction. Identification of the 'authority' of such a focused reality does not depend, as Sykes is to assert, upon 'self-assertiveness' but upon the assumption of plenitude, that is the totality of a prior, given essence – in theological terms the power of God. 'Self-assertiveness' belongs, as becomes apparent, not to the essential being, Hegel's 'Lord', but to the 'slave' or 'bondsman' who has to struggle *ab ovo*.

The one is independent, and its essential nature is to be for itself; the other is dependent, and its essence is life or existence for another. The former is the Master, or Lord, the latter the Bondsman.[12]

This characterisation of the foundation of human existence in assertion and negation has entered the structure of modern thought in many forms, not least through Marx, Freud, Sartre and Michel Foucault (not to mention feminist theory through Simone de Beauvoir). In Christian theology it is also present, be it in the epistemology of Protestantism (for example in Karl Barth) or the ontological hierarchy of Catholicism, and the pattern persists in the genteel ambivalence of Anglican polity. What comes next in the Hegelian conflict is less well understood and acknowledged. The Master exists for itself and mediates itself through the Other which becomes what it is through designation as a subordinate thing. The proof of essence, of being *through* the Other by the Master, strikes

---

[10] *Vorlesungen über die Philosophie der Religion*, Glockner, xv, p. 80, as cited by G. A. Kelly, 'Notes on Hegel's "Lordship and Bondage" ', in A. MacIntyre (ed.), *Hegel: A Collection of Critical Essays* (Notre Dame: University of Notre Dame Press, 1976), p. 217.

[11] Hegel, *Phenomenology of Mind*, p. 229.

[12] *Ibid.*, p. 234.

fear into the Slave, who is, despite the Master, a consciousness experiencing the threat of negation, of reduction to mere thinghood (*Dingheit*). In this 'trial by death' the Master in triumphing passes into the ultimate irony: at the moment of effectively achieved Lordship he finds that he is not fully independent but dependent; it is only *through* negation and isolation, the extinction of the Other as a *means* to self-fulfilment, that the Master attains to his exaltation. Correspondingly, the Slave enters a life-and-death struggle in the face of negation, the death embodied in the Master who comes to swallow him into mediate thinghood. He must in effect fight back; he must labour to assert himself or face subsumption into the mediation, the self-projection of the Master. The theological affinities are obvious.

Hegel, unlike Sykes, is of course engaged in an analysis of the transcendental presupposition of reason, and in this he is the successor of Kant. The parallel to be drawn here is limited: we are in the first instance concerned to juxtapose the archaisms of both Anglican hierarchy and the Lordship and Bondage passage with the critical 'modernisations' afforded by Hegel and by Sykes. The Hegelian polarity is not explicitly presented as a socio-historical entity or process but in terms of the mutual reality of the consciousness, which 'finds that it is and is not another consciousness, as also that this other is for itself only when it cancels itself as existing for itself, and has self-existence only in the self-existence of the other'.[13] The correlate of this in theological terms is, as I have argued, the situation of the unchallenged *ordo*, a priesthood that mediates, unchallenged, on behalf of others and in terms of which a laity must understand itself, that is as negated. We find a potent example of this in the dubious repristination of the doctrine of the essential priesthood embodied in the episcopate in *The Apostolic Ministry* of 1946, where it is conceived as the theological presupposition without which the dependent presbyterate and the even more remote lay non-entity (or *Unding*) do not respectively exist.

In this section we have seen how the parable of the Lord and Bondsman provides an informative parallel with the structure of traditional Anglican (and indeed Catholic)[14] ecclesiology; both represent anachronistic archaisms in the modern world. Hegel provides a

[13] *Ibid.*, p. 231.
[14] Yves M. J. Congar's assessment of the position of the laity in the opening sections of *Lay People in the Church: A Study for a Theology of Laity* (London: Bloomsbury, 1957) informs the approach taken in this chapter, especially the juxtaposition of an estimation of the laity as religious proletariat in the church and of a theology of laity as a theology of the *whole church*.

subversive account of this polarity in which Lord and Bondsman, Master and Slave co-exist in deadly conflict and with remarkable fluidity exchange attributes as the 'moments' of the *coincidentia oppositorum* engage in what amounts to a secularised *perichoresis*. Hegel's ontology and epistemology understand identity as the protest against a given, unreflective domination. Indeed, the theologically trained genius of Hegel was to understand the essence of enlightened modernity in terms of the necessity of recognising the inevitability of assertion in the context of the void and even, in the final account, the identity of being and nothingness (*Nichtigkeit*). As we shall see, there are further similarities between this position and modern Anglican attempts at self-definition. In the context of an abrogation of the historical transmission of identity through tradition and the nihilistic and analytical reduction of metaphysical claims, what can be done to reassert identity? Not surprisingly, tackling the analogous context involves a re-engagement with the question of power. Integrity (the question of method) and identity (the assertion of a definition or the postulation of the conditions of achieving definition) issue in the consideration of power: it is only, it would seem, through the latter that the vacuum can be filled and meaning imposed upon the tradition. Thus we now see that a full reading of the *Integrity* and *Identity* texts may now represent the contemporary dilemma of Anglicanism. On this basis we may later return to the question of power, informed by the parallel we have developed.

INTEGRITY: THE QUEST FOR METHOD

The Integrity of Anglicanism begins with a definition of systematic theology: 'By "systematic theology"', Sykes maintains, 'I mean that constructive discipline which presents the substance of the Christian faith with a claim on the minds of men.'[15] This is but one of several definitions of the nature of 'systematic theology' which have an important bearing on the course of the exposition. It is fundamental to Sykes' whole argument that the demand for *substantive* definition has, however, to be translated into a *functional* quest; thus the phrase 'the substance of the Christian faith' has to be understood throughout as the struggle for definition which becomes the definition itself. There is, it need hardly be emphasised, no reference made here to those contextual, structural and conflictual factors which are in reality presupposed by the phrases 'constructive discipline' and 'substance of the Christian faith'.

[15] *Integrity*, p. ix.

The 'integrity' for which Sykes strives has two meanings: it is first 'the capacity to recognise the whole identity of the aspect or "institution"', and 'to inquire into the identity of Anglicanism is to ask whether there is any internal rationale binding Anglicans together as a "Church"';[16] and second, it is to recognise that 'stage of moral soundness' characteristic of an institution that knows what it believes in when it accepts and moulds Christian allegiance. That 'integrity' in both senses is at the very least endangered within Anglicanism is of central importance. Whilst it is important to recognise that Sykes is consistent in his commitment to Anglican theology as the informed reflection of a world-wide communion, that is a body 'in communion with, and recognising the leadership of the see of Canterbury',[17] it is also notable that his argument is focused upon a specific articulation of the distinctiveness of Anglicanism by the English theologian, the late Bishop A. M. Ramsey. Writing in *The Gospel and the Catholic Church* Ramsey saw in the Anglican Church a balanced witness to 'Gospel and Church and sound learning', but beyond this

its greater indication lies in its pointing through its own history to something of which it is a fragment. Its credentials are its incompleteness, with the tension and turmoil at its soul. It is clumsy and untidy, it baffles neatness and logic. For it is sent not to command itself as the 'best type of Christianity', but by its very brokenness to point to the universal Church wherein all have died.[18]

This apologetic invites the riposte that mere turmoil is elevated to the level of theory; Sykes' postulation of conflict as a defining characteristic of Christianity is, however, the translation of tension and turmoil into a rationalisation of conflict manageable through a theory of power. Thus what we find in the *Integrity* text is a sophisticated, up-dated repristination of Ramsey's position, qualified by the careful distinction that 'incompleteness is something other than incoherence',[19] and complemented with insights drawn from a variety of sources. This is then worked out in its wider application to the complex quest for the 'essence' and 'identity' of Christianity. Reformulating the earlier and pointed questions of A. E. J. Rawlinson and Hensley Henson, Sykes asks:

Is there an Anglican theology, a proposal many have denied? Is there an Anglican method in theology, which some have affirmed while denying that there is an Anglican theology? And what in any case is the present state of the Anglican

---

[16] *Ibid.*, p. 1.
[17] *Ibid.*, p. 2.
[18] (London, 1936), p. 220.
[19] *Integrity*, p. 3.

study of the doctrine of the church, and why is there so little deliberate cultivation of doctrinal or systematic theology?[20]

The answers to these questions constitute the main body of the *Integrity*, but they are all ultimately underlaid, so Sykes argues, by a single issue that emerges in the final chapter, where he attempts 'to face directly the question which lies behind the whole Anglican hesitancy about its self-understanding, namely the question of authority in Anglicanism'.[21] It is the transmutation of the concept of 'authority' and its eventual identification with 'power' that unites the *Integrity* and the *Identity*. It is our purpose to map out critically this structure that unifies and informs the texts in the belief that there is an insufficiently explicit consistency in a position that merits further exploration in terms of the hermeneutic of power. The focus of conflict in Anglicanism is not understood by Sykes as structural but located in the diversity of theological positions that subsist in the church. *The Integrity of Anglicanism* is therefore presented as an exercise in the 'ethics of belief', which takes as axiomatic the Anglican mode of ecclesial subsistence with its institutionally sustained cohabitation of theologically incommensurable traditions. Sykes' response to this is a demand for an adequate, formal justification for this state of affairs:

A Christian Church, which is aware of a wide variety of diverse theological positions and which deliberately decides not to adopt one or other of them, but rather to tolerate diversity, has still to offer a definite reason for doing so and to justify that reason in the face of objection. If a Church both enforces the use of a liturgy which is thoroughly stamped by a particular doctrinal inheritance, and also permits wide latitude in the professed belief of its officers, then, again, there ought to be a thorough analysis and explanation of that dual position. And my complaint against the Church of England, in particular, is that its attempts to do so hitherto have been muddled and inadequate, partly by reason of the continued use of an apologetic which patently no longer meets the situation (if it ever did) and partly because of deeply rooted failures in its programme of theological education.[22]

In this passage the basic strands of Sykes' apologetic emerge: a diversity of theological positions co-exists with the enforced use of a liturgy which is itself the vehicle of the doctrinal inheritance. It is in effect necessary to redefine and clarify the relationship between freedom and authority so embodied in the Anglican Church. It is not only that 'Toleration of

[20] *Ibid.*, p. 5.
[21] *Ibid.*
[22] *Ibid.*, p. 6.

diversity itself need(s) to be justified theologically if it is to be able to claim any kind of integrity',[23] but that this toleration has to be conditioned by its relation to the redefined 'authority' invested in the control of, and participation in, the continuing liturgy of the church.

Sykes begins his argument with an account in chapter 1 of the origins of the idea of 'comprehensiveness', which in the context of Anglicanism 'means simply that the church contains in itself many elements regarded as mutually exclusive in other communions'.[24] In relation to the discussion of fundamental articles and the articulation of the *via media* Sykes launches what are for him ferocious attacks upon F. D. Maurice (and to a lesser extent Bishop Gore). Maurice's romantic commitment to the union of opposites and to the exclusion of systematic reflection appears, so Sykes argues, to have done little more than sanction lazy and inadequate thought and what amounts to self-deception. Most questionable was Maurice's use of the 'principle of the complementarity of apparently opposed truths',[25] and at this juncture Sykes erects theoretical criteria in the form of a realist challenge supposedly superior to that operating in the sub-rational Maurician tradition:

Lots of contradictory things may be said by those with a vested interest in refusing to think straight. What complementarity requires, if it is so to be used in a *rational* manner, is the demonstration that both of the alleged truths are true and necessary to the proper depiction of the reality being studied.[26]

Maurice's attempted containment of the liberal impulse by its confinement to a third church party in a supposed reconciliation of conflicting viewpoints only takes place in virtue of a 'suitable process of emasculation of controversial content'.[27] This in turn has led, so Sykes fears, to the propagation of 'a tame and Anglicised *tertium quid*' alien to each of the consistent traditions it purports to represent.

In chapter 2 of the *Integrity* Sykes reviews the significance of liberalism as expressed in Anglican modernism and concludes that its radicality was more appearance than reality. Thus Sanday and his associates produced what amounted to a mediating theology between 'hard line orthodoxy and wild radicalism'.[28] Notwithstanding this, Sykes endorses T. S. Eliot's view that 'liberalism is a negative phenomenon, a finding of the courage

---

[23] *Ibid.*, pp. 6–7.
[24] *Ibid.*, p. 8.
[25] *Ibid.*, p. 19.
[26] *Ibid.*
[27] *Ibid.*
[28] *Ibid.*, p. 27.

and the grounds *not* to hold views frequently held in the past and invested, it may be, with the venerable authority of tradition'.[29] Anglican 'comprehensiveness' is an abuse of the principle of complementarity when it is used to permit the cohabitation of views that may be really opposed and, moreover, the effort and courage required to be positive is greater than that invested in mere negative criticism. Realism has its own higher demands and Sykes finds evidence of these in the doctrine Report of 1976, *Christian Believing*, where it was argued that:

The issues here – on the one hand loyalty to the formulae of the Church and obedience to received truth, on the other adventurous exploration and the Church's engagement with the contemporary world – appear to point in very different directions and to reflect different conceptions of the nature of religious truth. It is, to say the least, very difficult to explain away divergences of this fundamental kind merely as complementary aspects of the many-sided wisdom of God.[30]

The polarity emerging here between obedience to truth and adventurous exploration lends support to Sykes' contention that liberalism is not a 'party' subsumable within a structure containing 'Catholic' and 'Protestant' groupings but a phenomenon that presents, as becomes apparent, an alternative mode of management undertaken on the assumption that, 'tolerant though the Anglican Communion has become, it has a standpoint on matters of doctrine which is firmer than seems to be the case at first sight, even if it stands in need of articulation and development'.[31] The consequent articulation of the Anglican standpoint in chapter 3 consists of an examination of the revised 1975 Declaration of Assent at ordination and the 1976 Report *Christian Believing*, which is spelt out in terms of the latter's attempt to formulate a common 'pattern', a framework within which Anglicans might cooperate; yet the Report

seems to have no conception of the fact that it is in itself nowhere near producing such a pattern and demonstrating how it operates, and no conception that the Anglican communion seems never to have produced a demonstration of this pattern properly applicable to its contemporary situation. The question, what binds Anglicans together, remains unanswered.[32]

Sykes' own resolution of the Anglican difficulty comes in the programmatic conclusion to the chapter: breadth of toleration of internal

---

[29] *Ibid.*, p. 32.
[30] *Christian Believing* (London: SPCK, 1976), p. 38.
[31] *Integrity*, p. 35.
[32] *Ibid.*, p. 41.

doctrinal diversity (even to the point of contradiction) is recognised, but the focal point of what the Anglican Church stands for as an institution is moved firmly onto the level of liturgy and canon law, the content of which is to be subject to 'rigorous criticism'.[33] Thus, by a subtle shift of emphasis, the repeated affirmation of certain doctrines, above all that of the Incarnation understood as 'the basis of dogma', is not to be understood primarily as a disputed item on the agenda of theological discussion but as that on which the church publicly stands. Thus the public liturgical transmission of the dogma provides as it were a functional justification: positive theology would in effect have to be the scrutiny of the 'function' of the dogma in the context of worship rather than through the conflictual discourse of the theologian. These aspects of Sykes' argument are combined in a contextual definition of the constructive theological task:

> Anyone can observe that the doctrine of the incarnation is basic to Anglican liturgical life as enforced by canon law. Almost anyone can, on the strength of a little theological education, write essays attacking or defending it. But it takes real theological skill to see how this doctrine both underlies and is interpreted by a worshipping body at once tolerant of theological criticism of it and yet aware of the responsibility as a matrix for the nurture of Christian character.[34]

Whether this definition is wholly true of the cohabitation of contradictory elements is open to doubt. It is questionable if any worshipping body has this level of consciousness and here we have, seen from a Hegelian standpoint, an 'optimistic' account of the reflection possible in the context of the dependent, passive *Knecht*-like status of the 'worshipping body'. Perhaps an even more apt analogy at this point would be Lukàcs' notion of 'imputed class consciousness': that is what the leadership chooses to attribute to the led. What this improbable set of assertions undoubtedly sanctions on Sykes' behalf is a pointed attack in chapter 4 upon an earlier document crucial to Anglican self-understanding, the *Report on Doctrine in the Church of England*, upon which William Temple set his stamp. The defence of the 'English mind' attributed to Temple and the 'poisonous arrogance' of the English dismissal of foreign influences are bad enough, but the betrayal goes further in that the complacent laziness of Anglican theologians leads Sykes to ask if it is not the case that 'their reluctance to formulate and defend Anglican theology is a serious disservice not only to their own communion, but also to the universal Church of Christ'.[35]

---

[33] *Ibid.*, pp. 51–2.
[34] *Ibid.*, p. 52.
[35] *Ibid.*, p. 61.

In chapter 5 Sykes reviews Anglican theological method, beginning once more with a declaration by A. M. Ramsey. In 1945 the latter wrote that Anglican theology is 'neither a system nor a confession . . . but a method, a use and a direction' that resists definition, but nevertheless it 'has been proved, and will be proved again, by its fruit and its works'.[36] Ramsey's setting of his reassertion of the Anglican cultivation of scripture, tradition and reason over against the appropriation of either neo-Thomism or Barthianism in a transcendence of 'isms' Sykes treats with polite scepticism, for he maintains that:

Anglicanism has a specific content, and that it ought to expose that content to examination and criticism; it ought also to encourage specific individuals to write systematic theologies or extended treatments of Christian doctrine.[37]

This call for intellectual action is made without any serious attention to the socio-structural factors which control the production, distribution and exchange of knowledge, save for a passing comment on the excessive burdens imposed upon tutors in theological colleges. What is, however, interesting and important is a commitment to an enhanced definition of the nature of systematic theology which emerges from the critique of Temple, whose denial of the necessity and the desirability of a 'system of distinctively Anglican theology' is countered by Sykes' demand for reflection organised in the following terms:

The *systematic* character of any systematic theology derives from a massive attempt at consistency in reasoning, an attempt whose seriousness can be gauged either by the sophistication of its philosophical equipment or by relation of each and every feature of the doctrinal structure to a fundamental understanding of divine revelation.[38]

Such reflection should, moreover, have an epistemology and an ontology and, in addition, express the attempt to create a uniform vocabulary. Sykes set a high standard for those like himself who would venture out of the narrow English parochialism epitomised by Temple into the higher reaches of a putative Anglican systematic theology.

The concluding chapters, 6 and 7, of the *Integrity* contain a modest and as it were experimental enactment of the reinvigoration of the theological tradition with regard to the doctrine of the church and 'authority', respectively. The effective educational relegation of ecclesiology to

---

[36] 'What is Anglican Theology?', *Theology*, 48 (1945), 2, cited *ibid.*, p. 63.
[37] *Integrity*, p. 68.
[38] *Ibid.*, p. 57.

'non-fundamental' status because of its contentious nature did not impede, as Sykes rightly notes, the long-standing and highly questionable defence on both theological and historical grounds of the institution of the threefold ministry. Regarded in historical perspective, Sykes' only comment upon these pretensions, that whereas 'it is true that Anglicans have consistently defended the retention of episcopacy for a variety of reasons, it is an innovation to suggest that Anglicans have regarded any particular theological interpretation of episcopacy as essential',[39] has proved highly judicious, almost prescient in the light of intervening events. Sykes' exposure of the polemical use of the 'appeal to the historic Episcopate' as a 'direct challenge to the traditional theory of fundamentals' by Anglicans associated with the volume *Catholicity*[40] would appear to make it impossible to invest in the office of bishop anything remotely approaching an absolute validation of theological meaning or truth, given the emergent subordination of free theological reflection to the critical guardianship of the liturgy. This relatively low view of the episcopate would explain, in principle, Sykes' non-intervention in the bitter public controversy surrounding Dr David Jenkins' (the present Bishop of Durham) apparent dismissal of certain doctrines regarded as central to the tradition by significant groups in the church. The truth-functional apparatus erected around the office of the bishop in the minds of those whose religious security was rocked in the controversy could be seen as a mistaken conception when seen from Sykes' standpoint precisely because it did not touch upon the real 'power-base' of the church in the liturgy and its management. Consistent with this concentration upon the dichotomy between theological reflection (and thus public controversy) as such and the pragmatics of ecclesiological power invested in the governance of the liturgy is an emphatic concentration upon the interpretation and magisterial theological rationalisation of existing structures and practice:

The weakness of modern Anglican ecclesiology may be in part traced to the disrepute into which certain passionately held dogmas fell when exposed to historical criticism; but it must also be traced to the chronic reluctance of Anglicans to accept the fact that what they have inherited as institutions and practices in the Church unencumbered with sharply defined theoretical baggage has profound theological, especially ecclesiological, significance *as such*. And it is only the theological exploration of the significance of such an inheritance which will begin to establish Anglicanism on lines significant for the future of the

---

[39] *Ibid.*, p. 84.
[40] *Catholicity: A Study in the Conflict of Christian Traditions in the West* (Westminster: Dacre Press/A. & C. Black, 1947).

world-wide Church, not only on the bogus grounds of its status as a so-called 'bridge church', but on the grounds of its capacity to submit its inheritance to a searching theological appraisal.[41]

It is at this juncture that the local, internal difficulties within Anglicanism and the distinct gift that this tradition brings forth to the wider ecumenical community distinguish themselves. Thus, on the one hand, the church has to devise new means of containing the conflict between the pursuit of theological reflection and the imperative demands of the 'norm of tradition' transmitted within the liturgy; and, on the other, Anglicanism by virtue of its wholehearted recognition of the inevitability of conflict within the church offers this realisation to a wider ecclesial public. In the seventh and final chapter on authority in Anglicanism Sykes starts out with qualified approval from the 1948 Lambeth Conference Report on authority and paraphrases it as follows: 'authority is both singular, in that it derives from the mystery of the divine Trinity, and plural, in that it is distributed in numerous, organically related elements',[42] and he thereby gives a distinct interpretation to the notion of 'dispersed authority' that the statement contains. The realistic recognition within this text of the inevitability of conflict within the church and the control placed upon potential tyranny through the 'mutually supporting, and mutually checking, life-process'[43] of dispersed authority contrasts, so Sykes argues, with the documents of the Second Vatican Council, one of whose chief weaknesses is a conspicuous failure to expect conflict in the church. It is 'in such a situation that the whole Anglican history of the experience of conflict is of potentially great service'.[44] Sykes' second major book, *The Identity of Christianity*, is effectively the translation of formal reflection upon the inevitability of conflict within the church (evident from its New Testament origins) into a proposed resolution of the quest for the 'essence' or 'identity' of Christianity itself.

The major thesis adumbrated above is subordinated in Sykes' text to the immediate conclusion in which he clarifies the emerging juxtaposition of the theological reflection that manifests acute conflictual diversity on the one hand and, on the other, the contingent, managerial necessities of sustaining the continuity, direction and stability of the liturgical enactment of the tradition and its norms. The second cluster of issues is

---

[41] *Integrity*, p. 85.
[42] *Ibid.*, p. 87.
[43] *Ibid.*
[44] *Ibid.*, p. 89.

dealt with first in such a way as to implicate, however implausibly (along lines directly reminiscent of Newman), the laity:

The point which I am concerned to sustain is that it is of the essence of the Anglican view of authority that it should be maintained in principle that the means of judging matters concerning the faith are in the hands of the whole people of God by reason of their access to the scriptures; and further, that it is distinctly Anglican that this means is given to them in the liturgy of the Church, backed by canon law.[45]

It is not our concern at this juncture to determine what precisely might be the socio-ecclesiological cash-value of the maintenance 'in principle' of the means of judging matters concerning the faith, except to observe that the role of the 'whole people of God' is in effect identified with passive receptivity over against the agency of the donor. The reasons for conflict in matters of faith arise, so Sykes argues, not least from the inadequacy of language: 'those who preach the gospel are committed to making plain in words, and words are inherently and necessarily ambiguous'.[46] Whether this is a general remark about the imperfect character of all human verbal communication or a defect peculiar to theological reflection is not made clear. Much is made of the duty of careful discernment incumbent upon the Christian: both laity and clergy are as it were underpinned by the 'essentially conservative' character of liturgies and hymns, which, Sykes asserts, puts them in a 'very powerful position when there break out, in the ordinary course of events, controversies as to Christian belief and practice'.[47] That such an assertion has, given the passive receptive role of those implicated in a conservative-tending liturgy, a misleadingly rhetorical tone is apparent to Sykes, who concedes that this is 'essentially a conservative position, unless steps are taken to ensure the theological education of the laity and their incorporation into the corporate decisions of the Church'.[48] This account of the role of the whole church in relation to the liturgy is conceived almost exclusively in terms of the logic of conferral, marginally tinged with sympathy for the unrealisable and un-Anglican congregationalist ideal. Sykes characterises the place of the laity with succinct clarity: their role is essentially conservative as 'an element checking the power of church leaders and theologians or, at the most, sharing (as in contemporary synodical government) in the process

---

[45] *Ibid.*, p. 93.
[46] *Ibid.*
[47] *Ibid.*, p. 95.
[48] *Ibid.*

of decision-making on a carefully restricted basis'.[49] In its fundamental structure this relationship is in the main one of agent and patient, of actor and reacted upon, of definer of theological reality and one upon whose behalf reality is defined; it is in short that of Lord and Bondsman. It is an asymmetrical polarity peripherally modified by the power of the inferior party to block excess, but it is never their power to act or innovate. A semantic collision takes place between the ever more strident rhetoric used to 'empower' the essentially static and conservative character of the liturgy itself and the actual decision-making processes affecting particular liturgies:

> Thus, for Anglicans, it still remains the case that the liturgy of the Church creates the power base for the Christian community as a whole. This was so in the early Church, and with the gift of the scriptures in the vernacular, it becomes still more the case in Anglicanism. And the conclusion for contemporary Anglicanism must be that what is enforced in the liturgies of the Church is the most powerful tool in the hands of ordinary clergy and the laity for resisting innovations which have no right to parity of esteem or equality of consideration when compared with the established traditions. Hence the decision-making process whereby liturgies are changed, as they must be with time, is the basic seat of authority in the Anglican Church, and the basic exercise of that authority is the power to enforce the liturgy.[50]

This somewhat heavy-handed exposition of the pragmatics of liturgical power, which moves from the near rhetorical exaltation of the static conservative, resistive 'power' of the ordinary clergy and the laity by a series of steps to the statement of active *espicopal* power hidden in the final sentence, contrasts markedly with the depiction of the theologian, whose creative discrimination generates what may prove troublesome attempted innovation. The Christian, and here Sykes must surely have in mind the Christian with informed theological understanding,

> must exercise his judgement . . . But to put some flesh on the bones one might add that this judgement is like the judgement a novelist has to exercise when he or she brings a character to a particularly dramatic set of circumstances and must offer a plausible account of the character's response. It must be plausible in the sense that the character must act out of the resources which the novelist has created in earlier parts of the book and within the general limits of human psychology. In such a judgement there is both a predictable and a creative element, and the skill of a novelist lies in his ability to make the most of the fact that characters are interesting not because their actions can be predicted with

[49] *Ibid.*, p. 96.
[50] *Ibid.*

certainty, but because the interaction of event and character creates genuine novelty.[51]

Whilst this analogy is readily adaptable to the pursuit of theology in the narrative mode, and the 'church has to act in character'[52] in relation to such resources, the latter are not in and of themselves authorities. Again resorting to the notion of 'process' introduced into the Anglican context in the Lambeth Conference Report of 1948, Sykes advances what can be construed as an eschatological dialectic of authority, a relationship with 'authority' which is subtly but significantly redefined in passing as 'norms of authority'. A behavioural and functional account of unending engagement with these 'norms' expands and arbitrarily displaces 'authority' itself onto the plane of the transcendental:

> While formally speaking, scripture, tradition and reason are norms of authority, the processes of decision-making in the Christian Church are never completed. Decision-making is not, therefore, a matter of balancing one authority against another nor of holding authorities in tension, as Anglican writing has sometimes suggested. There is only one source of authority which is the freedom and love of the Triune God. In human life, in scripture, in the creeds, in the decisions of councils, in the liturgical order and canon law, in Church leadership, there is only the discovery of authority, not its embodiment.[53]

This amounts to a *reductio ad absurdum* of the idea of 'authority'; the concept is driven into a dialectical impasse as problematic in its own way as the extreme immediate pre-Reformation nominalist doctrine of justification. In this quasi-nominalist account of authority, the 'norms of authority' identified with the dispersed elements of the Christian church are understood as the diverse occasions of the 'discovery of authority'. One reading of this position would be to regard Sykes' argument as a quasi-Barthian investiture of the broken fragments of Anglicanism with an occasionalist authoritarianism. The 'dispersal' of the 'norms of authority' is effected with some thoroughness, notably as regards the episcopate, which is strictly reduced, in a reworking of brokenness reminiscent of Ramsey, to 'oversight' (*episcope*) and to 'the interpretation of a partial and broken symbol of the continuity of faith'.[54] So perish episcopal pretensions inasmuch as they purport to depend upon authority in terms of a historical transmission or continuity of embodiment or possession of a

---

[51] *Ibid.*, p. 97.
[52] *Ibid.*, p. 98.
[53] *Ibid.*
[54] *Ibid.*

peculiar donation of the Holy Spirit. Conversely, the ground is prepared for the rebirth of 'authority' as immediate, that is as 'real' power.

So we may initially conclude that what Sykes has in effect executed is analogous to a dismissal of any realist theory of *transmitted* authority within Christianity. It is in the context of a broken, incomplete collectivity at the centre of which is celebrated the continuing liturgy of the Word that an authority-directed activity nevertheless takes place. There is, however, nothing which in and of itself *is* authority (it is merely a 'norm of authority'); but on occasion, authority is 'discovered'. The latter discernment is not assimilated to a fully consistent 'Barthian' position, that is to the divine foreordination and construction of the subjective receptive capacity as well as its objective correlate in the Word. The 'discovery of authority' demands the capacity of discernment; that which is authoritative must be identified on the basis of its having an identity. The very dispersed nature of authority in Anglicanism universalises at a stroke its translation into 'norms of authority'; thus the alternative locations of authority taken up within other traditions are all equally open to this critique. Sykes, through his pursuit of the 'integrity' of Anglicanism, has confronted the wider church and Christianity with the question of its identity. The role of the theologian as the informed agent of discrimination emerges out of the romantic intuition of the analogy of novelist into the actuality of becoming the vehicle of life-giving insight into the identity of Christianity itself. This is an ambitious reformulation of the historic theological destiny of the Anglican Communion in relation to the world-wide church. The dismissal of received authority as the basis of identity has now taken place, and the conflict-laden quest for identity is to become the identity of Christianity itself. These proposals are of profound and far-reaching consequence, not least for the understanding of 'power' which is itself the leitmotif that will in turn displace the preoccupation with identity as such. How the judicious reader ought to interpret this progression is an issue yet to be addressed.

IDENTITY: THE ASSERTION OF ESSENCE

The Identity of Christianity is a substantial work consisting of three sections: the first is primarily theoretical; the second contains detailed studies of relevant aspects of the work of Schleiermacher, Newman, Harnack and Loisy, Troeltsch and lastly Barth; the third is largely a reworking and clarification of the earlier material. There is on all levels an increase in conceptual complexity in comparison with the *Integrity* in that the consideration of 'authority', transformed at the end of the earlier work, is now displaced into an explicit 'sub-plot'[55] involved in the analysis and prescriptive exposition of the concept of 'power'. Thus we learn in the introduction that although there is an apparently old-fashioned ring about the 'essence of Christianity' controversy, the author's specific purpose is to excavate from this discussion lessons applicable to the present. This is, as compared with the *Integrity*, theology in a new key, for the criteria employed are not merely historical but philosophical: in particular, recognition of the decline of the quest for the essence of Christianity into the 'essentialist fallacy', here interpreted as an error characteristic of those who place too high a premium upon modes of cognition, is axiomatic. Thus the 'essence' quest stands as an unresolved dilemma, that is as threatened by the hostile alternatives of historicism and the descent into subjectivism. The necessarily conflictual character of this dilemma and its emergence (as illustrated by the historical examples) provides the main scenario in the *Identity*. As in the *Integrity* it was necessary to ask whether there was a distinctive Anglican theology or method, so on this more exalted level two basic and analogous questions emerge: 'What, then, *is* Christianity? Another way of putting the same question would be to ask directly, Do the differences between Christians matter?'[56] There is, however, a deeper intention, what Sykes calls a 'sub-plot', and this is an extended preoccupation with 'power' which consistently reflects the transitional interface between 'authority' in the *Integrity* and its corresponding transvaluation in the *Identity*:

> One of the themes of the book concerns the responsibility of the Christian theologian in his exercise of power in the Church, a power which resides in his or her articulacy, or power to communicate. I hold that a theologian must communicate to other than fellow theologians, and that clarification of meaning is one of the few justifications for occupying valuable time and money in the production and reading of works of scholarship.[57]

This characterisation of 'power' moves in some respects beyond the polarity that became visible in the *Integrity* between theology as free-ranging creative reflection upon the Christian character in the context of the narrative mode on the one hand, and on the other the strict control and interpretation of the 'norms of authority' dispersed within the church but focused primarily in the liturgy and worship. Here the

---

[55] It is this 'sub-plot' that is here interpreted as the 'structure' of Sykes' text: see n. 3 above.
[56] *Identity*, p. 4.
[57] *Ibid.*

understanding of power bears some affinity with Habermas' conception of power as communicative action, exercised here in relation to semantic clarification undertaken on the part of a wider community. Such an explication does of course presuppose a complex set of social relations related to educational access and the distribution of resources; for the intellectual hegemony here articulated is apparently regarded as 'value-free' as regards its context in social stratification (and this is perhaps a little surprising on the part of a socialist writer). The effective formulation of a theory of power expressed in 'communicative action' and 'instrumental reason' (the 'power to communicate' and 'clarification of meaning', respectively) reflects a 'managerial', interpretative approach to social polarisation, not surprisingly alien to a more critical Marxist or Neo-Marxist analysis. Seen from the latter standpoint, Sykes' conception of the theologian has a strongly ideological ring to it: the theologian orchestrates and refines the ideological superstructure of the church; indeed, hierarchy is conceptually translatable into intellectual hegemony.[58] It is, of course, precisely this latter danger, seen in the possibility of a 'tyrannous use of intellectual power',[59] to which Sykes is alert, but his explanation of the phenomenon takes the form of an incomprehensible allusion to the fragmentation of knowledge in the modern era understood as a cause of a theologian's over-estimation of his or her significance. There is here yet again no critical awareness of the hegemony embodied within the text itself: this is effectively suppressed by the diversion into pluralism. It is the intrinsic character of the interconnection of knowledge and power as *domination* that can provide a far more realistic account of the basis of this 'tyranny' than Sykes is prepared to concede. Thus it is that the essence/identity discussion overlies a sub-plot concerned with power and directed at the reconstruction of Christian praxis; it is the prescriptive, rather than the merely analytical and illustrative, status of this proposal that encourages me to accord it ultimacy in the appraisal and construal of the strategy present in the *Identity* text:

The purpose, therefore, of the sub-plot is to place the discipline of theology and the expertise of the theologian in an explicitly new relation to the total phenomenon of Christian identity, concerned as a body with unavoidable and restless internal conflicts.[60]

---

[58] Antonio Gramsci's conception of 'hegemony' as a group or class creating a state of affairs in which their leadership and privileged position seem natural is relevant here.

[59] *Identity*, p. 7.

[60] *Ibid.*, p. 8.

The exploration of the 'identity' issue is in effect the illustration and justification of the necessity of this relocation of the expertise of the theologian and thus of his or her power. The 'sub-text' of the *Identity* has thus a dual role: on the one hand it functions as a structure in relation to which the illustrative, clarificatory material concerned in the 'identity' is organised; on the other it provides the prescriptive conclusions, the translation of theory into practice. The 'structure' determines the direction of the argument which is reinforced and justified by oblique excursions into the 'identity' exemplifications in which the concept of 'conflict' is encapsulated as in a 'mediation', ostensibly an encounter with that which constitutes reality. Indeed, in apparent contradiction to Sykes' own definitions of the nature of *systematic* theology,[61] he resists global consistency: 'I do not claim here to have any general theory up my sleeve to explain why these features of Christian profession . . . should be of such importance.'[62] It will be suggested that this hesitancy *has* to be part of the strategy in the *Identity* if Sykes is to resist the discovery of the latencies within his text and to retain a grasp upon a position so radically equivocal in the light of the wider contextual critique formulated below. In other words, undue recognition of the real 'structure' of the text would demand an interpretative act, the consequences of which might well contravene the overt conclusion drawn by Sykes on the basis of a skilful, but ultimately misguided concatenation of proposals. As will become clear, the peremptory dismissal of contra-indicative evidence or conflicting standpoints becomes comprehensible when the restrictive, artificially contained character of the argument is analysed in the structural context of the hermeneutics of power, understood in terms of the universality of the Hegelian dialectic of aggrandisement. As against this, the virtual dismissal of the 'will to truth' – that is the textual subordination of the pursuit of truth to the manipulation of 'meaning' – and the marginally limited theory of the management of theological power constitute the least acceptable aspects of these proposals.

The first part of the *Identity* begins with an extended account of identity and conflict in early Christianity in which Sykes, using recent sociological

---

[61] 'The systematic character of any systematic theology derives from a massive attempt at consistency in reasoning, an attempt whose seriousness can be gauged either by sophistication of its philosophical equipment or by relation of each and every feature of the outward structure to a fundamental understanding of divine revelation', *Integrity*, p. 57. Judged by his own criteria Sykes can be understood to have succeeded in part, provided 'divine revelation' is identified with 'power'.

[62] *Identity*, p. 8.

studies of the New Testament, demonstrates that conflict is intrinsic within the tradition. Consequently:

I shall argue that any realistic account of the Christian phenomenon strongly suggests the inconceivability of there ever being complete agreement about the identity of Christianity. That is not to say that Christians may not be able to contain disagreement within reasonable boundaries. But contained diversity is, in fact, what unity amounts to.[63]

Sykes integrates into his study an analytical model of religion drawn from Ninian Smart, and this serves him well. Smart's six-dimensional model is admirably suited to Sykes' approach because it expands the structure of a given religion and distinguishes categories and aspects without admitting excessively complex accounts of how these aspects might interact. Thus the distinction, crucial to the argument, between the 'inner' and 'external' aspects of Christianity draws upon Smart's approach without the charges of mutual reduction or antagonism inevitable should a less 'value-free' and incommensurable set of analytical insights (drawn from Marx, Weber, Durkheim, Freud, Lévi-Strauss et al.) have been built into the model. Thus whilst Sykes' method as applied to the 'generalisation' of New Testament material would, according to his own criteria, indicate that he is writing 'systematic theology',[64] his use of the Smart schemata would indicate that he is not, at this stage at least, prepared to function in terms of a wider intellectual dialogue. The presentation of the New Testament materials is suggestive and illuminating, especially in the demonstration that stratified developments involve ambiguity. There is no primal unity in the tradition from which diversity is a deviation; even the teaching of Jesus 'has certain ambiguities which will give rise to different interpretations'.[65] The hermeneutical correlation between the New Testament era and Sykes' understanding of the present task of the theologian is remarkable (even if, perhaps, unintended):

The view of Jesus' intentions ... is one which emphasises the possibility for the transformation of a religious tradition by a simultaneous retention of the core-meaning of a familiar term combined with novel treatment of its conventional associations, supported by particularly significant actions.[66]

Where Sykes is less satisfying is in his evaluation of St Paul's constant, seemingly obsessive concern with unity in a Christian context which

[63] *Ibid.*, p. 11.
[64] *Ibid.*, pp. 12–13.
[65] *Ibid.*, p. 23.
[66] *Ibid.*, p. 19.

has, the reader is informed, always and everywhere only been susceptible to unity understood as contained diversity. The juxtaposition of the
Pauline lust for unity and the conflictual diversity of the empirical early
communities can only be understood in terms of the quasi-sociological
explanation later educed on the basis of Troeltsch's understanding of
the transitional steps in the development of the church. There is no
eschatological 'discovery of unity' proposed here corresponding to the
'discovery of authority' posited at the end of the *Integrity*. This hesitance
is the more significant when the extraordinarily important role of the
Pauline language and conceptuality of unity in Eucharistic, liberation
and ecumenical theology is taken into account. Moreover, given the earlier isolation of the 'one source of authority which is the freedom and
love of the triune God' in the *Integrity*,[67] the contrast between Pauline
'unity' and Sykes' realistic and pragmatic 'contained diversity' is uneasy
and would merit further critical exploration. In addition, consistent construal of Christianity as Schleiermacher envisaged it, that is as through
and through polemic, carries with it obvious dangers of retrojection and
retrospective over-determination.

So far Sykes has argued that the sources of conflict are understood to
stem from the inadequacy of words as a medium of communication and
from the ambiguities inherent in a tradition transformed by the 'simultaneous retention of the core meaning of a familiar term combined with
novel treatment of its conventional associations'.[68] Whilst under certain
circumstances *some* sources of conflict *might* so originate, it is fundamental to an informed sociological and critical perspective that the sources
of conflict lie outside language and are *perceived* in the inadequacies of
language. In concrete terms the sociological interpretation of the contemporary church and its forerunner in the New Testament depends
upon the analysis of class structure and hierarchy and their influence
upon belief and adherence. It is difficult to understand Sykes' resistance
to theory at this juncture given his definition of the nature of systematic
theology.[69] An even more implausible source of conflict is postulated
which again diverts attention away from the structure of power implicit
within the *Identity* text. This purportedly more potent source of conflict is
a dialectic intrinsic within Christianity which consists of the tension between the inner and external aspects of the phenomena of the Christian
religion. For Sykes, the primary thrust of Christian polemicism is located

[67] *Ibid.*, p. 98.
[68] *Ibid.*, p. 19.
[69] See n. 61 above.

in inwardness; for Christianity, 'its only chance of making clear what its own innermost nature is is by unmasking every false morality, or corrupt thinking, or impoverished religion'. So it is that the polemical character is not merely as it were external, but internal, for as Jesus himself (authentically) indicated, he brought a sword 'and by that he meant that the religion he founded would essentially be characterised by an unrelenting struggle for purity of intention'.[70] Out of these elements is constructed the core dialectic of Christianity, which is to be understood as a struggle between inwardness and external manifestation spelt out in terms of the following schematic cycle. The first moment consists of the inevitable conflict; the second moment is the serious struggle for purity of intention in response to diversity; the third moment is the enactment of the guidance necessary in cases of dispute; in short, 'authority' is 'discovered'. Once more the 'conflict' here outlined is interpretable in Hegelian terms of a premature resolution of the dialectic in favour of the Lord's 'moment', in which reality is discovered and thus imposed, without passage through the full cycle of self-discovery postulated in the full theory of power.

In the second chapter of the *Identity*, concerned with the tradition of inwardness, Sykes enlarges upon the factors that justify his isolation of 'inwardness' as the determinative core of the tradition. That virtual *autonomy* is accorded to inwardness (justified in relation to its origins in the teaching on the 'heart' in Old and New Testaments) is a step taken that demands some additional justification without which the material that follows remains the illustration of a carefully unexplored position.[71] The autonomous status of inwardness and the spirituality of conversion derived from the Psalms and Paul's conception of 'the inmost self' is qualified through an alternative scheme provided by H. Mol's study of identity and the sacred,[72] a work of considerable importance to any theologian or church official entrusted with the functional maintenance of a religion in a hostile, secularising context. Mol's analysis provides Sykes with some sense of a wider setting, but this is strictly subordinated to the formulation of an account of Christian reflection showing 'a characteristic oscillation between emphasis upon inward transformation, and an emphasis

---

[70] *Ibid.*, p. 29.

[71] For a critical treatment of 'inwardness' see T. W. Adorno, 'Kierkegaards Konstruktion des Ästhetischen', *Thomas Wiesengrund Adoono Gesammelte Schriften*, vol. II (Frankfurt-on-Main, 1962), chs. 2 and 3.

[72] H. Mol, *Identity and the Sacred: A Sketch of a New Social-Scientific Theory of Religion* (Oxford: Blackwell, 1976). The conservative orientation of this book admirably reinforces Sykes' position in a defence of religion as structural integration as opposed to alienation.

upon the importance of the cult, with a large number of possible ways of conceiving the relationship between the two'.[73] Despite the use of Mol's analysis, Sykes' argument is grounded upon a restricted categorial basis, scarcely expanded when he makes his first substantial references to Augustine and his understanding of the relation of heart and sacrifice in worship.[74] Sykes' narrow dual categorial plank projects over the abyss of legitimate complexity such as that explored, for example, by John Bowker in *The Sense of God*,[75] a book which tends to expose the non-dialectical character of Smart's six-dimensional account of religion. The reader is bound at this juncture to inquire after the existence here of a developed epistemology and ontology, the necessary components of a true systematic theology in the terms indicated by Sykes himself. In earlier post-Enlightenment generations the assumption by a theologian of a narrow categorial base and the consequent 'reconstruction' of all the loci was a permitted strategy; it is a rank implausibility to attempt this procedure within the confines of a restricted and largely uncritical advocacy of Anglican piety as rearticulated in terms of the assertion of the dimension of 'inwardness'. The absence of a theory of knowledge operable within the context of the human sciences and the purely assertive basis upon which theological claims are made place enormous weight upon the solution Sykes is to propose: the theory of theological power.

POWER: THE TRANSVALUATION OF AUTHORITY

It is the third chapter of the *Identity*, on power in the church, which contains the pivotal arguments; it is here that the fundamental hypothesis comprised in the sub-plot emerges most fully. Having established to his satisfaction that conflict was inevitable in a Christian movement containing inherent ambiguities from its inception, and that Christianity itself suffers from the pressure of constant revision of its externals on the basis of its inwardness, Sykes repeats the less than satisfactory inadequacy-of-words argument and concludes that 'diversity . . . is the

---

[73] *Identity*, p. 42.

[74] It is not clear how Sykes would reconcile his anthropological account of sacrifice made elsewhere with the principle of self-extinction proposed in the *Identity*: see 'Sacrifice in the New Testament and Christian Theology', in M. F. C. Bourdillon and M. Fortes, *Sacrifice* (London: Academic Press, 1980), esp. pp. 8off.

[75] John Bowker, *The Sense of God: Sociological, Anthropological and Psychological Approaches to the Origin of the Sense of God* (Oxford: Clarendon Press, 1973). The major works of Eliade and van der Leeuw are also relevant.

norm for Christianity',[76] a state of affairs overlaid often enough by the
rhetoric of unity. The main body of the chapter and its four-stage argument contain: first, a consideration of the problems of authority following the death of St Paul; second, an account of Troeltsch's explanation
of how the concentration of power took place in the early community;
third, a general presentation of the theme of power in the New Testament; and fourth, the development of the implications of these factors
for the contemporary management of power in the Christian church.
Before embarking upon this, Sykes proposes a crucial *identification* of authority with power, without which the whole general hypothesis would
collapse. As noted earlier, the dissolution of authority into 'norms of authority' took place at the end of the *Integrity* in conjunction with a move
from essentialist definition to the designation of meaning through use.
The functional definition of 'power' demonstrated in the control of the
liturgical 'power-base' of the church displaced any essentialist fictions
contained in the notion of a historically transmitted authority. It is therefore entirely consistent that the conceptual definition of 'authority' and
'power', drawing upon the wider discussion of the concepts in sociology
and political philosophy, should comprise an effective *identity* between
the terms and reveal, moreover, a shared intrinsic meaning which is
compatible with and assimilable into the remaining steps in argument of
the *Identity*. The earlier theological replacement of 'authority' by 'power'
through the quasi-nominalistic reduction of the former and its displacement by the functionally defined latter are therefore underpinned by a
further, somewhat brief, conceptual survey which merits close examination because it is the fulcrum around which the whole argument of the
sub-plot, latent in the *Integrity* and explicit in the *Identity*, in fact turns.[77]

In this brief transitional passage Sykes would appear to succeed in
reinforcing his emancipation of Christianity from the trammels of its
now disputed past by a reformulation of a 'discovery of authority' embodied in a new spirituality of real, managerial power exercised in the
discriminating agency of the theologian and through the rejuvenated
command structure of the church itself, that is of the higher clergy.
The embodiment of authority in its 'command-obedience connotation'
in the authority of the clergy as 'quite frequently legitimate, that is based
in the mutual acknowledgement of the divine sense of authority, and
then the right to command and obligation to obey'[78] might perhaps be

[76] *Identity*, p. 52.
[77] *Ibid.*, p. 54.
[78] *Ibid.*

surprising to the less than percipient reader; however, given the absolutely crucial *identification* of authority and power, it is entirely consistent,
and evidence of the integrity of the *systematic* drive and *structure* within the
text itself. It is on this basis that a newly found confidence in the power
of God is won and a consequent celebration of power may take place.
There is proposed a renewed fusion of charismatic power with church
office in a 'repetition' of the Christian Gospel in principle adequate to
our chaotic, pluralistic times. All of this would only seem possible both in
theory and in practice if we acknowledge, following Sykes, the identity
of authority and power. Are we bound, however, to accept such a crucial
identity? Are there not indeed certain dangers in such a redefinition of
charismatic 'authority' as power in the Christian church? How, indeed,
might such a theology of the celebration of power develop as the latter
clearly offers a category far more suggestive, complex and pervasive in
human experience than a theology determined through mere inwardness might indicate?

Sykes' treatment of the distinction of power and authority is brief but
decisive and consists of the reiteration of D. H. Wrong's definition of
power and the listing of the sub-headings of the third chapter of the
latter's recent book.[79] The sheer complexity of the history, contextual
determination and analytical treatment of authority and power is, however, revealed in Lukes' survey,[80] to which reference is also made in
footnotes. Contextual factors are particularly important in the religious
understanding of the authority–power relation, and the emergent conception in the *Identity* has affinities with a number of other examples, for
instance: Hobbes (the 'Great Definer'), Simmel (the stress on super- and
sub-ordination), Luhmann (a systems theory approach in which power
can be conceptualised as a medium of communication), Weber (inequal-
ity and dependence as phenomena of the distribution of power within a
community), Daniel Bell (authority based upon competence), and so on.
The initial many-sidedness of Sykes' discussion of the authority–power
relation up to this point is then decisively simplified. The relatively weak

---

[79] D. H. Wrong, *Power: Its Forms, Bases and Uses* (Oxford: Blackwell, 1979), ch. 3.
[80] Stephen Lukes, 'Power and Authority', in T. Bottomore and R. Nisbet (eds.), *History of Sociological Analysis* (London: Heinemann and New York: Basic Books, 1979), pp. 631–76, takes up a contextual approach as opposed to Wrong's more discursive line of analysis. The many-sided, even eclectic character of Sykes' proposals about power is evident given the partial applicability of so many concepts of power to them. Future work will have to take account of Michael Mann's *The Sources of Social Power: A History of Power from the Beginning to AD 1760*, vol. 1 (Cambridge: Cambridge University Press, 1986), esp. ch. 10, which puts strong emphasis upon the role of Christianity as a means of ideological integration.

definition of power (derived by Wrong from Bertrand Russell) and re-iterated by Sykes, that power is simply 'the capacity of some persons to produce intended and foreseen effects on others', does not in fact correspond with the demands of the identity of authority and power promulgated in the *Identity*, which would in reality be far better served by the stronger Weberian definition. Weber maintains that power is 'the probability that one actor within a social relationship will be in a posi-tion to carry out his own will despite resistance, regardless of the basis upon which this probability rests',[81] and this would be congruent with the distinctive 'command–obedience connotation' attributed by Sykes to 'authority'. Thus the categorisation of types of authority and the struc-ture and justification of its enactment have implications which verge upon the authoritarian. Sykes asserts that:

Authority may be coercive, induced, legitimate, competent, or personal. In reli-gion the authority of the clergy is quite frequently legitimate, that is based on the initial acknowledgement of the divine source of authority, and thus of the right to command and obligation to obey. It may also be personal, indeed charis-matic in the precise sense; quite often personal and other forms of authority are combined in a single instance.[82]

'Accordingly', Sykes concludes, 'so far as the use of terms in this chap-ter is concerned, Paul's authority is an exercise of power.'[83] The above extended statement is descriptive rather than analytical; but, beyond this, it certainly has prescriptive implications. In terms of the overall conception it is impossible to interpret this passage as anything other than a straightforward identification of authority and power. The basic point made is that there cannot be a '*mutual* acknowledgement of the divine source of authority' grounded in a historically and socially trans-mitted source (because this is ambiguous and conflictual), but only a quasi-charismatic assertion and reception, a discovery and an acknowl-edgement of divine power; this is the equivalent in the new context of the 'discovery of authority' proposed at the end of the *Integrity*. Sykes' formulation of the conception of authority and its trans-valuation into a depiction of power bears a more than passing resemblance to his under-standing of Jesus' own hermeneutical method, which, it may be recalled, 'emphasises the possibility for the transformation of a religious tradition

---

[81] Max Weber, *Economy and Society: An Outline of Interpretative Sociology* (2 vols., Berkeley, CA: University of California Press, 1979), vol. I, p. 53.
[82] *Identity*, p. 54.
[83] *Ibid.*

by a simultaneous retention of the core-meaning of a familiar term combined with novel treatment of its conventional associations as supported
by particularly significant actions'.[84] Sykes' sensitive remarks that 'It is
a common misunderstanding that in order to be powerful one has to be
self-assertive' for 'On the contrary, great power can be exercised by those
who locate the origin of their authority outside themselves, in God',[85]
are fully commensurate with his sophisticated reinstallation of the charis-
matically endowed but institutional and legally sanctioned office-bearer
who will discern and define the identity of Christianity in his context
and act (i.e. command) accordingly.

The following analysis of the highly complex and contentious area of
the interpretation of the history of the organisation of the early church
consists of a critical review of Hans von Campenhausen's distinction
between Paul and Clement's understanding of authority and the sacralisation of subordination: 'order here for him [Clement] became an abstract and autonomous principle of an abstract [sic] kind'.[86] According to
Sykes, von Campenhausen removed Paul's theological position from its
social setting and underestimated the chronic power vacuum left by the
departure of the so-called 'Apostles'.[87] The real difficulty in Clement's
claims to authority (the setting of which is remarkably similar to Sykes'
depiction of the present situation) is 'that *all* external norms, including authoritative persons, have to exercise their discrimination on matters concerning the inwardness of the Christian life'.[88] The sociological
deficiencies of von Campenhausen were to a considerable degree reme-
died by Troeltsch, whose three-stage theory of early church development
earns wholehearted approval. Troeltsch's scheme has three stages: first,
Jesus' teaching focused in the idea of God; second, the rise out of this of
a Christ-cult enjoining faith in Christ; and third, most crucially, a displacement of the Pneuma-Christ by the episcopate. This displacement
is of considerable importance as it brings Sykes' own argument to the
point at which it is possible to isolate and define the locus of the power
that is itself the agent of definition. In Troeltsch's words:

In a concrete way the episcopate was substituted for the earlier faith in the
Exalted Christ and the Spirit: it is the succession of Christ and of the Apostle,
the Bearer of the Spirit, the extension or externalising of the Incarnation, a

---

[84] *Ibid.*, p. 19.
[85] *Ibid.*, pp. 54–5.
[86] *Ibid.*, p. 57.
[87] *Ibid.*, p. 58.
[88] *Ibid.*, p. 59.

visible and tangible proof of the Divine Truth and Power, the concrete presence of the sociological point of reference.[89]

It was precisely an analogous attempted repetition of such a displacement in the face, not of the departure of Jesus, the death of the Apostles and the consequent power vacuum, but of an ambiguous decline in the reality of a high Christology in the face of historicism, philosophical critique and secularising pressures, which was, it was suggested at the outset of this chapter, a fundamental feature of twentieth-century English Anglican theology. Sykes' apparent reluctance to concede any particular theory of the episcopate in the face of the many earlier attempts at such a formulation was but a hesitation in the face of undue particularism. Being aware of the dangers implicit in the consequences of Troeltsch's acute analysis of displacement, Sykes asks (but significantly does not answer) the question whether it is true that 'the episcopate *replaces* faith in the exalted Christ'. Troeltsch's account is not disputed in principle; it is, he argues, inadequate to the complexity of the question of power in the primitive church. In the third section of his consideration of power in the church, Sykes' generalised presentation of the New Testament materials appears as a lightly modified schematic structure borrowed from Troeltsch: first, the power implication of the kingdom teaching of Jesus; second, the power conferred on Jesus' followers; third, power as understood in the Pauline and deutero-Pauline writings. The review of the New Testament materials is informed by the appropriation of C. K. Barrett's analysis of the distinction between *exousia*, understood as a potential energy or divine resource, and *dunamis*, its actualisation. The depiction of power in terms of high cosmic drama evinces the conclusion that 'Seen, therefore, from the standpoint of the power involved, we may hold that Paul's aggressive understanding of the authority lying behind his preaching of the gospel involves no radical transformation',[90] that is to say of Jesus' own experience and conception of power, given the ample evidence in Paul's letters for the centrality of the conception of the 'power of God'. The process of exposing the centrality of power is seen as initiated in Paul's interpretation of Jesus: 'Perhaps with sharper insight into the essentially veiled nature of Jesus' own exercise of power, Paul perceives that the crucifixion itself, and the weakness of Christ, is a message of great power (1 Cor. 1.18 and 24).'[91] The consistency of

---

[89] *The Social Teachings of the Christian Churches*, tr. O. Wyon (2 vols., London: Allen & Unwin, 1931), p. 32, cited in *Identity*, p. 63.
[90] *Identity*, p. 71.
[91] *Ibid.*

Sykes' interpretation emerges in that where Paul's power fails that of God takes over and sustains unbroken continuity:

Here one must note particularly the dialectic of weakness and power in Paul. It is not that human weakness is identical with divine power; rather that human weakness constitutes a vacuum which the power of God can fill.[92]

There is here distinct evidence of an emergent systematic theology of power, a 'consistent potency' which becomes the category, the criteria of which are employed as hermeneutical principles in relation to Paul's experience. This in turn reflects the integration into three stages of the continuous unfolding and changes in the organisation and management of divine power in the New Testament as a whole. Thus, seen in its totality, the handling of the theme of power in the New Testament brings Sykes to conclude without reservation that 'the early Christian communities were highly power-conscious bodies'[93] and that 'to be a Christian is to be equipped with power, real power, as distinct from the outward form of piety'.[94] It would now appear that any traditional, static conception of the historical transmission of authority would be inadequate in the face of the 'real power' of Christianity:

This power is the divine power, the power of the Spirit. It dwells in the gospel, and is evident at the points where it overcomes challenge, opposition and conflict. It is the power to convince, to bring about new life, to create loving harmony in the Community, to withstand persecution, and to triumph over death; it is powerful, in other words, over indifference and rejection, over law, over internal dissent, over external oppression, and over the last enemy itself.[95]

This triumphalist theological rhetoric is open to a variety of interpretations: it may be 'read' in different ways. As outlined here, 'power' is centralised, all-embracing, the onrush of enforced unity; it is, in short, potentially totalitarian. We learn that inwardness, the focal point of 'real power', is localised in the 'powerful people' who lead ritual and liturgical action – indeed, 'Totally diffused power is indistinguishable from no power at all.' It is here that the inner integrity and the consistent character of the structure of Sykes' argument are evident: the apparent declension of authority and its dispersal into the multifarious norms of authority have been sublated by the 'discovery' of authority as *power*. Despite the recurrent difficulties of finding structures adequate for its embodiment

[92] *Ibid.*
[93] *Ibid.*, p. 72.
[94] *Ibid.*
[95] *Ibid.*

(and here the New Testament itself is evidence enough), it is in the reality of power that is to be found the open secret of Christianity itself. Most disquieting of all is that no real analysis of this power is offered: it is, in effect, the power that itself defines; it is not definable, except, as we duly see, in terms of the rhetoric of conquest and the negation of anything that smacks of 'depotentiation'.

The centrality of power in Christianity allows Sykes to celebrate its presence and ability to sustain combat in the cosmic struggle with evil and to generate self-sacrifice. There is evidence, we are told, of a rather unhealthy, even craven evasion of the themes of power and authority, which is apparent when, for example, the spread of secondary education brings abuses of power perpetrated in the name of the churches to the attention of a wider public. This oblique gesture in the direction of Donald MacKinnon's sensitivities to the long history of the corrupt abuse of power in the history of the Christian church is not here accompanied by its familiar correlate. MacKinnon repeatedly returned to the theme of *kenosis* (even calling, rightly in my judgement, for a *'kenosis* of establishment'),[96] whereas Sykes will have none of this. Although a long-standing concern with the humanity of Christ is evident in Sykes' thought (and this fits in with the schematic outline of English theology in section 1 of this chapter), he nevertheless distances himself from *kenosis* and, as categorically stated in the *Identity*, from the 'theological celebration of powerlessness'. In a passage remarkable for its intuitive rather than evidential insight the reader learns that:

The theological celebration of powerlessness, based on what appears to be a misunderstanding of Paul's theology of the cross, has an altogether suspicious air of *post factum* justification for loss of political influence.[97]

The depotentiated theology of the cross (and here Sykes has the Tübingen theologian Jürgen Moltmann in mind) has its roots in 'the diminished political influence exercised by the Church in western societies', and although such correlations are 'notoriously difficult to verify',[98] Sykes attempts what amounts to a sociological reduction. There is, on the contrary, considerable evidence to suggest that Sykes' hypothesis is false. First, the West German experience of the Third Reich renders all uncritical celebration of power questionable and ambiguous in principle,

---

[96] This chapter is at least in part inspired by Donald MacKinnon's Gore Memorial Lecture, 'Kenosis and Establishment', in *The Stripping of the Altars* (London: Collins, 1964), pp. 13–40.

[97] *Identity*, p. 75.

[98] *Ibid.*

and no one is more aware of this than Moltmann. Second, in a further example, the history of the Roman Catholic Church following the loss of the Papal States and thus of political influence in the nineteenth century went hand in hand with the grosser forms of ecclesiological and papal aggrandisement. Moreover, it is plausible to interpret the Anglican theology of the Episcopate as the essential ministry in the face of secularisation along analogous triumphalist lines. Third, by extension, it would be equally plausible to apply our counter-hypothesis (effectively verified in the other contexts) to Sykes' own position and regard the 'celebration of power' in glittering, adamantine Christian inwardness as an overcompensated spiritual triumphalism encapsulated in a highly distinctive interpretation of Paul's words in Ephesians 1.19: 'the immeasurable greatness of his power in us who believe'. Sykes' remark that 'one is inclined to ask whether there are social reasons why modern theologians fail to make any such claim' (i.e. to power)[99] invites the converse response, that the reader ask why some theologians *do* make such claims. In all events the dismissal of 'depotentiated theology' and thus, by implication, of the kenotic motif, is entirely consistent with Sykes' position. A price has to be paid, and it is the *exclusion* from this distinctive Anglican theological position and its correlative praxis of anything remotely associated with a 'theology of liberation' which might well bear traces of depotentiation, or, even more dangerously, make visible social stratification and the ecclesiological equivalent of class polarisation within the church.[100] For Sykes, God's kingly power is that which unites and animates the church with a single corporate will:

If one of the functions of the mythological language of God's kingly rule is the mobilisation of the person to total commitment and to a sense of confident participation in an ultimate victory of the divine intention over contrary forces, then any response to that language which fails to elicit a corresponding confidence may be justly regarded as inadequate.[101]

This kind of language can be interpreted in a number of ways; evangelical zeal can under certain linguistic conditions have a less than salubrious resonance. As theological rhetoric directed at the admonishment

---

99 *Ibid.*
100 Those acquainted with Boff's *Church, Charism and Power* will recognise an affinity of intention with the contents of this chapter. See chapter 5, 'The Power of the Institutional Church: Can it be Converted?', and especially Boff's question: 'Is it true that the Gospel needs power, prudence, concessions, the typical tricks of pagan power, all criticised by Jesus (Matthew 10:42), or does its strength lie precisely in weakness, renunciation of all security, prophetic courage, as practised in the church of the first three centuries?', and his remark, pp. 55–6, on the relation of inwardness and institutional structure.   101 *Identity*, p. 76.

and activation of the Christian community it succeeds; but if absorbed into the structure of the 'sub-plot', the call to 'mobilisation', 'total commitment' and 'ultimate victory' could become the homiletic aura surrounding a theory of power with the authoritarian tendencies to which allusion has already been made, that is to a full-blown celebration of power.

It is at this juncture that evidence of pervasive problems within Anglican theology and indeed English cultural identity emerge. Neither Anglican theology nor English culture really knows where it is now 'placed' in historical or geographical terms. Even within the Church of England local identities are forged and micro-ideologies created on the basis of reconstructions arbitrarily inspired by episodes in the history of the church, be it the primitive Palestinian community, a supposed Pauline hegemony, patristic orthodoxy, Reformation piety or the unfettered egoism of neo-Romantic catholic medievalism. In this setting Sykes' sophisticated, well-informed argument is, it is suggested, a hermeneutic of power ideally suited for the reformation of the Anglican Church along lines which transcend the fragmentation of historically localised ideologies. The theme of emergent, later routinised and rationalised, charismatic and kingly power is deeply rooted in the biblical materials and in the subsequent history of the church. This 'power' has been ambiguous, not just, as Sykes would have his readers believe, in terms of a dialectic of inwardness and externality, but in a far more complex set of relations between spiritual and temporal power, between classes within the church stemming from at least the early distinction of *ordo* and *plebs Dei*, and between ideological superstructure and socio-economic base, and so on. Sykes' refusal of this 'complexity' (explicit with regard to Troeltsch – the 'complexifier with a conscience') and his development of what amounts to a monopolistic theory of divine power, albeit moulded and mediated through changing structures of church government, are not an adequate substitute for this further, and to my mind indispensable, critical framework. The role of the theologian envisaged by Sykes not surprisingly conforms with the preceding argument and the hypothesis in the 'sub-plot', which contains, so far as ecclesial theory and praxis are concerned, the real substance of *The Identity of Christianity*. Here a new problem arises concerned with the nature of truth and the theologian's conflicting responsibilities. The theory of power that emerges in the sub-plot of the *Identity* confronts the theologian with the possibility of a dilemma latent in the following statements:

It is . . . very rare to discover a theologian who has taken full stock of the power which he or she exercises. Theological responsibility is commonly defined solely in terms of obedience to the truth . . . But even if it be true that obedience to the truth is one of the aspects of the theologian's responsibility, it is demonstrated that other aspects entail the formidable use of power in the modern Church.[102]

In short, should the theologian's integrity be expressed in the pursuit of truth or in commitment to the management of power in the church? This is no simple choice: it may in fact be a false dilemma if the argument is pressed too hard. But, given Sykes' absolutely uncompromising advocacy of the management and deployment of power, that is the power of God's kingly rule at the centre of Christianity, the theologian has, at the very least, to exercise some caution with regard to these proposals.

We have outlined the vertebral logic of the dominant sub-text of Sykes' argument. What follows in the middle section of the *Identity* is skilled historical appraisal of the essence of Christianity controversy and a demonstration of its continuing relevance. Sykes' answer to the difficulty exposed by the conflictual character of the Christian quest for identity is, however, already fully evident: it lies in the wholehearted appreciation and appropriation of the role of power understood as practical management in theology and church government. From the examples examined in the second part of the book are drawn qualifications of the power hypothesis; but by and large the 'sub-plot' is reinforced and unaltered. The presence of the historical material is justified in terms of the clarification of theological meaning: it does not directly pertain to power and managerial responsibility.

The *Identity* has a sandwich-like structure: outlying theoretical and analytical chapters enclose an extended central section which consists of a detailed scholarly appraisal of individual treatments of the essence/identity theme, subject, as Sykes himself concedes, to 'manipulation' in order to suit the thesis of his book. The latter concession does not appear out of place provided that it is always borne in mind that the exploration of the essence controversy is directed at the reinforcement of the hypothesis concerning power. In consequence, a series of illustrative beads are threaded onto the theoretical cord that binds together the three main sections of the *Identity*. There is first of all, in Schleiermacher, the concern

---

[102] *Ibid.*, p. 77.

to escape from the 'externality tradition' and to replace this with the determination of the essence of Christianity through the establishment of its 'inner structural coherence', that is its 'particular mode of faith' (*Glaubensweise*). The methodological decisions Schleiermacher made determined in turn the structure of his dogmatics and, indeed, informed his understanding of the permanent relationship of theology with the non-theological disciplines. Second, Newman is shown to have proceeded along lines analogous to those of Schleiermacher, and his approach is an example, *par excellence*, of the prominent exercise of theological responsibility. Third, the dispute between Harnack and Loisy provides contrasting accounts of the relation between the 'kernel and husk' of direct relevance to Sykes' own interpretation of the inward and external aspects of Christianity. Both tackle the theme of power and represent it in non-political terms: for Harnack it is the power of personality, a reality into which 'no research can carry us further',[103] whereas Loisy believed that 'ecclesiastical authority is not in true nature domineering, but educative'.[104] Each writer was above all else committed to the recovery of the original force of the Gospel, an act itself the exercise of responsible theological power, whatever might be the inadequacies of the results achieved.

Of particular importance for Sykes' supportive arguments is a juxtaposition of Troeltsch and Barth. Troeltsch set out precisely the relationship between historicism and epistemology in the form determinative of modern discussion and offered a strategy in direct opposition to that developed by Barth. Despite what is referred to as an unfortunate tendency to complexify issues, Troeltsch saw the necessity of Christianity's retaining its naivety[105] in the face of the qualitative discontinuity of pre- and post-Enlightenment thought. Troeltsch's understanding of the social-psychological character of Christianity as a communal reality contributed to an epistemology which complemented historical research into the reality of Jesus' life and teaching. The exercise of the former insight demands highly developed theological discrimination – hence the interrelation of the power and status of the theologian with epistemology. In sharp contrast, Barth reinstated the power and primacy of the Word over against Troeltsch's combination of the socio-psychological and historical approaches. Barth's emphasis upon radical novelty and discontinuity

---

[103] *Ibid.*, p. 141.
[104] *Ibid.*, p. 142.
[105] *Ibid.*, p. 150.

in the renowned second edition of the *Römerbrief* and the expressing of this through the central ecclesial act of preaching is of particular importance to Sykes as he distances himself from a purely archaeological approach to Christianity. The demand for immediacy is singularly uncompromising, for, as the reader has learned earlier: 'Hermeneutics must under no circumstances become a sophisticated way of clinging to the evacuated shell of a once living religion.'[106] This statement is one of the more memorable dicta in the *Identity*, and the justification of this standpoint is largely in terms of a subtle and original exposition of Barth which is particularly illuminating with regard to the Christological treatment of power in volume IV/1 of the *Church Dogmatics*, which attains a level of 'confidence' sustainable only on the basis of a 'parallelism of language'.[107] This parallelism (what we might term the juxtaposition of rhetorical excess and the realism relatable to actual social and historical context) demands an interpretative strategy different from that of Sykes,[108] who notes Barth's consistent repudiation of the hierarchical concept of the ministry and yet his high view of the theologian. The assumption of Barth's dialectical 'parallelism' into Syke's own position is problematic: Barth is 'so radical a representative of the inwardness tradition that nothing external can be said unequivocally to be an actual sign of the presence of divine power'.[109] It is at this juncture that Sykes distinguishes the realism of his own position and indeed that of Anglican theology from what he understands as Barth's 'unrealistic' dialecticism. The latter has in my view a fundamental, and from the English Anglican standpoint, an incomprehensible emphasis upon grace: the words are invested with the Word as an act of divine invasion, a justifying grace that for ever denies the proclaimer the possession of that Word or indeed, the manipulation of it in terms of human achievement. By contrast, Sykes reinvolves the Anglican principle of *via media* in a form of direct synthesis, more accurately a syncretic synergism:

The language of sociology and the language of theology may be separate, but the reality of divine and human power is not. It is not parallel or merely coordinated, it is inevitably, and dangerously, mixed.[110]

---

[106] *Ibid.*, p. 76.
[107] *Ibid.*, p. 203.
[108] See R. H. Roberts, 'Theological Rhetoric and Moral Passion in the Light of Mackinnon's "Barth"', in K. Surin (ed.), *Christ, Ethics and Tragedy: Pursuing the Thought of Donald Mackinnon* (Cambridge: Cambridge University Press, 1980), pp. 1–14 for an account of such 'parallelism' in the English context.
[109] *Identity*, p. 207
[110] *Ibid.*

Sykes' subsequent promulgation of 'the challenge of a more balanced and realistic interpretation of the identity of Christianity'[111] falls ironically into precisely that errant tendency he isolated and exposed in the *Integrity*, that is the taming and domestication of theological impulses within a manageable institution, which, when all is said and done, demands a theology able to serve within rather than challenge its context.

In the third concluding section of the *Identity* the basic issues are reworked and clarified. The dialectic of inwardness and externality is regarded as fundamental and presented in terms of three models: foundation–superstructure; spirit–body; and centre–circumference. Deep anxiety is expressed in Sykes' concern for the maintenance of a stable unity within Christianity sufficient to evince and sustain effective commitment on the part of believers. The question of the relation of the pursuit of truth to the quest for identity is raised once more,[112] and it passes yet again into a critique of 'depotentiated Christianity'.[113] Sykes' own position is expressed in terms of an elegant, pragmatic compromise:

It is perfectly reasonable to enquire under what conditions Christianity is one thing. Such an enquiry performs a useful service in bringing into the open the natural assumptions about its diachronic and synchronic unity. The specification of these conditions would be a conscious construction or standpoint in Christian history, neither ruled out of court by historical relativism nor convicted of being a subtle deviation from the question of truth.[114]

To chronic disagreement about the Christian tradition as a whole there are, Sykes maintains, only three possible responses: the first is simply straightforward affirmation; the second the abandonment of the defence of even minimal continuity in the Christian tradition; the third, taken up and developed, is that of 'dialectical' management of the dispute through the incorporation and development of W. B. Gallie's notion of an 'essentially contested concept'.[115] This advocacy of the 'genuinely creative dispute' would, if taken on its own, appear to leave Christianity and indeed Anglicanism treading the theological water in perpetuity. It is now surely apparent that this is *not* the intended conclusion: the rescue can be performed by the ordained theologian. Here the new 'prince of the Church', in whom 'a religious concern and a scholarly spirit are finely conjoined for the purposes of theoretical and practical activity

111 *Ibid.*, p. 208.
112 *Ibid.*, pp. 247–8.
113 *Ibid.*, p. 249.
114 *Ibid.*, p. 250.
115 *Ibid.*, p. 251.

alike',[116] must step forward and take up his authoritative relation to the community of worshippers. Thus the internal experience of new life can be interrelated with the external factors of story, myth and doctrine; it is, Sykes concludes,

in the process of interaction between this inward element and the external form of Christianity that the identity of Christianity consists.[117]

The final definition of the identity of Christianity in terms of the relation of its inward and external aspects is incomprehensible to me. In the light of analysis of the structure of the dominant sub-text, the 'sub-plot' of which Sykes himself speaks, such a conclusion would appear to be a diversion and a foreshortening of perspective (possible as part of a negative strategy) imposed upon a concrete situation far more complex and problematic than is admitted in either the *Integrity* or the *Identity*. Sykes' overall argument is thus severely and unnaturally limited by a careful process of the inclusion and the exclusion of key issues. Most fundamental to Sykes' exclusion zone is that concern, central to liberation theology, and indeed present long before this in certain aspects of the English Reformation and Dissent, with the highly problematic relation of secular and spiritual power in the Constantinian and medieval, post-Reformation and established church. Sykes' advocacy of the inevitability of power within theology is presented in terms of the 'dialectic' of inwardness and externality as though this bore no intrinsic relation to the *contextual* factors implicit in ideology, social structure and the distribution of wealth and educational resources and opportunities, and not least the concentration of patronage. Sykes' solution to the problem of the identity of Christianity is a shrewd and sophisticated recognition and reworking of the role of the theologian (and, it would be not unreasonable to assume, the theologically informed ordained holder of senior church office, that is ultimately the bishop) which is undertaken uncritically within the given structures of Establishment and the continuing crisis in British higher education.

The unchallenged centralised hegemony implicit within Sykes' proposals falls all too well into a national, government-led, strategic return

---

[116] *Ibid.*, p. 88. Schleiermacher's conception of the 'prince of the Church' appears to have had an unmistakable influence upon Sykes' understanding of the role of the theologian: 'If one should imagine both a religious interest and a scientific spirit conjoined in the highest degree and with the finest balance for the purpose of theoretical and practical activity alike, that would be the idea of a "prince of the Church"', F. D. E. Schleiermacher, *Brief Outline of the Study of Theology*, tr. T. N. Tice (Richmond, VA, 1966), par. 9, p. 21.

[117] *Identity*, p. 261.

to the contemporary analogue to the social structures that underlaid 'Victorian values'. Despite Sykes' gestures in the direction of a limited democracy in the church (a vestigial lay veto on liturgical extremities), the threads of power lead back into the hands of a magisterial elite which, aware of its power, defines the reality in relation to which the believer is to sacrifice himself or herself. It might well be that such measures are necessary if communities of endurance and a clerisy are to be sustained in the new Dark Age in England; if this is the case, then there is no point in disguising or unduly mollifying proposals which are in reality to do with the dominative, hegemonic management of power and the organisation of belief in a threatened church and religious tradition. It may well also be that the relation of the theologian to the embodied religious tradition of worship can condition and restrain the potential intellectual tyranny of the intellectual,[118] but this is not, it would seem to me, a *necessity*, but merely a contingent consequence of the minimal discipline incumbent upon the ordained theologian bound by the canon law governing worship. We have here a skeletal, centralised ecclesiology, built around a hermeneutic focused through the power of established and informed judgement that expresses itself both in the pursuit of theology as such *and* in the minds of those who control liturgy. There is, however, no full ecclesiology, no sense of the reality of the people of God, except insofar as it exists as a passive, organised liturgical entity with a consciousness structured, as it were, from 'above'. In epistemological terms a nascent theology of power confronts us, which, not to put too fine a point on it, is an ideology of 'kingly rule'; it is, to use the unadorned language of Hegel, Simmel and Weber, the renewed reality of *Herrschaft* reborn in a judicious, elegant form sufficient, perhaps, to English Christianity's hour of need.[119]

CONCLUSION

It now remains for us to draw together the threads of our argument, in which we have set out some of the fundamental issues in the situation

---

[118] *Ibid.*, pp. 7, 285–6.

[119] My elaborate argument corresponds with the gentle plea by John Bowker for less centralisation of power in the Church of England: see *Licensed Insanities: Religion and Belief in God in the Contemporary World* (London: SCM, 1987). In commenting on 'The Individual and the System' he concludes: 'The systematic nature of systems is undoubtedly open to abuse and exploitation. All too easily the system becomes the end in itself, instead of the means towards an End which lies beyond itself. The responsibility of all Christians, in any generation, is to transform – or to allow God to transform through them – the dry bones of the system into a living presence which in turn touches, heals, restores, sustains many lives far beyond its own', p. 142.

of contemporary Anglicanism and examined at some length one highly influential and representative response. Through an exposition of the historical context, an outline of method and a 'reading' of the integrity, identity and power hypotheses that are contained in the structure of the now Bishop Sykes' 'sub-plot', in our terms the dominant sub-text of his work, we are now in a position to synthesise the methodological and substantial aspects of our argument.

If the revival of Christianity implies its recapitulation or 'repetition' at each new juncture in history, then the attempt to define the identity of Christianity we have subjected to critical analysis has involved the reworking of archaic, inherited structures which bear an undeniably analogous relationship with Hegel's representation of the Lordship and Bondage relation: the structure of power that entails domination and subjection. Despite the specific authorial disclaimer, a denial of a dominative understanding of power, we have shown that Sykes' re-endorsement of the legitimate power of the ordained ecclesiastic, the bearer of authority understood as the power to command and anticipate obedience, is wholly congruent with the structural sub-plot of his texts. In a partly redundant intellectual mediation, Sykes has tried, unsuccessfully in my view, to divert attention away from the latent integrity of the structure of his own position through his constant emphasis upon the conflictual character of Christianity as ostensibly generated through the difficulty of historical transmission and the intrinsic imprecision of language. Inasmuch, however, as the power-conscious theologian, a re-embodiment of Schleiermacher's 'prince of the Church', exercises his (or her) discrimination and defines Christian identity *for others*, this 'princedom' manifests itself as Lordship, that is a *Herrschaft* in Hegel's sense. In fact, to pursue the analogy further, Sykes' argument takes the dialectic from the merely unconscious assumption of inherited essence, as in the case of a pre-critical embodiment of a transmitted *authority* in tradition, to its active postmodern assertion as *power*. In other words, we move from the static, frozen authority of the ancestral juxtaposition of *ordo* and *plebs*, that is from a canonical authority conveying a deposit of faith (possibly modified through a hierarchy of truths), to a dynamic self-defining authority that self-consciously legislates reality for and on behalf of the *other*. When seen in the context of Hegel's presentation of the dialectic of power, this represents merely the first 'moment' related to the third 'moment' in the progression: we thus move from the static assertion of authority directly to the active exercise of pre-emptive power by the sublated Lord; but at the same time this is a misrepresentation: there is, in reality, no engagement with the middle 'moment', the 'other', that is with the Bondsman, the Slave, the *plebs*, in this case the spiritual proletariat, the laity. It has been my aim to articulate the position of the elided 'moment', the invisible Bondsman identical in terms of our analogy with a voiceless laity subsumed into a false mediation, a Christian foreshortening of the dialectic which prematurely assumes such conflict into a false 'reconciliation'. The dialectic is paralysed by 'containment' prior to the administration of the *coup de grâce* through the 'discovery of authority', that is through the reassertion of power on a new 'Real-theologie' of spiritual 'Herrschaft'.

If Christianity then persists in foisting a false reconciliation or 'containment' upon 'conflict', what, then, are the immediate consequences? Not least we may see that the Christian 'dialectic' can only subsist on a restricted plane assimilable into the post-Enlightenment pattern of 're-constructionist' theologies; it can in effect only take up a position at an alienated distance from the real fabric of life. If it were to enter into the latter, then the encounter (informed ideally by the full panoply of the human sciences) would expose the most painful discordance between these conditions and the residual, crucial 'rhetoric' of the Gospel. The suppression or elision of the rhetorical *topos* or commonplace which posits (however unrealistically in Sykes' terms) an eschatological unity of humankind, that is, its construal as 'one in Christ', is evidence of a pervasive failure to recognise the conflict and relationship between different kinds of rhetorical discourse within theology, a problem which might be elucidated through the use of tools drawn from literary theory, not to mention the other relevant areas of discourse.

Sykes' downgrading of such Pauline conceptuality and his consistent avoidance of a sociological definition of the church in terms of a quality of human relation, other than as super- and sub-ordination, is doubtless 'realistic', but do they do justice to the demands of the theological task? The displacement of original and final unity, the Alpha and Omega of the Christian rhetoric of salvation, has disastrous consequences: Christian identity is put entirely and exclusively at the mercy of the informed virtuoso, the writer of Christian character, the Prince-Lord of the church legislating for the identity of Christianity. To 'mix' the parallel languages of Paul and of Karl Barth in a new theological 'realism' puts 'God' finally at the mercy of the constructive ambition of the theologian, male or female. This is a false mediation, a sophisticated diversion made possible only because of a manifest curtailment of the understanding of conflict and enabled by a theology that baulks at the prospect of a doctrine of 'total depravity', the universal fallibility of *all* human agency. To draw a veil over this is in reality not only to deny humanity its inheritance, and indeed, its need for an anticipated solution, however wrought, but it is also to incur the risk, indeed the inevitability, of the corrupt, obfuscatory manipulation of others through the management of power at the most fundamental and insidious level, that is in the construction of the self-consciousness of the other. It is this 'other' that dies in the Christian representation of the dialectic as embodied in the structure of *ordo* and *plebs*. This is not normally a violent public act but the quiet ecclesial practice of spiritual abortion, the unprotesting infantilisation of countless millions of embryonic believers upon whose behalf an essential ministry presumes to interpose.[120] In the brutality of Hegel's dialectic there are to be found the means that may effect the raw exposure of wounded psychic flesh, the cry for existence embodied in the slave, the *Knecht*, the non-entity (*Unding*), deprived in the Christian context of the gift of Life itself. To disinter Hegel's terrifying dialectic at this juncture is, I believe, to unsheathe once more what Hoskyns called the 'dagger of the Incarnation'. What is found here in Hegel's argument is a true and brutal reflection of that tension, even contradiction, traceable in Christianity to Philippians 2.5–7, rendered with uncompromising lucidity by Luther:

Jesus Christus . . . welcher, ob er wohl in göttlicher Gestalt war, nahm er's nicht als einen Raub, Gott gleich zu sein, sondern entäusserte sich selbst und nahm Knechtsgestalt an.

Such theology is neither genteel nor '*salonfähig*'; it exists in a negative relation to the ambiguities of the positions we have subjected to critical examination in this chapter.

In the final analysis our concern in this long chapter has been not merely with the limitations and the questionable tendencies of two representative texts, but with the larger situation in English and Anglican theology. We have in effect compared the arguments of texts which in different contexts struggle to come to terms with the relation of ancestral tradition and modernity. If, following Ernst Bloch, we test the texts in order to establish their progressive or regressive orientation, an interesting parallel is apparent.[121] Hegel represents and subverts in narrative form

---

[120] A full decade after first writing this chapter, I am now (2000–1) more than ever convinced of the basic validity of the position I took up earlier. In the fully managerialised church that we analyse in the next chapter, this mechanical approach to religion may, at its worst, lead to what Ken Willber has described as the spiritual 'killing-jar' of main-line religion.

[121] See R. H. Roberts, *Hope and its Hieroglyph: A Critical Decipherment of Ernst Bloch's 'Principle of Hope'* (Atlanta: Scholars Press, 1990).

the logic of epistemological dominance in the ontological parable of the Lord and Bondsman; Sykes likewise restates but ultimately re-endorses a theology of dominance despite all the cosmetic diversions which overlie the structure of his texts. Hegel was, at least in 1807, progressive; Sykes is, according to our analysis, *regressive*, despite valiant efforts at modernisation. What Hegel (and, following him, the critical theoreticians of a humane Enlightenment) have all understood is that the emancipation of humanity is to do with the realisation, through affirmation or through revolution, of the 'other'. The history of the disjoined, secularised relics inherited from the Christian consensus in socialism, even in its healthier forms, has doubtless been in many respects disastrous; the 'dialectic of Enlightenment' is itself a sombre intellectual episode in the history of the modern period. Nevertheless, if the Christian Gospel has to do with freedom, love or grace, then it has to do with the affirmation of the other.

Neither the traditional Anglican ecclesiology with which we began nor the sophisticated rethinking of authority as 'real power' and the unneurotic celebration of such power in an Anglican Church of the future can, by any stretch of the intellectual imagination, be regarded as a theology of liberation. If the Christian church in its Anglican form has not yet even discovered or recognised the form of the other, that is in the bondspersons or laity, then it has no right to legislate for a reality explicitly or implicitly, theologically or otherwise, on their behalf. The rediscovery of the doctrine of the church, the beginning of an answer to the ecclesiological question in Anglicanism, begins here with the theological invisibility of the laity, and thus with the consequent climb into active, stirring consciousness of the *plebs Dei*, God's own proletariat, the people of God. The fuller form of an answer would be the formulation of a doctrine of the church and the enactment of a corresponding theological and institutional repentance which served to build structures of anticipation rather than merely to promote regression and conserve hierarchical power. Such a development we await.

CHAPTER 6

Ruling the Body: the care of souls in a managerial church

In the first part of this book we traced out aspects of the process through which British, and in particular English, society under Prime Ministers Margaret Thatcher, John Major and Tony Blair has absorbed and imposed upon itself the new paradigm of a managerial modernity. In the last chapter a centrally important Anglican attempt at self-definition was critically examined in some depth in relation to ecclesiology. Now, in this chapter, it will become apparent that with characteristically Erastian impulse the Church of England would appear to have followed contemporary trends and to be involved in the process of managerialising its mission and ministry. Given the historical context, this transformation can be seen as offering a beleaguered senior Church leadership in the so-called 'essential ministry' a long-sought-for identity, in exact terms the opportunity to regain what Bishop Sykes called the 'real power' of the Gospel, which, although problematic and ambiguous, has, he argued, nonetheless to be grasped and operationalised. The aggregation of the Church of England to societal trends has, it will be argued, fateful consequences within the wider setting of a world order in which invasive commodification is rampant and where the future of the human is placed under a multiplicity of threats. Can, indeed should, a managerialised church serve the wider religious and spiritual needs of humankind, or should it simply acquiesce in its reconfiguration as a 'quality'-bound, 'supply-side' organisation dedicated to the well-marketed and efficient delivery of what amounts to a pre-determined English Anglican 'Gospel^{TM}' in limited (because privileged) competition with other outlets in the spiritual market-place? These are controversial questions posed primarily in relation to both English and Scottish church experience, but which have implications for all main-line religion at the outset of the twenty-first century.

INTRODUCTION

The Church of England has taken steps at both executive and middle-management level to aggregate itself to the global and national paradigm of managerialism.[1] Thus the 'body', at the various levels of the individual physical body, the corporate organisational body – and the mystical 'Body of Christ' – is committed to the appropriation and deployment of instruments of coordination and integration of what is, for members of that body and in a sense to be specified, a systemically irresistible power.[2] This consolidation of top-down efficacy and efficiency, that is the enactment within the church of the managerial revolution that has been imposed upon business, education, the health and social services sectors and parts of the culture industries, will, if the foregoing analysis has validity, have distinct and characteristic features and consequences.

As applied across British society, 'modern management' in its Neo-Fordist form involves, as we have observed in a range of settings, the loss of relative autonomy and the assimilation of all operatives into 'provider–receiver', 'provider–customer' relationships, SWOT analysis, 'transparent' performance appraisal, the enforcement of 'Quality circles', and 'benchmarking'. All ends–means relationships are thereby transformed. In such managerialised contexts, strategic objectives are the prerogative of executive management; 'mission statements' inform the aims and objectives in terms of which middle managers secure the conformity of front-line operatives; the latter encounter the 'receivers', consumers or 'customers' in rationally pre-determined and supervised of modes of relationality. The ultimate reductive paradigm of this mode interaction may, as noted earlier, be represented as 'McDonaldisation', that is the systematic application of the means of securing ever greater *efficiency, calculability, predictability* and *control*.[3] Under such managerialised

---

[1] This chapter has been developed and presented in a range of contexts. The Scottish material was first presented in an extra-mural lecture at the University of St Andrews in 1992. I then, as acknowledged earlier, engaged regularly in a continuing discussion of the religious appropriateness of creating a managerialised Church of England. I am grateful to the Revd Dr Ken Leech for an invitation to deliver the Jubilee Group Annual 'Christ the King' Lecture entitled 'Ruling the Body: The Care of Souls in a Managerial Church' at St John on Bethnal Green, 25 November 2000, immediately after which this chapter took its present form.

[2] See Clegg, 'Circuits of Power: A Framework for Analysis' in *Frameworks of Power* (London: Sage, 1989) for an account of the systemic nature of power in modern organisations and the difficulties of 'outflanking' such power. R. H. Roberts provides a basic outline of the issues in 'Power', in Andrew Linzey (ed.), *The Routledge Encyclopaedia of Theology and Society* (London: Routledge, 1996), pp. 673–8.

[3] See George Ritzer, *The McDonaldization of Society: An Investigation into the Changing Character of Contemporary Social Life* (Thousand Oaks, CA: Pine Forge Press, 1993) and by the same author, *The McDonaldization Thesis: Explorations and Extensions*, London: Sage, 1998).

conditions, which have successfully imposed uniformity across many apparently diverse sectors of society and culture, local cultures are captured, rationalised, regularised and then redirected by managers, who then present their reconstruction of reality to be accepted and 'owned' by operatives. On occasion, a yawning dichotomy between executive goals and control may open up, and the contingent requirements of local cultures of safe and appropriate performance can be neglected to a disastrous – even catastrophic – degree.

The extension of an apparently 'rational' mode of working and existing to so-called 'professionals' is based upon the implementation within 'brain-', 'heart-' and 'soul-' work of the transfer of knowledge and agency from the operative to the manager as originally envisaged by Frederick W. Taylor as early as 1911 in research based upon Ford factory practice. The Taylorisation or 'modernisation' of the *mind* is now following that of the *hand* in factory work. This extension of rational managerial control from the hand to the head has been implemented without serious resistance in British education at all levels. As argued above, this regime has now been imposed upon higher education in Britain and Australasia in particularly radical forms. Whilst this is a procedure that involves a severe loss of relative autonomy and the non-consensual destruction and reconstruction of local cultures, the threat of the withdrawal of funding has been sufficient to secure conformity. The next stage in this 'modernisation' is the rational management of the 'heart' and 'spirit' or 'soul'; and it is this, as will become apparent, that is now in train in context of the organisation of church life. As ever, it is our contention that the implicit distinction between the 'form' of a given management system and the 'content' of that which is to be managed is unsustainable, given the self-interest of an expanding managerial elite and the inherent momentum of managerialism as a distinct form of bureaucratisation.[4]

The British New Labour predilection for 'modernisation' is similar in many key respects to Taylor's programme as it is extended to all areas of human life implied by 'hand', 'head', and now, as it were, the 'heart' and even the 'soul'. There are no limits to this process of managerial normalisation, and as a mode of systematic organisation the maintenance of contemporary Taylorism or Neo-Fordism requires constant vigilance. Moreover, as seen earlier with regard to the universities, for it to work

---

[4] Max Weber's classic account of the routinisation of charisma and of bureaucratisation is, as ever, relevant at this juncture. See Gunther Roth and Claus Wittich (eds.), *Economy and Society* (Berkeley: University of California Press, 1978), pp. 246–54, 1121–3.

effectively it has to be 'owned' by its victims.[5] Given the present British government's commitment to the ideology of 'modernisation', and if we call to mind the comprehensive embrace of modernity itself, the 'triumph of capitalism', the facile eclecticism of a postmodern consumerist culture, and modern management techniques, then is there, can there be, should there be, any real alternative to this infinitely elastic 'cage', the clinging body-stocking of the 'reality' that invites, indeed increasingly compels, our submission and integration?

It is here my contention that the *uncritical* incorporation of managerialism within the Church of England amounts to a betrayal. The 'rule' of the Body in all its aspects, on the one hand, and, on the other, the practices of managerialism amount to a crushing pincer movement. In terms of the title of this chapter, the assimilation of managerialism into an organisation whose leaders have been – and remain – in a state of prolonged identity crisis endangers the 'care of souls', that is the fostering of that delicate ecology of spiritual opportunity that constitutes the fabric of real human community, *koinonia*, itself.

In this chapter the various components of this managerial revolution as it comes to impact upon the Church of England are reviewed under the following headings. At the outset, taking up the theme explored in the foregoing chapter, connections are forged between a long-standing crisis of identity and authority within English Anglicanism and the legitimation and actualisation of power provided by the prerogatives of managerialism and its employment as means of ecclesial restoration. This restoration is analysed in terms of two stages. The first is the reinauguration of the ecclesial version of the managers' 'right to manage' seen in the restructuring of an 'executive Church', and the second is the introduction and implementation of the culture of performance and appraisal which may consolidate the oversight of *episcope* into an ecclesial Panopticon of other- and self-administered surveillance. This twofold pattern of ecclesial renewal is then related back to an ever more managerialised modernity, which, it is argued, contains distinctive forms of the 'closure of transcendence'. Such opportunities as there are for religious and spiritual exploration, and for the 'care of soul(s)', exist in what must increasingly be understood as a competitive spiritual market-place in an increasingly

---

5 Whether church management is 'post-Fordist' or, as seems more likely, an intensification of Fordism into 'neo-Fordism' as Michael Aglietta argues is a difficult question. The emphasis of the latter is upon control rather than realisation, and this better fits ecclesial experience. See Paul Bagguley, 'Post-Fordism and Enterprise Culture: Flexibility, Autonomy and Changes in Economic Organisation', in Russell Keat and Nicholas Abercrombie, *Enterprise Culture* (London: Routledge, 1991), p. 153, n. 16.

de-traditionalised society. In conclusion, the issues that arise when a 'supply-side' main-line religion encounters the 'primal religion' of our time are briefly explored, and the theological question is then posed as to how Christian churches might respond in 'ecologies of the Spirit' to the challenges that arise.

FROM CRISIS OF AUTHORITY TO LEGITIMATION OF POWER: MANAGERIALISM AS ECCLESIAL RESTORATION

Given the long-standing nineteenth-century Anglican quest for episcopal and priestly legitimacy in an authentic apostolic succession of unbroken lineage and a historically contemporaneous modification of Christology in the direction of a 'modern', human – even kenotic – Christ, the question of the religious and theological identity of the Church of England has been, as argued in chapter 5, a sensitive issue for many generations of priests.[6] As Bishop Stephen Sykes argued in two notable books, *The Integrity of Anglicanism* and *The Identity of Christianity*, for Anglicans the question of authority remains intractable in the face of what is, for traditional theology, that form of modernity represented by historicism, the doctrine that all history is in the final analysis an infinitely complex causal nexus in which truths conveyed by tradition are a matter of mere probability. Given the fact that historical continuity as bearer of absolute significance is impossible to achieve, and that because it is likewise difficult to anticipate agreement upon what the comprehensive 'identity' is that is to be transmitted, Bishop Sykes saved the day by resorting to a performative definition of the power that lies at the heart of the Gospel. On the basis of Ernst Troeltsch's analysis of the transformations of charismatic faith into a visible institutional reality,

In a concrete way the episcopate was substituted for the earlier faith in the Exalted Christ and the Spirit: it is the succession of Christ and of the Apostle, the Bearer of the Spirit, the extension or externalising of the Incarnation, a visible and tangible proof of the Divine Truth and Power, the concrete presence of the sociological point of reference.[7]

Sykes proceeded to examine the handling of the theme of power in the New Testament and came to the unreserved conclusion that 'the early

---

[6] In this chapter I once again assume the basic validity of Willard F. Enteman's hypothesis in *Managerialism* that 'managerialism' as a societal *topos* succeeds J. A. Schumpeter's triad of 'capitalism, socialism and democracy'.

[7] Troeltsch, *Social Teachings*, vol. II, p. 32, cited in S. W. Sykes, *The Identity of Christianity* (London: SPCK, 1984), p. 63.

Christian communities were highly power-conscious bodies'[8] and that 'to be a Christian is to be equipped with power, real power, as distinct from the outward form of piety'.[9] Thus any theologies which weaken this awareness of 'real power' are suspect. In criticising then influential contemporary views, Sykes asserted that:

The theological celebration of powerlessness, based on what appears to be a misunderstanding of Paul's theology of the cross, has an altogether suspicious air of *post factum* justification for loss of political influence.[10]

Apart from the historicist questions raised by Troeltsch, the traditional, static conception of the historical transmission of authority would be inadequate in the face of the 'real power' of Christianity:

This power is the divine power, the power of the Spirit. It dwells in the gospel, and is evident at the points where it overcomes challenge, opposition and conflict. It is the power to convince, to bring about new life, to create loving harmony in the Community, to withstand persecution, and to triumph over death; it is powerful, in other words over indifference and rejection, over law, over internal dissent, over external oppression, and over the last enemy itself.[11]

In the 1980s such advocacy of institutionally embodied charismatic power doubtless might well have appeared somewhat implausible, as it was, not least, at variance with the then liberal ethos of much Anglican theology and with the secularised and marginalised status of the church. Yet in 1984 Sykes nonetheless argued in an uncompromising way for the unashamed rehabilitation of power:

If one of the functions of the mythological language of God's kingly rule is the mobilisation of the person to total commitment and to a sense of confident participation in an ultimate victory of the divine intention over contrary forces, then any response to that language which fails to elicit a corresponding confidence may be justly regarded as inadequate.[12]

Now, with hindsight, we can see how, indeed, Bishop Sykes exercised a 'prophetic' ministry in that he foresaw and prepared the way for the 'reform' and 'modernisation' of the church.[13] In the fullness of time

---

[8] Sykes, *Identity*, p. 72.
[9] *Ibid.*
[10] *Ibid.*, p. 75.
[11] *Ibid.*
[12] *Ibid.*, p. 76.
[13] When developing the connections made in this paper it is significant to recall that Bishop Stephen Sykes was theological consultant for the Turnbull Report, *Working as One Body*.

the managerial imperative enacted across British society would provide the means for realising a return to the exercise of 'real' ecclesial power. Sykes dared to reinvolve the Anglican principle of *via media* in a form of direct synthesis, an anticipation of what is to the modern manager a real 'synergesis':

> The language of sociology and the language of theology may be separate, but the reality of divine and human power is not. It is not parallel or merely coordinated, it is inevitably, and dangerously, mixed.[14]

From where might the means for risking the dangerous but necessary remixing of these two distanced discourses come if 'reality' is to be encountered? The answer can be found, it will be argued, in two related stages of the aggregation of English Anglican polity into a wider societal managerialism. These steps in aggregation are summarised prescriptively in two recent texts, the first with official status, the so-called Turnbull Report, *Working as One Body*,[15] and the second a joint effort by the retired senior naval officer and university vice-chancellor (or Chief Executive) Professor Derek Burke, and the sociologically trained theologian Professor Robin Gill in their book *Strategic Church Leadership*,[16] the truths of which have fallen upon the open and eager ears of ecclesiastical authority.

These related and complementary steps on the path towards the rational management of the church are now to be briefly examined in the light of their apparent resolution of long-standing theological difficulties. According to this 'rational' view, managerial modernity has gifted to the church the means of regaining *real power*: the church has but to grasp the latter as *means* and dedicate them to the *end*, the Gospel itself. In terms of recent history I may claim a little credit for having sensed what was to come when I concluded in 1989 that:

> In fact, pursuing the analogy further, Sykes' argument takes the dialectic from the merely unconscious assumption of inherited essence, as in the case of a precritical embodiment of a transmitted *authority* in tradition, to its active postmodern assertion as *power*. In other words we move from the static, frozen authority of the ancestral juxtaposition of *ordo* and *plebs*, that is from a canonical authority conveying a deposit of faith (possibly modified through a hierarchy of truths) to

---

[14] Sykes, *Identity*, p. 76.
[15] *Working as One Body: The Report of the Archbishop's Commission on the Organisation of the Church of England* (London: Church House Publishing, 1995).
[16] Robin Gill and Derek Burke, *Strategic Church Leadership* (London: SPCK, 1996).

a dynamic self-defining authority that self-consciously legislates reality for and on behalf of the *other*.[17]

This 'other' has, as it happens, turned out to be the *managed* 'other', a subject other subordinate to those whose *right to rule* is identified with the manager's *right to manage*. To achieve this state of affairs, it is first necessary to establish and to consolidate the executive and supervisory power of the manager. As regards the Church of England, this has been achieved, at least in principle, in two stages, first through the (re-)establishment of executive hegemony and then through the implementation of the 'Quality' culture of managerial control of staff. These steps are now examined in turn.

THE MANAGER'S 'RIGHT TO MANAGE': RESTRUCTURING
AN EXECUTIVE CHURCH

As it happens, a sudden and unexpected financial crisis caused by an unfortunate property investment policy on the part of the Church Commissioners created a situation in which fundamental reappraisal of the church's function and purpose became possible.[18] A vacuum had to be filled, and the Report of the Archbishop's Commission on the Organisation of the Church of England, *Working as One Body*, the Turnbull Report, proposed remedies of far-reaching significance.

Working as One Body contains an innovative and brilliantly conceived plan for the systematic restructuring of the Church of England. Central to the Report was a vision of the church as an executive-led, highly unified organisation, in many respects similar to a business corporation. There would in effect be a World President (the Archbishop of Canterbury), a Company Chairman (again the Archbishop of Canterbury), an Executive Board (the proposed National Council of senior bishops and appointees) and a Chief Executive with considerable powers (the Secretary General) and many key, leading positions would be occupied by archiepiscopal appointees. The plan involved the effective subordination of other important bodies to the Executive. Most notably, General

---

[17] See p. 62 above.
[18] In fairness to the Church Commissioners it is important to note Sir Michael Coleman's (First Church Estates Commissioner) observation in a Press release (May 1996) that, 'A total return of 19.5% on the Commissioners' investments and an increase in value of over £300 million to £2.7 billion continues the strengthening of the Church of England's historic assets.' This improvement has continued, but it has not allowed for a reversion to the previous funding arrangements, in particular as regards clergy pensions.

Synod was to become an advisory and legislative body representative of other stakeholders which would (rather like the periodic meetings of shareholders in a public company) keep the Executive in indirect touch with wider realities. The Church Commissioners would have a restricted financial function and be brought under Executive remit.

Taken together, the Turnbull proposals were regarded by some as the most far-reaching changes to be enacted in the Church of England since the Reformation. Under the terms of the Turnbull Report, the National Council would become the Executive core of the church; theologically speaking, it might be difficult to resist the temptation to conclude that in reality it would also become the 'Head' to which the 'Body' of the church would be responsible.[19] The managerial culture envisaged by the Report offered both real power and 'empowerment' to its senior practitioners and the seductive possibility of harnessing the motivation of others using religious and spiritual means as shown earlier.[20] Indeed, we might ask, should the Church of England not be 'reformed' along with the National Health Service, the social services, the universities and all other areas of education? Are there any good reasons why the church should not be thus 'normalised'?

In beginning to address such questions, it is first important to remark upon the carefully wrought rhetorical structure of the document in which the 'shape' of the text is reminiscent of that of a well-planned liturgy. The church's executive and managerial deficit is addressed in terms under which the managerial and organisational reform is implicitly sanctified through explicit references to the Eucharistic context,[21] to the 'theology of the gracious gift'[22] and invocation of the Holy Spirit.[23] Worthy of particular note, however, is the mixture of discourses. This could be illustrated at length, but the opening paragraph of the two Archbishops' foreword is representative. Those responsible for the Report were invited

to recommend ways of *strengthening the effectiveness* of the Church's *central policy making and resource direction machinery*. They were encouraged not to shrink from *radical ideas*. Their report is forthright about the *challenges* which face the Church; *much needs to be changed* if the Church is to be *effective* as one body (italics in the original).[24]

---

[19] The very suggestion of this possibility was denounced as 'blasphemy' by Bishop Turnbull. See his letter in the February 1996 issue of *New Directions* in reply to R. H. Roberts, 'Towards an Executive Church?', *New Directions*, January 1996.

[20] See chapter 3 above.

[21] *Working as One Body*, p. xii.

[22] *Ibid.*, pp. 4ff.

[23] *Ibid.*, pp. 2–4.

[24] *Ibid.*, p. ix.

The foreword continues in the same vein as the Archbishops write of creating a 'new mechanism', 'securing coherence' and 'mov(ing) purposefully to implement' in order to avoid 'prolonged uncertainty'. This discourse employed is of course that of the new managerial *classe dirigiste*, and this may have its place – even in a church. There is an odd juxtaposition of a mechanical, functional language and the organic, theologically derived imagery of the 'body'. The *topoi* of 'modern', Taylorian and human resources management co-exist with residual theological conceptions in what is a typical modern/postmodern way. Corresponding discursive sutures are evident at important points throughout *Working as One Body*; the text has the marks of skilful surgery directed towards the creation of a single-headed creature from diverse and contrasting raw materials. The Turnbull Report is thus representative of a distinctive persuasive genre, and it incorporates in an all too obvious way fragments of discourse welded together by executive and managerial intent. In a strange way, *Working as One Body* is a classic example of conservative postmodern thinking.[25]

The theological justification of *comprehensive leadership* and *trusting followership* is, however, at every point underpinned by 'organisational theory'. In succeeding paragraphs the discourse of theology in 'polity',[26] God's relational and personal love for humanity,[27] the Trinitarian life of the church,[28] and the identification of the 'aims and tasks of the Church of England' with those of the 'one, holy, catholic and apostolic Church'[29] flow together without interruption. In paragraph 1.8 the reader is suddenly informed that the church 'must be a learning community'.[30] Here once again a key term of contemporary management theory is introduced, drawn from that of the 'learning organisation'; it is casually slipped in to be followed immediately with an interesting suture between the two levels of discourse. We are informed that 'the *aims* of the Church of England have already been given to it, it has continually to formulate and reformulate its specific *objectives* with a view to their being consistent with these fundamental aims and also being appropriate and relevant

---

[25] This is in the sense employed by David Harvey where he excoriates 'the condition of postmodernity' as embodying serious and comprehensive political intent in *The Condition of Postmodernity: An Enquiry into the Origins of Cultural Change* (Oxford: Blackwell, 1989). I likewise regard John Milbank's *Theology and Social Theory* as conservative postmodern theology, despite its alleged socialist radicality. See chapter 7 below.

[26] *Working as One Body*, paragraph 1.4.

[27] *Ibid.*, paragraph 1.5.

[28] *Ibid.*, paragraph 1.6.

[29] *Ibid.*, paragraph 1.7.

[30] *Ibib.*, p. 3.

to the conditions of our land in our time (italics in the original)'.[31] Here, however, much is at stake: *who* is to define these aims and objectives? Is this latter distinction an adequate basis for the connection between (as it were) the transcendental given and the imminent pragmatics? The power to define the terms of the discussion is transcendentally encoded in the argument: the reader's duty is that of receiver, and not partner – never mind questioner. This is a 'theology from above' that precludes and excludes movement or initiative from below, as did the ecclesiology reviewed in the preceding chapter.

The integral logic of the remainder of paragraph 1.9 is clear: there is a stable 'given' which can be more or less efficiently transmitted in each generation. In a sense one might say (in retrojecting the managerial realism back into the theological preamble) that the warehouses are full of the Gospel: the problem is simply to shift the product in the most efficient and economically accountable way possible. Thus again another suture is apparent at the end of this section, where

To speak of the Church's 'direction' and 'effectiveness' (as do the terms of our enquiry) is to imply a grasp upon the mission which God has given to the Church; but at the same time it demands a critical and imaginative insight into current failures and future possibilities. What is asked of the Church at this particular moment is a combination of fidelity and expertise of various kinds in the formulation of its current objectives.[32]

In effect, the last sentence means that a given *aim* (the Gospel) requires new means for the operationalisation of *objectives* (the delivery of that Gospel). We have here to pose the question: does this juxtaposition really reflect in an adequate way what Christianity and the church should really be about today? The reality of the 'aim' underlying the text is that of an uncritically routinised charisma embodied in institutional practices legitimised by reference to 'tradition'.[33] The task spelt out in 'objectives' is the pursuit of institutional and organisational efficiency, rather than active prophetic interpretation, or indeed the less spectacular but wholly central task of effective pastoral care, both of which require a degree of professional relative autonomy and the exercise of much discernment. Moreover, it could well be argued, were this analysis to have begun either with a theology of the laity (of the kind implied by that strand

[31] *Ibid.*
[32] *Ibid.*, p. 4.
[33] Max Weber's classic discussion of this conception is to be found in *Economy and Society: An Outline of Interpretative Sociology* (2 vols., Berkeley, CA: University of California Press, 1979), vol. I, ch. 4, paragraphs iv and v.

of the thought of Second Vatican Council as the 'people of God' found in the Dogmatic Constitution on the Church, *Lumen Gentium*[34]) or in an exploration of the ministerial remit at parish level, then the technique of presentation adopted in *Working as One Body* might well appear even more implausible to the hard-worked practitioner.

As the distinguished historian Edward Norman has argued,[35] the episcopal elite in the Church of England has almost invariably tended to absorb and transmit the dominant ideology of its peer group. This is now largely composed of the senior executives and managers who increasingly control all significant sectors of society. Thus a pillar-box church is fed with ruling ideas from the top which percolate downwards in constant tension with the reality experienced at the base. What is new about the present situation of the Church of England is that the ideology of managerialism being appropriated by its elite is infinitely more subtle and invasive than any of its clumsier predecessors.[36] Indeed, the outstanding success of managerialism as an ideology is that it fights off all comers with the charge that any resistance to the prerogatives and practices of managerial control is simply the expression of vested interests and an unwillingness to be efficient and accountable and to be 'flexible' and open to change. The implementation of the latter, so-called 'accountability', almost invariably implies outright *control*. Whilst the basic rationale of the Turnbull Report expressed in terms of the need to gain efficiency may seem reasonable enough, in reality, the importation into the church of what James Burnham called the 'managerial revolution' involves the ecclesial deployment of the sophisticated means of enforcement now characteristic of the creeping sovietisation of a managed, rather than an actively democratic, Britain.

Taken as a whole, the proposals in the Turnbull Report (once properly supplemented with appropriate managerial control measures) will ensure not merely that effective social hermeneutics may gradually cease (as informed social criticism has tended to be eliminated in the universities), but that they also clear the way for the Church of England to

---

[34] Austin Flannery (ed.), 'Dogmatic Constitution on the Church, *Lumen Gentium*', in *Vatican Council II: The Conciliar and Post Conciliar Documents* (Leominster: Fowler Wright, 1975), pp. 350–426.

[35] Edward Norman, *Church and Society in England 1770–1970: A Historical Study* (Oxford: Oxford University Press, 1976).

[36] This, however, requires qualification. Stewart Clegg recalls that E. P. Thompson cites Andrew Ure (1835), who maintained in *The Philosophy of Manufactures* that human beings had to be trained to 'renounce their desultory habits of work, and to identify themselves with the unvarying regularity of the complex automation', *The Making of the English Working Class* (Harmondsworth: Penguin, 1968), p. 395.

become an efficient, product-led service organisation meeting the pre-defined spiritual requirements of the residually Christian part of the English population with a regularised and marketable 'Gospel'. Thus once more, in the words of Michael Novak, the 'empty shrine' of our particular local form of capitalism will thereby be filled.[37] Does, however, such a limited task correspond with human needs? Is this where the task of the church should begin – and end? Aware of the outline plans for managerial control implied in *Working as One Body*, we next need to acquaint ourselves with the fine-grained management proposals spelt out with exemplary clarity in Burke and Gill's supplementary, *Strategic Church Leadership*.

CULTURES OF PERFORMATIVITY AND APPRAISAL: *EPISCOPE* AND THE ECCLESIAL *PANOPTICON*

In their short but far-reaching book, Professors Robin Gill (Adviser to the Archbishop of Canterbury) and Derek Burke (former senior naval officer and Vice-Chancellor of the University of East Anglia at Norwich) have moved the vision of the managerial integration of the Church of England a step beyond the executive restructuring proposed by the Turnbull Report towards the implementation of a system of Quality Audit and performance appraisal. Gill and Burke argue that:

If church leaders had looked to the modern university or business worlds during the same period of time, they might have seen how finances and strategy could have been managed more effectively and accountably in a similar period of change (italics in the original).[38]

Taking the recent experience of British universities as a worthy example, and the Book of Acts as their biblical mandate, Gill and Burke propose the revitalisation of the church through 'SWOT analysis' of the strengths, weaknesses, opportunities and threats facing the organisation, the organisationally 'owned' mission statement and correlative goal setting, strict quantificatory accountability, a comprehensive Audit culture, and so on. The proposed mission statement for the churches

[37] For an account of Novak's conception of the (to my mind) ambiguous individual empowering role of Judaism and (Roman Catholic) Christianity in a 'democratic capitalist' world order, see R. H. Roberts, 'The Spirit of Democratic Capitalism: A Critique of Michael Novak', in Jon Davies and David Green (eds.), *God and the Marketplace: Essays on the Morality of Wealth Creation* (London: Institute of Economic Affairs, 1993), pp. 64–81.
[38] Gill and Burke, *Strategic Leadership*, pp. 12–13.

(which closely follows the requirements of the Turnbull Report) runs as follows:

The central aim of the churches in modern Britain is the communal worship of God in Christ through the Spirit, teaching and moulding as many lives and structures as deeply as possible through this worship (italics in the original).[39]

Correspondingly, resource allocation should always be: 'absolutely in line with agreed priorities; as fair as possible; open and accountable: there must be no secret pockets'. The enactment of this aim requires the church to adapt itself to a new mode of organisation. Thus Gill and Burke ask:

What does strategic leadership mean? Quite simply it means taking the change that affects us all, and channelling it so that it takes us in the way we want to go.[40]

Whilst I do not wish in any way to deny the need for *appropriate* forms of accountability, such ecclesial responsibility should be the result of properly informed negotiation and fully compatible with the inherent character of the task in hand. The all too obvious inclusions implied by the 'us' and 'we' in the above statement require careful interrogation. Gill and Burke's assumption that all parties are automatically included in and endorse the process of managerialisation through their use of an imputed and transgressive 'we' is questionable; they continue with the assertion that,

The changing world calls for a new style of leadership – but one that is rather closer to that of Acts than is the consensus style of leadership which still pre-dominates in British churches.[41]

In classic Taylorian terms, Gill and Burke have handed over imagination, thought, agency and control to management (in their case the bishops).

On this new understanding, church leaders would be free to provide and foster vision – theological, moral and strategic – and to enable this vision to be realised by the whole church. It would be their job as strategic leaders to think, plan prayerfully, to coax, to monitor, to help others to learn, and, above all, to identify and enhance opportunities for qualitative and quantitative growth and to be firm about subsidised projects that do not promote growth. Only by carefully

---

[39] *Ibid.*, p. 48.
[40] *Ibid.*, pp. 12–13.
[41] *Ibid.*, p. 74.

monitoring outcomes, both quantitatively and qualitatively, would they be able to do their job effectively.[42]

According to Gill and Burke, it is necessary to move from consensus leadership and incremental budgeting to a strategic, vision-led and 'owned' through 'learning' style. In justification they cite (very selectively) the management guru Peter Senge:

> The new view of leadership in learning organisations centers on a subtler and more important task. In a learning organisation, leaders are designers, stewards and teachers. They are responsible for building organisations where people continually expand their capabilities to understand complexity, clarify vision, and improve shared mental models – that is they are responsible for learning.[43]

Following this line of argument, the Church of England is to move from consensus leadership and incremental budgeting to a strategic, vision-led and 'owned' style. As Peter Drucker has recently argued, it is only now that the full application of Taylor's ideas to intellectual production has become possible. Gill and Burke have shown that there are yet further opportunities for the implementation of the Taylorian vision in both organised religion and the spiritual life. The introduction of the customer–provider principle in churches, as in the universities, implies the elimination of the 'thoughtless use of subsidy',[44] and the setting in place of the 'owned', enforceable mission statement which provides the framework for the introduction of a quantifiable Audit culture.[45] Such 'Total Quality Management' is, we might do well to recall, both a total and a totalising system: it requires the willed conformity of mind – and the soul. Simple mechanical subordination in a command–obedience relationship is inadequate: 'ownership' implies the assumption on the part of the employee of the identity required by the organisation and as it is transmitted through the manager. Thus, Gill and Burke advance their agenda for reform:

> However difficult it is to write clear, unambiguous criteria for such professionals as university lecturers or parish priests, it does need to be done.[46]

[42] *Ibid.*, p. 86.

[43] Peter Senge, *The Fifth Discipline: The Art and Practice of the Learning Organization* (London: Random House Business Books, 1990), p. 340. Senge's use of the term 'metanoia' as the centrepiece of his exposition of the 'learning organisation' has a fatal attraction for the power-hungry ecclesiastic looking to managerialism for the 'real power' of the Gospel and for the legitimation of personal identity.

[44] Gill and Burke, *Strategic Leadership*, p. 17.

[45] *Ibid.*, p. 43.

[46] *Ibid.*, p. 84.

Let us summarise. In effect, the ecclesial 'Quality' circle is to be closed with the introduction of the equivalent of 'benchmarking': the priest (like the nurse, secondary school teacher, university lecturer, telesales-person – and the staff at a McDonalds outlet) is to be locked into the performance and quantitative measurement of a grid of pre-determined, benchmarked outcomes. The authors concede that for those who identify too closely with their prior roles and identities as priests (or, as we have seen, for many other de-professionalised operatives), the process of man-aging the change that they claim 'we all want' may have catastrophic outcomes. The future does not, however, lie with such inflexible em-ployees. At this juncture biblical authority may be invoked. The Book of Acts provides us with exemplary parameters of the degree of resolution that genuinely effective management may require; hence the instructive character of the example of Ananias and Sapphira, who are both struck down dead for the concealment of fraud.[47]

Can the church – can any form of Christianity – be said to lose any-thing once its 'Quality' is improved in these terms, which imitate the 'reforms' and 'modernisation' that many parishioners have themselves undergone in their work lives? What place, if any, should be left for spon-taneity and creativity 'from below'? Can the latter no longer be risked in a low- or no-trust society – or church? Should this fusion of theol-ogy, management theory, and so-called 'good practice' be understood as an authentic manifestion of the love of God in the world, or is it fundamentally flawed?

MANAGERIAL MODERNITY AND THE CLOSURE OF TRANSCENDENCE

At this juncture it is salutary for us, indeed for all those encaged in man-agerialised systems to recall the words of Jean-François Lyotard from his classic account of the 'postmodern condition':

Technology is therefore a game pertaining not to the true, the just, or the beautiful, etc., but to efficiency: a technical 'move' is 'good' when it does better and/or expends less energy than another.[48]

This is how legitimation by power takes shape. Power is not only good performativity, but also verification and good verdicts. It legitimates science

---

[47] Acts 5, 1–11.
[48] J.-Fr. Lyotard, *The Postmodern Condition*, in L. Cahoone (ed.), *From Modernism to Postmodernism: An Anthology* (Oxford: Blackwell, 1996), p. 495.

and the law on the basis of their efficiency, and legitimates this efficiency on the basis of science and law. It is self-legitimating, in the same way a system organized around performance maximisation seems to be.[49]

Whenever efficiency (that is, obtaining the desired effect) is derived from a 'Say or do this, or else you'll never speak again', then we are in the realm of terror, and the social bond is destroyed.[50]

Should societal conformity around the principles of managerialism (however much represented as secondary to mission goals) be extended into the church understood as the context in which radical *Otherness* may supposedly be encountered?

Given Lyotard's account of a postmodern condition ruled by the 'performative absolute', might it not be the case that instead of exploring and learning, and becoming critically and empathetically responsive to societal and cultural demands encountered in the culture of any given ministry that may be unpredicted, indeed unpredictable, a ministerial and priestly elite may simply adopt the identity and execute the role ascribed to it by managerial policy, and thereby accrue approval points on the relevant performance indicator ratings? In other words, once executive management becomes (as it all too easily may do) an end in itself, then it is easy and profitable for all institutional operatives simply to follow directives and relapse into rule-governed behaviour rather than engage in demanding, critically reflexive action for which they may well be penalised.[51]

From looking back over previous chapters, it becomes apparent that given the many important changes in the relation between the public and private spheres brought about since Mrs Thatcher's accession to power in 1979, any individual active in the context of organisational life now faces the likelihood of the repeated reconfiguration of his or her personal identity. The operationalisation of the managerial revolution in contemporary Britain has proceeded with scant regard for the inherent integrity of the different spheres of activity that together make up a humane civil society. Seen in terms of the modern/postmodern debate, the modernity which we now inhabit no longer offers even the interstitial 'breaks' (*Brüche*) in social reality sought by artistic and philosophical modernism. Genuinely open sacred space and time are in short supply.

[49] *Ibid.*, p. 498.
[50] *Ibid.*
[51] There is much to be learnt by the theologian and priest from Pierre Bourdieu's concept of 'critical reflexivity': see Pierre Bourdieu and Loïc J. D. Wacquant, *An Invitation to Reflexive Sociology* (Chicago: University of Chicago Press, 1992).

If main-line religion, and the established church, ceases to offer and benignly to interpret such space and time as opportunity for encounter freed in certain respects from universal performance appraisal and the seamlessness of managerial and commodified capitalism, then it is little wonder that the 'sacred' is lost, or can be said to 'migrate'.

Whereas Protestant and then Roman Catholic theologies struggled with the vicissitudes of Kantian limits upon knowledge and with historicism as an infinite but ultimately closed system of causal connections, their debate with the sociologically constituted construals of modernity has been, as will be argued in the following chapter, less than wholly satisfactory. In the setting of the modernity outlined above, religion may offer one of the few areas of remaining societal space possessing a continuing counter-cultural potential, even, under certain circumstances, because of the archaic character of much main-line religious practice; yet nostalgic regression is not the answer. On the other hand, the growing salience of religious or quasi-religious factors is also apparent in what George Steiner once called the 'after-life' of religion. In overall terms we live in an era in which there is a complex and ambiguous 'return' or 'resurgence' of religion. As one example, Lynn Revel writes, in a way strongly reminiscent of Lyotard, that

The self may have become God, but it is an isolated and lonely self, limited by the fragmentary nature of its own parochial experiences and dreams, and impoverished by its inability to communicate with any other soul than its own.[52]

Correspondingly, Paul Heelas has developed the ideas of the 'sacralisation of the self' and of 'self-religion' as core concepts of so-called New Age practices. The seeming elimination of all grounds of spiritual opportunity other than those present in the manipulation and expansion of the self would appear to be evidence of a claustrophobic closure of opportunities for liminality and transcendent possibility. Rather in the way the English Enclosure Acts of the sixteenth to the eighteenth centuries removed the use of common land from the lives of the propertyless, so rational modernisation encroaches upon residual zones of human renewal. The managerialisation of society along the lines described earlier removes and reallocates agency, and regularises contextual cultures; the parallel process in main-line religious activity may contribute to the final consolidation of the process of the exclusion of anything

---

[52] Lynn Revel, 'The Return of the Sacred', in Suke Wolton (ed.), *Marxism, Mysticism and Modern Theory* (London: Macmillan, 1996), pp. 111–31. For a full account see Paul Heelas, *The New Age Movement: The Celebration of the Self and the Sacralization of Modernity* (Oxford: Blackwell, 1996).

whatsoever that does not attain its objectivity through performance and its appraisal. There, in reality, is a 'performative absolute' that makes ultimate demands.

Yet, as has also become apparent in earlier chapters, managerial modernity is both regulatory and 'hard' as well as 'empowering' and 'soft'. Managerialism commands both aspects; like the combination of brutal and sympathetic interrogators in a police investigation, it is all the more effective when both dimensions are deployed as interactive partners. In other words, fully developed post-Fordist management is not simply the replication of Max Weber's famous 'steel-hard casing' or 'jacket' (*ein stahlhartes Gehäuse*, freely translated by Talcott Parsons as the famous 'iron cage'[53]) understood as something outside the agent. It is more like a garment that fits so closely that we may learn to fail to notice its existence as we find that it has become the skin-tight armour that accompanies and dictates all our flexions. When such a body stocking becomes skin, then to remove it is to be skinned alive. The experience of the disintegration of an identity which is truly and self-sacrificially 'owned' can be excruciating. The truly postmodern self should wear its identities lightly; but the historic task of religion is to secure deep change, *metanoia*. For those who have not yet learnt to invest and divest themselves of identities with rapidity and apparent ease life can indeed be difficult. Here the real struggle is over the ownership and control of the means of production of human identity itself. Consequently, in my view, battles may have to be fought against the unconstrained organisation and societal abuse of such identities as are won by hard-pressed individuals: in what sense, yet again, do we have any 'right' to an identity?

THE CARE OF 'SOUL(S)' IN THE SPIRITUAL MARKET-PLACE

The Christian church originated in pre-modernity; its energies have been sapped with a continuing and abortive struggle in and with modernity; it now exists in an era characterised by the 'postmodern condition'. The situation may be summarised as follows on the assumption that each of the concepts employed to depict the modernity–postmodernity matrix is subject to constant debate and interrogation. We risk simplification. Thus in *pre-modernity* religion and society existed in relative

---

[53] See Max Weber, *Die protestantische Ethik und der 'Geist' des Kapitalismus* (Hain Hanstein: Athenaum, 1993), p. 153. It is interesting to note, not least when we are aware of Novak's spirituality of capitalism, that a permissible translation of *Gehäuse* is 'shrine'.

harmony, and despite the coercive aspects of patently pre-modern cultures this state is often romanticised as a pre-lapsarian 'golden age'[54]; in *modernity* religion and instrumental reason exist in a state of deadly conflict and society underwent and continues to undergo secularisation, and new religious movements (for example the Unification Church, Sokka Gakkai, the House Church movement) emerge; in *postmodernity* 'religion' is displaced, migrates and may transmute into 'quasi-religion' (for example in this chapter Michael Jackson, or Amway[55]) and diverse religiosities and innovative spiritualities (New Age, so-called Self Religions, and (Neo-)Paganism[56]).

In the contemporary world, and not least in Britain, pre-modernity, modernity and postmodernity presented as ideal typological characterisations or interpretative categories co-exist uneasily as 'moments' in an unresolved dialectical interplay, often structured in accordance with the distribution of economic and cultural capital in systems of social stratification (i.e. class structure) and clustered around resurgent national aspirations. In an ever-expanding market society driven forward by the rhetoric of 'choice', and a globalising world order reflecting the power of multinational capitalism, cultural capital is mediated for present purposes through two main channels: the market and the educational system. The market informs postmodernity: humanity as a whole is differentiated and targeted transnationally with cultural artifacts through fashion and styles, cultural identities embodied in cult personalities, and commodified sex and violence mediated through film, television, video and the Internet, all distributed according to researched and manipulated predilections and desires. The education system has become, as argued earlier, the 'knowledge industry' operating in a largely closed and manipulated 'market'. This system is dedicated to meeting centrally directed production quotas of bearers of 'packaged knowledge' which has a mandatory content assured through centrally defined national curricula and benchmarking, and enforced through models of modern line-management that have, often enough, migrated from failure in British manufacturing industry. This mode of production ironically

---

54 Examples are Pagan Monica Sjöö and Barbara Mohr's idealised pre-metallic matriarchy and the Roman Catholic theologian Yve Congar's depiction of 'Christendom' discussed in chapters 8 and 10 below, respectively.

55 See David G. Bromley, 'Quasi-Religious Corporation: A new Integration of Religion and Capitalism', in R. H. Roberts (ed.), *Religion and the Transformations of Capitalism: Comparative Approaches* (London: Routledge, 1995), ch. 7.

56 See Arthur L. Greil and Thomas Robbins (eds.), *Between Sacred and Profane: Research and Theory in Quasi-Religions* (Greenwich, CI: JAI Press, 1994).

bears a strong similarity to conditions in democratic centralist pre-1989 eastern Europe.

In the context outlined above, the established Christian churches and main-line religions stand between 'lost, defeated tradition' (Alasdair MacIntyre) and what is for them an increasingly alien and alienated human and social reality. Yet the established churches and main-line religions have not yet been fully integrated into the new market order, despite the energetic and earnest efforts of some to achieve that reviewed earlier in this chapter. Can main-line religions grounded in traditions in de-traditionalised societies and cultures *both* relate to their theological identities *and* meet human needs? This, in the terms employed by the German Reformed theologian Jürgen Moltmann, is yet one more example of the identity/relevance dilemma,[57] considerably complicated by the fact that twenty years ago the boundaries between the religious and the secular in western European cultures seemed more obvious than they now are. This new complexity in the increasingly marketised field of culture and identity-renewal may be approached from different directions; for, as seen earlier, managers may appropriate spirituality and instrumentalise quasi-religion in their unceasing quest for 'transformation' and total performance, and bishops may also, but conversely, find in management the 'real power' that facilitates the achievement of their objectives. A parallel mutual convergence is also apparent in the market-place itself, to which we now turn our attention.

My initial thoughts on this matter were provoked by a report in *The Independent* on the General Assembly of 1991. In this article declining membership of the Church of Scotland was noted,[58] but more serious perhaps was the fact that a poll in *Scotland on Sunday* had revealed 'an alarming lack of confidence among many ministers and elders, portraying the church as an ailing institution whose days were numbered'. I did not then (or now) propose to enter the dangerous area of demographic prediction on the basis of age profiles, or to tackle the more specific question why certain groups did or did not respond to the church. At the time my thoughts began to turn to what the retiring moderator, the Very Revd Robert Davidson, spoke of as 'an identity crisis' which centred 'around what we mean by claiming to be a national church' and the

---

[57] Jürgen Moltmann, *The Crucified God: The Cross of Christ as Foundation and Criticism of Christian Theology* (London: SCM, 1974), ch. 1.

[58] Diana Hinds, Religious Affairs Correspondent, 'Church's Gloom over its Dwindling Congregations', *The Independent*, 23 May 1991.

kind of relationship worshipping communities ought to have to the life
of the community as a whole.

As it then happened, I wrote to *The Independent* and the letter was published. It included the following remarks, some of which, with hindsight,
I now regard as imprudent:

> During the Thatcher era, and especially since the revolutionary events of
> late 1989 in Central Europe, we have gradually become more aware of the
> role of the market as an enabling means of energising and enabling human
> life, both individual and collective. However, the national churches of both
> Scotland and England display many of the sclerotic symptoms that mark
> nationalised industries: and an all embracing rhetoric of monopoly and ser-
> vice to the whole nation disguises an actual failure to discern the market
> and to prepare goods and services required by the customer in, or outwith
> the pew.
>
> Ministers and religious professionals (like academics) have much to learn from
> some experience of the active democracy of the marketplace. Theologians and
> their students will have to devise means of honouring ancestral traditions whilst
> at the same time thinking and enacting them through the dominant reality of
> our age, the market.
>
> Here, like Abraham, the church and theologians will have to set out as risk-
> takers in covenental faith on the path that leads to a truly enterprising religion.
> Moreover, we might do well not to forget that St Paul himself chose to launch
> Christianity in the marketplace of Athens (Acts 17:17).

Much water has passed under the bridge since May 1991, and whilst
some aspects of my views have changed radically, others remain the
same. I still consider that use, albeit limited, should be made of the market metaphor in order to understand what the conditions might be for
the emergence of an 'enterprising church' which might be better able
to understand its societal location and the cultural strategies open to
it in the global market-place of the modern/postmodern condition.
What I then sought to demonstrate is that the 'migration of the sacred' and its reconstitution in various forms of quasi-religion can be
extremely radical. The human desire for experience that transgresses
boundaries of a banal modernity is far from dead: mythic narrative,
ritual, forms of corporate worship and ecstatic self-prostration take
place, not least within the globalised popular 'culture industry'. The
phenomenon is best understood by reference to the refunctioning of
religious artifacts. A very remarkable and prominent example of the
latter was the performer Michael Jackson's Bucharest concert of 1990
and the album *Dangerous* which, taken together, presented in a peculiarly

extreme form the characteristics of quasi-religiosity in the 'after-life' of religion.[59]

The context and content of this performance are significant: Romania had just liberated itself from the corrupt communist regime of the Ceauşescus, and the event amounted to a celebration of liberation in which a global performer combined narrative fragments in an extended moment of intertextual globalised fusion. This remarkable Bucharest concert was underpinned by a redeemer myth embodied in the performer and entextualised in the lyrics of 'Heal the World'. At the beginning of the performance Jackson made a sudden mysterious entry into the historical order with the technological bravura of a contemporary *deus ex machina*; his renowned physical ability enacted the 'miracle' of the famous 'moon-walk', a veritable 'walking on water'; as redeemer figure he repeatedly worked through the stages of collapse, death, resurrection, entombment and ascension, guarded by protective technological 'angels'; he performed a 'dance of death' sequence with skeletal figures, and so on. As a performance, the totality was a corporate quasi-religious act involving mass local observance and a corporate identity; it enjoyed fully global participation and showed every sign of being a carefully crafted ritual involving ecstasis and mass hysteria. All in all, the narrative may be read as an incarnational juxtaposition of the frail (yet extraordinary) flesh of Michael Jackson and the 'divinity' provided by technological universalisation and mediatic 'transfiguration'. Jackson's subsequent collapse and decline as a public performer need not here concern us. What is important to note is that such an event as the Bucharest concert was constructed around the blatant capture of a whole conceptual vocabulary of images and artifacts taken indiscriminately from a range of religious sources and their refunctioning in a new (yet simultaneously archaic) mythic narrative in which Jackson to all intents and purposes became an *avatar* of Dancing Shiva.

The ritual event was focused around a self-realising, globalised and quasi-religious artifact: the person and work of Michael Jackson. It is significant to note the self-modifications and adaptations which turned an individual entertainer limited to a niche in the culture industry into a supremely successful global cultural commodity. Thus careful analysis of Jackson's performance *persona* indicates that he combined the following

---

[59] Madonna would have provided an alternative, but the character of the audience for which the original lecture was prepared made this inadvisable. Here the contents of Michael Jackson's performance are described at some length; at the lecture some eight minutes of edited video were played together with overheads.

carefully crafted attributes. For example, in a way confirmative of Anthony Giddens' depiction of the purely residual and voluntaristic character of gender difference in advanced modernity, Jackson was thoroughly androgenous, with the consequence that in a gender-polarised world he might appeal equally to both sexes and not alienate, *a priori*, a large market sector. Moreover, Jackson's performance exemplified explicit physical sexuality, ambiguous skin colour status (the theme 'black on white' together with possible skin colour treatment maximised cross-racial appeal), extraordinary control of the body in a highly body-conscious culture, personal identification with and embodiment of a quasi-salvific message, and the most advanced technology deployed as the means of transgressing human bounds. Assessed from an economic standpoint, Jackson exemplified the total maximisation of the *persona*, the personality and all physical, mental and affective resources. In market terms the positive was expanded and the negative modified or eliminated. All in all, this amounted to a form of quasi-religion, the extraordinary, albeit relatively short-lived, global success of which indicated that human needs are being tapped and indeed exploited, however perversely. It was perhaps only Pope John Paul II or the Ayatollah Khomeini in their prime who could rival such a remarkable functionalisation of affective mass religiosity in the domain of main-line religion.

The paradox consists in this: established churches in western Europe often find themselves to be victims of their own conceptions of modernity with which they are locked in a fruitless struggle, and, correspondingly, they frequently believe that 'religion' is dying or dead; yet, in reality, religion and forms of religiosity, especially spiritualities, are very much alive and answering human needs in a global and local market-place from which many established churches have explicitly or tacitly retreated. Bodies like the national Churches of England and Scotland exhibit the following features. They tend to have congregations with age structures which indicate that demographic processes will involve inevitable and increasingly spectacular decline. They service the requirements of social constituencies which are not, generally speaking, representative of the population at large and from which, given present socio-political trends, they may well be increasingly alienated. They may be ill-equipped to confront progressive differentiation of culture away from literary or literate forms of mediation and reception readily adaptable to the ancestral verbalised 'Word of God' mode of communication especially characteristic of Scottish culture. Often enough there has been general paralysis at the centre owing to fear of internal division and a failure to understand and respond to external socio-demographic factors. As we have seen above, one way out of this situation is to managerialise the church organisation and marketise the practice and message of any given ecclesial body. The cultural inheritances of Scotland and England differ markedly. North of the border, there is what the theologian Ian Bradley has called militant 'presbyterian atheism' and often enough a powerfully hostile reaction to a tradition which involved forms of affective, cultural and sexual negation now out of touch and dissonant with a contemporary mass culture, which prioritises feeling over the intellect. In England, what the sociologist Grace Davie has sagely described as 'believing without belonging' seems to be characteristic of post-formal religiosity. Within both churches there tends to be the idea and the reality of religious culture understood as patriarchal and dynastically transmitted tradition which prevents the emergence of the critical reflexivity essential to the comprehension of, and a creative response to, present circumstances.

There are a number of consequences and strategies which emerge in the situation outlined above. First, there is the traditionalist religious response, which remains locked in a battle with a reluctant modernity in order to recover the past, a strategy which finds fulfilment in qualified regression.[60] Second, there is the residual response, which involves little effective contact with the latent human and religious needs of the general population, except, that is, on the level of residual rites of passage and a corresponding (and relatively cheap and easy to operate) displacement of the universality of the Gospel onto the rhetorical level of 'serving the nation', largely on the level of political intervention. Third, as regards the religious 'market', there would seem to have been limited attempts to engage in fundamental appraisal of a declining demand, to review a problematic 'product', and to revivify a labour force largely trained in 'care and maintenance' of plant, rather than in the dangerous and creative skills of religious 'enterprise'.

In short, established churches are trapped between institutionalised tradition and the market-place of human needs and wants in an increasingly de-traditionalised society. This is not, however, a neutral environment. As we have argued above with regard to Michael Jackson's self-deployment, vast resources are poured into a globalised culture and entertainment industry which refunctions anything and everything which might possibly undergo profitable reproduction, up to and including religion and theological ideas and motifs. This flexibility is without bounds; contemporary expectations are such that narrative structure

---

[60] This corresponds with 'fundamentalism'. Martin Riesebrodt has provided one of the most convincing accounts of radical conservative religion in *Pious Passion: The Emergence of Modern Fundamentalism in the United States and Iran* (Berkeley: University of California Press, 1993).

is shattered repeatedly and a plethora of cultural artifacts and fragments of cultural identity can be juxtaposed with virtuoso intensity. A hard technological core, information transfer, virtual reality and cyberspace create worlds which exist on the basis of expanding electronic and informational resources. They provide the 'real' (in virtual terms) in forms of immanent quasi-transcendence, in which the analogues of omnipresence, multiple location, omniscience and forms of omnipotence appear as practical possibilities limited only by the imagination of the empowered practitioner.

In such an era, any organisation which purports to bear a message or reality of universal import cannot afford to ignore the marketisation and commodification of the world order. Any such body that does so is by a sociological and cultural necessity locked into a social niche market, let us say retired people who still live with a sense of metanarrative – the Christian story, albeit heavily secularised. To go beyond strategic retreat (the equivalent of the gradual abandonment of manufacturing industry), to engage once more in the real world of religious need, would require a religious and theological revolution. As we have seen earlier in this chapter, in England the executive and managerial strategy has been implemented which adds up, together with such schemes as the Alpha Programme of marketised evangelism, to what might be called the Tupperware Party solution to the threat of secularisation. In the early and mid 1990s in Scotland there seemed to be but few signs of re-engagement with the societal market-place. Such figures as Professor William Storrar, now of the University of Edinburgh, have, however, developed the religious correlate to cultural nationalism in the setting of devolution.[61] Yet, strangely, Storrar's typology of Scottish Christianity (and with it Scotland's religion) begins with medieval Catholic Scotland, and for unstated reasons it pointedly ignores the early Celtic Christian and non- or pre-Christian heritage, which are, paradoxically, contemporary forms of religiosity resonant with the contemporary conditions of the spiritual market-place. Others in Scotland, notably, for example, the environmental activist Alastair McIntosh, have pioneered a radical revival of Celtic spirituality in the setting of 'human ecology'.[62]

When this situation is observed from the standpoint of the individual committed to an ecclesial tradition, a responsible approach for a postmodern church would involve a *principled eclecticism*. This involves

[61] See William Storrar, *Scottish Identity: A Christian Vision* (Edinburgh: Hansel Press, 1990).
[62] See Alastair McIntosh's bardic and shamanic epic the *Gall-Gael*, reproduced with commentary in Pearson, Roberts and Samuel, *Nature Religion Today*, ch. 14.

a balance between authority and freedom, and between contextual framework and interpretation; but it is difficult if not impossible to conceive of established Christianity making any impression upon the national and global market of cultural capital and human identities unless it is prepared to mobilise *all* its resources. This means looking once more at the totality, and training well-grounded religious professionals to look upon the whole inheritance as a potential resource: the tradition as a whole in its variety may well offer enormous possibilities, symbolic, mythic, narrative, experiential, ethical and, not least, theological.[63] Such contexts present considerable risks if, as is the case in England, an established church simply 'buys in' and instrumentalises managerialised and thus transmuted religious and theological conceptions from quasi-commercial sources rather than nurturing and developing its genuine indigenous managerial sources. There notions of 'vision', 'mission' and the 'mission statement' are obvious and problematic examples of 'out-sourcing' the means of renewal. Fundamental strategies of religious and thus societal renewal will not be found through parasitic dependence upon expertise from outside agencies, drawn in on analogy with the management consultant.

As will be argued in ensuing chapters, the modern/postmodern matrix presents Christian churches, main-line religions, innovative spiritualities and indeed all human beings of goodwill with immense challenges which, if they are to be met, will require ruthless self-appraisal, a com-mitment to reflexive socio-cultural analysis and a willingness to venture out in a newly defined enterprise of faith. Within the setting of a religious field which is undergoing radical change and recomposition there is a need for the kind of contextually appropriate 'meta-theory' which David Harvey has rightly called for in terms of politics. Without such principled effort, all those who remain engaged with the religious dimension will be at the mercy of forces over which they have no control and, even worse, they will be in acute danger of sprinkling the holy water of religious legit-imation upon alien powers of social construction they may have wilfully failed to comprehend.

CONCLUSION: PRIMAL RELIGION AND THE ECOLOGIES
OF THE SPIRIT

It has been my contention in this chapter that an uncritical assimilation of managerialism may resolve after a fashion ancestral problems of the

---

[63] I am now less sanguine about such idealised possibilities. See chapter 11 below.

loss of theological identity by church leaders under conditions of secularisation by the restoration of a form of performative absolutism, for
'Managers have the right to manage' – and others have a duty to follow and to 'perform'. Yet, in an engaging historical irony, as democratic
centralism moved westwards from the former Soviet Bloc to inform
the invasive capitalism of a globalised world system, so the managerial revolution continues to displace truth-seeking with naked concern
with performance within an ever-extending 'surveillance society'. This
loss of rootedness cannot simply (as Burke and Gill would have it) be
replaced by the allocation of management attention to the 'qualitative'
dimension of quantitative performance appraisal. As argued earlier, the
problems run far, far deeper. Once again it is Vaclav Havel who provides
the leitmotif for our thoughts as we see churches seduced by managerialism and unable critically to respond to the current differentiation of
individual human and societal religious requirements. In this chapter
we have examined yet one more facet of the 'profound crisis of human identity' that is the result of what Vaclav Havel calls living within
the lie:

> The crisis brought on by living within a lie, a crisis which in turn makes such
> a life possible, certainly possesses a moral dimension as well; it appears, among
> other things, as a deep moral crisis in society. A person who has been seduced
> by the consumer value system, whose identity is dissolved in an amalgam of the
> accoutrements of mass civilization, and who has no roots in the order of being,
> no sense of responsibility for anything higher than his or her own personal
> survival, is a *demoralized* person. The system depends on this demoralization,
> deepens it, is in fact a projection of it into society.[64]

This, it is my contention, is our present state, both in the universities, as we saw in chapter four, and now in the churches. Havel wrote
of the decaying communist system; now, alas, his words apply to our
own condition, as regards both society and the Church of England. In
its *uncritical* assimilation of managerialism the Church of England has,
in Havel's terms, been seduced by the reality and promise of power
restored over a subject 'other', a pattern all too tempting in a managerialised society. Against such a plangent appeal for human depth, one
of the most distinguished figures in the management world (now almost

---

[64] Vaclav Havel, 'The Power of the Powerless', in Jan Vladislav (ed.), *Living in Truth* (London:
Faber & Faber, 1987), p. 62.

co-terminous with the world itself), Peter F. Drucker asserts the sheer externality of what the managerialised world now requires:

> The knowledge we *now* consider is knowledge that proves itself in *action*. What we now mean by knowledge is information effective in action, information focused on results. Results are *outside* the person, in society and the economy, or the advancement of knowledge itself (italics in the original).[65]

In the face of these assertions we face choices: do we with Havel seek depth and roots in the order of being, or do we obey the dictates of managerialism and assume that externality, superficiality and the vacuity of identity envisaged by Drucker as the precondition of the efficient, knowledge-based society? Our present state demands consideration of the 'primal religion' that might be found in the context of late capitalism and advanced modernity, and, from a Christian point of view, the discernment of an 'ecology of the Spirit' in which that religion may be discovered in practice. Such consideration and discernment will demand, not least, the deployment of the whole armoury of the interdisciplines of religious studies and theology. This, however, is another story. We now turn to the analysis of the relationship between theology and the social sciences in the modern/postmodern matrix. The next chapter will provide the focal point of the rejection, enacted throughout this book, of theological flight into any cultural-linguistic refuge or intellectual condominium of those who will happily hibernate until history delivers the anarchy out of which the eschatological clerisy will emerge to rule the world.

[65] Peter F. Drucker, *Post-Capitalist Society* (London: Butterworth-Heinemann, 1993), p. 42.

CHAPTER 7

Theology and the social sciences

INTRODUCTION

At first sight, as observed from the standpoint of the social scientist, the relation of theology to the social sciences looks somewhat unpromising.[1] The history of social science presents itself as a narrative of divergence from, and the surpassing of, both religion as such and the idea of there being a revealed core to Western culture. Modernity (*Neuzeit*) has witnessed the long and sometimes tortuous relinquishment of the central role of theology in culture and society. Indeed, sociology understood in terms of 'grand theory' may plausibly be viewed in a certain sense as the successor to theology as 'queen of the sciences'. There is something of a natural progression from the *mentalité* of the once all-knowing theologian to that of the ambitious contemporary social scientist who aims not merely at comprehensive interpretation of human life-worlds, but also to promote the emancipatory role of social science as itself the agent of enlightened modernity. By contrast, the theologian would now seem to occupy a shrunken and marginalised residual territory confronted by a hostile secularised reality; such theology lives on in reduced circumstances. This is, of course, a simplification, not least because the theologies of main-line religion now face pluriform postmodern and New Age recompositions of the religious field.

From the early seventeenth century, as scholastic philosophy was confronted by early natural science and philosophy moved in Cartesian and empiricist directions, so the theological residuum was gradually whittled away. Correspondingly, from the early nineteenth century onwards, disciplines in the social and human sciences differentiated themselves and this

---

[1] This chapter is a lightly revised version of 'Theology and Social Science', in David Ford (ed.), *The Modern Theologians*, 2nd rev. edn (Oxford: Blackwell, 1996), pp. 700–19. As such, it represents a stage in the evolution of my reflection on the relation between religion, theology and the human sciences when the question concerning the capacity for reconstruing the tradition from, as it were, within was a paramount issue.

further usurped the territory of theological thought. Kant's magisterial attempt to stave off the nihilistic implications of an abstract juxtaposition of empiricism and idealism has now, some argue, reached the limit of its use. In an era of nihilism, the possibilities for theology seem both extreme and contradictory, for, if we are to believe some commentators, there can be no common ground between theology and secular thought. Those who start out from such an uncompromising standpoint regard all mediating and liberal theologies as mistaken, even perverse, and have little respect for much of the reflection set out in this book.

In the setting outlined above, it is possible to explore the relation of theology and the social sciences along two lines of approach. On the one hand, there are the efforts made by a number of theologians from Ernst Troeltsch and Dietrich Bonhoeffer onwards who have sought to take account of sociological insights in their work. On the other hand, however, there is the larger question of how the divergence of and subsequent relation between two inherently complex and contrasting (and in many respects antagonistic) traditions of reflection should be understood, once other factors are taken into account. I therefore adopt the following procedure. First, through a brief survey and typology I outline five strategies of negotiation employed by representative theologians who have attempted to develop relationships between theology and the social sciences. Then, second, key issues are drawn out and related to current debates which provide the basis for a more general appraisal of the relation of theology to the social sciences in the light of contrasting responses to modernity. In conclusion, a tentative agenda for theology in relation to the social sciences is proposed. The latter involves the formulation of a framework for the *episteme* of theology conceived as an emancipatory 'human science'.[2]

The engagement between theology and the social sciences has by and large been relatively one-sided. Some theologians have been committed to the use of socio-scientific insights, whereas social scientists have characteristically resisted normative styles of thought and favoured modes of rationality which valorise critical, interpretative, quantitative and theoretical skills, as opposed to concerns with ultimate, value or transcendental questions. The sociological imagination as classically deployed undercuts religious and theological pretensions. Recently, however, the

---

[2] The term 'human sciences' includes not only the social sciences but also other fields, notably discourse, law, history, literary theory and literature, and so on. See the introduction to R. H. Roberts and J. M. M. Good (eds.), *The Recovery of Rhetoric: Persuasive Discourse and Disciplinarity in the Human Sciences* (Charlottesville, va: University of Virginia Press, 1993).

very extremity of twentieth-century history has provoked a number
of sociologists into more explicit ethical and normative reflection.[3]
Moreover, resurgent religion and religiosities, the ethnic revival and the
all-encompassing character of an 'outer-directed' social order have provoked a revived socio-scientific interest in religion that goes well beyond
the limits of the sub-discipline of the sociology of religion. Other theoretical developments within post-structuralist cultural theory and associated
sociological thought invite the posing of questions which, if they are not
explicitly theological, certainly have a quasi-theological character. The
representation of the human condition as susceptible to interpretation
as pre-modern, modern and postmodern also has considerable import
for the construal of the relation of theology and the social sciences.
Entrenched and doctrinaire oppositional stances may no longer be appropriate, but what alternative modes of intellectual cohabitation might
now be appropriate is a contested question.

THEOLOGIANS AND THE SOCIAL SCIENCES: SURVEY AND TYPOLOGY

From the side of Christian church and academic theology it has long
been recognised by some theologians that they cannot operate effectively without recourse to the social sciences. In 'practical' or 'pastoral
theology' eclectic appropriations of insights and methodology often take
place, and pragmatic syntheses are arranged which enhance instrumental insight into the ministerial task and the continuing life of the church.
Moreover, in such areas as Old and New Testament studies, church
history and Christian social ethics the use of material drawn from the
social sciences has become increasingly common. Much more difficult
issues arise, however, when we consider the role of social science in relation to systematic theology, for it is here that the immanent critique
and relativism of sociological thought clashes with the re-enactment
(or even the re-creation) of tradition(s) in given socio-cultural contexts.
Under post-traditional or 'de-traditionalised' social conditions the very
idea of tradition is regarded as problematic; yet for others it remains
indispensable.[4]

---

3 For example, Zygmunt Bauman, *Modernity and the Holocaust* (Cambridge: Polity, 1989); Stjepan
G. Mestrovic, *The Barbarian Temperament: Toward a Postmodern Critical Theory* (London: Routledge,
1993) and Mestrovic, *Postemotional Society* (London: Sage, 1997).
4 See Paul Morris, 'Community Beyond Tradition', in Paul Heelas, Scott Lash and Paul Morris
(eds.), *Detraditionalization: Critical Reflections on Authority and Identity* (Oxford: Blackwell, 1996),
pp. 223–49.

The 'turn to the subject' initiated by Martin Luther and furthered by later theologians, not least Friedrich Schleiermacher, intensified religious experience whilst loosening the hold of theological explanation upon the 'outer', physical world. Such a development serves as a prelude to the growth of individualism and modern self-identity.[5] Whilst Protestant theology thus willingly ceded socio-cultural space in return for an intensification of religious consciousness, its battle with modernity was largely fought out elsewhere, notably in the long struggle with the implications of the historical-critical method and historicism. Having accepted an increasingly individualistic and subjective role in social reality (an option most consistently worked out in the history of Pietism), Protestant theology had to suffer the virtual destruction of the scripture-principle and the problematisation of its chosen textual foundations. Lacking the diachronic stability provided by the institutional hierarchy of Catholicism, German Protestant theologians were nonetheless culturally licensed to provide religious legitimation for a nascent and ascendant Germany. This theological and cultural role was based upon a transmutation of religious consciousness and the evolution of forms of enlightened religious inwardness (pioneered by Schleiermacher) which were compatible with the ethos of progress. In its turn, Protestant liberalism became a fundamental feature of the socio-cultural compact between church and state (that as a consequence of Bismarck's *Kulturpolitik* also eventually came to include the Catholic Church), an arrangement which endured until the catastrophic collapse of Germany at the end of the First World War.

The 'first postmodernity' of the culture of the Weimar Republic[6] was the origin not only of twentieth-century Protestant theology but also of many other strands of thought (and notably of those conducted in dialogue with Marxism). For the intellectuals of Weimar, many of whom were Jews later to be scattered following Hitler's coming to power, it was Marxism which became the bearer of hope. Now, however, in the so-called 'postmodern condition', and after the collapse of communism (albeit recognised to be an ideology long drained of authenticity), the present state of affairs in certain respects mirrors the inner-European vacuum created by the implosion of Germany after the Armistice of 1919. In both contexts human beings confront rapid economic and technological change and socio-cultural instability; now under the conditions

---

5 The classic account is to be found in Charles Taylor, *Sources of the Self: The Making of the Modern Identity* (Cambridge: Cambridge University Press, 1989).

6 See Roberts, 'Barth and the Eschatology of Weimar', *A Theology on its Way: Essays on Karl Barth* (Edinburgh: T. & T. Clark, 1992), ch. 6.

of 'advanced' or 'high' capitalism they are seemingly obliged to shop for life-style options in competitive markets of human identity.[7]

As a consequence of the Reformation and the Enlightenment, both Catholic and Protestant theologies retrenched and retreated in distinctive ways. As regards the Catholic Church, the totalising ambitions of scholastic theology were eventually reborn in reduced form in Neo-Scholastic Thomism underpinned by the authority of Pope Leo XIII in response to the threat of immanentist thought. Speculative abstract theological reflection within Protestantism underwent a form of revival in German (above all Hegelian) idealism. The Western and Enlightenment aspiration towards the totalisation of knowledge (paradigmatically represented in Goethe's *Faust* and its philosophical parallel, Hegel's *Phenomenology of Mind*) was transmitted to Marxism and to social science. Michel Foucault mapped with an uncompromising clarity the battle for the *episteme* which took place both between and within the emergent human and social sciences; yet within this struggle, religion and theology have an intensely problematic status.[8] In the most general terms, 'religion' and the 'sacred' underwent marginalisation and migration, and the history of aesthetics and the 'sublime' is one point of entry into understanding this process. Significantly, as regards theology, not only did Wilhelm von Humboldt exclude the divinity faculty of the University of Berlin from the faculty of humanities, but this marginalisation was repeated in Wilhelm Dilthey's configuration of the human sciences (*Geisteswissenschaften*) in the early twentieth century.[9] Paradoxically (given its extraordinarily well-funded base in Germany), such has been the degree of cultural isolation of theology that the New Testament theologian Ernst Kasemann could write of the status of theological thought as a 'nature reserve' in European culture. This is an apt but alarming image.

As noted earlier, the relationship between theology and the social sciences is problematic and as a first step we examine briefly, and in highly simplified terms, a typology of five possible strategies of appropriation enacted by theologians. First, the fundamentalist option involves the repudiation of modernity and concomitant patterns of regression; second, theology can tend towards reductive absorption into the social

---

[7] Anthony Giddens, *Modernity and Self-Identity: Self and Society in the Late Modern Age* (Cambridge: Polity, 1991), pp. 85–6.

[8] Michel Foucault provided the seminal account of this problematic in *The Order of Things: An Archeology of the Human Sciences* (London: Tavistock, 1970).

[9] Wilhelm Dilthey, *Introduction to the Human Sciences: An Attempt to Lay the Foundation for the Study of Society and History* (Brighton: Harvester Wheatsheaf, 1989), is essential reading in this regard.

scientific perspective (Ernst Troeltsch); third, the theologian may draw upon and use sociological categories as part of his or her essentially theological project (Dietrich Bonhoeffer, H. R. Niebuhr); fourth, theological and sociological categories can be regarded as coinherent aspects of an integral 'form of life', 'life-world' or 'phenomenology of tradition' (Edward Farley) which subsists at a remove from the question of modernity; fifth, the theologian may repudiate sociology as heretical secular thought and posit the persuasive option of commitment to the Christian cultural-linguistic practice (John Milbank). As I shall indicate in the sections that follow, I consider that no one of these strategies should be considered adequate as it stands: further factors have to be taken into account.

Theology repels the social sciences: fundamentalism

It is a mistake to confuse fundamentalism with pre-modern thinking as such. Fundamentalism involves in large part the rejection of modernity, or its manipulation. Thus in recent studies Gilles Kepel and Martin Riesebrodt have depicted global fundamentalism as attempts at reconquering the world and patriarchal protest movements, respectively.[10] Biblical (and other, for example Koranic) scriptural literalism, the creation of consistent sub-cultures, the coercive imposition of distinctive gender roles for men and women, and so on are characteristic. It is, however, easier to discern the conflict between fundamentalism and modernity than between active conservatism and so-called 'postmodernity'. Under postmodern conditions of fragmentation rational choice gives way to 'seduction' by the rhetorics of discourses which recognise no final hegemonies. Thus, curiously, the distinction between naive Protestant fundamentalism and the sophisticated quasi-fundamentalism of our fifth strategist, John Milbank, is more a question of reflective awareness than substance: the former might be unaware of the full implications of modernity; but the latter certainly is so aware, but he persists nonetheless in demanding decisions on the basis of an either–or choice between exclusive alternatives. If and when fundamentalism encounters social science, it is most often where fundamentalism makes instrumental use of social psychological or other techniques in order to facilitate conversion

---

[10] See G. Kepel, *The Revenge of God: The Resurgence of Islam, Christianity and Judaism in the Modern World* (Cambridge: Polity, 1994) and Martin Riesebrodt, *Pious Passion: The Emergence of Modern Fundamentalism in the United States and Iran* (Berkeley: University of California Press, 1993) for well-informed starting-points.

and other religious experience. The functional compatibility between instrumental reason as employed in technology and fundamentalist beliefs is well documented, where (for example) the latter serve as means of social empowerment over against an invasive, Western-dominated modernity. Postmodern or quasi-fundamentalism is, as it is argued below and elsewhere in this book, altogether more problematic.

Ernst Troeltsch: sociology overcomes theology

Ernst Troeltsch, the polymath sociologist and theologian-historian (and close associate of Max Weber), pioneered the application of sociological method to the study of Christian origins. Thus the history of dogma (as paradigmatically represented by Adolf von Harnack) became the model for a sociological interpretation of the interdependent relation between the transformed socio-ethical teachings of the church and the changing socio-political context of an organisation that grew from its status as an obscure religious minority group with strong eschatological beliefs into the state religious monopoly of the late Roman Empire.[11]

Troeltsch's thought was dominated by a prolonged intellectual and personal struggle with historicism. This conception of history asserts the universality of cause and effect in the nexus of events, and excludes *a priori* the 'absolute truths' necessary to religious faith from objective historical study. In essence, Troeltsch argued that the modern idea of history depended on critical source analysis and psychological analogy, and that history was many narratives of the development of peoples, cultures and the components of cultures. According to this approach, all dogmas dissolve into the flow of events, none of which is accorded a status of priority on the basis of extra-historical presuppositions. The historian works up from appropriate comparison through combination of material drawn from evidence in order to drive towards a comprehensive account of any given context.[12]

Troeltsch experienced a severe crisis of faith and then famously exchanged faculties. He was left with a residual and individualistic commitment to Christian values and with the scientific conviction that all historical truth was relative and conditioned. For Troeltsch, there was no escape (as with Karl Barth) from the rigorous constraints of *Historismus*

---

[11] See Ernst Troeltsch, *The Social Teachings of the Christian Churches* (2 vols., London: George Allen & Unwin, 1931), and Michael Mann, *The Sources of Social Power: A History of Power from the Beginning to AD 1760*, vol. 1 (Cambridge: Cambridge University Press, 1986).

[12] Ernst Troeltsch, *The Absoluteness of Christianity and the History of Religion* (London: SCM, 1972).

into the dialectics of crisis, and the reappearance of the Word in the supra-historical *Momente* existentially perceived in the interstices of the historical order. As a consequence, many twentieth-century Protestant theologians faced a dilemma: should they opt for Troeltsch and reductive ascesis of historicism, or follow Barth on the dialectical and hermeneutical path and renegotiate theologies of the Word?[13] In reality, this dilemma accords too dominant a role to historicism as the mediator of modernity, for, as is argued below, Christian theology has undergone an aborted and unsatisfactory encounter with 'modernity'. This is the product, at least in part, of the institutional arrangements that have compounded the isolation of theology in the Anglo-Saxon world.

Ernst Troeltsch and his friend and colleague Max Weber were jointly responsible for the initiation and development of an organisational ty-pology, the celebrated church–sect distinction, which related the social structure of religious organisations to belief and religious behaviour. The dichotomies formulated by Weber and Troeltsch have been employed in systematic study of the whole Western Christian tradition. The further refinement of this theoretical approach proved particularly fruitful in the study of differentiated North American Protestantism, religious sects and new religious movements. More recently, the church–sect typology and stratification theory have been applied to the study of the New Testament church.

H. R. Niebuhr took up the Weberian church–sect typology and ap-plied it to the analysis of the growth of denominations in a way typ-ical of the pragmatic appropriations made by theologians.[14] It is sig-nificant that Niebuhr's text is repeatedly cited within the theological literature, whereas, by contrast, the later sociological discussion of so-cial movements has largely failed to make a transition to theology. Thus whilst this latter discussion has considerable importance for understand-ing the dynamics of religious group behaviour and is thus of relevance to contemporary theology, it has remained largely within the sphere of influence of the sociology of religion. In such particular contexts, disciplinary differentiation and the corresponding protective, interest-driven strategies of disciplines (and sub-disciplines like the sociology of religion) may distort and fragment what should ideally be a more

---

[13] For an unmatched account of this crucially important era in the history of modern Protestant the-ology, see Christoff Gestrich, *Neuzeitliches Denken und die Spaltung der dialektischen Theologie* (Tübingen: J. C. B. Mohr, 1977).

[14] H. R. Niebuhr, *The Social Sources of Denominationalism* (New York: Holt, 1929; reprinted New York: New American Library, 1975). This is a rare example of informed sociological work from within theology.

comprehensive and integrated approach. Such failures of connection have had an impact not only upon the continuing task of theology, but also upon the informed study of religion. As a specific example, whilst the French sociologist Alain Touraine's studies of new social movements and of 'post-industrial society'[15] have had important implications for research conducted by, for instance, the sociologist James Beckford into new religious movements in 'advanced industrial society',[16] the further step of applying such work in the field of theology has proved harder to achieve.

The Weberian influence extends far beyond the much-cited 'Protestant Ethic' thesis and the economic sociology of *Economy and Society*. The theoretical work of the American sociologist Talcott Parsons (who did much to transmit Weber's ideas to the United States) and the structuration theory of the English sociologist Anthony Giddens, to take but two examples, both owe a considerable debt to Weber. The sociological tradition of grand theory has until relatively recently had minimal impact upon the practice of theology. Our fourth type, the mutual assimilation of theological and sociological categories, does express a greater measure of appropriation of Parsonian systems theory, but, as will become apparent, this is achieved at the cost of downplaying the substantive content of the theology in favour of phenomenological and systemic description. In reality, confrontation with modernity exacts a higher price, and this is perhaps nowhere more apparent than in our third type, Dietrich Bonhoeffer's attempt to correlate a theology of the Word with a convincing analysis of the social being of the Christian community.

Dietrich Bonhoeffer: theology recruits sociology

Dietrich Bonhoeffer was raised in the elite centre of German cultural life, and he thus absorbed the major theological and cultural influences of his time. After early experience as a pastor he became convinced that there were profound flaws in a theology which seemingly failed to equip Christians to act effectively and in a distinctive way in a hostile social reality. Worse, this theology later proved incapable of resisting its political abuse by the German Christians. In his doctoral thesis *Sanctorum*

---

[15] Alain Touraine, *The Post-Industrial Society: Tomorrow's Social History, Classes, Conflicts and Culture in the Programmed Society* (New York: Random House, 1971; London: Wildwood House, 1974) and *The Self-Production of Society* (Chicago/London: University of Chicago Press, 1977).

[16] James A. Beckford, 'Systems, Symbols, Societalisation, Secularisation, Subjectivity', in *Religion in Advanced Industrial Society* (London: Unwin Hyman, 1989), pp. 74–107.

Communio Bonhoeffer engaged with the question whether Christianity has a sociologically definable essence.[17] Taking up Ferdinand Toennies' famous categories of community (*Gemeinde*) and association (*Gesellschaft*), Bonhoeffer tried to understand how the Church might enact itself in the context of a post-organic, associative modernity, and whether, furthermore, it had a distinct sociologically definable essence which Bonhoeffer identified (in debate with K. L. Schmidt) as that of an agapeistic community. *Sanctorum Communio* is a pioneering work, but it remains a relatively isolated example of the recruitment of specifically sociological conceptuality in the service of a theology of the Word. In terms of both substance and methodology this text remains an erratic and an undeveloped element in Bonhoeffer's curtailed theological achievement. Besides the term *sanctorum communio* others such as 'ethics as formation', 'presence' in Christology, 'religionless Christianity', and the 'ultimate' and 'penultimate' in theological ethics passed into post-Second World War theological reflection in Europe and North America. Bonhoeffer's sensitivity to the all-pervasiveness of totalitarian social systems, which first became apparent in his observation of the German émigré community in Barcelona and was later developed in confrontation with National Socialism, is still of immense relevance. This was demonstrated not least in the struggle against apartheid in South Africa, but now in the post-communist era, when capitalism is without effective critique or constraint, Bonhoeffer's assertion of the penultimacy of all things over against the ultimacy of the divine has gained a new and urgent relevance, and not least in the face of an invasive managerial modernity.

A second important aspect of Bonhoeffer's theological legacy consists of his confrontation with the progressive secularisation of Western society and culture, an issue which not only provoked the so-called 'secular theology' of the sixties, but also provided within theological reflection the major parallel with the issue which dominated much post-war sociological study of religion. In much-quoted passages in the *Letters and Papers from Prison*, Bonhoeffer set out an agenda in which he accepted and ingested the implications of secularisation, albeit with highly paradoxical consequences for theology. It was apparent to Bonhoeffer that the emergence of the world's autonomy which had origins in science, religion, philosophy, politics and natural law was an inescapable reality. He concluded that 'God as a working hypothesis in morals, politics or science, has been

---

[17] Dietrich Bonhoeffer, *Sanctorum Communio: A Dogmatic Enquiry into the Sociology of the Church* (London: Collins, 1963).

surmounted and abolished."[18] Thus any yearning for a lost golden past
in the Middle Ages would be mere despair cloaked by an infantile nostalgia. Bonhoeffer takes with absolute seriousness Kant's strictures on
maturity as emergence from heteronomy, and the latter's injunction,
Sapere aude, dare to know, is incumbent not least upon Christians. Rather
than side with either Barth (whose ontology Bonhoeffer had criticised
in *Act and Being*) or with Nietzsche (and relinquishing theological language altogether), Bonhoeffer admits the reality of secularisation and
modernity and strives to interpret this theologically.

> And we cannot be honest unless we recognize that we have to live in the world *etsi
> deus non daretur*. And this is just what we do recognize – before God! God himself
> compels us to recognize it. So our coming of age leads us to a true recognition
> of our situation before God. God would have us know that we must live as
> men who manage our lives without him. The God who is with us is the God
> who forsakes us (Mark 15.34). The God who lets us live in the world without
> the working hypotheses of God is the God before whom we stand continually.
> Before God and with God we live without God. God lets himself be pushed out
> of the world on to the cross. He is weak and powerless in the world, and that is
> precisely the way, the only way, in which he is with us and helps us. Matt. 8.17
> makes it quite clear that Christ helps us, not by virtue of his omnipotence, but
> by virtue of his weakness and suffering.[19]

Whilst it would be idle to pretend that Bonhoeffer's response to secularisation was to play a large role in the post-war research or theoretical
work of mainstream sociologists, his account did set an agenda worked
out by theologians who sought further to explore the idea of a so-called
non-religious Gospel and a 'secular city' in which throughgoing secularity could itself provide the basis of theological celebration.[20] Above all,
and despite the relatively outdated character of the sociological theory
he used, Dietrich Bonhoeffer provides an enduring theological prototype
of critical and responsible reflexivity in the face of modernity. As will be
argued further in the conclusion of this chapter, it is the development and
reinforcement of such a reflexivity that has to be a central feature of a
socio-scientifically informed reconstitution of the theological task today.
Whereas, however, it is arguable that Troeltsch capitulated to modernity

---

[18] See, for example, Dietrich Bonhoeffer, letters of 8 and 30 June and 8, 16 and 18 July 1944 in
E. Bethge (ed.), *Letters and Papers from Prison*, rev. edn (London: SCM, 1967), pp. 324–9, 339–47,
357–63.

[19] Bonhoeffer, *Letters and Papers*, pp. 360–1.

[20] Harvey Cox, *The Secular City: Secularization and Urbanization in Theological Perspective* (New York:
Macmillan, 1965) is perhaps the most notable expression of this theological genre.

as he understood it and that Bonhoeffer sought to create a dialectical cohabitation which preserved the tensions in the confrontation, our next example, the work of Edward Farley, proposes a mutual absorption which blunts the substantive edges of both theology (as grounded in tradition and authority) and social science (as bearer of modernity).

Edward Farley: theology and social science mutually merged?

It is not my purpose here to analyse or evaluate in detail the theological proposals of Edward Farley. What is of major concern here is how this representative thinker has assimilated socio-scientific insights and made them mutual and intrinsic aspects of a method that seemingly overcomes any contested divergence between theology and the social sciences. Farley endorses theological proposals which reverse both the Barthian tendency to polarise 'faith' and 'religion' and the whole post-Enlightenment predilection for reconstructionist theologies which adhere to and amplify a single category of ethical or affective experience which then becomes the medium of theological construction. In this he is directly assisted by broadly phenomenological methods.

In *Ecclesial Man* Edward Farley tackled the problem of foundations, the ways in which realities are pre-given to theology,[21] whereas *Ecclesial Reflection* concerns judgement, the ways in which those realities lay claim to truth.[22] The task of foundations is, according to Farley, 'that of describing faith, the faith world, the community of faith (ecclesial existence) as the matrix of reality-givenness'.[23] The 'criteriology' expounded in *Ecclesial Reflection* begins with an 'archaeology' of the 'house of faith' which is analogous to Heidegger's critique of the history of ontology. Furthermore, Farley propounds a 'phenomenology of tradition', that is a phenomenology of 'ecclesial process and its bearers'.[24] The implications of this are spelt out clearly and pertain directly to our interpretation, for

the move from foundations and pregivenness to theological judgement is not simply a move into philosophy of religion nor from the determination of faith to the general level of ontology. Theological judgements are made from a historical

---

[21] Edward Farley, *Ecclesial Man: A Social Phenomenology of Faith and Reality* (Philadelphia: Fortress, 1975).
[22] Edward Farley, *Ecclesial Reflection: An Anatomy of Theological Method* (Philadelphia: Fortress, 1982).
[23] *Ibid.*, p. xiv.
[24] *Ibid.*, p. xv.

faith-community which has a determinate corporate memory carried in a
determinate network of symbols. The bearers of that determinacy, even written
collections from the past, play some role in judgement. And the nature of that
role is established not by authority but by the structure of the ecclesial process
itself. This is why a phenomenology and even sociology of tradition plays such
a central part in this prolegomenon.[25]

This sort of approach emancipates theology from the constraints of
historicism and overcomes differences posed by alternative principles used by the ancestral 'houses' of authority of Protestantism and
Catholicism. More seriously, however, whilst it ostensibly liberates theology from the 'house of authority', it thereby side-steps the critique of
power. Theology comes into existence at the point of correlation between the 'meaning and proper function' of the literature of the ecclesial
community and the 'nature of ecclesiality and its duration over time'.[26]
Thus theological reflection consists in 'the depiction of ecclesiality
(portraiture), the truth question, and reflective praxis'.[27] In effect, the
description and analysis of the means of 'social duration' (Pitirim
Sorokin) of ecclesial bodies replaces the prescriptive role of outdated,
unacceptable tradition. It is an open question why such an approach
should result in a distinctively Christian theology as opposed to the highly
general, even reified description of 'ecclesial being'.

The intention here is not to test the adequacy of this sophisticated
sociological and phenomenological synthesis as such, but to raise questions which stem from the broader context of the disjunction of theology
and the social sciences. Thus the phenomenological approach exploited
by Farley makes full and free use of apposite sociological conceptuality, but as *theology* it would seem appropriate to ask if it is more than
a religiously nuanced 'portraiture', and thus simply a phenomenology
of religion. George Lindbeck's use of the idea of a 'cultural linguistic
practice' is similar in some ways to that of Farley; both are enabled by
their American background of pragmatism. There is a parallel between
the phenomenological approach and recent reconstruals of Christian
theology through the medium of theories of the origin and nature of
language.[28] Both use theory as the basis for constructive proposals that
appear to emancipate theological reflection from the Enlightenment

---

[25] *Ibid.*
[26] *Ibid.*, p. xvii.
[27] *Ibid.*, p. xviii.
[28] See, for example, Graham Ward, *Barth, Derrida and the Language of Theology* (Cambridge: Cambridge University Press, 1995).

critique. Once again we need to ask if the Enlightenment principle can be banished so easily, and could it not be that the descriptive phenomenological approach (or indeed the linguistic turn) is in some way an evasion? Our answer to such questions begins with an exploration of some of the wider issues affecting the relation of theology and the social sciences touched upon in the following section.

Postmodern quasi-fundamentalism (John Milbank)

One drastic and influential response to the whole problematic of the relation of theology and the social sciences is that advocated by the English theological thinker John Milbank in his monumental work, *Theology and Social Theory*. Milbank provides an extended 'archaeology' of the 'heresy' of secular (i.e. sociological) thought as it has diverged from Christian truth and then poses an uncompromising either–or. Secular social theory and Christianity in effect stand in contradiction to each other. All the main components of secular social theory have a (usually genetic) relation with Christianity, and the bulk of Milbank's work is dedicated to exposing these connections. Because there is no ultimate foundational basis in *rationality* for distinguishing between the claims of Christianity and those of secular reason, the project consists of an 'exercise in sceptical relativism'. Ultimacy is not a matter of rational choice; the Christian *perspective* is *persuasive* and not conveyed through 'the apologetic mediation of human reason' (that is, to put it less ambitiously, through *argument* as such). Correspondingly, in a Nietzschian postmodernity the Christian perspective is offered to theologians for their positive appropriation.

Thus according to Milbank, the meta-discourse and cultural-linguistic practice of 'Christianity' relativises modern (i.e. 'liberal') theology, which is seen to be an immanent idolatry (the 'oracular voice of some finite idol' stemming from history, psychology or transcendental philosophy). Any 'liberal' theology construed as an adjunct of secular reason faces a dilemma: it *either* fuses idolatrously with a particular immanent field of knowledge *or* it is effectively alienated and 'confined to intimations of a sublimity beyond representation'.[29] Taken in the latter sense, theology as a 'sublimity beyond representation' negatively affirms a (from Milbank's point of view questionable) autonomous secular realm open to rational understanding. The situation is, however,

---

[29] John Milbank, *Theology and Social Theory Beyond Secular Reason* (Oxford: Blackwell, 1989), p. 1.

further compounded by another complexity. Whilst theology is not to be identified with secular reason, it is nevertheless a wholly contingent historical construct embedded in 'semiotic and figural codings'; in other words, its horizons are always those of cultural-linguistic practice. This state of affairs is conceded and endorsed: there can be no return to, or restoration of, the pre-modern position of Christianity. Christianity must *neither* accommodate *nor* adapt itself to the space apparently left to it within social reality. Any such involvement weakens Christianity as *faith* and as radical *praxis* by (mistakenly) searching for common ground.

It is at this juncture that Milbank notes a fundamental conjuncture, i.e. the postmodern *necessity of myth*: Nietzsche has shown that all cultural associations are traceable to the will-to-power. Nietzsche further indicates that the basis of *all* social and economic power is 'religious' inasmuch as myth masks the will-to-power. Thus social theory and theology subsist on the same ground: to pass *beyond* Nietzsche is to recognise 'the necessity and yet the ungrounded character of some sort of metanarrative, some privileged transcendent factor, even when it comes disguised as the constant element in an immanent process'.[30] There can be no significant 'sociological' representation of religion and theology precisely because *religion* is the ultimate transcendental.[31] All forms of secular reason (and thus social science) can be traced archaeologically to, and then deconstructed into, their *theological* progenitors. This can be understood as the *inversion* (not merely the reconstrual) of Hans Blumenberg's account of the 'legitimacy' of modernity (as opposed to the perverse Christian obstruction of human *curiositas*).[32] Seen thus, secularity and secular discourse are *heresy* in relation to orthodox Christianity, and the archaeological investigations will show that all 'scientific' social theories are in fact 'theologies or anti-theologies' in disguise.

We hear two 'voices' in Western culture. The first is classical and medieval, the voice of an Alasdair MacIntyre speaking in Platonic-Aristotelian-Augustinian-Thomist terms.[33] The second is the nihilistic, Nietzschian voice which historicises and seeks to show that 'every

---

[30] *Ibid.*, p. 2.

[31] How the 'religious transcendental' is to be understood is an intriguing matter. In essence, Milbank makes 'theology' function as a kind of 'religion', whilst denying the latter its full, multi-layered constitutive potential, which is only made available to critical reflection through interdisciplinary religious studies.

[32] Hans Blumenberg, *The Legitimacy of the Modern Age* (Cambridge, MA: MIT Press, 1983).

[33] See Alasdair MacIntyre, *After Virtue: A Study in Moral Theory* (London: Duckworth, 1981), chs. 12 and 15.

supposedly objective reasoning simply promotes its own difference, and disguises the power which is its sole support'.[34] In the final analysis the first, the voice of 'Christian virtue', triumphs. In such a setting, a total scenario implying a reading of the whole Western tradition, Christianity may reassert its total originality:

> Christianity, however, recognises no original violence. It construes the infinite not as chaos, but as harmonic peace which is yet beyond the circumscribing power of any totalising reason. Peace no longer depends upon the reduction to the self-identical, but is the *sociality* of harmonious difference . . . Christianity . . . is the coding of transcendental difference as peace.[35]

At the very last moment Christianity subverts and exposes the Nietzschian assertion that 'difference, non-totalisation and indeterminacy of being necessarily imply arbitrariness and violence'.[36] In conclusion, Milbank posits a 'third voice' which pursues the above 'argument', which amounts in effect to a 'choice', an effective *seduction* by one encoding as opposed to the other. This is what we might call the ecclesial supercession, a sublation in which a 'historicist and pragmatist, yet *theologically* realist' position is advanced in which

> no claim is made to 'represent' an objective social reality; instead the social knowledge advocated is but the continuation of ecclesial practice, the imagination in action of a peaceful, reconciled social order, beyond even the violence of legality.[37]

On the assumption that 'truth is social', a 'lived narrative' projects and 'represents' the triune God who is 'transcendental peace through differential relation'.[38] This is the 'ultimate "social science"' and the sole offer that may establish theology, give content to the idea of 'God', and impress itself upon the world through practice. For Milbank, the metadiscourse of theology understood as the 'discourse of non-mastery' is that which may alone save us from nihilism. In the final analysis this is a *theological* transvaluation of all 'theology', myth and 'religion' (and the nihilistic human condition that they mask). Social science is at best a signpost to the root from which there has been a catastrophic deviation; at worst it, that is to say the whole conspectus of the human and social sciences, is a heretical perversion.

[34] Milbank, *Theology and Social Theory*, p. 5.
[35] *Ibid.*, pp. 5–6.
[36] *Ibid.*, p. 5.
[37] *Ibid.*, p. 6.
[38] *Ibid.*

Milbank posits an abstract, quasi-Manichaeistic (yet mutually involuted) opposition of false alternatives which entails abuses of both 'theology' and 'social theory'. In effect, both 'theology' and 'social theory' (equivalent for present purposes with the social sciences) are reduced to the *rhetorics* embedded in and expressive of cultural practices in a way that universalises Nietzschian perspectivism. But this procedure rules out through *a priori* occultation the wide variety of rationalities, epistemological strategies (not least induction), and epistemic resolutions that characterise both these areas of intellectual activity. Construed thus, theology becomes the imposition of *stasis*, a rearward-looking construal paradoxically rooted in eschatology, which has consequences which paralyse theology as embedded, grace-driven reflection entrenched in the real conflict and injustices of the human condition. *Active* theological thinking *from the future*, the anticipatory consciousness of the Spirit, is excluded. In somewhat extravagant, but not altogether misleading terms, John Milbank may be said once more to enact the infinite cunning of reason that extinguishes itself and migrates in order to survive as 'theology'.

Sociology as a discipline should not be construed *reductively* and *exclusively* in terms of the perverse metanarrative of secular reason. Sociology and the social sciences may also be classically understood as the *critical representation* and *clarification* of the patterns of social organisation necessary to the sustenance of humane societies, rather than (as Milbank would have it) the partner in the promotion of an allegedly necessary and totalitarian violence of order. The tasks of theology and sociology are mutual at least inasmuch as they address the human condition in exploratory and interpretative terms, and do not subsume (in however virtuosic a fashion) *everything* under the dance of death and totalitarian logic of Western secular reason. Moreover, sociology and theology which embody concerns for the other cannot afford to neglect or express contempt for ethnography, that is the effective representation and interpretation of what is actually happening in human lives. Both theology and the social sciences should be concerned in their distinctive ways with life and with how things are – and might be.

On a scale of proximity and modes of negotiation and assimilation between social science and theology, fundamentalism tends to flee modernity (and thus the social sciences), but in so doing it may be tempted to exploit social scientific insights in instrumental ways to facilitate conversion experiences. Troeltsch tended to absorb theological questions into historicism and early social science, Bonhoeffer attempted (not least under the influence of Karl Barth) to maintain a dialectical cohabitation of theological and sociological categories, and Edward Farley has expressed theology in terms of a throughgoing appropriation of the phenomenology of ecclesial being. John Milbank drives a wedge between theology and the social sciences, and demands that we resist all accommodations and decide upon one or the other in what amounts to a despairing postmodern quasi-fundamentalism of paradoxical sophistication. This depiction of possible ways of configuring the relation of theology and the social sciences is in no way exhaustive, but it is representative of a range of possible strategies in a fraught borderland.

THEOLOGY'S USE OF SOCIAL SCIENCE: SOME OBSERVATIONS

The exceptionally high profile of Protestant theology in German thought and culture is unique in Europe, if not the world. Moreover, many of the sub-disciplines within Christian theology either originated or were given vital impulse in Germany throughout the post-Enlightenment period. The contextual character of this widely disseminated and thereby universalised theological tradition cannot be left out of account. It is only recently that a leading role appears to have passed to the United States, and in consequence, it is reasonable to anticipate the assimilation of distinctively American concerns and insights. The ascendency of American theology is remarkable as regards both Protestant theology from the North and Catholic liberation theology from the Latin South, respectively. This growing, albeit differentiated, hegemony is also evident in the proliferation of feminist and other special interest and communitarian theologies. These developments incorporate societal changes of profound significance. The shift of interest away from the archetypically 'male' paradigm of all-embracing, hegemonic theologies of largely German inspiration towards the contemporary pluralism of *theologies of* gender, race, ethnicity, sexual orientation, poverty, and so on, is contemporaneous with a major crisis in the ethnic 'melting-pot' of the United States. The responsible use of such theologies is, however, improbable apart from the just and intelligent deployment of social scientific insight which defines the constituencies to which each type of theological reflection may primarily relate. In a 'glocalized' (Roland Robertson) world, liberal values, conceptions of universal human rights and theologies which imply catholicity are now prone to systemic crisis and readily attacked as postcolonial hegemony, cultural neo-imperialism or regressive patriarchy.

Without, however, effective means of representing human universals there is a danger that it will become impossible to represent any interests over and above those of special groups. It is at this juncture that religious and theological insights once more become important resources.[39]

The brief typology presented in section 1 of this chapter and the differentiation and pluralism in contemporary theology alluded to above are illuminating dimensions of the changing relationship between Christian theology and the social sciences. On a more abstract level what concerns us is the implications of what the English sociologist Anthony Giddens means when he asserts that '*Modernity is deeply and intrinsically sociological.*'[40] In other words, if sociological (that is to say reflexive, as opposed to tradition-dominated) self-understanding is a defining feature of modernity, then theology is faced with the requirement that it engage in the comprehensive negotiation of its relationship with the social sciences. Whilst some forms of liberation theology may have attempted this inasmuch as they sought to build contextual theological foundations influenced by Marxist insight (thereby invoking the consequences of a less than problematic alliance), the Western engagement has been fragmented and incomplete. The mediation of modernity and theology's response to it is, however, a matter of central importance around which cluster many aspects of the issues relating to theology and the social sciences.

Christian theology remains, and it should remain, church- or community-related theology. Despite its many ambiguous (and largely successful) attempts to gain and retain academic legitimacy, theological thought often subsists in social and economic contexts which distance it from any need to reckon not merely with secularisation but also with the fuller impact of modernisation and modernity. 'Modernity', itself a much-disputed concept, has been opposed to 'tradition'. For some social scientists the very idea of 'tradition' is not merely seen as inherently problematic, but as a primary and defining characteristic of a superseded pre-modern condition.[41] Contemporary culture and society may thus be regarded as post-traditional. Other sociologists

---

[39] An important countervailing attempt to restate universal values in the context of growing pluralism is the Global Ethic coordinated by the Swiss German theologian Hans Küng and promulgated at the Parliament of the World's Religions held in Chicago in 1993. See chapter 9 below.

[40] Giddens, *Consequences of Modernity*, p. 43 (italics in the original).

[41] See Philip A. Mellor, 'Reflexive Tradition: Anthony Giddens, High Modernity and the Contours of Contemporary Religiosity', *Religious Studies*, 29/1 (1993), 111–27.

have argued for the continuing force of the idea of tradition in ways which, for example, in part endorse Farley's formulations.[42] What greatly complicates the situation that we now encounter is two further factors. On the one hand, social reality has not remained static as 'the sacred' and 'the religious' have undergone ambiguous displacements and transmutations in reaching accommodations with modernity in what, for example, George Steiner has suggestively described as the twentieth-century 'after-life of religion'. On the other hand, the Barthian critique of 'religion' and the scission between theology and the academic study of religion have tended to disable the former's ability to come to terms with the resurgence of religion and its ambiguous 'after-life'.

A theology uninformed by engagement with the social sciences may well persist as a form of 'false consciousness', but it will do so at a dangerous distance from what the German Reformed theologian Jürgen Moltmann once referred to as the 'dialectic of the real'.[43] This 'real' now includes a range of new possibilities and challenges. For example, post-structuralist intimations of theology (or *a*theology), New Age 'self-religion', globalised spiritualities, gender-specific goddess-centred Neo-Paganism, varieties of fundamentalism, and environmental spiritualities all tend to outflank a wearied Christian theology often mainly concerned with the internal politics of its own decline. Thus Christian theology not only has to face up to its own partially aborted reception of modernity and its correlative fear and ignorance of new developments which meet human religious needs the world over. In addition, it must confront and come to terms with acute and profound problems with regard to gender, power and the status of nature that it will only begin adequately to comprehend if it successfully relocates itself at the conjuncture of pre-modernity (where its origins lie), modernity (where it underwent crippling damage) and the 'postmodern condition', or, less contentiously, 'high' or 'late' modernity, in which new possibilities open up on an almost daily basis. The idea and the reality of 'tradition' has to comprehend and manage these dialectically cohabiting dimensions. If theology fails to achieve this, then it may persist as *mauvaise foi* for as long as the relevant funding continues, but it will not be answering the challenge posed by the history and present state of the human and social sciences.

---

[42] Edward Shils, *Tradition* (London: Faber, 1981).

[43] Jürgen Moltmann, *The Crucified God: The Cross of Christ as Foundation and Criticism of Christian Theology* (London: SCM, 1974).

To these challenges and opportunities we shall shortly return in concluding remarks.

The argument pursued so far in this chapter does not imply that no
effective collaborations between sociologists and theologians have taken
place.[44] My contention is, however, not only that such collaboration
is marked more by discontinuity than coherence, but that underlying
alliance or conflict there are major unresolved issues. These stem from
the historical differentiation of disciplines and adjustments which relate
to modernisation, secularisation and the nature of the Enlightenment
project. It will therefore require thoroughgoing methodological renewal
within theology (rather than occasional intellectual transfers by unusu-
ally energetic theologians) before the disjunctions between theology, the
sociology of religion and main-line social theory are better understood
and more well-founded working relationships are established.

THEOLOGY AND THE SOCIAL SCIENCES: A TENTATIVE AGENDA

The current identity crisis of Christian theology does not lack precedent,
and that necessarily strange discipline is not the only field of study marked
by an identity crisis. I have already alluded to Michel Foucault's depiction
of the interlinked 'deaths' of God and man at the very heart of the
evolution of the human and social sciences (*les sciences humaines*).[45] Human
identity itself, and the means of grasping and expressing our knowledge
of the human, the *episteme*, is not possessed by any one discipline or
field of knowledge precisely because of the evolutionary differentiation
and changing basic configurations of the disciplines in the absence of
overarching means of integration. In even more basic terms, it is of
the essence of human being that identity is not pre-defined. There is,
however, no shortage of agencies and powers queuing up and striving to
impose their demands upon the human agent; in more formal terms, we
are all the victims of social construction. On the other hand, the necessary
condition of the sustenance of civilised life demands a degree of willed
conformity to agreed norms. The fact that theology or metaphysical
philosophy may once have provided the basis of coherent identity and
legitimation does not now sanction regressions into a mythic past or the
invocation of a utopian futurity when we are faced with the challenge of
secularisation and modernity. On the contrary, other means have to be

---

[44] See, for example, David Martin, John Orme-Mills, and W. S. F. Pickering, *Sociology and Theology:
    Alliance or Conflict* (Brighton: Harvester-Wheatsheaf, 1980).
[45] Foucault, *Order of Things*, pp. 384ff.

found through which tradition(s), Enlightenment and critical reflexivity may be creatively coordinated anew.

We have seen how the relation between social science and specifically Christian (besides religious) thought is fraught with difficulties. Humankind now exists in the extremely complex nexus between an invasive world system that transforms ever more effectively all facets of human life into marketable commodities and, on the other hand, the resurgence of local identities, be they marked by ethnic, cultural, gender or national specificities. Moreover, the interlinked processes of globalisation and localisation are overshadowed by the environmental crisis, a veritable 'ecological eschaton'. Market choice, informational integration, and global competition have, it is arguable, replaced the struggle of monolithic hegemonies, all the more so since the near-total collapse of Marxist socialism. Yet, even this does not fully comprise the difficulties. Theology will require practitioners who, like 'postmodern saints', will be able to extinguish themselves in seeking to enter this dialectical complex. There is no easy way forward.

On a pragmatic level, a responsible postmodern theology of integrity must recognise and own new affinities and new allegiances if it is to grapple in effective ways with the contemporary orgies of collective tribal power or the manipulation characteristic of marketisation in an increasingly divided, yet globalised, and ever more powerful world system, and the crisis of male gender identity. This involves a re-engagement with the real on every level: we must begin with the effective understanding that human 'life-worlds' are constituted; yet socio-scientific analysis informed by critical reflexivity is insufficient on its own. Theological reflection must understand itself in this matrix, yet here it can do little without the unpredetermined gift, the charisma that comes with a vocation. At the base of this complex we must seek new and active fusion of the human sciences together with the articulation and admission of the human right, following the example of Bonhoeffer, to express a self-transcending identity. It is ironic that in empirical terms the realisation that the human sciences should be employed in inner-directed and emancipatory, rather than outer-directed and hegemonic terms occurs at core points within management theory and practice where it critically differentiates itself from its shadow side, managerialism. In a so-called rationally managed reality (now being uncritically extended to the life of the churches) we may find the paradigmatic societal microcosms in which the theologian might first test his or her renewed skills and vision. This is where the subversive emancipation of the Gospel may be enacted to good effect.

In this brief study of the relation of theology to the social sciences I have argued on the basis that the latter should be understood within the overall conspectus of the human sciences (*les sciences humaines/die Geisteswissenschaften*). At the heart of the human sciences there is a combative void from which essential human concerns have been banished. The twofold death of God and 'man' of which Foucault writes is one influential way of characterising a multiplex crisis of human identity. This crisis has many aspects, and it is spread world-wide with the invasive power of global capitalism before which all cultural particularities seem to bend, if not break. Religion, and the self-critical reflexive discourses of religion, theology, provides a form of resistant cultural capital. There are those, like the American Catholic theologian Michael Novak, who would wish to use religion as a means of filling the 'empty shrine' of the global economic system.[46] According to this view, Christianity and Judaism are supremely well suited to such a role. My contention is that assimilation of this kind may well involve a betrayal.

Fundamentalists may react with equal vehemence for such an integration into the aims of the dominant economic system and advocate prosperity theologies.[47] Conversely, quasi-fundamentalists may react against capitalism, advocate political impossibilism, and await revolution in a state of Adornian 'hibernation'. Correspondingly, the day of the theological reductionist is largely over; liberalism that trades upon the infinite extendability of the death by a thousand small cuts holds little attraction in an era of catastrophe. Yet, as Edward Farley has shown, the diachronic continuity of the meaning-systems of ecclesial communities may be understood through phenomenology and a mutual assimilation of theology and social science, but this may take place without either evincing Christian or other theological particularity or confronting the full rigours of modernity. Of the strategies reviewed it is Bonhoeffer who, despite the archaism of his sociological appropriations, offers most inspiration, even if his insights into social science are extremely dated. Unflinching in confronting modernity as he experienced it, Bonhoeffer embodies the supreme adventure of the sovereign rights of the life of the mind and heart that is theology rightly understood. He was prepared to risk the unpredictable consequences that follow any sincere obedience to the command: 'Follow me'. All

---

[46] Michael Novak, *The Spirit of Democratic Capitalism* (London: Institute of Economic Affairs, 1982).
[47] R. H. Roberts (ed.), *Religion and the Transformations of Capitalism: Comparative Approaches* (London: Routledge, 1995), introduction and chs. 7 and 10.

truth-seekers take such risks, but Christians and Christian theologians draw upon an identity and hope for a future that is life promised only on the basis of death. The substantive content of Christian traditions (understood in the most comprehensive sense) is a resource, but to regard the future as open and to act is a supreme test of the resolve of faith.

We inhabit a desert, yet somewhere there are rocks that may be touched and from which sustenance will flow. Each who is aware of such possibilities may seek out sources from within his or her own faith-tradition; ecumenism must now become an ecumenism of religions, not merely that of the belief systems present within any given tradition. It is not the case that in pre-modernity the touching places were wholly obvious, nor is it true to think that reflexivity is the sole prerogative of modernity. Neither, again, should we believe that religion and theology die off on the margins in a secularised modernity; indeed, the resurgence of religion and religiosity precludes such naivety. The theological task of our day should not consist simply of attempts (however sophisticated) to recapture a lost past; yet 'tradition' is a resource as refunctionable in postmodernity (or 'late modernity') as are all other cultural artifacts. How this reappropriation is responsibly to be conducted is a task we are only beginning to learn. The mechanical recapitulation of Christian doctrine merely as items in an inherited belief system, undertaken as though nothing had happened, is indefensible.

The reconfiguration of the theological task requires immersion in the dialectics of identity as they emerge from the history and evolution of the social and human sciences in the transitions of modernity. Religion and the expression of its critical and responsible reflexivity, theology, can become methodologically equipped to address this enigma of identity. They will have to do so, however, whilst willing to confront the absolute contrast of the individual and the collective, the relative and the absolute and the immanent and the transcendent. These and other contingencies touched upon in this chapter are inherent in our condition as human beings. This means that all theology should be contextual and should relate to human needs, be it at the level of basic communities or the global condition. It should also be stirred by an articulate hope that things could be other than they are. Anything less is a deviation. Understanding must be grounded in such correlations, but it is misleading to suppose that co-responsibility of this kind implies a contempt for the intellect. As Antonio Gramsci argued for socialism, so for a theology informed by the social and human sciences, the theologian should be an organic intellectual, a risk-taker, an entrepreneur of the mind and heart who is willing to withstand the systemic marginality that afflicts all those who are willing to cross boundaries in the borderlands that are normative in the contemporary human condition.

PART 3

Religion and social science: identity, globalisation and the transmutation of the religious field

CHAPTER 8

The souls of Europe: identity, religion and theology

INTRODUCTION: 'DIVINITY' AND ITS DISCONTENTS

My topic, that of the conflicting identities of Europe (a theme that I have focused metaphorically as the 'souls of Europe'), is one which shows how 'divinity' might now operate today, in what has been influentially represented by Jean-François Lyotard as the 'postmodern condition'. I am also concerned to show how 'divinity' understood as the study of religion and theology, whilst fraught with difficulty, is simultaneously and equally a task full of promise; that is when, as I shall argue, the term 'divinity' is rightly understood.[1]

Given my experience as a Professor of Divinity in Scotland, this chapter has a relative focus through which an array of major issues can be refracted, in part at least, on the basis of participant observation. What, then, is 'divinity'? In the ancient Scottish university divinity faculties as founded, or refounded at the Reformation, this term came to comprise dogmatic or systematic theology, philosophy of religion and 'apologetics'. Through this subdisciplinary triad it was possible to articulate 'faith' in dogmatic or systematic theology; to explore the nature and limits of 'reason' as applied to central conceptions of faith in the philosophy of religion; and then to articulate *both* in forms answerable to the world in 'apologetics'.

One purpose here is to show how the disciplinary range and remit of 'divinity' has in effect been changed and extended almost beyond recognition by force of circumstance, not least through cultural transformations taking place at the heart of European culture and society in which the quest for and the rebuilding of identities has become a matter

---

[1] This chapter originated as my Inaugural Lecture when I was Professor of Divinity at the University of St Andrews. It was entitled 'The Souls of Europe' and was published as 'The Construals of "Europe": Religion, Theology and the Problematics of Modernity', in Paul Heelas (ed.), *Religion, Modernity and Postmodernity* (Oxford: Blackwell, 1998), pp. 186–217. The text is lightly revised.

of central importance. From the early modern period, and certainly since the Enlightenment, a gradual and increasingly complex process of secularisation has taken place which has involved not only the marginal-isation of religion and theology but also the occultation and migration of the sacred. The immediate context of the study of religion and theology has, furthermore, also been radically affected, in particular since 1989, by a largely unanticipated global resurgence of religion and of forms of religiosity. Thus on the levels of locality, Europe, and the world system, there are interconnected phenomena which have to be understood and interpreted within a common theoretical framework.

The contemporary situation now confronts us with a fundamental challenge which may be expressed in the form of a dilemma: *either* retreat ever more into the diminishing and fragmented redoubts of traditional religious discourse forced by secularisation to the margins of social life and problematically rebirthed in the sub-cultures of fundamentalism and New Age; *or* redefine in a comprehensive way the remit and tasks of divinity.

In our era in which, as Karl Marx once remarked, 'All that is solid melts into air', it is not, however, religion and theology alone that have experienced crises of identity and relevance, for the representation of 'life' itself in the human and social sciences is also in a relatively fluid and undecided state.[2] The French philosopher-historian Michel Foucault has put it thus: the 'death of God' is attended by the death of man:

> Rather than the death of God – or rather in the wake of that death and in profound correlation with it – what Nietzsche's thought heralds is the end of his murderer; it is the explosion of man's face in laughter and the return of masks.[3]

The *explosion of man's face in laughter* and the *return of masks* are terrifying and perplexing features of our age. Moreover, the *religious* condition is affected. In the resonant image of the distinguished literary critic and comparativist George Steiner: 'It is to the ambiguous after-life of reli-gious feeling in Western culture that we must look, to the malignant energies released by the decay of natural religious forms.'[4] We now live in the 'after-life' of religion, an era of 'post-religion'. Under these

---

[2] From a Reformed theological standpoint the German theologian Jürgen Moltmann provided an effective if now somewhat dated exposition of this dilemma. See Moltmann, *The Crucified God: The Cross of Christ as Foundation and Criticism of Christian Theology* (London: SCM, 1974), introduction and ch. 1.

[3] Michel Foucault, *The Archeology of Knowledge* (London: Tavistock, 1972) pp. 385–6.

[4] George Steiner, *In Bluebeard's Castle: Some Notes Towards the Re-definition of Culture*, T. S. Eliot Memorial Lectures (London: Faber, 1971).

conditions 'tradition' quails in the face of 'de-traditionalisation'; and new religious growths, *masks of identity*, return, not least in forms of fundamentalisms and new forms of religiosity which all in their turn invite critical interpretation.[5] The student and teacher of divinity are, however, faced with a further challenge: whilst new religious growths sprout fungi-like on the stumps and trunks of the fallen trees of tradition – and humanity dances with its new spiritual masks – the traditional main-line denominations of the Christian church in western European culture are for the most part in decline.[6]

As Richard Dawkins has recently – and in a certain measure rightly – pointed out,[7] the institutional functionalisation of a mere dictionary definition of 'theology' (in his case the *Oxford English Dictionary*) as the study of God, his nature and attributes, is scarcely defensible as it stands.[8] For we live in an era in which the existence of God is widely disputed, and the presence of many gods (or even in some quarters of goddesses) is asserted.[9] Furthermore, we now operate in an environment in which budget centre and managerial methods demand well-defined remits. In consequence, what is now at stake is the presuppositions and composition of the inner core of the designated zone of the study of religion and theology, and how this is to be addressed by competencies which – in the absence of an explicit and publicly justifiable remit – might just as well be broken up and, where possible, redistributed.

THE 'SOULS OF EUROPE' AND THE POSTMODERN PROBLEMATIC

If we grant in initial terms the reality of the new constraints and possibilities introduced above, then what might a problem look like to which

---

[5] For an introduction to the growing literature, see Martin E. Marty and R. Scott Appleby, *Fundamentalism Observed* (Chicago: Chicago University Press, 1991) and again Martin Riesebrodt, *Pious Passion: The Emergence of Modern Fundamentalism in the United States and Iran* (Berkeley: University of California Press, 1933).

[6] See Michael Northcott, *Identity and Decline in the Kirk* (Edinburgh: Centre for Theology and Public Issues, 1992) and chapter 6 above.

[7] Richard Dawkins, *The Selfish Gene* (Oxford: Oxford University Press, 1989), ch. 1.

[8] In this book and other works Dawkins proposes a consistent theory of culture in terms of genetic survival. This approach is strongly reminiscent of Ernst Haeckel's *Der Welträtsel*, which was highly influential during the 'first postmodernity'. Dawkins has recently staged a series of attacks upon the continued teaching of 'theology' in British universities, above all at Oxford.

[9] See, for recent examples, Pam Lunn, 'Do Women Need the GODDESS? Some Phenomenological and Sociological Reflections', *Journal of Feminist Theology*, 4 (1993), 17–38, and the Neo-Pagans Monica Sjöö and Barbara Mohr, *The Great Cosmic Mother: Rediscovering the Religion of the Earth* (San Franscisco: Harper & Row, 1987; 2nd edn, 1991).

'divinity' could legitimately address itself? It is to this end that we examine the topic adverted to in the metaphorical title of this text, the 'souls of Europe': that is the problem of European identity, or rather of a range of European *identities*, understood from a standpoint in which religious and theological factors are acknowledged as significant. And this is *despite* the marginalisation and migration of the sacred in European culture evident during the last two centuries.

It is precisely the changed status, the diminished socio-cultural and societal space of religion and theology, that must become fully part of any critical, yet positive, argument designed to sustain the continued pursuit of the study of religion *qua* religion, and theology *qua* theology in the academic setting. Both the context and changes in approach do, of course, have consequences for the church and for ministerial training which are in the longer term inescapable.

'Divinity' now appears to lack a defensible *episteme* or 'the total set of relations that unite, at a given period, the discursive practices that give rise to epistemological figures, sciences, and possibly formalised systems'.[10] We set out on the assumption that underlying the politics of representation involved in the formation and practice of all disciplines there is a universal problem concerning the nature of the human. This crisis is commonly associated with post-structuralism and the depiction of the human as a *postmodern* condition. This implies tacit knowledge. Again in the words of Foucault:

Man has not been able to describe himself as a configuration in the *episteme* without thought at the same time discovering, both in itself and outside itself, at its borders yet also in its very warp and woof, an element of darkness, an apparently inert density in which it is embedded, an unthought which it contains entirely, yet in which it is also caught ... [that is] the Other and shadow.[11]

Religion and theology – and thus divinity – have much thinking of their as-yet *unthought* to do.

The image of the 'souls of Europe' resonates with the conflictual identities that both afflict 'Europe' in an extended and as yet unspecific sense and also affect Scotland as a relatively small, yet important – we may add *paradigmatic* – country on the geographical periphery of Europe.[12]

---

[10] Foucault, *Archeology of Knowledge*, p. 191.

[11] *Ibid.*, pp. 326–7.

[12] The topical importance of Scotland in Europe consists not least in the continued, though much-threatened, existence of 'wilderness', the close proximity of widely differing local cultures, a remarkable layering of languages and dialects, and a distinctive constitutional tradition. Scotland is a societal retort in which the assertion and transformations of cultural identity can be studied

Indeed, for present purposes, Europe and Scotland may be understood as the macrocosm and microcosm, respectively, of a series of interrelated problems. Both dimensions can be analysed as regards the historical and sequential emergence of conflicting identities; and both contexts demand methodological self-awareness. Such self-awareness requires theorisation, which in turn permits the comparison of types based upon the isolation of historical stages in traditions (and the classification of such periodisations) to be transformed into a discussion of *metanarratives* operating in the *conflictual field of forces* that gives rise to identities in the contemporary world. This is a world which now manifests the *postmodern condition*.

Jean-François Lyotard expresses the contemporary state of *metanarratives* in a well-known passage to do with 'incredulity towards metanarratives':

This incredulity is undoubtedly a product of progress in the sciences: but that progress in turn presupposes it. To the obsolescence of the metanarrative apparatus of legitimation corresponds, most notably, the crisis of metaphysical philosophy and of the university institution which in the past relied on it. The narrative function is losing its functors, its great heroes, its great dangers, its great voyages, its great goal. It is being dispersed in clouds of language narrative elements – narrative, but also denotative, prescriptive, descriptive, and so on. Conveyed within each cloud are pragmatic valencies specific to its kind. Each of us lives at the intersection of many of these. However, we do not necessarily establish stable language combinations, and the properties of the ones we do establish are not necessarily communicable.[13]

What is at stake here is this: what happens to identities when traditions pass into an era of *de-traditionalisation* and into *postmodernity*,[14] in which

---

at first hand, fortunately without, as yet, the violent and disastrous characteristics manifested elsewhere in the United Kingdom. Scotland is thus exemplary in the European context: premodernity, modernity and postmodernity closely co-exist – and the socio-political dialectics of Lordship and Bondage are alive in the 'subaltern consciousness' of the nation and its re-emergence. There is a pervasive concern with cultural identity on the part of many Scottish intellectuals; this contrasts markedly with contemporary England, where it seems that *identity is to have no identity*. See David McCrone, *Understanding Scotland: The Sociology of a Stateless Nation* (London: Routledge, 1992); David McCrone, Stephen Kendrick and Pat Shaw (eds.), *The Making of Scotland: Nation, Culture and Social Change* (Edinburgh: Edinburgh University Press/The British Sociological Association, 1989), and David McCrone, *The Sociology of Nationalism: Tomorrow's Ancestors* (London: Routledge, 1998).

[13] Jean-François Lyotard, *The Postmodern Condition: A Report on Knowledge*, 2nd edn (Manchester: Manchester University Press, 1984).

[14] See, for example, Zygmunt Bauman, *Intimations of Postmodernity* (London: Routledge, 1992); Ulrich Beck, *Risk Society: Towards a New Modernity* (London: Sage, 1992); and Anthony Giddens, *Modernity and Self-Identity: Self and Society in the Late Modern Age* (Cambridge: Polity, 1991).

such identities become 'clouds of language narrative elements' which we can only strive to hold together as pragmatic valencies in language combinations? Moreover, how should we transmit and negotiate identities composed of artifacts (including those of religion and even theology) that are exchanged as cultural or symbolic capital in the European marketplace of a globalised world system?[15] This presentation of the context of the problem of identity presupposes a set of fundamental cultural insights implicated in the modern/postmodern problematic, which we shall approach in stages.

We therefore now investigate under the rubrics of 'archaeology' (Michel Foucault) and 'genealogy' (Friedrich Nietzsche) the historical emergence of the 'souls' or cultural identities of 'Europe' as a way of construing in a contextualised way the problematic interactions of *pre-modernity* (Christendom, tradition and the *ancien régime*), *modernity* (the dialectic of Enlightenment, communism, instrumental reason and European integration), and *postmodernity* (inaugurated by the progressive triumph of the market, fluidity of identities, the collapse of communism and the 'End of History'). A thread that links the themes of tradition, conflictual metanarratives and dialectical contemporaneity can be found in the thought of the philosopher Hegel; it is no accident that on an international scale a movement *back to Hegel* is now taking place. So to a brief depiction of Hegel's prefiguration of the present confrontation of pre-modernity, modernity and postmodernity.

In the Hegelian parable of the Lord and Bondsman to be found in the *Phenomenology of Mind* of 1807 Hegel provides an extraordinary and compelling account of the growth of consciousness into a mature and tested self-consciousness. The *Phenomenology* underlies and is received in the work of such thinkers as Karl Marx, Friedrich Nietzsche, Edmund Husserl, Jean-Paul Sartre and Michel Foucault, who all in their respective ways recapitulate and resolve the 'moments' in the knowledge–power nexus.[16] In Hegel's text the dialectical conception of the achievement of full personhood over against the 'other' is represented as a 'trial by death', for

The individual, who has not staked his life, may, no doubt, be recognised as a Person; but he has not attained the truth of this recognition as an independent

---

[15] The most recent survey of the ground is to be found in Peter Beyer, *Religion and Globalization* (London: Sage, 1994). See chapter 9 below.

[16] The contrasting receptions and resolutions of the Hegelian dialectic allow us primary insight into a profound problematic that has worked itself out in later nineteenth- and twentieth-century events. See R. H. Roberts, 'The Reception of Hegel's Parable of Lord and Bondsman', *New Comparison*, 5 (1988), 23–9.

self-consciousness. In the same way each must aim at the death of the other, as it risks its own life thereby; for that other is to it of no more worth than itself; the other's reality is presented to the former as an external other, as outside itself; it must view its otherness as pure existence for itself or as absolute negation.[17]

What is true of consciousness may now also be applied to the emergence of cultures in an era in which cultural identity and cultural agency (or lack of them) appear to displace class as a medium of analysis and empowerment. In Hegel's *Phenomenology* the traditions of *pre-modernity* (associated with ancestral sacralised social hierarchy) come into conflict with *modernity* (the total – and totalising – emancipation of reason and ambiguous *Geist*); yet in Hegel's early dialectic the agonistic emergence of the metanarratives in an unresolved consciousness also prefigures the dynamics of self-creation characteristic of the *postmodern self*. The contrasting receptions and resolutions of the Hegelian dialectic permit insight into the problematic that has worked itself out in the events of the later nineteenth and twentieth centuries. A renewed Hegelian interpretation of European culture after the fall of Marxism may facilitate the thinking of the 'unthought' – and the uncovering of what some of a Eurosceptical turn of mind might well prefer to remain the *politically unthinkable*.

We here touch upon what George Steiner has called the 'theory of aggression'[18] residing in the very heart of European culture; it is the depiction of this dialectic discerned in the successive and then layered identities of 'Europe' that is the focal point of our analysis. It is this problematic that in turn has burdened – and still afflicts – the inner core of Christian theology in the Western world, for 'All recognition is agonistic. We name our own being, as the angel did Jacob, after the dialectic of mutual aggression.'[19]

'EUROPE' AS PERIODISATION AND TYPOLOGY

Approached from the standpoint of history, 'Europe' is a deeply ambiguous term. On the one hand it may be understood as the 'New Europe', in which a configuration of nation states cede sovereignty, and elements of cultural identity – and thus hegemony – to a greater whole, to the extent required by political and economic integration. 'Europe' also, however, implies an uneasy confrontation with the conflictual identities of the 'Old Europe'. As part of a greater conflictual totality these identities

---

[17] Hegel, *The Phenomenology of Mind*, tr. J. B. Baillie (Landon: Macmillan, 1910), p. 233.
[18] Steiner, *In Bluebeard's Castle*, p. 46.
[19] *Ibid.*

emerged, differentiated themselves, enjoyed a near global triumph, and then 'declined'.

In the contemporary context, then, complex tensions now arise between the modernising conformity required by multi-national capitalism expressed in European integration and its 'Europe', on the one hand, and on the other, the 'old' Europe of nationalisms, ethnic diversity, anti-Semitism, fear of Islam, and the renewed Roman Catholic ideology of 'Christendom'. Religious and theological elements have been of importance (both positive and negative) in the successive transformations of the 'idea' and the identities of the 'old' Europe.

The origins of the idea and of the identities of Europe are shrouded in myth.[20] In particular, the myth of Europa presented in its fullest form in the poem of Moschus of Syracuse (c. 200 BC) represents the earliest manifestation of a persisting mythopoeic or myth-creating tendency.[21] In the time of Homer the name 'Europe' applied to Middle Greece, but also, according to other texts, to Thrace and Epirus. Gradually the designation spread to the whole Greek mainland, and then in the colonisation period it referred to one of the three great journey directions away from the homeland (the others being Asia and Libya). Through the later Greek and then the Roman period the sense of this known mainland extended north and west. The historical evolution of Europe prior to the Christian era was profoundly influenced by migrations of Indo-Germanic peoples and population movements. There is now lively argument stimulated by Martin Bernal's monumental two-volume work *Black Athena*,[22] in which he argues for the non-European origins of the civilisation that extended itself from mainland Greece throughout Europe and beyond.

However, neither investigation of the question of historical origins nor the mythopoeic transmutation of those origins is our central concern at

---

[20] K. Hübner provides a wide-ranging account of theories of myth in *Die Wahrheit des Mythos* (Munich: C. H. Beck, 1985); see ch. 3, 'Zur Geschichte der Mythos-Deutung'.

[21] 'The maiden Europa sleeps in her father's palace, dreams that two women are struggling over her and awakes in great fear as the dream seems real. She plays with her friends in a meadow (and the poet recounts the story of the three golden baskets and the history of Zeus). Zeus sees the playing girls, transforms himself into a bull, crosses the meadow, where the girls pass the time with him. Europa trustingly rides on the back of the animal, which runs away with her and swims over the sea to Crete. Europa laments and prays to Poseidon, "Oh woe is me the deeply unhappy one, who has left the house of my father"; Zeus reveals who he is and prophesies her wedding. The poem concludes with the fulfilment of the words of the father of the gods: "So he spoke, and what he spoke was fulfilled".' This is based upon part of the article 'Europa', in *Literatur Lexikon* (Zurich: Kindler Verlag, 1964), vol. II, columns 2513–14.

[22] Martin Bernal, *Black Athena: The Afroasiatic Roots of Classical Civilization* (2 vols., London: Free Association Press, 1978; 2nd edn, 1991).

this point. The various constructions placed upon the historical emergence and geographical consolidation of Europe in late antiquity, the so-called Dark Ages and the early Middle Ages, mapped, amongst others, by Theodor Steinbuchel (1953),[23] Denys Hays (1968),[24] Judith Herrin (1987),[25] and most recently Robert Bartlett (1993),[26] inform our approach, but our focal point is the decipherment of what I shall call the 'politics of representation'. In other words, 'Europe' is always *someone's* representation, and designed to construe, to include – and to exclude.

An awareness of the complexity of the task of isolating European identity is not new. Systems of management of this complexity that involve periodisation are normative in this domain. Thus 'tradition' (*paradosis, traditio*), the paradigm of pre-modern European identity, may be understood as an active 'handing on' that can be traced and constructed through a sequence of linked events. These 'events' are subsequently prioritised, thus becoming the *topoi* or commonplaces of an identity which may achieve normative status for a community, ethnic group, or even, more ambitiously, an entity as large as that of 'Europe' itself. Such transhistorical identities when they purport to attain universal status in the face of modernity may be construed in the terminology of contemporary theory as competing 'metanarratives'. Each such metanarrative seeks to appropriate authority and hegemonic status as a bearer of the authentic European identity.

The passage from pre-modern tradition to modernity was experienced in theology above all as a crisis of history, expressed in the doctrine of *historicism*. In historicism the connection with a secure past becomes problematic: all historical events were seen to be part of a seamless causal chain of probabilities, from which revelation and the supernatural were banished *a priori*. The relation of modernity to postmodernity is never, however, a sequential *transition*, but rather a *dialectical* relation. This is expressed with brilliant economy by Lyotard: 'A work can become modern only if it is first postmodern. Postmodernism thus understood is not modernism at its end but in the nascent state, and this state is constant.'[27]

---

[23] Theodor Steinbuchel, *Europa als Idee und geistige Verwirklichung* (Cologne, 1953).
[24] Denys Hays, *Europe: The Emergence of an Idea in History* (Edinburgh: Edinburgh University Press, 1968).
[25] Judith Herrin, *The Formation of Christendom* (Oxford: Blackwell, 1987).
[26] Robert Bartlett, *The Making of Europe: Conquest, Colonization and Cultural Change* (London: Penguin, 1993).
[27] Lyotard, *Postmodern Condition*, p. 79

PRE-MODERNITY IDENTITY: CATHOLIC TRADITION

Two representative Roman Catholic figures, the English historian Christopher Dawson[28] and the present Pope, John Paul II, may be used in order to illustrate the *thesis* of a European pre-modernity grounded in tradition as opposed to the *antithesis* of modernity. Even within the Roman Catholic apologetic standpoint, it is, however, important to note significantly different resolutions of the problem of identity as periodisation. Christopher Dawson has expressed an extreme Eurocentric standpoint:

The existence of Europe is the basis of the historical development of the modern world, and it is only in relation to that fact that the development of each particular state can be understood.[29]

In the aftermath of the then recent European disaster of the Second World War, Dawson argued that consciousness of nationality and the nation-state had tended to leave 'Europe in the background as a vague abstraction or as nothing more than a geographical expression'.[30] Furthermore, he maintained that the conception of *Europe* as such never held a definite place in a tradition of education that had been effectively dominated, at one level, by the history of the ancient world of Greece and Rome, and, at a much lower level, by consciousness of an individual's own country. These were factors unfortunately linked in the British public consciousness by such works as Gibbon's *Decline and Fall of the Roman Empire*. Indeed, Dawson directly attributed the European catastrophe to this misguided double focus:

To ignore Europe and to concentrate all our attention on the political community to which we belong, as though it was the whole social reality, leads in the last resort to the totalitarian state, and National Socialism itself was only this development carried out with Germanic thoroughness and Prussian ruthlessness.[31]

For Dawson, democratic European states had ignored the 'existence of Europe as a social reality' and they thus stood irresolutely between the nation-state and the 'ideal of a cosmopolitan liberal world order'.[32]

---

[28] See the series of books by Christopher Dawson, *The Making of Europe: An Introduction to the History of European Unity* (London: Sheed & Ward, 1932); *Religion and Culture*, Gifford Lectures (London: Sheed & Ward, 1948); *Understanding Europe* (London: Sheed & Ward, 1952).

[29] Dawson, *Understanding Europe*, p. 24.

[30] *Ibid.*

[31] *Ibid.*

[32] *Ibid.*

The latter, embodied in the League of Nations and its failure in the interwar period, was theoretically co-extensive with the human race. But in practice it was dependent on the realities of international trade and finance. Thus according to Dawson:

Europe is more than the sum of the nations and states of the European continent, and it is much more than a subdivision of the modern international society. In so far as a world society or a world civilisation can be said to exist, it is the child of Europe, and if, as many peoples believe to-day, this ideal of world civilization is being shipwrecked before it has achieved realization, then Europe remains the most highly developed form of society the world has yet known.[33]

Dawson developed his distinctively Eurocentric standpoint in the broad 'Christendom' tradition. Europe as such is defined as

a community of peoples who share in a common spiritual tradition that had its origins three thousand years ago in the eastern Mediterranean and which has been transmitted from age to age and from people to people until it has come to overshadow the world.[34]

For Dawson, Europe can only be understood by the study of *Christian* culture: for 'it was as Christendom that Europe first became conscious of itself as a society of peoples with common moral values and common spiritual aims'.[35] Dawson then develops a seven-stage account of the history of Western culture which is dominated by transitions that become the *topoi* or *loci* – the commonplaces – of a tradition that aspires to the status of total trans-national cultural system.[36]

Dawson's stages are: (1) the pre-Christian (and thus pre-European) stage, which is to be regarded as the source of the intellectual and social traditions of the West; (2) the time from Alexander to Augustus, and from the death of Augustus to the conversion of Constantine, which saw the growth of Rome and a cooperative effort between the two great Mediterranean peoples that enabled Christianity successfully to transplant a sacred tradition of immemorial antiquity into the Roman-Hellenistic world; (3) the formation of Western Christendom

---

[33] *Ibid.*, pp. 25–6.
[34] *Ibid.*, p. 26.
[35] *Ibid.*
[36] Ernst Troeltsch tackles this problematic comparatively in his work of 1922, where he reviews the periodisations offered by Hegel, Ranke, Guizot, Harnack, Weber and Sombart, amongst others. See Ernst Troeltsch, 'Der Europäismus' and 'Das Problem einer objektiven Periodisierung', sections 2 and 3 of ch. 4, 'Über den Aufbau der europäischen Kulturgeschichte', of *Das logische Problem der Geschichtsphilosophie*, bk 1 of *Der Historismus und seine Problem, Gesammelte Schriften*, vol. III (Tübingen: J. C. B. Mohr (Paul Siebeck), 1922; reprinted Darmstadt: Scientia Aalen, 1961).

through the conversion of the barbarians and the subsequent transmission of Mediterranean culture by the Church; (4) the expansion of Christendom from the eleventh century onwards through cultural activity inspired by the Carolingian conception of Christendom as a social unity, the society of the Christian people, which transcended the lesser unities of nation and kingdom and city in an ideal of the universal Christian empire which (although corrupted) survived long enough to inspire the fourteenth-century poet Dante.

After reaching the high point of European development in the work of Dante, the remaining stages in Dawson's periodisation constitute a regrettable falling away from the ideal of Christendom. Thus (5) both the Renaissance and the Reformation, (6) post-Renaissance Europe until 1914, and (7) the period from 1914 to 1950 are lesser adjuncts.[37] These are all a record of contingent imperfection against which the authentic would-be bearer of European identity has to respond through a *return to*, or *recovery of*, Christendom.

Any contemporary scheme of periodisation undertaken in strictly diachronic and sequential terms would now, of course, require the addition of (8), the Cold War and of European integration in the EC (1949–89); and (9) the era from 1989 onwards, with the reality of a renewed but unresolved greater Europe, in which the question of identity once more holds centre stage.[38] But the simple addition of further contemporary periods is pointless if it is not attended by a theorisation which recognises that the recent transitions involve *qualitative disruption* and the subsequent *dialectical interaction*, indeed the *functionalisation* of pre-modernity and modernity in the postmodern condition. Here our concern is above all with the critique of a particular periodisation and typology.

The Roman Catholic Church has of course traditionally invested heavily in the conception of a unified Christian Europe, and this idea has undergone systematic renovation and indeed reassertion on a number of levels during the pontificate of Pope John Paul II. To take one example, an important and unambiguous expression of papal strategy is to be found in two statements concerned with the spiritual patronage of the

---

37 For further reading relating to historical schematisation, see Steven Ozment (ed.), *Culture and Belief in Europe, 1460–1600: An Anthology of Sources* (The Hague: Van Leeuwen, 1990); Theodor Arend, *Christianity and World History* (London: Edinburgh House Press, 1964); J. M. Wallace-Hadrill, *Bede's Europe* (Jarrow: St Paul's Rectory, 1962); and Werner Weidenfeld and Wolfgang Wessels (eds.), *Die Identität Europas* (Bonn: Goldmann, 1981).

38 Here we follow the inspiration of Hayden White, *Metahistory: The Historical Imagination in the Nineteenth Century* (Baltimore: The Johns Hopkins University Press, 1973), and his analysis of the rhetorical constitution of historical periodisation as the commonplaces or *topoi* in a comprehensive analysis of nineteenth-century strategies of historical representation.

European totality, 'Cyril and Methodius'[39] and 'Europe and the Faith',[40] issued in 1981 and 1985, respectively.[41]

In the earlier document the Pope set out the theological ground-rules for a historic decade during which several important anniversaries of the millennium of the conversion of eastern Europe would take place (for example the conversion of the Rus of Kiev in 988). Thus in 'Cyril and Methodius', the Pope made a strategic ideological pre-emptive strike by bringing into conjunction the patronage of western Europe by St Benedict, declared by Paul VI in 1964, with his own declaration of the patronage of eastern Europe by the Thessalonican brothers Cyril and Methodius (who died in 869 and 885, respectively). Subsequent developments have indicated the apparent wisdom of this commitment, now that inter-denominational and inter- religious struggles – suppressed by Marxism-Leninism and exacerbated by economic crisis – have once more broken out after the collapse of communism in 1989–90.

Few contemporary institutions can claim such historical legitimation as that grounded in the undivided church, that is the church prior to the Photian Schism and the separation of Rome and Byzantium in the ninth century.[42] Constantinople (which sent the brothers) and Rome (which confirmed their mission) are thus presented as *one in intent and purpose*; and when this partnership is placed in the same context of co-patronage with Benedict, 'protection' is seen to apply to the 'whole of Europe'. It is at this juncture that Europe appears in its true form:

Europe, in fact, as a geographical whole, is, so to speak, the fruit of two currents of Christian traditions, to which are added also two different, but at the same time deeply complementary, forms of culture.[43]

The proclamation of the co-patronage of Cyril and Methodius combines historical justification with the future eschatological reference of the 'signs of the times'. Thus the new-born Europe of the Dark Ages 'ensured the Europe of today a common spiritual and cultural heritage'.[44] Now, in a new Dark Age of Europe, that primal resource must be reasserted.

---

[39] Pope John Paul II, 'Cyril and Methodius', 31 December 1980.
[40] Pope John Paul II, 'Europe and the Faith', 11 October 1985.
[41] Key sources are: Pope John Paul, Apostolic Letter 'Egregiae Virtutis', 1981, proclaiming the Apostles to the Slavs, SS Cyril and Methodius, co-patrons of Europe along with St Benedict; and John Paul II, 'Cyril and Methodius' and 'Europe and the Faith'. See also J. P. Willaime, *Strasbourg, Jean-Paul II et l'Europe* (Paris: Cerf, 1991).
[42] This is an extremely complex and disputed set of events. See F. Dvornik, *The Photian Schism: History and Legends* (Cambridge: Cambridge University Press, 1948).
[43] John Paul II, 'Egregiae Virtutis', p. 17.
[44] *Ibid.*, p. 18.

And all these levels of legitimation combine in a highly distinctive form of discourse:

> Therefore, with certain knowledge and my mature deliberation, in the fullness of apostolic authority, by virtue of this Letter *and for ever*, I constitute and declare saints Cyril and Methodius heavenly co-patrons of the whole of Europe before God, granting furthermore all the honours and privileges which belong, according to law, to the principal Patron Saints of places (my italics).[45]

The second Apostolic Letter, 'Europe and the Faith', is a document that provides a fuller account of the papal understanding of contemporary Europe and the relevance to it of its 'Christian roots'. The Pope begins with a characterisation of the contemporary Europe whose destiny is at stake:[46]

> The Europe to which we are sent out has undergone such cultural, political, social and economic transformations as to formulate the problem of evangelization in totally new terms. We could even say that Europe, as she has appeared following the complex events of the last century, has presented Christianity and the Church with the most radical challenge history has witnessed, but at the same time opened the way today to new and creative possibilities for the proclamation and incarnation of the Gospel.[47]

The programme of the Roman Catholic Church implied in these documents is not so much dialogical as *evangelistic* in orientation. The consistent lack of allusions to any fundamental crisis affecting the church, or indeed to Protestantism, is remarkable: the latter is here seemingly regarded as an irrelevance, an aberration over which Catholicism leaps without great effort back to a primal unity, a cultural *fons et origo*.

It is significant that here once more a succession of distinctive *topoi* (involving both exclusions and inclusions) articulate a narrative identity grounded in tradition. The Roman Catholic discourse of identity undergoes rhetorical development in preparation as it were for the last battle at the 'End of History'. A binary scission is acknowledged; plurality is eschewed in the sphere of Christian values, as living tradition confronts modernity. It is, however, Pope John Paul II's apparent 'resistance to

---

[45] *Ibid.*

[46] It is remarkable that given John Paul II's expert acquaintance with phenomenology he rejects the construal of the European condition as 'crisis'. Thus Husserl (Karol Wojtila's intellectual mentor) lectured on 7 and 10 May 1935 in Vienna with the original title of 'Philosophy in the Crisis of European Mankind'. Pope John Paul's Letter of 1985, 'Europe and the Faith', might perhaps be understood as a deliberate repudiation of Husserl's representation of the idea of Europe. See Edmund Husserl, *The Crisis of the European Sciences and Transcendental Phenomenology: An Introduction to Phenomenological Philosophy* (Evanston: Northwestern University Press, 1970), pp. 269–99.

[47] John Paul II, 'Europe and the Faith', p. 279.

theory', expressed in a *retreat* from periodisation of the history of
the divided church – the Renaissance, the Reformation and the
Enlightenment – that tends to isolate and consolidate contemporary
Catholic teaching at some distance from the dynamics of *self*-creation that
constitutes *postmodernity*. The postulation of a seamless trans-historical
identity is itself an act of spiritual and theological politics, part of whose
rhetoric is to be the *ars theologica artem celare*: the theological art that seeks
to conceal its artfulness.

The Roman Catholic and papal vision is that of ancestral tradition,
the inner principle of the *ancien régime*, a conception of continuity and
interpretative *topoi* that constitutes the *pre-modern* thesis in our argument,
and, if we once more appropriate Hegel's parable, may be regarded as
the *mentalité* of unconscious spiritual Lordship (*Herrschaft*) that sees no real
need to recognise the other, other than to negate it through evangelical
love – and the exacting of 'docility in the Spirit'.

Before we turn to the real antithesis of Catholicism, the European
modernity of the unambiguous Faustian and Promethean self-assertion of
Marx and Nietzsche, and for our purposes, Oswald Spengler, we must
briefly touch upon the uneasy and unstable accommodation effected
by Liberal Protestantism. Both the original Protestant Reformation and
the later accommodating synthesis between pre-modern tradition and
modernity in the guise of 'progress' attempted by Ernst Troeltsch's
'Liberal Protestantism' are effectively ignored in the papal documents in
question. The constructive processes underlying this papal strategy are
perhaps best seen in the fate of the 'Others' that fall outside tradition,
and thus outwith the now newly *recreated* Roman Catholic metanarrative
of European spiritual as well as the cultural *unity* of East and West (and
the elision of historical discontinuity), which is secured on the level of
theological ideology and religious cultural politics.

IDENTITY AS ACCOMMODATION: LIBERAL PROTESTANTISM[48]

In 1912, when confronting the then contemporary significance of the
Reformation for Germany – and for civilisation itself – the historian and
sociologist Ernst Troeltsch considered the question of cultural identity at

---

[48] See Roger Mehl, *Das protestantische Europa* (Stuttgart: Fischer, 1959); Karl-Heinz Pfeffer, 'Der
Protestantismus in Europa: Dokumente', *Zeitschrift für internationale Zusammenarbeit* 13 (1957),
171–4, 183–278; Hans Roser, *Protestanten und Europa* (Munich: Claudius Verlag, 1979); Trutz
Rendtorff (ed.), *Europa: Theologische Versüche einer Ortsbestimmung* (Gütersloh: Gerd Mohn, 1980);
Trutz Rendtorff, 'Universalität oder Kontextualität der Theologie: eine "europäische" Stel-
lungnahme', *Zeitschrift für Theologie und Kirche*, 74 (1977), 238–54; and Hans Hermann Walz,
Der politische Auftrag des Protestantismus in Europa (Tübingen: J. C. B. Mohr, 1955).

the high point of European self-confidence. In *Protestantism and Progress*,[49] Troeltsch touched upon the deepest currents of the specifically German and thus Protestant contributions to the identities of Europe. In 1912, when the old order was about to disappear, Troeltsch sought to gain insight into the intellectual and religious situation of his day, assessing it as that 'from which the significance and the possibilities of development possessed by Christianity might be deduced'.[50]

In outright contrast to the representative Roman Catholic commentators we have considered above, Troeltsch held that 'the living possibilities of development and progress are to be found on Protestant soil',[51] and thus specifically *not* within Catholicism, which remains for him an essentially non-progressive phenomenon. Troeltsch sought to distinguish the perennially valuable elements in modern civilisation from the temporary, and on this basis to establish a position of stable compromise:

to give the religious ideas of Christianity – which I hold to be the sole really religious force in our European system of civilisation, and which I also believe to be superior to the religions of the East – a shape and form capable of doing justice to the absoluteness of religious conviction, and at the same time in harmony with the valuable elements in the modern spirit.[52]

Troeltsch proceeds to expound the ambiguous role of Protestantism in the history of western Europe and North America. Protestantism appeared as a 'revival and reinforcement of the ideal of authoritatively imposed Church-civilisation' which served to revive the Catholic idea and relaunched the 'medieval spirit'[53] for a further two centuries.[54] It was only in the late seventeenth and the eighteenth centuries that the struggle for freedom took place which effectively terminated the Middle Ages. There is thus an ineradicable paradox embedded in the historical career of Protestantism, and this is best explored if 'we seek its influence at first not in a universal regeneration or reconstruction of life as a whole, but mainly in indirect and unconsciously produced effects, nay, even in

---

[49] Ernst Troeltsch, *Protestantism and Progress: A Historical Study of the Relation of Protestantism to the Modern World* (London: Williams & Norgate, 1912); see also Troeltsch, 'Der Europäismus'.

[50] Troeltsch, *Protestantism and Progress*, pp. v–vi.

[51] *Ibid.*, p. vi.

[52] *Ibid.*, pp. vii–viii.

[53] *Ibid.*, pp. 85–6.

[54] The pathos of the Reformation was well expressed in the words put into Cajetan's mouth by John Osborne in his play *Luther*: 'You know, a time will come when a man will no longer be able to say, "I speak Latin and am a Christian" and go his way in peace. There will come frontiers, frontiers of all kinds – between men – and there'll be no end to them', *Luther* (London: Faber, 1961), p. 74.

accidental side-influences, or again in influences produced against its will'.[55]

The Protestant heritage in Europe is therefore consistently ambiguous. It recapitulates Christian identities in forms fraught with compromise. Even as Luther had abandoned the world to the worldly authority, so Troeltsch accepted that the world as such fell under the unchallengeable sway of historicism.[56] He consequently believed that an uneasy tension existed between historicism and a residual inner conviction that Christian values were superior to those of other cultures. In contemporary terms, we might say that as a provisional synthesis made between Christian antiquity and modernity, Protestantism purported to hold the middle ground: but this does not now furnish the dialectical integration that is an imperative requirement in the face of *postmodernity*.

The political and existential weakness of the *retreat* or *turn to the subject* characteristic of Protestantism was not lost on one strident commentator, Francis Fukuyama, whose work has recently come once more to wider public attention in the new *Zeitgeist* of postcommunism.[57] The redoubtable cultural historian and disciple of Nietzsche, Oswald Spengler, wrote in *The Decline of the West* (1926):[58]

> I have the same view that the cause of all our troubles is Christianity . . . As a view of life Protestantism in comparison with Judaism, Catholicism, and Bolshevism, is a nullity. Nevertheless, it carries with it the immense danger that it has a passive effect upon people. From this comes the lack of self interest, of independence, of capacity of self defence, of instinct for danger.[59]

What is then that modernity with its instinct for danger with which Troeltsch had to strike his compromise? What is the modernity against which Roman Catholicism now directs itself in fundamental antithesis? What is this reality in relation to which Protestantism is but a mere interlude – or, in Spengler's terms, a *nullity*? It is here that we encounter that other Europe, a Europe that repudiates its Christian heritage in order to strike back into different bedrock. This is a 'Europe' that advocates explicit power, a Europe that is unambiguously Promethean – and modern.

[55] Troeltsch, *Protestantism and Progress*, p. 87.

[56] See Troeltsch's celebrated article 'History', in James Hastings (ed.), *Encyclopaedia of Religion and Ethics* (Edinburgh: T. & T. Clark, 1926).

[57] See Fukuyama, *The End of History and the Last Man* (London: Hamish Hamilton, 1989) and chapter 1 above.

[58] Oswald Spengler, *The Decline of the West: Form and Actuality* (London: George Allen & Unwin, 1926) and *Man and Technics* (London: Murray, 1931).

[59] Spengler, *The Decline of the West*, p. 62.

PROMETHEAN MODERNITY: THE NEGATION OF 'EUROPE'

In characterising European, indeed global 'modernity', as Promethean, it is possible to adopt a number of approaches.[60] Thus both Marx and Nietzsche afford receptions and developments of Enlightenment reason that emphasise the recovery of the lost, thwarted grandeur of man. I have chosen instead to focus upon the lesser-known and ambiguous figure of Oswald Spengler (1880–1939).[61]

Spengler, a former *Gymnasium* (grammar-school) teacher turned private scholar, published *Der Untergang des Abendlandes* in Munich (1918–22). *The Decline of the West* was conceived before and finished during the First World War, and had an immense impact upon a defeated German population, which had – with unprecedented unity – fought and lost the War. Spengler has never been a fully respectable figure in academic terms, but his significance is nonetheless very considerable. This advocacy of Goethe and Nietzsche, his endorsement of ruthless entrepreneurial capitalism (epitomised by Cecil Rhodes) and his hatred of Bolshevism resonated strongly with the then *Zeitgeist*, a *first postmodernity* of Weimar culture, and thus with our own era – the *second postmodernity*.[62] Spengler expresses what is now a topical post-Marxist perspective *prior* to the full-flowering of Marxism-Leninism and Stalinism, and the collapse of communism. As Francis Fukuyama has rightly discerned, Spengler *pre-*thought those parts of the once *unthinkable* that now resurface in the Neo-Darwinian warrior ethos of resurgent capitalism.

Many of the major German-speaking Protestant theologians of the first half of the twentieth century, for example Karl Barth, Emil Brunner, Rudolf Bultmann, Paul Tillich and Friedrich Gogarten (all collaborators in the journal *Zwischen den Zeiten*, 1922–33), were inescapably aware of the impact of Spengler's text as '*the* philosophy' of their time.[63] Spengler's success stemmed not least from his presentation of the history of the

---

[60] For general background see Franz Ansprenger, *The Dissolution of the Colonial Empires* (London: Routledge, 1989); Jean Beacher, John Hall and Michael Mann, *Europe and the Rise of Capitalism* (Oxford: Blackwell, 1988); Max Beloff, *Europe and the Empires* (London: Chatto & Windus, 1957); Karl Jaspers, *Vom europäischen Geist: Vortrag gehalten bei den Rencontres Internationales de Génève September 1946* (Munich: Piper Verlag, 1947); Paul Kennedy, *The Rise and Fall of the Great Powers* (London: Collins, 1989); J. M. Roberts, *The Triumph of the West* (London: BBC, 1985); Eugen Rosenstock-Hüessy, *Die Europäischen Revolutionen und der Charakter der Nationenen* (Stuttgart: W. Kohlhammer Verlag, 1931; reprinted 1951).

[61] W. Dray, *Perspectives on History* (London: Routledge & Kegan Paul, 1980); H. S. Hughes, *Oswald Spengler: A Critical Estimate* (New York: Scribner, 1952).

[62] This distinction is developed in R. H. Roberts, 'Barth and the Eschatology of Weimar', *A Theology on its Way: Essays on Karl Barth* (Edinburgh: T. & T. Clark, 1992).

[63] Spengler, *The Decline of the West*, p. xv. The comment dates from December 1917.

West as a 'natural philosophy', so that responsibility for national failure is attributable neither to the nation nor to the individual but to the cyclic character of the historical process itself.[64]

All branches of a culture are bound together in the 'morphological relationship', in what Spengler calls the 'logic of space' within which 'Man' is a meaning-forming conscious organism faced with the continuing problem of securing 'world-formation'.[65] Spengler dismisses the traditional subdivision of history into 'Ancient', 'Medieval' and 'Modern' which universalises the ancestral Christian time-scale. These are terms which distort the immensity of world history as the history of many cultures. The very word 'Europe' comes in for pointed attack. Spengler stresses the constructed and transient character of all characterisations of 'Europe'. Indeed:

The word 'Europe' ought to be struck out of history. There is historically no 'European' type, and it is sheer delusion to speak of the Hellenes as 'European Antiquity' . . . It is thanks to the word 'Europe' alone, and the complex of ideas resulting from it, that our historical consciousness has come to link Russia with the West in an utterly baseless unity . . . 'East' and 'West' are notions that contain real history, whereas 'Europe' is an empty sound.[66]

Spengler's historical Copernican revolution involves a radical de-centring of the European subject and its conceits. This is a form of deconstruction *avant la lettre* which, moreover, presages in a 'first post-modernity' the contemporary dynamics of the so-called 'postmodern condition'. For Spengler, the self-assertion of a culture in its own context becomes the blameless norm; the organic growth of a particular cultural species takes place in a competitive environment:

I see in place of that empty figment of one linear history . . . the drama of *a number* of mighty Cultures, each springing with primitive strength from the soil of a mother-region to which it remains firmly bound throughout its life-cycle; each stamping its material, its mankind, in *its own* image; each having *its own* idea, *its own* passions, *its own* life, will and feeling, *its own* death.[67]

The 'Decline of the West' has thus become the problem of '*Civilisation*'; the latter state is the routinised petrifaction of that which *has become*, and it

---

[64] Karl Löwith addresses related problems in *Meaning in History* (Chicago: Chicago University Press, 1946).

[65] Spengler, *The Decline of the West*, pp. 6–7.

[66] *Ibid.*, p. 16. Said's arguments also have a particular relevance here. Spengler stresses the historical construction of identities and deconstructs local pretensions.

[67] *Ibid.*, p. 21.

succeeds the vitality of *becoming* expressed in a true Culture. Thus 'Civil-isations' are external and artificial, the death that follows life. With a challenging and unadorned honesty casting his mind as it were beyond the interlude of Bolshevism, Spengler remarks that in 'Civilisation' it is *money* that comes to the fore as dominant cultural phenomenon. For Spengler it is Cecil Rhodes (rather than, as has been the case in our own time, Margaret Thatcher, 'Tiny' Rowland, Ivan Bowsky or Rupert Murdoch) who is the symbol of the woman or man of imperialism and capitalism. In Civilisation the energy of such hero-leaders is directed outwards, rather than inwards, as in the case of the outdated, even ef-fete 'culture-man'[68] – that is, what in England Right-wing politicians might designate a member of the 'chattering classes'. As a then present-day Caesar, Rhodes exemplified the power that precedes the inevitable Nemesis of the over-extension, petrification and decay that will ultimately result from the slogan 'Expansion is everything.' Like Francis Fukuyama in *The End of History and the Last Man*, Spengler concentrates upon the apotheosis of the capitalist conqueror, the economic and technological warrior-hero, the veritable *master* for whom others will be *slaves* in the aggressive social Neo-Darwinianism of post-Marxist modernity.

According to Spengler, West European man must relearn his place within a general cultural scheme, be warned, and devote himself prag-matically to 'technics instead of lyrics, the sea instead of the paintbrush, and politics instead of epistemology' in the *early winter* of Civilisation.[69] In this particular 'Back to Basics', renewed scepticism is informed by the 'universal symbolism' of the 'Morphology of world-history'[70] and thus the World War itself becomes part of a greater scheme, 'the type of a historical change of phase occurring within a great historical organism of definable compass at the point preordained for it hundreds of years ago'.[71]

It now becomes apparent that our investigation of the identities of 'Europe' involves a struggle for, as it were, the very soul of a continent and its cultures. Spengler's identification of the modern evolution of Western

---

[68] *Ibid.*, p. 37.

[69] *Ibid.*, p. 41.

[70] *Ibid.*, p. 46.

[71] *Ibid.* The quasi-theological undertones of Spengler's argument are apparent in his citation of Goethe's correspondence with Eckermann in the English text of *The Decline of the West*, p. 49, n. 1: 'I would not have one word changed in this: "the Godhead is effective in the living and not in the dead, in the becoming and the changing not in the become and the set-fast, and therefore, similarly, the reason (*Vernunft*) is concerned only to strive towards the divine through the becoming and the living, and the understanding (*Verstand*) only to make us of the become and the set-fast."'

civilisation with the single motif of the Faust legend and the organic naturalism of Goethe, combined with the subversive impulse of Nietzsche and energised by rampant technological capitalism, leads to a *caesura*:

The insatiable historical voracity of the Western mind began with Hegel. He himself relied entirely on the traditional view of history (antiquity–Middle Ages–Modern Times). Actually an 'extensive knowledge of history finally leads of necessity to a perception of the void – in the artistic language of Goethe 'the beautiful purposeless game of Living Nature'...The standard of knowledge in 1820 supported the belief in something 'Absolute' *behind* single individual historical events. Today, however, we see India and China and Mexico with their dead cultures.[72]

With historical hindsight, modernity – and instrumental reason – has now to be reconceived after the Third Reich, the Holocaust, the discovery and use of atomic weapons and the collapse of communism. In the midst of the iniquities of the present we require a more dialectical and theoretical representation of the nature of European identity, that is if 'Europe' is not, in Spengler's words, to be *struck out* of history. In order to attempt this, we return to the radical Hegelian impulse and trace out anew the representation of 'Europe' from the standpoint of its 'others', that is from the standpoint of the *slave* rather than the Lord or Master.

'EUROPE' AND THE *OTHER*

'Christendom' as a conception exists most powerfully in the constructive imagination of those who propound its virtues. The defence of 'Christendom' has from the time of Augustine involved coercive enforcement as a means of sustaining its integrity. As regards Europe's and Christendom's 'others', two important areas of concern stand out: the treatment of the Jews and the relationship with Islam.[73] With respect to the former, some feminist theologians – for example Rosemary Radford Ruether in *Faith and Fratricide*[74] – have argued that Christianity is deeply

---

[72] A. Helps (ed.), *Spengler Letters 1913–1936* (London: George Allen & Unwin, 1966), pp. 72–3.

[73] For background information see Stephen Castles, Heather Booth and Tina Wallace (eds.), *Here for Good: Western Europe's New Ethnic Minorities* (London: Pluto Press, 1984); Paulo Cecchini, Michel Continat and Alexis Jacquethar, *The European Challenge 1992: The Benefits of a Single Market?* (New York: Wildwood House, 1988); John Edwards, *The Jews in Christian Europe* (London: Longmans, 1988); Herrin, *Formation of Christendom*; A. G. Lehmann, *The European Heritage: An Outline of Western Culture* (London: Phaidon, 1984); W. Montgomery Watt, *The Influence of Islam on Medieval Europe* (Edinburgh: Edinburgh University Press, 1972); A. D. Wright (ed.), *The Counter-Reformation: Catholic Europe and the Non-Christian World* (London: Weidenfeld & Nicolson, 1982).

[74] See Rosemary Radford Ruether, *Faith and Fratricide: The Theological Roots of Anti-Semitism*, (New York: Seabury Press, 1974).

and irrecoverably anti-Semitic. This argument is now being played out in a most acute form in the diverse Jewish, Christian and secular responses to the Holocaust.[75] Outcomes are intrinsically related to recent discussion of modernity, and its expressions in the 'dialectic of Enlightenment' and its cultural antecedents.[76]

It is, however, the 'Orientalism' debate provoked by the distinguished Palestinian Christian literary critic Edward Said[77] which affords us a vital clue in the present argument in which we seek to go beyond the mere periodisation of traditions – or even – as with Troeltsch and Spengler, to go beyond the typologies of consciousness or *mentalités* into the dynamics of cultural agency.

In thinking the *unthought* implicit in the formation of the identity of Islam as presented in 'Orientalism', Said makes explicit reference to Hegel in his analysis of the *construction* of a cultural identity and its *imposition* upon a living culture. Said thus subjects the construction of *discourses of representation* of both 'Orientalism' and the resultant scholarly method to deconstructive analysis out of which emerges his understanding of the politics of representation.[78] Said begins by designating the Orient and its special place in European experience in the following way:

> The Orient is not only adjacent to Europe; it is also the place of Europe's greatest and richest and oldest colonies, the source of its civilizations and languages, its cultural contestant, and one of its deepest and most recurrent images of the Other. In addition, the Orient has helped to define Europe (or the West) as its contrasting image, idea, personality, experience.[79]

Said's designation of the Orient as 'the other' resonates with Hegelian overtones and the explicit assimilation of the dialectics of lordship and

---

75 The literature is vast. See, for an introduction, Richard L. Rubenstein and John K. Roth, 'The Silence of God: Philosophical and Religious Reflection on the Holocaust', in Richard L. Rubenstein and John K. Roth (eds.), *Approaches to Auschwitz: The Legacy of the Holocaust* (London: SPCK, 1987), pp. 290–336.

76 See Zygmunt Bauman, *Modernity and the Holocaust* (Cambridge: Polity, 1989). The problematic consequences of the Enlightenment and its core role in Western thought are confronted in Max Horkheimer and T. W. Adorno, 'The Concept of Enlightenment', *Dialectic of Enlightenment* (London: Allen Lane, 1972), pp. 3–80.

77 Edward Said, *Orientalism: Western Conceptions of the Orient* (Harmondsworth: Penguin, 1978; 2nd edn, 1991).

78 See Michel Foucault, 'Representing', *The Order of Things: An Archeology of the Human Sciences* (London: Tavistock, 1970), ch. 3; and Michel Foucault, 'Archaeology and the History of Ideas', *Archeology of Knowledge*, part IV, ch. 1. Maxime Rodinson, *Europe and the Mystique of Islam* (London: I. B. Taurus, 1988) provides a complementary account of Western misconceptions of Islam.

79 Said, *Orientalism*, pp. 1–2.

bondage drawn from the *Phenomenology of Mind*.[80] The metaphors and the parable provide the language and interlocking conceptions used to designate and represent the discourses of culture and identities as *constructions* based on *interest*. Thus Orientalism, which presents itself as an allegedly scientific and purely objective study, is dealt with

as the corporate institution for dealing with the Orient – dealing with it by making statements about it, authorizing views of it, describing it, by teaching it, ruling over it: in short Orientalism as a Western style for dominating, restructuring, and having authority over the Orient.[81]

The representation and interpretation of Islam within the ambit of Orientalism is thus understood as the exercise of a form of cultural hegemony, in Gramsci's (1971) understanding of the term through *self-assimilated* ideological control. Conversely and reciprocally, this is directly relevant to the formation of *European* identity itself, for:

Orientalism is never far from what Denys Hay has called the idea of Europe, a collective notion identifying 'us' Europeans as against all 'those' non-Europeans, and indeed it can be argued that the major components in European culture are precisely what made that culture hegemonic both in and outside Europe: the idea of European identity as a superior one in comparison with all non-European peoples and cultures.[82]

Said maintains that the flexible strategy of cultural dominance through definition of the 'other' is closely associated with anti-Semitism: 'I have found myself writing the history of a strange, secret sharer of Western anti-Semitism.'[83] The rise of Orientalism as the charged study of the 'other' culture is traced back to the Council of Vienne (1312). The Islamic invasions beginning in the seventh century served to shift the centre of European culture northwards away from the Mediterranean and into a form of enclosure: the Romano-German civilisation of the Holy Roman Empire. Consequently, as Pirenne has argued, 'Christendom' became the 'one great Christian community, conterminous with the ecclesia . . . The Occident was now living its own life.'[84]

Said regards Orientalism as the product of a political master–slave relationship the terms of which are applicable, by direct transfer, to

---

[80] Hegel, *Phenomenology of Mind*, pp. 228–67; see also Roberts, 'Reception'. It is significant that Francis Fukuyama entitles ch. 18 of *The End of History* 'Lordship and Bondage'.
[81] Said, *Orientalism*, p. 3.
[82] *Ibid.*, p. 7.
[83] *Ibid.*, p. 27.
[84] H. Pirenne, *Mohammed and Charlemagne* (New York: W. W. Norton & Co., 1939), pp. 234, 283.

the decipherment of the construction of the idea of 'Europe' as such. In the Enlightenment, and in particular in that side of the German Enlightenment imbued with Romanticism, the construction of the Oriental and Islamic 'other' took place. Yet we must recognise that this was the same intellectual and social context which gave rise *both* to modern post-Enlightenment German Liberal Protestant theology *and* to the poly-aspectual Romantic quest for primal sources of *European* identity and the possibility of a cultural dynamic freed from Christianity. Here the tensions between the inner-European struggle for cultural hegemony (exemplified supremely by the nineteenth-century conflict between France and Germany), the formation of modern disciplines in the humanities, and imperialism (both political and cultural) converge within a context characterised by rapid and pervasive industrialisation and the secularisation of culture.[85] Here is a central nexus in the struggle for the 'soul of Europe'.

Said argues that with the loss of confidence in the biblical texts as the primal source and justification of the cultural hegemony of Christendom, the Romantics and their associates turned eastwards and applied in transplanted form the Christian motif of dying and rising to a renascent Orient. Thus (and this is surely not without irony) a culture of Indo-European origin, exposed and displayed through the paradigmatic discipline of philology, could in turn service the needs of a culture in crisis. Increasingly deprived of its ancestral epistemological assumptions through Kantian thought in the Enlightenment, and of its Christian mythic history through historicism, the declining metanarrative of 'Europe' needed to draw upon and assimilate the 'others' it had both created and imposed.[86] Thus the negation of the other was simultaneously a creative act – the creation of the other.[87] Such procedures of negation and creation are an *intimation of postmodernity*, the era in which the capacity to self-create is the condition of cultural existence. Indeed, according to Said, 'the Orientalist could celebrate his method, his position, as that of a secular creator, a man who made new

---

[85] Owen Chadwick, *The Secularization of the European Mind in the Nineteenth Century* (Cambridge: Cambridge University Press, 1975; reprinted 1991). It is important to recognise that 'secularisation' is not to be understood solely as a loss of the religious and the sacred but as its complex transmigration and reconstitution. For a recent, purely sociological account, see K. Dobbelaere, 'Church Involvement and Secularization: Making Sense of the European Case', in E. Barker, J. A. Beckford and K. Dobbelaere (eds.), *Secularization, Rationalism and Sectarianism* (Oxford: Clarendon Press, 1993), ch. 3.

[86] Said, *Orientalism*, p. 115.

[87] *Ibid.*, p. 120.

worlds as God had once made the old'.[88] At the foundation of a *discipline*, a collection of texts – in effect a 'canon' of normativity – emerged, which was a social and cultural creation executed in what Ernest Renan called the *laboratoire philologique*, often at a remove from the 'reality' it purported to represent. In terms of a basic leitmotif of nineteenth-century European scholarship and intellectual life, *the ideal had displaced the real*.

The strategy of the construction of the 'other' outlined above equally fits the era of the poet Novalis, who (by contrast with Heine) in *Die Christenheit und Europa* (1799) accused the Reformation of enthroning reason through the admission of literalism into the philological study of the *Word* of God, thereby losing hold of the spiritual unity of Europe.[89]

Far from being unquestionable givens, the various identities of Europe are the products of the politics of representation. In terms of the Scottish microcosm of the European problematic it would doubtless be possible to generate a similar analysis of Scottish cultural identity as assimilable to a 'Britishness' created as an imposed or partially acknowledged identity. To imagine that any of these processes is simply bipolar would be simplistic: all such processes of identity involve collusions as complex and intimate as the evolution of *both* Master *and* Slave within a single self-consciousness that we find in Hegel's parable. Contemporary Scottish cultural politics, for example, amply exemplify these convoluted difficulties.[90]

THE 'NEW EUROPE' AND A 'GREATER EUROPE'

The 'New Europe' which has evolved since the Second World War was created in order to resolve a historical problem: the conflictual character of a continent divided by the Rhine corridor.[91] In the relatively

---

[88] *Ibid.*, p. 121.

[89] In Ronald Taylor, *The Romantic Tradition in Germany: An Anthology* (London: Methuen, 1970), pp. 131ff.)

[90] See the anguished journalism of Tom Nairn: *Auld Enemies: Essays from the Nairn on Monday Column in The Scotsman* (Glasgow: Common Cause Declarations, 1992). For informed background see Tom Gallagher (ed.), *Nationalism in the Nineties* (Edinburgh: Polygon, 1991); Christopher Harvie, *Scotland and Nationalism: Scottish Society and Politics 1707–1977* (London: Allen & Unwin, 1977), and see n. 12 above.

[91] See Abel Aganbegyan, *The Challenge: The Economics of Perestroika* (London: Hutchinson, 1988); Timothy Garten Ash, *We the People: The Revolution of '89 Witnessed in Warsaw, Budapest, Berlin and Prague* (Cambridge: Granta Books, 1989; reprinted 1990); Lord Ralf Dahrendorf, *Reflections on the Revolution in Europe* (London: Chatto & Windus, 1990); Karen Dawisha, *Eastern Europe, Gorbachev and Reform* (Cambridge: Cambridge University Press, 1988); Mikhail Gorbachev, *Perestroika: New Thinking for Our Country and the World* (London: Collins, 1987); David Lane, *Soviet Society Under*

reduced circumstances of the post-war Europe, William Nicoll and Trevor Salmon have traced the idea of the 'New Europe' back to its sources, not least, for example, to Carlo Cataneo (1801–69) and his idea of 'subsidiarity' as a means of reconciling conflicts of interest in which decentralisation and federation are combined in a layered distribution of competence, responsibility and power.[92] The career and writings of Jean Monnet (1888–1977) provide essential commentary upon these processes of integration.

In the course of European integration the question of the *identity* of Europe has been until now a relatively peripheral issue. It is precisely the historical identities of Europe which have made the *pragmatic* trans-nationalism of the processes of European integration so important. The 'European Identity' document published in Copenhagen in 1973 spoke of a definition of identity,[93] but little was done. The Single European Act of 1985 refers to 'a European identity in external policy matters',[94] and even this has proved extremely difficult to sustain, as the Maastricht Summit of 1991 and its painful aftermath continue to show. Although the ideas of Sully, Penn, Simon and Cateano 'have been transformed into living institutions and systems',[95] Nicoll and Salmon remark that 'the European destination is still unknown'.[96] Since 1989 the destabilisation of this vision of gradual (if slow and painful) progress is now crisis-laden by the collapse of the Soviet Union. Yet at the heart of the European endeavour the word 'community' has not been excluded or abandoned. In the era of *glasnost* and *perestroika*, Mikhail Gorbachev wrote in 1987 of a new Europe constructed of 'enlightened' principles which was co-extensive with the papal 'greater Europe':

Europe 'from the Atlantic to the Urals' is a cultural-historical entity united by the common heritage of the Renaissance and the Enlightenment, of the great philosophical and social teachings of the nineteenth and twentieth centuries. These are powerful magnets which help policy-makers in their search for ways to mutual understanding and cooperation at the level of interstate relations.

Perestroika (London: Unwin Hyman, 1990); and Pedro Ramet (ed.), *Religion and Nationalism in Soviet and East European Politics* (Charleston, NC: Duke University Press, 1989).

[92] William Nicoll and Trevor Salmon, *Understanding the European Communities* (London: Harvester Wheatsheaf, 1990).

[93] 'The European Identity', 14 December 1973, *Bulletin of the European Communities*, 12 (1973), 118–22.

[94] Article 36 (a).

[95] Nicoll and Salmon, *Understanding the European Communities*, p. 232.

[96] *Ibid.*, p. 229.

A tremendous potential for a policy of peace and neighborliness is inherent in the European cultural heritage. Generally, in Europe the new, salutary outlook knows much more fertile ground than in any other region where the two regions come into contact.[97]

The collapse of communism has been attended by marked, but locally differentiated, changes in religious activity throughout the former socialist countries of eastern Europe and the former Soviet Union. The interpretation of these phenomena is, however, not a simple matter. Many kinds of religious and theological identity are now struggling for survival in a situation reminiscent in certain respects of that in defeated Germany after the First World War. Far from being the 'End of History', as Francis Fukuyama has argued, this new situation brings with it myriad renewals of national and ethnic identity, often with highly disruptive consequences which fall far short of the idealised vision of European identity ventured earlier by Mikhail Gorbachev.

The situation in the re-emergent Europe following the 1989–90 revolutions invites a range of theoretical explanations. But no one interpretative scheme would appear to suffice. The processes within the overall scheme of things might, for example, be theorised in terms of globalisation and world system theory, international relations and European integration theory, social psychology and social identity theory, and so on. But we have argued that the construction of the 'idea' and the 'identities of Europe' also involves the dynamics of religious and theological change and transmutations of chthonic myth grounded in problematic historical constructions and justifications.

We conclude that the only adequate methodology will be one which operates on the level of the *politics of representation* and takes account of the global and local factors we have outlined. This in turn may serve to enhance *cultural agency* and the just distribution of *cultural capital*, that is to promote the *emancipation* of the human condition. It is only upon such a basis, which makes human freedom a central consideration, that the claims to inaugurate *theological* argument should be grounded.

Our analysis leads us to conclude that our concern should not be solely with political relations between states, nations and peoples, or indeed with such a problematic and dangerous conception as 'Europe', but with human relations as embedded in local and national cultures and with the 'cultures' and root paradigms of all human communities,

---

[97] Gorbachev, *Perestroika*, p. 198.

which are rapidly becoming colours to be reworked on the palette of resurgent, transnational and globalised capitalism.

What, however, in more specific terms, does 'divinity' potentially have to offer? What is the positive dimension that religion and theology might add to the problem of European identity construed, as we have attempted to construe it, as a major manifestation of the pre-modern, modern and postmodern problematic?

'DIVINITY' AND ITS TASKS

We have attempted to respond to the question 'What, then, is "divinity"?' We have proceeded on the assumption that the traditional formulation of its remit and tasks needed to change, and to change for good reason. Through the presentation of a single, but interestingly complex issue, that of the 'souls of Europe', we have explored the identities of a continent, showing how these originated in pre-modern traditions which then entered into metanarrative conflict with the onset of modernity. It would, however, be sociologically misleading to represent the *tertium quid* of a postmodern reconstitution of European identities in the religious field in the sloganistic terms of the de-traditionalised circulation of narrative fragments. The reality is more complex.

In the parable of the Lord and Bondsman in Hegel's *Phenomenology of Mind* we found a metaphorical and real representation of this conflict, and, moreover, a prefiguration of the possibility of an active *postmodern translation* (in effect an *Aufhebung*), that is a passing beyond sterile opposition into the realm of *supercession* or *sublation*. The Scottish intellect and sensibility (with its instinctive lust for contradiction) is probably better equipped than the English mind (with its residual love of *via media*) to cope with this contingency. In the zone of the critically reflexive, *self-creating* self, the responsibility of *becoming* is grounded; in a trial by death, consciousness strives for full self-consciousness or accepts the negated status of *thinghood* (*Dingheit*). This is a universal dialectics which resists the totalising appropriation of the possibilities and rewards of persecution by any one interest group, be it identified with ethnicity, gender or sexual orientation.

We have argued that the *thesis* of ancestral Catholic Christian tradition (as well as Janus-faced Protestant Reformation) and the *antithesis* of secularising modernity were uneasily reconciled in the progressivist accommodation of Liberal Protestantism. By contrast, in the realm of *postmodernity*, prefigured in Hegel's parable and in the idea of the 'Unhappy

Consciousness', this consciousness is in a state of dialectical irresolution. It is

itself the gazing of one self-consciousness into another, and itself is both, and the unity of both is also its own essence; but objectively and consciously it is not yet this essence itself – it is not yet the unity of both.[98]

Yet this irresolution affords the *possibility* of a creative life lived in the midst of antitheses. It is in the residual eschatology, in the *necessity* of living proleptically, at the juncture where pre-modern theological tradition, critical modernity and the ethical and religious demands of postmodernity coincide, that the remit of 'divinity' is now to be located. Once more we live *between the times (zwischen den Zeiten)*; it is in *difference* that new life will emerge.

The contemporary task of 'divinity' is both religious and theological. It is *religious* in the very traditional sense of *religio*, that is in a concern with the binding together of humankind on the level of the claim that ultimate cultural *universals* manifest themselves, paradoxically, in the *particularities* of the extraordinary diversity of socially embedded cultural practices of religion. It is *theological* in that this ultimacy has frequently presupposed a transcendent reference point in relation to which *all* human activity is experienced as *relative*. 'Divinity' is also rhetorically committed to *Christian* theology as the distinctive tradition and a central metanarrative source of European, and indeed Scottish culture.

As William Storrar has shown in his study of Scottish Christian identity we might well reconstruct an argument parallel with that pursued in this chapter for the metanarratives of contemporary Scotland.[99] In the latter, the suffering pathos and Europeanism of an Edwin Muir might be set over against the chthonic urges and Lenin-hymning modernism and 'greater Christ' of Hugh MacDiarmid, in a newly contextualised juxtaposition of Christ and Prometheus. Now, however, each culture must write the narrative of its own identity within the ambience of postmodernity. The theologian stands at the confluence of these streams, where he or she must strive to enunciate, symbolise and enact principles of human cohabitation in a pluralist and particularist environment.

Theology understood as the uncritical advocacy and proclamation of a logocentric 'God' conceived apart from such a critical framework

---

[98] Hegel, *Phenomenology*, p. 251.

[99] See William Storrar, *Scottish Identity: A Christian Vision* (Edinburgh: Hansel Press, 1990). I owe much to Professor William Storrar and the Revd Jock Stein, who invited me to take part in a series of Carberry Conversations after the 1991 General Election organised by the Mair Institute at Carberry Tower, Midlothian at which the future of Scotland was considered at length.

as we have outlined might well involve what Ernst Bloch once called with regard to Karl Barth a *Herrschaftstheologie*, a theology of Lordship. Theology is difficult; it implies engagement with a purpose largely obscured in contemporary culture. It would be easy – indeed painless – to relinquish the task and substitute for it a variety of *technai*, technical skills and competences. Alternatively, overt postmodern theological strategies can look little different from regression and sophisticated fundamentalism.

In what the distinguished sociologist Stewart Clegg has called the 'multi-dimensional pleasure dome of postmodern society', the assumption of tradition as *privilege* by any denomination or religious grouping is to infringe the 'postmodern democratic freedom of the market' and to make a compact with obsolescence.[100] This may be the militant obsolescence of fundamentalism or the planned obsolescence of a fatalistic adjustment, made without adequate self-interrogation, to demographic decline of church membership. Either way, this involves a failure of active intergenerational transmission that paradoxically takes place in an era in which religions and religiosities are thriving.

Until, and unless, the increasingly marginal vested interests represented by the Christian churches are prepared to enter, albeit self-critically, into the dialectics of the human community as we have presented them, this decline may well prove terminal. There is, of course, always the possibility of that special form of continued existence as commodified 'heritage' – even prison camps may survive in this form – or even of re-creation – as theme parks. As in the former eastern Europe, where obsolete industries face extinction, so the dying spiritual monopolies of the West should hope for a planned transition, rather than a slow or rapid death. Yet, and this is crucial, in abandoning blatant hegemonies and in going through an experience analogous to 'market-testing', the Christian church must relearn – even recreate – whatever it might be that it has to offer.

This act of self-exposure is a learning process to be conducted in a spirit inspired by the President of my fatherland, Vaclav Havel, who wrote in 'The Power of the Powerless',

> The profound crisis of human identity brought on by living within a lie, a crisis which in turn makes such a life possible, certainly possesses a moral dimension as well; it appears, among other things, as a deep moral crisis in society. A person who has been seduced by the consumer value system, whose identity is dissolved

---

[100] S. R. Clegg, *Frameworks of Power* (London: Sage, 1989), p. 275.

in an amalgam of the accoutrements of mass civilization, and who has no roots in the order of being, no sense of responsibility for anything higher than his or her own personal survival, is a *demoralized* person. The system depends on this demoralization, deepens it, is in fact a projection of it into society.[101]

It is not possible intelligently or authentically to distinguish oneself from something of which one has no knowledge. *Regaining roots in the order of being* is a moral task, yet it is also religious and theological. As the poet Friedrich Hölderlin put it: 'Wo die Gefahr ist, wächst das Rettende auch' – where danger is, there lies salvation.

Divinity is far from being an option for refugees fleeing from the core of life; its remit and task involve a degree of self- and contextual interrogation few can perhaps consistently sustain. Yet without risking – even on occasion passing through – death, we cannot attain full life. The specific Christian hope in the resurrection of life should strengthen the resolve of those prepared, as Havel would have it, to exhibit a sense of responsibility for something higher than an individual's personal survival. It is at this very basic level that religion and theology should operate. It is here that the critical and facilitative remit and task of divinity should be dedicated to the creation of the responsible autonomy of the theologian. We may also add that the training of so-called religious professionals entails immersion in the problematic depicted above.

Such relative autonomy may now be regarded by some as incompatible with the all-pervasive commodification of knowledge and with the invasive power and the false ultimacy of an inadequately relativised and triumphalist capitalism, the veritable 'jealous God' of our age. But there can, in the final analysis, be no compromise. Anyone active in 'divinity' must daily face the following dilemma: in the light of the conflict at the core of my own personal and my disciplinary existence do I choose to retreat into pre-modern tradition, or do I escape into the textual technology of a philological or historicist modernity? Or, alternatively, do I grasp the ethical and theological dialectics of the postmodern condition, and seek, as Vaclav Havel wrote from the prison cell, to *live in truth*?

---

[101] Vaclav Havel, 'The Power of the Powerless', in Jan Vladislav (ed.), *Living in Truth* (London: Faber, 1987), p. 62.

CHAPTER 9

Globalised religion? The Parliament of the World's Religions (Chicago, 1993) in theoretical perspective

INTRODUCTION

In the late summer of 1993 I was able to attend the Parliament of the World's Religions, held in the Palmer House Hilton, Chicago. This event, planned over some five years by a Council (chaired by Cardinal Joseph Bernardine of Chicago), celebrated and re-enacted the first Parliament held in 1893. The first Parliament is generally credited with having introduced Eastern world religions to the United States in ways which were to have a growing impact on the level of mass culture and society, rather than upon a small eccentric or academic elite. The traditions then planted underwent an enormous boost in the 1960s, when esoteric religious and mystical religious experience began to feature in global popular culture, not least following the Beatles' association with the Maharishi. The second Parliament of 1993 was a global event in which indigenised religions from within the United States and Canada, including official representatives of Buddhism, Christianity (mostly Roman Catholic) and Judaism (predominantly Liberal), Hinduism, Islam, Sikhism and so on, encountered their root communities and traditions of origin. There was also an impressive array of more esoteric groups of many kinds. The much-remarked and controversial participation of Neo-Pagans was indicative of the opening up of the religious 'market' at the Parliament. Co-religionists from all over the world converged upon Chicago in a highly diversified, complex, and sometimes conflictual encounter.

Michael York provided an admirable report on the Chicago 1993 Parliament of the World's Religions in *Religion Today*.[1] The event itself was on an overwhelming scale, and participants inevitably took from it highly individual impressions. Indeed, the personal impact upon

---

[1] Michael York, 'Parliament of the World's Religions', *Religion Today*, 9/2 (1994), 17–20.

any participant not wholly indifferent to religion was inescapable.[2] Nonetheless, the purpose of this chapter is to place the 1993 Parliament of the World's Religions in a theoretical setting, and to test the hypothesis that it may be understood as a paradigmatic example of emancipatory 'globalised religion'. Thus whilst the affective aspects of the Parliament should not be minimised or denigrated, it is possible to argue, contrary to some critics, that there are more substantial grounds for attributing to it a longer term and exemplary significance. I shall argue that as a globalised religion, the Parliament successfully juxtaposed, even if it did not fully integrate, global values and human universals, on the one hand, with, on the other, cultural particularities of the most diverse kind. These extremities, held in creative tension, correspond with and answer to certain emancipatory requirements that are to be found in recent social theory. It is my purpose to locate these points of correspondence and outline their consequences for the study of religion.[3]

The scale of the Parliament was so great that any interpreter faces a problem: how is it possible to represent – without misrepresentation – an event involving some 6,500 participants and hundreds of meetings held in a single intense week of activity? Methodologically, it was important to proceed in a way that respected the need for several interconnected levels of analysis but that also recognised the limitations of any brief interpretation. First, a short personal narrative gives some sense of what happened, and how this affected one of those present. Second, as a means of conveying the scale of the meeting, a brief content analysis and interpretation of the programme show how (within certain limits) collaboration was made possible. Third, three insights are drawn from current sociology that facilitate an informed, albeit preliminary, evaluation of the Parliament as emancipatory event. These are: (1) recent globalisation theory of the world system (Roland Robertson and Peter Beyer); (2) differentiation in a social reality understood as an 'economy of signs and space' (Scott Lash and John Urry); and (3) the search for 'meta-theory' in the 'condition of postmodernity' (David Harvey). Fourth, some implications of the analysis and interpretation are then drawn out which suggest that religion can be understood as a differentiated global resource, an ambiguous,

---

[2] Indeed, for this (male) writer the experience was extremely intense, and it has subsequently required longer-term reflective ingestion.

[3] Russell T. McCutcheon attacked the paper upon which this chapter is based in 'The Economics of Spiritual Luxury: The Glittering Lobby and the Parliament of Religions', *Journal of Contemporary Religion*, 13/1 (1998), 51–64, and I responded in 'The Dialectics of Globalized Spirituality: Some Further Observations', *Journal of Contemporary Religion*, 13/1 (1998), 65–71.

yet dynamic form of 'cultural capital' of vital import in an era of post-materialist value-formation. Fifth, in conclusion, it is argued that thus understood the globalised religion represented by 1993 Parliament of the World's Religions has wider implications for the study of contemporary religion and forms of religiosity. Religion returns from the theoretical and cultural periphery (a marginalisation promoted by traditional secularisation theory) into a close relation to the core issues of our time. This is an optimistic interpretation of an event, the significance of which, in my opinion, should not be underestimated in the evaluation of religion as global resource in a threatened world.

THE 1993 PARLIAMENT: A PERSONAL NARRATIVE

I attended the Parliament as a member of team of ethicists (mainly employed in business and management schools) who met with business leaders at an adjunct meeting some half-mile from the Palmer House Hilton where the Parliament itself took place. This group sponsored one of the main non-plenary meetings of the Parliament, which was addressed by the Swiss theologian Hans Küng on the subject of the Global Ethic. The physical distance between the fortress-like and forbidding half-light of the Midland Hotel with its grey-suited businessmen and anonymity, and the golden-tiled, glowing lobby of the Palmer House Hilton was important; it obliged a participant to make the symbolic transition between two very different centres of power (those of the capitalist world system, and global religion, respectively), passing through the canyon-like streets of Chicago, there encountering the human dereliction of junkies and crazies – besides an ordinary humanity going about its daily business. Furthermore, this first-time visitor to Chicago felt overwhelmed by the grid-iron plan of the city, which runs north–south and east–west, thus imposing a brutal, rational logic upon the transverse so-called Indian trails that had preceded the arrival of the white man. This juxtaposition was mirrored when the Native or First Nation American participants in the Parliament began to focus on and express a largely suppressed and lost but now renascent spiritual consciousness, which was to be of great importance in the enactment of the conference.

The ambience of the Palmer House Hilton was significant. It was a magnificent and grandiose hotel; its lobby was simultaneously both like a gilded sarcophagus and a womb-like, fecund beehive of religious activity. Here, in an enclosed, windowless and secure environment what took place could perhaps be best described as a global religious 'happening', a temporary suspension of physical distance as many life-worlds converged in the ultimate postmodern religious bazaar. In the temporary sacred space of the Palmer House it was possible to observe many intimate human encounters taking place across many a cultural abyss.

Particular examples remain impressed on the memory: one evening in the cavernous entrance lobby of the Palmer House Hilton, crowded with an interactive global mix (drawn from the 6,500 participants and one count of some 147 religions), an old Hopi chief quietly seated in order to rest would be venerated by a Zen Buddhist, who on parting drew the Native American's hands onto his shaven head and positively demanded a blessing. During the youth evening two young Hindu women enacted a sacred dance to Shiva which was quite the most exquisitely beautiful religious performance art I have ever witnessed. After a meeting to commemorate the life of Dom Bede Griffiths an anonymous Aids sufferer appeared, embraced an intensely charismatic Christian-Hindu syncretic woman prophet (of New York Brooklyn Jewish origin) – and then disappeared. This was functional religion as a myriad ministries took place in a vast and essentially unpredefined range of encounters. It was possible to be conscious of the exceptional and the quietly ecstatic character of what was occurring. Bliss was happening amidst the formal programme, and the enactment of religious virtuosity of the highest order took place, despite the politics of difficult encounters, such as when, for example, Master Chungling Al Huang led a remarkable Tai Chi session involving more than a thousand participants during the intermission in a gruelling plenary.

As Michael York and media commentators have pointed out, there was both public and private disagreement at the Parliament.[4] Thus, for example, in the course of a plenary dedicated to 'voices of the dispossessed', there were explosive and painful disruptions when two (highly provocative) speakers representing the Sikhs and Kashmir were interrupted by other representatives from the Indian sub-continent, and the peace-seeking goals of the Mission Statement of the Parliament were placed in jeopardy.[5] The angry cry of an African American woman rang

---

[4] For example, 'Religious Differences Heat up a Conference Aimed at Unity', *Chicago Tribune*, 31 August 1993, p. 1.

[5] The Mission Statement of the Council for a Parliament of the World's Religions comprised the following objectives:

To convene a Parliament of the World's Religions in Chicago in 1993.
To promote understanding and cooperation among religious communities and institutions.
To encourage the spirit of harmony and to celebrate, with openness and mutual respect, the rich diversity of religions.

out: 'This is America! Let him speak!' When the security guards and police moved in to ease the clashing participants away for talks, the elderly Hopi Chief Burton Pretty on Top and the Native Americans led 2,000 participants in the main ballroom in a collective peace and healing dance. It was apparent that one dynamic universal at the Parliament was a practical spirituality, in this case an individual and collective response to the cosmic heart-beat of the drum.

The event was focused around a combination of main concerns, perhaps best summarised on a popular level in the slogan printed on plastic carrier bags provided with the compliments of the Association of Sikh Professionals: 'There is ONE GOD; We are ALL ONE.' Of course, not everyone, in particular, for example, some Buddhists, could agree that there was a God or gods (or indeed the goddess or goddesses). In what real sense were all those present 'one'? What was holding the participants together in this simmering cauldron of diversity?

INTEGRATION STRATEGY: GLOBAL VALUES AND PARTICULAR RELIGION

A provisional answer to the question how relative integration was achieved is provided by drawing attention to five factors which were essential to the cohesion and success of the event. These were: (1) a universalist religious discourse, most explicitly expressed in Sikh and Bahai statements, but evident in much other documentation generated by both organisers and participants; (2) a universally shared and rationally articulated sense of the need to bring about a unified global religious response to the ecological crisis; (3) the universal necessity of meditation and prayer on a regular basis (the injunction to pray or meditate without ceasing was constantly repeated); (4) the exhortation (in Joseph Campbell's words) to 'follow your bliss' or religious option with integrity, but with respect for the 'bliss' of the other; (5) a conviction that human beings exist to love and be loved and, furthermore, to find themselves forms of self-realisation enacted through ecstatic death to the lower self. This

To assess and to renew the role of the religions of the world in relation to personal spiritual growth and to the critical issues and challenges facing the global community.

To promote and sponser conferences, workshops, and studies; interfaith encounters, conversations, and exchanges; publications; exhibits and festivals of religious art, music, dance, and ritual; and other appropriate activities, in anticipation of and preparation for the 1993 Parliament.

To develop and encourage interfaith groups and programs which will carry the spirit of the Parliament into the twenty-first century.

latter form of self-negation was expressed in a strong cross-religious commitment to total sexual abstinence, exemplified by the renunciants of all persuasions who clearly enjoyed high status amongst participants. These characteristics are educed in part from content analysis of the Parliament documentation[6] and the materials presented by stall-holders, and were confirmed by participant observation in representative settings at the event.[7]

On the level of overall organisation, examination of the Parliament programme indicates that careful thought had been invested in the creation of a balance between structure and content in the main plan. The fact that the detail of the plan relating to the many sub-sessions was extremely difficult to follow and that the logistics began to falter (owing not least to financial strain) towards the end of the week was relatively unimportant. This was because the main programme involved a sound ritual and dramaturgical structure sufficiently strong to sustain the conviction and drive of the event regardless of local failures.

Closer examination of the programme also indicates the following. As regards the whole week, the event was initiated and brought to a close with spectacular collective ceremonies. The opening plenary on Saturday 28 August with its procession, invocation and blessing was (significantly) addressed by Native American elders. Their active presence institutionalised the 'other' and facilitated the formal and symbolic representation of all those whose identities were felt to be suppressed by Anglo-American global hegemony. On the Sunday morning, the diversity of participants was recognised by incorporation in a wide range of welcoming services held throughout the multi-religious and multi-cultural community of Chicago. Once the Parliament was in progress in the Palmer House Hilton, the timing of plenaries was unaffected by the contrast of light and darkness, night and day, save for one (rather coy) reference in the main programme to 'sunrise' as the starting point for daily prayer and meditation.

The central issues sponsored by the conference organisers were addressed in plenaries on the first two days of the Parliament (Sunday 29 to Monday 30 August). The Sunday afternoon plenary confronted the issue of environmental degradation as the main issue affecting humankind

---

[6] The various publications associated with the Parliament, notably Joel Beversluis (ed.), *A Source Book for the Community of Religions* (Chicago: Council for a Parliament of the World's Religions, 1993), and the conference programme itself are vital sources.

[7] Enjoying Press accreditation, I exploited to the full the freedom this gave me to talk to participants and the remarkable effect the Press pass had upon their powers of self-expression.

in an impassioned address entitled 'Global 2000 Revisited: What Shall We Do?' delivered by Dr Gerald O. Barney of the Millennium Institute.[8] Before elaborating upon what he presented as the environmental 'Global Problématique', Dr Barney added the following hand-written paragraph to his address. This summarises in a succinct way both the historic position of the Parliament and its major inner dilemmas:

> We are here because we sense that earth and her people are in serious trouble, trouble *that is as* threatening to life on earth as a nuclear war. The origin of the trouble, we feel, is fundamentally spiritual, so we thank the Trustees of the Council of the Parliament of the World's Religions for the opportunity to describe the critical issues of the 21st Century and to hear your wisdom on our question: What shall we do?[9]

The shared fate of environmental extinction is regarded as the prime critical human universal which in effect succeeds the nuclear threat. In a long, illustrated lecture Dr Barney expounded the unsustainable consequences of present policies. He then outlined two contrasting outcomes: a violent and divided world of haves and have-nots, or an earth of 'sustainable, just, and humane development'. The establishment of the spiritual, economic, political and social conditions to limit the human population to 12 billion, eliminate over-consumption and waste, protect land and species, and establish a new energy policy would involve the abandonment of the standard development model. For many, according to Barney, the unsatisfactory character of many faith traditions as regards the Earth, the poor, women and future vision has 'become *a very central part of the human problem*'; thus any appeal to them is fraught. Dr Barney then put these questions to those present: did they represent a 'sustainable faith',[10] and would they be prepared to engage (where necessary) in a profound revision of ancestral assumptions based upon tradition? He then concluded:

> Then, with hope in our hearts, we can die in peace – all 6 billion of us – to our old, immature, 20th-century ways of being and thinking. We can cross the waters together. And we can celebrate Earth's arrival in a new era in a way that will be remembered forever.[11]

---

[8] A non-governmental organisation 'promoting long-term integrated global thinking' based in Arlington, Virginia responsible for the *Global 2000 Report to the President*, commissioned by President Jimmy Carter.

[9] Text of address by Gerald O. Barney (1993), released 29 August 1995, p. 2.

[10] *Ibid.*, p. 32.

[11] *Ibid.*, p. 39.

This was the conclusion of a remarkable speech, on any reckoning an outstanding piece of oratory, which combined Dr Barney's own Christian sense of a death to self with the image of the Chosen People crossing the Red Sea, shifted from the individual nation to a global transition in consciousness. The retreat from the reification of religious particularity (it is hoped without loss of distinctiveness) was an aspiration thoroughly characteristic of the Parliament and its objectives. Subsequent events have, however, indicated that main-line religious traditions have yet, for example, to come to terms with one of Dr Barney's major points, the need for limitation of human fertility.

The remaining plenaries in the first two full days, 'Visions of Paradise and Possibility', 'Voices of the Dispossessed' (already referred to above), 'Voices of Spirit and Tradition' and 'From Vision to Action', were video-recorded for posterity. The mid-week from Tuesday 31 August to Friday 3 September was packed with a vast number of presentations from which a participant had to pick with great care if he or she were to avoid utter exhaustion. The closing plenary began early and informally on the Saturday afternoon at the Petrillo Bandshell in the Grant Park with a 'Concert for the Twenty-first Century' and culminated in a lengthy closing ceremony with (and only highlights are mentioned) the chanting of Tibetan monks, a speech from His Holiness the Dalai Lama, the promulgation of the less than unproblematically formulated 'Declaration of a Global Ethic', and an 'Invocation on the Twenty-first Century' performed by a succession of religious leaders. The central role of womankind in the world was demonstrated in a powerful extended dance representing the four ages of women and accompanied by multi-cultural drums of the world beaten (as it happened) by men.[12] The Parliament ended with a recessional accompanied by the truly extraordinary African American Chicago Soul Children's Choir.

This, then was the basic structure of the event seen as a whole over the week. The passage from entry, encounter with the diverse and the extraordinary, and return to the mundane was successfully sustained. On a daily basis the pattern of prayer and meditation, meals, dispersal into plenaries or the differentiated programme and pre-evening worship likewise promoted the universal of spiritual cultural practice as a means of relation and integration. In more general terms, there was the heterogeneous cohabitation (if not integration) of reflexive modern, universalist

[12] Professor Ursula King has argued that the men drumming was an expression of male hegemony: under the circumstances at the time I interpreted their presence, possibly mistakenly, as more an expression of gender complementarity.

with particularist, mythopoetic discourse in both the major input of the plenaries Parliament and in many of the more specialised sessions. The pattern set by Dr Barney of urging an informed confrontation between the 'spiritual' and the scientific was thus characteristic of much that went on. There is not a great deal of evidence to suggest that these zones entered into closer intellectual integration on the macroscopic plenary level, and the results of the thematic sessions are difficult to determine. It might be possible to analyse the relation of these different levels of discourse in socio-linguistic terms, but that lies beyond the remit of this chapter.[13]

On the level of more immediate observation, however, it is important to note the general exclusions (both actual and apparently felt) that were characteristic of the Parliament. Most of those who failed to respond positively to the event (a small but discordant minority) were often strongly conservative or 'fundamentalist' in orientation (by this I mean that they refused to concede the relativisation of their religious claims in the face of the unconditional demands for respect for, and active toleration of, the existence of the other embodied in the agenda of the Parliament. In particular some Protestant Christians (as contrasted with Roman Catholics) seemed to have considerable difficulties, not least, perhaps, because of their uncompromising rejection of symbolic and mythic communication, and their equally rigorous emphasis upon the exclusive rationality of their particular faith narrative, asserted at the expense of the universality of religious experience as *religio*, a multifarious

---

[13] Some of the earlier socio-linguistic work of Mary Douglas and Basil Bernstein could well be useful at this juncture. See Mary Douglas, 'To Inner Experience', *Natural Symbols: Explorations in Cosmology* (London: Barrie & Jenkins, 1970), p. 43 for a Durkheimian study of levels of discourse and their sociological correlates:

Bernstein starts with the idea that there are two basic categories of speech, distinguishable both linguistically and sociologically. The first arises in a small-scale, very local social situation in which the speakers all have access to the same fundamental assumptions; in this category every utterance is pressed into service to affirm the social order. Speech in this case exercises a solidarity-maintaining function closely comparable to religion as Durkheim saw it functioning in primitive society. The second category of speech distinguished by Bernstein is employed in social situations where the speakers do not accept or necessarily know one another's fundamental assumptions. Speech then has the primary function of making explicit unique individual perceptions, and bridging different initial assumptions. The two categories of speech arise in social systems which correspond to those which Durkheim indicated as governed by mechanical and organic solidarity.

See also Basil Bernstein, 'A Socio-Linguistic Approach to Socialisation', in J. Gumperz and D. Hymes (eds.), *Directions in Socio-Linguistics* (New York: Holt, Rinehart & Winston, 1970). A comparative contextual study of the different discourses employed in the Parliament would require a considerable extension and modification of this approach.

binding together of humankind. There were also specific difficulties associated with the appearance of such controversial figures as Louis Farrakhan and the presence of Neo-Pagans, which led to the withdrawal of official Jewish and Orthodox representation, respectively.[14]

THEORETICAL CONTEXTUALISATION: EMANCIPATORY GLOBAL RELIGION?

What, however, can be made of the Parliament in a wider context? An evaluation on the level of political consequences or of an advanced synthesis between spiritual values and scientific discourse might well prove disappointing.[15] If, however, the Parliament is taken on its own terms as a global religious event, then there are sociological grounds for considering that its socio-cultural importance could be more considerable. It is this latter dimension that is now opened up to analysis in the three following sub-sections concerned with globalisation, an economy of space and signs, and postmodernisation, respectively.

Religion and globalisation theory

In an era after the 'End of History',[16] that is in a post-Marxist world order where 'capitalism has triumphed', the interpretation of religion as part of the socio-cultural capital of humankind involves the juxtaposition of the global (and globalisation) with the local (and with processes of localisation) in resurgent indigenous cultures.[17] It is at this juncture, in a fraught and complex tension between conflicting tendencies, that globalisation

---

[14] See York, 'Parliament of the World's Religions', for further comment.

[15] Subsequent experience in the field has consolidated my belief in the importance of large-scale ritual events and of their participant-observational study through appropriate ethnographic techniques.

[16] Francis Fukuyama, 'The End of History', *The National Interest*, 16/2 (1998), 3–18 and *The End of History and the Last Man* (London: Hamish Hamilton, 1989) is less than helpful on the religious issue: 'Religion has thus been relegated to the sphere of private life – exiled, it would seem, more or less permanently from European political life except on certain narrow issues like abortion', yet in the revival of nationalism, 'identity would be expressed primarily in the realm of culture rather than politics', p. 271. In other words, Fukuyama's prescriptive approach to contemporary history signally fails to grasp the integral character of the ethno-religious revival of nationalism.

[17] For a discussion of communitarian as opposed to individual and liberal, universal ethics see Charles Taylor, *The Ethics of Authenticity* (Cambridge, MA: Harvard University Press, 1991), ch. 5, 'The Need for Recognition'; and R. H. Roberts, 'Identity and Belonging', in Theo van Willigenberg, Robert Heeger and Wibren van der Burg (eds.), *Nation, State, and the Coexistence of Different Communities* (Kampen: Kok Pharos Publishing House, 1995), pp. 25–56.

theory advanced over the last decade by the sociologist Roland Robertson of Pittsburg,[18] and developed by the Canadian Peter Beyer,[19] proposes a more substantive role for religious beliefs, values and practices in the world system than had hitherto been sanctioned by both world system theory and post-war secularisation theory.[20] World system and globalisation theory (from the economic materialism of Sergei Eisenstadt, Immanuel Wallerstein and Leslie Sklair to the more 'humanistic' interpretations of Robertson and Beyer) has important relevance to the task of interpreting the relations between religious belief systems and religious cultural practices and the global economy and transnational business.[21] Peter Beyer has gone farthest in this direction and applied globalisation theory in a series of test cases.[22] Correspondingly, it is Beyer's ideas which touch most closely upon our concern with the Chicago Parliament.

[18] R. Robertson, 'The Globalization Paradigm: Thinking Globally', *Religion and Social Order*, 1 (1991), 207–24 and many other articles. Robertson's recent book, *Globalization: Social Theory and Global Culture* (London: Sage, 1992) draws together his thought. See also Mike Featherstone (ed.), *Global Culture: Nationalism, Globalization and Modernity* (London: Sage, 1990) and references in chapter 1, n. 19.

[19] Peter Beyer, *Religion and Globalization* (London: Sage, 1994).

[20] See S. Acquaviva, *The Decline of the Sacred in Industrial Society* (Oxford: Blackwell, 1979); G. Baum, 'The Secularization Debate', ch. 7 of *Religion and Alienation: A Theological Reading of Sociology* (New York: Paulist Press, 1975), pp. 140–61; H. Blumenberg, *The Legitimacy of the Modern Age* (Cambridge, MA: MIT, 1983; first published 1966); O. Chadwick, *The Secularization of the European Mind in the Nineteenth Century* (Cambridge: Cambridge University Press, 1975; reprinted 1991); Karel Dobbelaere, 'Secularization: A Multi-Dimensional Concept', *Current Sociology*, 29/2 (1981); Karel Dobbelaere, 'Some Trends in European Sociology of Religion: The Secularization Debate', *Sociological Analysis*, 48/2 (1987), 107–37; Richard Fenn, *The Dream of the Perfect Act: An Inquiry into the Fate of Religion in a Secular World* (London: Tavistock, 1987; P. E. Glasner, *The Sociology of Secularisation: A Critique of a Concept* (London: Routledge & Kegan Paul, 1977; T. Luckmann, 'The Decline of Church-Oriented Religion', in Roland Robertson (ed.), *Sociology of Religion: Selected Readings* (Harmondsworth: Penguin, 1969), pp. 141–51; D. Martin, *A General Theory of Secularisation* (Oxford: Blackwell, 1978); D. Martin, 'Towards Eliminating the Concept of Secularization', *The Religious and the Secular: Studies in Secularization* (London: Routledge & Kegan Paul, 1969), ch. 1, pp. 9–22; R. Stark and W. S. Bainbridge, *The Future of Religion – Secularization, Revival and Cult Formation* (Berkeley: University of California Press, 1983), ch. 2, pp. 19–37.

[21] Given the real power of these factors, the critical study of managerial and business ethics in the context of global managerialism becomes, contra Alasdair MacIntyre, a central rather than a peripheral issue.

[22] This is a very difficult area. Beyer's arguments for taking seriously the claim that culturally entrenched religious discourse is now taking on substantive significance in a post-Marxist world order merit very careful scrutiny. For present purposes it is assumed that the attribution of epiphenomenal status to religious (and many other) phenomena in an ideological 'superstructure' of *Überbau* is now under challenge. For comparative studies of global fundamentalism relevant to these considerations see: Gilles Kepel, *The Revenge of God: The Resurgence of Islam, Christianity and Judaism in the Modern World* (Cambridge: Polity, 1994) and Martin Riesebrodt, *Pious Passion: The Emergence of Modern Fundamentalism in the United States and Iran* (Berkeley: University of California Press, 1993).

Beyer's presentation of his conception of the role of religion in globalisation is constructed around an extended definition of the nature of religion that draws upon the insights of Niklas Luhmann:

religion is therefore, sociologically speaking, a certain form of communication. Many sociological definitions of religion operate with a basic dichotomy such as profane/sacred (Durkheim), natural/supernatural (Parsons), nomos/cosmos (Berger), and empirical/super-empirical (Robertson). Others speak about religion as dealing with ultimate 'problems' (Yinger) or a 'general... uniquely realistic' order of existence (Geertz), implicitly defining it by contrast to a more proximate and equivocal domain. The common thread through most of them is that religion is primarily about something beyond the normal, the everyday, the perceptible; and that somehow this radically other conditions human existence.[23]

Beyer maintains that religion comprises the juxtaposition of 'otherness' of transcendence with the 'indeterminacy of the immanent'. The latter term is perhaps not wholly satisfactory. This is because it is precisely the ever-extending power of the modern world system and its tendency to normalise individuals and social structures in terms of 'managerialism'[24] or, more contentiously, global 'McDonaldisation',[25] that threatens to create a totalised – even a totalitarian – reality from which the deviant and unpredictable should be excluded. Examined from this standpoint, the Parliament understood as a global religious event takes on significance as an exercise in benign deviance, a 'dangerous circumstance' (Roland Robertson), assimilable only with difficulty into a hegemonic managed modernity.[26] Beyer continues:

I prefer to use immanence/transcendence to label the central religious dichotomy. What is definitive about this polarity is the holistic nature of the first term. The immanent is the whole world, the whole of perceptible reality, all meaning communicable among human beings. The whole, however, cannot as such be the object of communication because we cannot distinguish it from anything that it does not encompass. The transcendent, as the polar opposite, serves to give the immanent whole its meaningful context. In this sense, it acts as the condition for the possibility of the immanent. The central religious paradox lies in the fact that the transcendent can only be communicated in immanent terms, and this by definition: communication on the basis of meaning

---

[23] Beyer, *Religion and Globalization*, p. 5.

[24] W. F. Enteman, *Managerialism: The Emergence of a New Ideology* (Madison, WI: University of Wisconsin Press, 1993).

[25] G. Ritzer, *The McDonaldization of Society: An Investigation into the Changing Character of Social Life* (Thousand Oaks: Pine Forge Press, 1993).

[26] For references relating to 'modernity' see chapter 1, n. 18 above.

is always immanent, even when the subject of communication is the transcendent. Religion, therefore, operates with sacred symbols, ones which always point radically beyond themselves. It deals simultaneously with the immanent and the transcendent.[27]

Global religion thus understood becomes a means, possibly one of the few remaining means, of outflanking globalised and totalising power. Placed in this context the Parliament of the World's Religions was correspondingly a corporate, yet also individual and differentiated act which reclaimed human values and interests through symbolic and mythopoeic functionalisation of immanence/transcendence distinctions (which are of course conceived in many ways). Beyer's contends that

religion posits the transcendent to give the immanent world meaning; and makes the requisite distinction between the two by further postulating that the transcendent is not subject to the root indeterminacy of the immanent[28]

and that

In sum then, religion is a type of communication based on the immanent/transcendent polarity, which functions to lend meaning to the root indeterminability of all meaningful human communication, and which offers ways of overcoming or at least managing this indeterminability and its consequences.[29]

According to the perspective outlined in this section, the Parliament of the World's Religions may be understood as a challenge to globalising hegemony inasmuch as it succeeded in enacting the emancipatory distinctions between immanence and transcendence central to much world religion in conjunction with the articulation of total global threats. Global religion confronts alienation, and even negotiates with it in special ways; but this engagement implies no capitulation either to hegemonic ideologies or to the seamless consumerism of late capitalism. It may function as a powerful and globally well-dispersed resource to be drawn upon when confronting the absence of an adequate immanent critique of the modern world system.[30]

---

[27] Beyer, *Religion and Globalization*, p. 5.
[28] *Ibid.*, p. 6.
[29] *Ibid.*
[30] John Milbank has attempted such a critique in *Theology and Social Theory*, but his solution is a Pyrrhic victory involving a retreat from engaged worldliness. See R. H. Roberts, 'Transcendental

Religion and differentiation in an 'economy of space and signs'

A second theoretical resource upon which this chapter draws is Scott Lash and John Urry's *Economies of Signs and Space*,[31] in which important connections are made between economic systems and their cultural analogues. Whereas some influential globalisation theorists ascribe more than an epiphenomenal role and status to religious beliefs and practices in the global system, Lash and Urry evince little overt interest in the socio-cultural role of religion in their magisterial study of the state of the world system after 'organised capitalism'.[32] This marked divergence is despite an implicit convergence of concerns between the study of religion and explorations in social science: religion may exemplify emancipatory differentiation. Lash and Urry seek out differentiation as the opportunity for emancipation. The following passage provides a sense of the postmodern context in which Lash and Urry are to propose an emancipation driven by an ever more efficacious 'reflexive modernisation':

Analyses of (such) postmodern economies and societies have dominated debate on the left and the right for the last decade. If modernism came to cut away the foundations of the Western tradition with the death of God, then postmodernism proclaiming 'the end of Man' removed even those few foundations that remained. The abstraction, meaninglessness, challenges to tradition and history issued by modernism have been driven to the extreme in postmodernism. On these counts neo-conservative analysts and many Marxists are in accord. In any event not just are the analyses surprisingly convergent, but so too are the pessimistic prognoses.[33]

In response to this scenario Lash and Urry stress subjectivity and a conception of 'reflexive modernisation' as agents of emancipation in a de-traditionalised postmodern world. Whilst it is possible to concur with the maximisation of critical reflexive consciousness, this is nevertheless an intellectualistic response, and they are arguably unduly optimistic when they consider that the social process can be challenged or changed simply at the level of consciousness. Lash and Urry supplement their argument and thus expose the basis of a congruence and a potential elective affinity between globalised religion as exemplified in the Parliament of the

Sociology? – Review Article of A. J. Milbank's *Theology and Social Theory*', *Scottish Journal of Theology*, 46/4 (1993), 527–35 and chapter 7 above.

[31] Scott Lash and John Urry, *Economies of Signs and Space* (London: Sage, 1994).
[32] See Scott Lash and John Urry, *The End of Organized Capitalism* (Cambridge: Polity, 1987).
[33] Lash and Urry, *Economies of Signs and Space*, p. 3.

World's Religions and their emancipatory intent. They continue:

Now much of this pessimism is appropriate. But is part of the aim of this book to argue that there is a way out. It is to claim that the sort of 'economies of sign and space' that became pervasive in the wake of organised capitalism do not just lead to increasing meaninglessness, homogenization, abstraction, anomie and the destruction of the subject. Another set of radically divergent processes is simultaneously taking place. These processes may open up possibilities for the recasting of meaning in work and in leisure, for the reconstruction of community and the particular, for the reconstruction of a transmogrified subjectivity, and for heterogenization and complexity of space and everyday life.[34]

There is insufficient space to take this argument much further at this juncture save to suggest that it is precisely global and globalised religion of the kind functionalised in the 1993 Parliament which not only, following Lash and Urry, provides 'heterogenization and complexity of space and everyday life' but also, as Beyer proposes, affords a dynamic way of articulating comprehensive issues concerning the human condition in ways accessible to groups lying outside the subjectivity of the virtuoso reflexive moderniser.

Religion, 'meta-theory' and the 'condition of postmodernity'

Whilst Beyer's approach requires modification, enlargement and a measure of recontextualisation, it nevertheless points to a way of satisfying the demand for post-Marxist 'meta-theory' articulated at the core of the debate concerned with the 'condition of postmodernity'. Likewise, it is necessary to take even greater liberties with Lash and Urry's procedure, which is narrow in its admission of real possibilities for emancipation in a differentiated world order. Nevertheless, in the two preceding subsections of this chapter the Parliament of the World's religions has been presented as a symbolic collective act that embodied a set of distinctions correlatable with those made in recent globalisation theory and in the idea of an 'economy of space and signs'. The Parliament may thus be construed as having a role in the world system which should not be underestimated, and which could well be developed further. In a third theoretical contextualisation the Parliament is further related to arguments concerning aspects of the so-called 'condition of postmodernity'. [35] Here the threads

---

34 *Ibid.*
35 See, for example, David Harvey, *The Condition of Postmodernity: An Enquiry into the Origins of Cultural Change* (Oxford: Blackwell, 1989), chs. 1 and 2 and Hans Küng, *Theology for the Third Millennium: An Ecumenical View* (London: HarperCollins Academic, 1991), pp. 1–12, 257–84.

can be drawn together in David Harvey's fuller argument for a political conditioning of postmodernity:

Postmodernism, with its emphasis upon the ephemerality of jouissance, its insistence upon the impenetrability of the other, its concentration on the text rather than the work, its penchant for deconstruction bordering on nihilism, its preference for aesthetics over ethics, takes matters too far. It takes them beyond the point where any coherent politics are left, while that wing of it that seeks a shameless accommodation with the market puts it firmly in the tracks of an entrepreneurial culture that is the hallmark of reactionary neoconservatism. Postmodernist philosophers tell us not only to accept but even to revel in the fragmentations and the cacophony of voices through which the dilemmas of the modern world are understood. Obsessed with deconstructing and delegitimating every form of argument they encounter, they can end only in condemning their own validity claims to the point where nothing remains of any basis for reasoned action. Postmodernism has us accepting the reifications and partitionings, actually celebrating the activity of masking and cover-up, all the fetishisms of locality, place, or social grouping, while denying that kind of meta-theory which can grasp the political-economic processes (money flows, international divisions of labour, financial markets, and the like) that are becoming ever more universalizing in their depth, intensity, reach and power over daily life.[36]

This is a humane and influential characterisation of the process of postmodernisation. There are many ways in which the global religion of the Parliament might be understood to intersect with, yet challenge Harvey's vision. Of these, perhaps the most important is that global and globalised religion confronts deconstructive fragmentation because it does not itself seek to avoid juxtaposition of the extremes of universality and particularity. Its management of this tension is both problematic and paradigmatic; yet it does not offer easy answers, for there are none, despite what a consumerist capitalism might lead us to believe. This global and globalised religion confronts deconstructive fragmentation because it does not itself seek to avoid juxtaposition and celebrates diversity whilst honouring and seeking to articulate universal exigencies. Harvey's demand for a 'meta-theory' that may grasp and resist totalising power is enabled by the admission of the global religion dimension when this is appropriated along the lines suggested by Beyer and implied (contrary to their explicit agenda) by Lash and Urry. This is not a question (as in, for example, the former East Germany, where religious societal space was temporally exploited) of using religiosity as a vehicle for political

---

[36] Harvey, *The Condition of Postmodernity*, pp. 116–17.

goals, but of understanding more fully the role of religion as a resource, as a form of 'cultural capital' that creatively yet ambiguously and unpredictably refracts the human condition through myth, ritual, symbol, narrative and complex cultural practices. The peculiar and distinctive ways in which religion represents the global condition acknowledges the relativity of all validity claims, yet it does not abandon them; it cannot, because tensions between universal and particular are endemic and acknowledged in religion.

RELIGION AS RESOURCE: A 'CULTURAL CAPITAL' APPROACH

In this chapter the argument has been advanced that in the 1993 Chicago Parliament, forms of consciousness which may be designated as 'reflexive mythopoesis' and 'reflexive spirituality' were apparent, which are analogous to the 'reflexive modernity' required by contemporary theorists as both the price of and the opportunity for emancipation in late modernity and postmodernity. In other words, seen from a socio-linguistic standpoint informed in a provisional way by the three theoretical positions outlined above, the Parliament was not characterised by regressive pre-modern traditionalism but a dynamic, emancipatory postmodern-tending discourse in which a variety of 'genres' (in the Bakhtinian sense) were dialectically combined, not least through a repeated yet transformed ritual diachronic structure.

It is possible to maintain, moreover, that the Parliament was more politically conscious in its own distinctive way than Lash and Urry in *Economies of Signs and Space*, despite their explicit emancipatory agenda. This was because the Parliament was able both to admit a truly extreme heterogeneity and complexity of space and signs way beyond anything conceded by these sociological writers and then to assimilate them, albeit proleptically, under a single global agenda. In other words, in the crudest terms, can 'reflexive modernization' on its own (albeit understood as an improvement on naked instrumental reason) be an adequate agent of emancipation in the context of global crisis such as that addressed by the Parliament?

THE CHICAGO PARLIAMENT AND THE STUDY OF RELIGION

The interpretation of such a global religious event raises important questions for the academic study of religion. The theorisation and interpretation of religion in such sub-disciplines as the 'sociology of religion' is, however, in a state of partially acknowledged crisis. The isolation of such a sub-discipline from the core activities of the parent disciplines is problematic. In this chapter I have tried to show that contemporary religion need not necessarily be understood as pre-modern residuum, of interest only to specialists in something close to intellectual pathology.

Furthermore, the socio-scientific study and normative evaluation of contemporary religious phenomena can now only be adequately undertaken in ways which imply a critique of internal, endogamous approaches to the study of religion. As the sociologist James Beckford has observed,[37] recent analyses of modernity neglect religion as a social factor, but this need not necessarily be the case. My contention has been that despite the distance between the study and analysis of religion and the socio-scientific representation of the contemporary human condition, there is evidence of the existence of important elective affinities between both fields of activity. I have tried to illustrate and expound this with regard to an extremely important recent example of global religion.

The move we have made from description to explanation in the foregoing account of the Parliament of the World's Religions confronts a problem elucidated by John S. Cumpsty in one of the most substantial recent contributions to methodology, *Religion as Belonging: A General Theory of Religion* (1991). Cumpsty's impassioned plea for a return from the disciplinary dispersal of 'religious studies' to its *Hilfwissenschaften* needs to be treated with some caution. Cumpsty asserts that:

Wherever Religious Studies has sought to move beyond description to explanation, it has been heavily dependent upon sociology, anthropology and psychology, for both definition and theory.[38]

In order to counter this tendency, which appears to endanger and lose the distinctiveness of 'religion' itself, Cumpsty proposes a systemic, self-referential method for the study of religion, based upon the assumption that, first, it should become truly a discipline in its own right, by second, defining its own object of study (however tentatively) in terms of the object itself, that is as non-reductively as possible, or it will not be in a position to fulfil the other criterion of a normative discipline, which is,

---

[37] At the Easter 1993 meeting of the Sociology of Religion Group of the British Sociological Association.

[38] John S. Cumpsty, *Religion as Belonging: A General Theory of Religion* (Lanham: University Press of America, 1991), p. xxxvi.

third, to develop and evaluate its own theory in terms of what enriches understanding of its own object of study.[39] Cumpsty concludes that, 'In short, one needs to have a feeling for what is the really real and some way of assuring one's relation to it. That, in human terms, is the religious drive.'[40]

Such a throughly *sui generis* definition of religion is problematic for obvious reasons. A definition of religion as appropriating the 'really real' directs us into at least three major areas of difficulty. The first is an evasion of an array of hidden and begged questions concerning realism and constructivism in the human and social sciences that confront any one seriously engaged in social representation and the construction of social facts in and through disciplines. The second is the danger of a confinement *ab initio* within the commonplaces of a discourse which may well then suffer from an immediate methodological foreclosure. The third is an uncontrolled slide towards the abyss represented by the search for a watertight definition of religion (was it 95 or 96 such definitions at the last count?). This is an unsatisfactory procedure, and one challenged long ago by Max Weber when he argued that the definition of 'religion' should be attempted, if at all, only at the conclusion of an investigation. In more positive terms, Ursula King's observations made some years ago in an important study of the historical and phenomenological approaches to the study of religion are worthy of reiteration:

the study of religion, as currently conceived, is undergoing a great deal of change involving much critical self-examination and a search for clearer definition.[41]

The approach adopted in this chapter has been conducted in the spirit of such critical self-examination. Indeed, it is basic to the foregoing argument that narrative and systemic, purely self-referential accounts of religion do not tell us much more about religious phenomena in the contemporary world than any informed student could construe on the basis of prolonged participant observation. When religious studies is involved in empathetic, yet critical participant observation, when it responsibly and flexibly practises the disciplines of the human and social sciences in ways recognisable and respected by main-line exponents of those disciplines, when it draws upon the history of religions and the

---

[39] *Ibid.*, pp. xxxvi–xxxvii.
[40] *Ibid.*, p. xxxvii.
[41] Ursula King, 'Historical and Phenomenological Approaches', in Frank Whaling (ed.), *Contemporary Approaches to the Study of Religion* (2 vols., Berlin: Mouton, 1984), vol. I, *The Humanities*, p. 71.

apposite linguistic tools, and last, but not least, when it is concerned with what Neville calls 'first-order normative issues in religion', then it may, I believe, play its part in engagement with problems of universal human import. In short, religious studies so understood is a most fascinating and salient multi-disciplinary practice. To achieve the latter is not easy, for it requires not least credibility within disciplines and across disciplinary boundaries, besides an awareness of the processes involved in the history and formation of those disciplines in the context of the modernisation process itself.[42]

In conclusion, in this chapter I have sought to show that the Chicago 1993 Parliament of the World's Religions was a remarkable expression of global spirituality which embodied and enacted forms of reflexive consciousness with important emancipatory potential. As such it lends substance to an eventuality sketched out by Peter Beyer:

All in all, then, we might provisionally conclude that 'global civil' religion is both possible and likely; but there will be more than one of them and these will simply be more religious offerings beside others, both systemic and cultural . . . We live in a conflictual and contested social world where the appeal to holism is itself partisan. That paradox alone is itself enough to maintain the religious enterprise, even if with more risk and less self-evidence.[43]

Ninian Smart remarks in his concluding reflections on global religion[44] in *The World's Religions* (1989):

though we may not achieve a global religion, we may achieve a global civilization in which values from the great traditions are woven together in a glittering net. Perhaps it will turn out like the jewel net of Indra, of which Hua-yen so eloquently speaks: each stone reflecting every other.[45]

This is an idealistic vision replete with imagery which recalls some aspects of the experience of the 1993 Chicago Parliament of the World's Religions. Since Smart wrote these words, it has become even less plausible to hope for a 'global civilization'. Nevertheless, although the

---

[42] See R. H. Roberts and J. M. M. Good (eds.), introduction to *The Recovery of Rhetoric: Persuasive Discourse and Disciplinarity in the Human Sciences* (Charlottesville, VA: University of Virginia Press, 1993) and Julie Thompson Klein, *Interdisciplinarity: History, Theory, and Practice* (Detroit: Wayne State University Press, 1990).

[43] Beyer, *Religion and Globalization*, p. 227.

[44] Note the six dimensions of religion: ritual; mythological; doctrinal; ethical; social; experiential, in Ninian Smart, *The Religious Experience of Mankind* (London: Collins, 1969), pp. 15–25.

[45] Ninian Smart, *The World's Religions: Old Traditions and Modern Transformations* (Cambridge: Cambridge University Press, 1989), p. 561.

Parliament of the World's Religions was not immune from the experience of the conflicts pervasive at both global and local level in the world system, there was evidence of serious, negotiated convergence of concerns. When global religion becomes a global religiosity, that is when as a form of critical reflexivity it has access to and refunctions the resources of ancient traditions and engages in diverse but commensurable cultural practices in the context of shared universal concerns, it becomes, as effective cultural capital, a dynamic resource for a modern/postmodern world system.

The 1993 Chicago Parliament of the World's Religions may be counted a significant step on the path towards the recovery of both the use and intrinsic values of religion in a threatened world. In the glittering lobby of the Palmer Hilton many jewels in the net of Indra reflected and refracted each other's light. World religion drew itself together for a moment; much of what it saw was good, not least in the experience of the multitude of 'others' who experienced each other both as difference and likeness – but also as complementarities within the greater community of religions and humankind itself.

CHAPTER 10

Time, virtuality and the Goddess: transmutations of the religious field[1]

Today the future has caught up with the present, but time, in-dividually and collectively, has remained limited. New resources of time are in demand. They are opening up through the extension of time in the present and through the availability at all times which technologies make possible. But the latter in their turn demand the temporal availability of human beings. So where is the time to be found?[2]

INTRODUCTION

At first sight the theme of 'time, virtuality and the Goddess' looks abs-truse in the extreme, yet exploration of this constellation of factors draws the reader into fuller, cross-disciplinary understanding of the contempo-rary transmutations of time and value and of distinctive aspects of the modern/postmodern problematic. Analysis of changes in the categories of time (and space) throws light upon transformations in contemporary sensibility,[3] not least, as will become apparent, those changes affecting

---

[1] The first explorations underlying this chapter appeared in a paper entitled 'Religion and Virtual Reality' delivered at the annual conference of the British Association for the Study of Religion, entitled Religion and the Media, and as a lecture entitled 'The Chthonic Imperative: Religion, Gender and the Battle for the Earth', given at the conference Nature Religion Today, both held in 1996. This material was then developed separately in two chapters, 'Time, Virtuality and the Goddess', in Scott Lash, Andrew Quick and Richard Roberts (eds.), *Time and Value* (Oxford: Blackwell, 1998), pp. 112–29, and 'The Chthonic Imperative: Religion, Gender and the Battle for the Earth', in Joanne Pearson, Richard H. Roberts and Geoffrey Samuel (eds.), *Nature Religion Today: Paganism in the Modern World* (Edinburgh: Edinburgh University Press, 1998), pp. 57–73, respectively. I intend to develop the latter in a separate project.

[2] Helga Nowotny, *Time: The Modern and Postmodern Experience* (Cambridge: Polity, 1994), p. 15. Originally published in 1984 under the title *Eigenzeit Entstehung und Strukturierung eines Zeitgefühls*, this work has attained wide recognition.

[3] See, for example, David Harvey, *The Condition of Postmodernity: An Enquiry into the Origins of Cultural Change* (Oxford: Blackwell, 1989), 'The Experience of Space and Time', Part III. This covers much the same ground as Nowotny but with an emphasis upon the visual arts, geography and architecture.

gender identity and constitutive human self-identifications which purport to be grounded in assertions of ultimacy and in new concretions of the sublime. Accordingly, in this context recondite and long-standing theological traditions in Western thought now find new relevance in relation both to contemporary social theory and to writing which seeks to articulate virtual reality. Thus ancient sources, such as those exploited in the time and eternity axis in systematic theology, can be brought into connection with the cultural practices, discourse and theory of spatio-temporal transmutation. In turn, this opens up innovative paths into the exploration and interpretation of contemporary transmutations of the religious field. This chapter represents my own first steps in such remapping; much remains to be done. The theme of temporality also completes another full circle bringing us in contact again with two of the key points of departure in this book, the pristine self-enclosedness of the dogmatic theology of Karl Barth and the eschatological reconstruction of transcendence of Ernst Bloch.[4]

FINDING TIMES: TRANSMUTATIONS OF RELIGION, TIME AND IDENTITY

The religious field (*le champ religieux*) now exhibits a new dynamism and salience; moreover, this field now comprises a set of strange junctures. Under these conditions there is evidence of a complex interaction between globalising integration and localised intensification which has been touched upon in chapter 9; but there is a further polarity, to which we turn our attention in this chapter. Here we return to the thematic of time as a postmodernised reality and in this setting describe an emerging cultural tension between virtual reality and cybernetic enhancement, on the one hand, and potent drives towards chthonic identification with the female principle, a psycho-spiritual and mythopoeic reality frequently designated as 'the Goddess' of chthonic consciousness, on the other. In summary terms, the former appears to promise a virtual omnipotence, and the conquest of the limitations of embodiment, respectively. The latter would seem at first sight to express a monumental regression into the primordial feminine.[5] Whilst these contrasting

---

[4] This reconnnects with core issues in my studies of Karl Barth and Ernst Bloch. See R. H. Roberts, *A Theology on its Way: Essays on Karl Barth* (Edinburgh: T. & T. Clark, 1992) and *Hope and its Hieroglyph: A Critical Development of Ernst Bloch's 'Principle of Hope'* (Atlanta: Scholars Press, 1990).

[5] I am of course aware of the difficulties in the use of terms such as 'feminine' and 'female', and 'masculine' and 'male'.

developments may be regarded simply as (for example) integral factors in cycles of cultural production in so-called advanced capitalist societies,[6] such limiting and even reductive strategies should not be allowed to submerge perception of a gender-suffused recomposition of the religious field in which decayed and disintegrating patriarchy and resurgent matriarchy display fascinating and important affinities and analogues with other areas of cultural change. In this chapter we set out to chart some areas of this complexity with a view to working towards the fuller explanation of the increasing salience of the religious and quasi-religious factors in contemporary life-worlds and their cultures.

Recent attempts to appropriate social theory in the interpretation of religion understood as 'tradition' through the adaptation of 'reflexive modernity'[7] to notions of 'reflexive tradition', and even to 'reflexive religion',[8] involve inconclusive accommodations with the dynamic oppositions between pre-modern fixities, attritive modernities, and fluid postmodernities that have been described in this book. Moreover, the positive representation of 'postmodernity' in terms of socio-ethical critique by such writers as Zygmunt Bauman,[9] besides the theoretical stretching of the imaginative possibilities prefigured in strands of science fiction, far outstrip the intermediate positions taken up by the critical reflexivists who seek to emancipate the sub-discipline of the sociology of religion from its absorption with the secularisation paradigm. In the *imaginaire* of virtual reality and cyber-cultures, time, space, self, body, gender, community, and modes of 'transcendence' (that is focal points of sublime identification) are all subject to visionary and revisionary treatment. These recompositions do not simply repel or distance pre-modern religion or contemporary religiosity grounded in the 'turn to the self',[10] but subject it to an unparalleled 'creative destruction'. Thus, in more general terms, the virtual as vehicle of the religious (or quasi-religious) does not simply function as (for example) a psychological or quasi-religious compensator

---

[6] See James Beckford, *Religion in Advanced Industrial Society* (London: Unwin Hyman, 1989), ch. 2.

[7] See the development of 'reflexivity' in Ulrich Beck, *Risk Society: Towards a New Modernity* (London: Sage, 1992); Anthony Giddens, *The Consequences of Modernity* (Cambridge: Polity, 1990); Anthony Giddens, *Modernity and Self-Identity: Self and Society in the Late Modern Age* (Cambridge: Polity, 1991).

[8] See Philip A. Mellor, 'Reflexive Tradition: Anthony Giddens, High Modernity and the Contours of Contemporary Religiosity', *Religious Studies*, 29/1 (1993), 111–27.

[9] See Zygmunt Bauman, *Intimations of Postmodernity* (London: Routledge, 1992), chs. 4 and 9.

[10] Paul Heelas, *The New Age Movement: The Celebration of the Self and the Sacralization of Modernity* (Oxford: Blackwell, 1996) and Paul Heelas, 'The Sacralisation of the Self in New Age Capitalism', in N. Abercrombie and A. Ware (eds.), *Social Change in Contemporary Britain* (Cambridge: Polity, 1992), pp. 139–66.

for disappointed and displaced aspirations,[11] but becomes the dynamic and problematic 'third nature' that succeeds both a primal raw 'first nature' and the industrially and technologically transformed 'second nature'. Simultaneously, virtuality and cyborgic enhancement undermine the reality and significance of *both* these former modes of nature. In reality, however, as pre-modernity, modernity and postmodernising processes may coincide in Hegel-like 'moments' in complex societal real world settings, so 'nature' may likewise be problematised.

In the context outlined above, 'postmodern religion', whether understood as 'shadow of spirit'[12] or as the 'after-life of religion',[13] is seemingly outrun by temporal possibilities which not merely loosen all ties with traditions and their transformations, but also distance human experience from the ritual cycles that underpin viable cultures, and thus devalue and banalise the *quotidian*, the repetitive tedium of untransfigured and commodified daily life in a managerialised world. Indeed, as will be argued below, the forced universalisation that stems from a virtual simultaneity may, as we shall argue, be understood as promoting yet further trivialisation of the cultural universals of myth, ritual and symbol that inform the experience of humankind. Thus in this chapter we examine the decomposition and recomposition of a cultural field in which the coalescence of reality and quasi-religiosity within the 'transcendence' afforded by virtual worlds and the transformations enabled by cybernetic empowerment draw us towards an end of the human, a 'posthuman' poised on the brink of escape from history and the human condition.[14]

There is, furthermore, an important parallel between the present time-based analysis of the role of virtuality and the apparent abolition of the time-order, and Francis Fukuyama's depiction of the 'End of History' after the triumph of capitalism with which we began.[15] Both the temporal analyses pursued by Helga Nowotny and earlier by me and the historico-cyclic analysis presented by Fukuyama assume the inescapable totalising power of the globalised world system. These affinities notwithstanding, the consistent virtualist, the aspirant cyborg, and the feminist theorist seeking respite for womankind, besides the transnational global

---

[11] As theorised by Rodney Stark and William Sims Bainbridge, *A Theory of Religion* (New York: Peter Lang, 1987).
[12] Philippa Berry and Andrew Wernick (eds.), *Shadow of Spirit: Postmodernism and Religion* (London: Routledge, 1992), introduction.
[13] George Steiner, *In Bluebeard's Castle: Some Notes Towards the Re-definition of Culture*, T. S. Eliot Memorial Lectures (London: Faber, 1971).
[14] Jean-François Lyotard, *The Inhuman: Reflections on Time* (Cambridge: Polity, 1991).
[15] See chapter 1 above.

ideologue with mythopoeic ambitions, part company as regards the solutions they propose for the problems of the posthuman and posthistorical conditions, respectively. Yet their respective solutions amount to a recapitulation of the matrix of modernity/postmodernity which exposes not only the recomposition of the religious field but also the migration of the sublime or, in more usual terms, the 'other' of religious encounter.[16]

The scenario sketched out above has serious consequences for the sub-discipline known as the 'sociology of religion' and the fraught interdisciplinary cluster that entitles itself 'religious studies'. Whilst there is a wide growing awareness of the increasing salience of the religious (or quasi-religious) factor in contemporary social and cultural change, and therefore also in the human and social sciences that have addressed and represented such change, the expert reaction has so far been less than impressive.[17] Formal disciplinary responses have for the most part been confined to lengthy discussion of the adequacy of the secularisation model which has dominated the sociology of religion since the end of the Second World War. Correspondingly, related and lengthy controversies concerning the validity of the categories of 'religion' and the 'sacred' have also divided the academic study of religion. The latter constituency has been split between functional reductionists (like Russell McCutcheon and Robert Segal, who see themselves as truly 'scientific' and true to Enlightenment principles) and empathetic substantivists (for example those influenced positively by Mircea Eliade or Ninian Smart, to name but two) for whom religion is regarded as possessing a fundamental and irreducible significance for human beings. These debates internal to the religious academy might, perhaps, be regarded as mere local difficulties when compared with the overall recompositions of the cultural field reviewed in this chapter, yet the question whether there is a fundamental religious function, a 'primal religion', remains of critical importance.

In more specific and applied terms, a further major purpose of this chapter is to show how effective analysis of the temporal aspects of the recomposition of the religious field under postmodernising conditions may undercut many of the main assumptions of the local (and sometimes rather parochial) study of religion in the academy. This is, however, not simply a matter of subverting the academic divide between the

---

[16] The word 'sublime' is used here with a measure of provisionality: such terms as 'sacred', 'religious' and 'spiritual' are too heavily laden with connotations and extensive meaning to be used here.

[17] There are, of course, some notable exceptions. See, for example, Philip A. Mellor and Chris Shilling, *Re-forming the Body: Religion, Community and Modernity* (London: Sage, 1997) and Paul Heelas, David Martin and Paul Morris (eds.), *Religion, Modernity and Postmodernity* (Oxford: Blackwell).

reductionists, who self-consciously perform a series of final acts in the demolitionary explanation of the religious category, and the historians of religion and the phenomenologists who remain empathetic. There are further, and indeed more dramatic, reassimilations that take place once the religion of residual traditions and of emergent religiosities and spiritualities is confronted with the 'quasi-religion' apparent in certain aspects of contemporary socio-cultural change. Not least, such developments may be traced through patterns of commodification and transmutation, as has become apparent in the course of this book. Effective socio-scientific analysis of context is the presupposition, indeed the necessary condition, of any re-engagement with the reflexive and self-critical discourse of religion, in other words with theological reflection. In consequence, this chapter may also be understood as part of a continuing attempt to engage in contextually relevant postmodern theological reflection on the indispensable assumption, contrary to all arbitrary takings of refuge in what Ernst Bloch, ironically echoing Luther, once called 'safe strongholds of transcendence'.

In the main body of this chapter, the following issues are briefly investigated; each has its own legitimate complexity. First, we briefly outline the use of the category of time in twentieth-century Western theology and religious thought and interpret this as a partial and distorted assimilation of modernity. Second, we develop and apply Helga Nowotny's account of the recent history of the concept of time so as to broaden the framework of interpretation. Nowotny explores the transformations of the time problematic from the standpoint of the juxtaposition of modernity/postmodernity, and this allows us not only to understand more fully the aborted mediation of modernity by theology and religious thought but also to create the theoretical setting in which some of the rather startling implications for religion of the assimilative power of contemporary cultural change may be understood. Third, central to such change is the growing (but as yet insufficiently explored) cultural prominence of a polarity between two alternative ultimate points of resolution of the human condition. The first sublime is the informatically sustained virtual reality and the prosthetic enhancement of the cyborg, which afford ways of escape from the limitations of both 'first' and 'second nature'; and these options appear to be gender-nuanced as regards their acceptability. Then fourth, a second sublime can be detected in the celebration of the resurgent matriarchy taking place in the appearance (or reappearance) of the gender-specific spirituality of Gaia and the Goddess in a chthonic, earth-related identification. Fifth, and in conclusion, we consider this polarity of the alternative *noetic* and *chthonic* sublimes that can be understood as focused in expanded, even virtual mind, and earth-centredness, respectively. This analysis serves as the prelude to a brief last chapter in which we outline the burden presented in this book, that the responsible seeking and creation of identity both individual and communal has been, and remains, a core task of religion.

THEOLOGY, MODERNITY AND THE TEMPORAL MATRIX

In historical terms, the socio-scientific study of religion is traceable to such texts as David Hume's *Dialogues Concerning Natural History of Religion*, where it originally distinguished itself from theology understood as the normative exposition of revealed truth expressed in sacred narrative. From the Enlightenment onwards, and most notably following Wilhelm von Humboldt's separation of theology from the *Geisteswissenschaften* as the correlate of the institutional organisation of the University of Berlin into separate faculties for theology and the humanities, the study of theology and of religion came to occupy largely unrelated disciplinary fields, that is until the development of 'religious studies' in the second half of the twentieth century. When interpreted from the standpoint of time, the evolution of modern Christian (and indeed Jewish) theology was obliged to respond to German idealist philosophy and to the challenge of historicism. The religious alternative thus stood between the idealising (for our purposes the noetic) tendency to resolve history into Absolute Mind or its surrogates, and a reductive historicist critique which eliminated absolute (originally revealed) truths in favour of an infinitely complex but in the final analysis closed system of contingency and historical causality, a position expounded *par excellence* by Ernst Troeltsch.

The Swiss-German Reformed theologian Karl Barth (1886–1968) attempted to overcome the dilemma between an idealist loss of time and the exclusion of absolute truths from the contingent realm. He did this first of all by the adoption of a radicalised eschatology, and then, after a prolonged intellectual crisis, he rebuilt his theology around the axis of eternity and time.[18] Barth thus moved from the theological equivalent of the dialectical *Momente* of the Hegelian *massif* to the refunctionalisation of the ancestral *totum simul*, the idea of divine simultaneity, originating in its classic form in Boethius' *Consolations of Philosophy*. Karl Barth's representation of eternity as 'God's time' for which the

[18] Roberts, *A Theology on its Way?*, ch. 1.

succession of past, present and future is not an insuperable obstacle presages and parallels the contemporary rebirth, under very special historical and technological circumstances, of what Helga Nowotny depicts as the patriarchal time of ancestral Western thought. Nowotny's stress upon the economically and informatically driven search for simultaneity in which reductions of nanoseconds count for a great deal in a globalised and virtually instantaneous system of exchange has a remarkable elective affinity with Barth's re-use of divine simultaneity. The temporal logics of theological patriarchy and hyper-advanced capitalism are remarkably similar, hence, perhaps, the tendency to refunction theological categories in the conceptuality of world system and globalisation theory.

In overall terms, nineteenth- and twentieth-century Protestant Christian theologies, and in particular their representations of time and space, may on a relatively superficial level be understood as manoeuvres played out in a long-standing strategy of retreat in the face of an aggressive modernity. It is also possible to subsume both the internal development and the external relations of Christian theology under a secularisation model in which the categories of time and space provide an effective means of mapping the disjunction of the theological sphere from other representations of reality. Now, however, the 'market' of theological and religious possibilities is far more differentiated and potentially democratic than the orthodox secularisation model might suggest, both within theological traditions and as found in new or revived forms of religiosity. Main-line Abrahamic religions are in persisting crisis, and part of their difficulty is apparent in the disintegration of patriarchy both in their theologies and in their relevant religious cultural practices. A peculiarly well-focused aspect of this process is what, following Helga Nowotny's analysis, can be now represented as the fragmentation and reconstitution of patriarchal time.

MODERNISM AS POSTMODERNITY: THE TIME/SPACE MATRIX

At the end of the twentieth and in the early twenty-first century, neo-apocalyptic consciousness, postmodern panic thinking, an 'ecological eschaton' and resurgences of religious activity are taking place against the background of the much-contested 'End of History', in which invasive capitalism seemingly knows no bounds. This array of factors, all individually contestable, forms part of a complex process of reconfiguration of society and cultures. In the framework of resurgent modernism perceived as postmodern, Helga Nowotny has argued for the centrality of the concept of time, or rather of *time*s, for

it is we human beings who make time. The more complex the society, the more stratified the courses of time also become which overlap, form temporal connections with and alongside one another... Time has become a fundamental issue for all sciences, since it raises problems central to the understanding of the phenomena under investigation.[19]

The differentiation of 'times' out of unified time, and what Nowotny depicts as the 'disappearance of the category of the future and its replacement by ... an extended present'[20] are central features of technological modernisation and of modernity as such. The world-wide drive for simultaneity now confronts a variety of cultural 'times' in the temporal manifestation of the global/local matrix. The capacity for and attainment of simultaneity within global markets is what differentiates the rich from the poor who are strictly localised in time and confined to duration. Attempts to attain simultaneity are (according to a law of diminishing returns) progressively more difficult, and are also associated with qualitative changes in the perception and utilisation of time. We might say (when permitted a neologism) that we inhabit a *nanocracy* in which the capacity to compress and accelerate temporal processes is a prime index of wealth and power. Thus distinctions between the pre-modern (characterised by a unified temporal order), the modern (exhibiting quantified and commodified time) and the postmodern (which manifests accelerated time tending to simultaneity) can be located in a differentiated continuum that tends towards a point of culmination in the abolition of both temporal succession and future reference:

Whilst in the phase of industrialization it was above all the equation of time and money which resulted from the industrial capitalist logic of production and made time a scarce commodity, time is becoming accelerated innovation.[21]

The latter equation of time with accelerated innovation is commensurate with Lyotard's classic definition of the 'postmodern condition' as dynamic yet persisting transition:

A work can become modern only if it is first postmodern. Postmodernism thus understood is not modernism at its end but in the nascent state and this state is constant.[22]

[19] Nowotny, *Time*, p. 7.
[20] *Ibid.*, p. 8.
[21] *Ibid.*, pp. 10–11.
[22] Lyotard, *Postmodern Condition*, p. 79.

Nowotny's two basic contentions concerning the disappearing future and the extension of the present are complemented by a further third axiom, the assertion that the boundaries between past, present and future are not universally valid. Thus as in Karl Barth's account of theological temporality, so with Nowotny, simultaneity threatens to overturn time as mere succession. This radical suggestion is grounded in difference of temporal judgement that is in turn correlatable with changing cultural conditions:

With the end of an age in which, by means of the time-structure of industrial production, both linearity and the belief in progress were sustained, the category of the future is losing much of its attractiveness. A present geared to accelerated innovation is beginning to devour the future. Problems which could formerly be deferred into the future reach into the present for their part, press for solutions which admittedly may not be on the agenda until tomorrow but demand to be dealt with today.[23]

If, as Nowotny suggests, linear time has 'died', then what might have replaced it? Is it plausible to hope that time will be stopped, or that the continuum will be replaced by the technological and temporal equivalent of the Kondratiev business cycle? The relation between the content of time and value has changed – and is changing. Further exploration and explanation of the cultural consequences of this change could well begin with a consideration of the temporal implications of Lyotard's declaration that '*Post modern* would have to be understood according to the paradox of the future (*post*) anterior (*modo*).'[24] As a feminist theorist, Nowotny crystallises her argument around the notion of 'one's own time' (*Eigenzeit*), which she associates with the emergence of women from the private (as opposed to a male-dominated public) temporal sphere of bourgeois society. Time and its disposal thus become a matter of rights and of the differentiated political sphere, rather than subject to the *imperium* of a patriarchal universal. Questions of time and identity are inexorably intertwined. As we shall see, technological developments permit the virtual and cybernetic extension and enabling of what has been exposed in the recent history of time. As a hard-headed materialist and feminist social scientist, Nowotny pursues a pragmatic line and avoids the excesses of the hyper-stimulated *imaginaire* of the *prosthesophiliac*.[25] Nonetheless, she does propagate the conceptual neologism of competing 'uchronias', ideal and as yet non-existent good times, within the patriarchal *chronos* of

[23] Nowotny, *Time*, p. 11.
[24] Lyotard, *Postmodern Condition*, p. 81.
[25] Celia Lury, *Prosthetic Culture: Photography, Memory and Identity* (London: Routledge, 1997).

modernity/postmodernity. Such is the intensity of the rational, maximising demands imposed upon the reserve of time that in practical terms a countervailing strategy is required if time is to be recovered:

Learning to handle one's own reserves of time better in the face of a limited term of life, resisting the pressure of time, presupposes an appreciative openness towards the strategically playful aspect in time. Some things may be learnable in seminars on time management, but there are innumerable playful approaches and strategies.[26]

Nowotny's ludic treatment of time, reminiscent of aspects of the spirituality and quasi-religion of the postmodernised management consultant we examined earlier in chapter 3, involves what we may aptly call the relearning of a considered slowness, and is similar in certain respects to the reappropriation of time through ritual to be found in the context of deep ecology and chthonic spirituality to which we turn later in this chapter. This further dimension does not, however, concern a theorist whose conceptual apparatus ignores the relevance of a resurgent pre-modern condition. Nowotny nonetheless regards the successful exploration and management of temporal transition[27] as a central human preoccupation of late or advanced modernity. She incorporates into her argument what is for her an implicit cultural tension within women's existence between the managerial self-maximisation enacted in enhanced, competitive performance in participation in the nanocracy of patriarchal time, and a woman's primal biological identification grounded in 'slowness'. This tension between the exploitation of simultaneity as the arena of performance and efficiency and a 'slow' biological time will recur in the innovative religiosities of New Age and Neo-Paganism to be examined later.

Nowotny's interest is concentrated upon the transformation of time-consciousness from early modernity onwards; she is pointedly uninterested in pre-modernity. The change from pre-modernity (although Nowotny does not use this term) begins, so she argues, at the turn of the twelfth and thirteenth centuries. Repeating the French historian Le Goff's assertion that it was at this juncture that God's time gave way to the time of the traders, Nowotny links social change to material relations. Reflecting, however, the influence of J. A. Schumpeter's (rather than Marx's) account of the rise of the entrepreneur, Nowotny argues

---

[26] Nowotny, *Time*, p. 14.
[27] See John Hassard, 'Images of Time in Work and Organisation', in Stewart R. Clegg, Cynthia Hardy and Walter R. Nord (eds.), *Handbook of Organisation Studies* (London: Sage, 1996), pp. 581–98.

that it is the risking of assets that becomes the starting point of development and nascent modernity. Curiously, according to Nowotny, it is only with the eighteenth century that the horizon of the future is activated and 'The idea of progress entered the history of the human race.' With this there also came about a pervasive disjunction between measured time difference and lived time, that is between 'world time' (*Weltzeit*) and 'life time' (*Lebenszeit*).[28] Nowotny's subsequent analysis largely ignores the continuing cultural impact of an active historic residue of ideas of time and the perspectives latent in the religious and eschatological dimensions of Western history explored, for example, in the historical works of Ernst Bloch. Thus if Nowotny were to have included the conceptual pre-history of the scenario of modernity/postmodernity, this would have provided the basic analogue to the loss of the future and growth of simultaneity that she regards as typical of the chaotic proliferation of 'times' characteristic of postmodernity. As was argued earlier, it is theological conceptuality which provides the appropriate analogue of spatio-temporal compression and its over-arching simultaneity.

There is, indeed, a marked deficit in Nowotny's work, which recalls that of Marx: the religious past of the West is either virtually ignored, or appears in derisory, even (and this is especially marked in the case of Marx) parodic forms. Thus the imposition of standardised time on a global scale associated with economic and political integration, transportation, informatisation, and so on approaches world-wide simultaneity, in response to which people '*want to have more time for themselves*'.[29] However brilliant Nowotny's mapping of social and cultural change that leads to this juxtaposition of globalised and localised temporal economy may be, her account is circumscribed. Nowotny has set to one side the question of God; but, by contrast with this exclusion, the 'history of God' in Western culture as depicted by (for example) Hans Blumenburg can be rendered concrete through the mapping of time change and the role of simultaneity in relation to economic and societal factors.[30] As Marx hints in percipient passages of the *Grundrisse*, the 'jealous God' of capitalist accumulation, in short, ontologised money, is the 'God' that once mediated Western culture.[31] Recent technological developments turn the omniscience, omnipotence, omnipresence and

---

[28] Hans Blumenburg, *Lebenszeit und Weltzeit* (Frankfurt: Suhrkamp, 1986).

[29] Nowotny, *Time*, p. 18, my italics.

[30] Hans Blumenberg, *The Legitimacy of the Modern Age* (Cambridge, MA: MIT, 1983) and 'Die Vorbereitung der Neuzeit', *Philosophische Rundschau*, 9 (1961), 81–133.

[31] Further analysis of this could begin with such passages as the following from the *Grundrisse*: 'There is no higher or holier, since everything is appropriable by money. The "*res sacrae*" and "*religiosae*",

simultaneity of 'God'/capital expressed by Marx and Simmel (amongst others) in conceptual terms into 'realities' accessible to a mass culture.[32] Thus rather than God 'giving way' to the time of the traders, God's time becomes the temporal empowerment incarnated in capital itself. For those concerned with the promotion and professional management of religion these developments require a critical reconstrual of their discourse and its role in relation to contemporary capitalism.

As both Nowotny and Harvey argue, the 'first postmodernity' of rampant cultural modernism[33] in the early decades of the twentieth century had two interrelated aspects, speed and simultaneity. Whereas speed was a central preoccupation of artistic modernism (which then becomes a universal feature of hyper-modernisation under the technological conditions of postmodernity), it is likewise a second, more intense, intoxication, what Nowotny calls 'the illusion of simultaneity', that affects – even afflicts – our own era, the 'second postmodernity', by way of permanent satiation.[34] This situation is not value-free, for 'Simultaneity has everyone under control.'[35] It is possible to parallel Nowotny's position by allusion to refunctionings of the ancient philosophical and theological notion of the *totum simul* and the distinctions between *kairos* and *chronos* and, as regards history, *Historie* and *Geschichte* in twentieth-century religious thought.[36] Given the modernist and materialist perspective that both Nowotny and Harvey substantially share, it is the expressionist, apocalyptic, eschatological and chthonic dimensions of the post-human condition which they both, correspondingly, neglect.

Having appropriated features of Nowotny's sober argument in the context of the development of temporal aspects of the history of modern theology, we now visit and enlarge the literature associated with the

---

which may be "*in nullius boni*", "*nec aestimationem recipere, nec obligari alienarique posse*", which are exempt from the "*commercio hominum*", do not exist for money – just as all men are equal before God. Beautiful that the Roman church in the Middle Ages [was] itself the chief propagandist of money.' *Grundrisse: Foundations of the Critique of Political Economy (Rough Draft)* (Harmondsworth: Penguin, 1973), p. 839. See also David McLellan, *Marx's 'Grundrisse'* (London: Macmillan, 1971).

[32] Paul Morris, 'Judaism and Capitalism', in R. H. Roberts (ed.), *Religion and the Transformations of Capitalism: Comparative Approaches* (London: Routledge, 1995), ch. 5.

[33] See also Glenn Jordan, 'Flight from Modernity: Time, the Other and the *Discourse of Primitivism*', *Time and Society*, 4/3 (1995), 281–303.

[34] Roberts, *A Theology on its Way?*, p. 30.

[35] Nowotny, *Time*, p. 30.

[36] Elmer Fastenrath, '*In Vitam Aeternam': Grundzüge christlicher Eschatologie in der ersten Hälfte des 20. Jahrhunderts* (Erzabtei St Ottilien: Eos Verlag, 1982); Werner Jaeschke, *Die Suche nach den eschatologischen Würzeln der Geschichtsphilosophie: Eine historische Kritik der Säkulisierungsthese* (Munich: Kaiser Verlag, 1976); Gerhard Sauter, *Zukunft und Verheissung: Das Problem der Zukunft in der gegenwärtigen theologischen und philosophischen Diskussion* (Zurich/Stuttgart: Theologischer Verlag, 1965).

emergence of virtual reality, cyber-space and cyborgic enhancement that inhabit the attempted simultaneity that, as it were, succeeds time. This is the sphere in which 'God/s' are reborn and refunctionalised. As indicated above, it is in the extraordinary developments within the *imaginaire* of recent media and cultural theory that are here of concern to us. From the stand-point of religious studies this process can be regarded as yet a further stage in the de-eschatologisation of experience and of the time-order, and its assimilation into a commodified, managerialised, closed – and ultimately internalised – reality.

VIRTUALITIES, CYBORGS AND REDEMPTIONS OF THE 'FLESH'

There is an extensive and sophisticated literature that extends the discussion of modernity/postmodernity into the reconfigurations and extensions of space and time that occur when 'third nature' proliferates in virtual reality and cyborg culture.[37] Klaus Eder focuses upon the consequences of this expansion in an undramatic, but nevertheless pointed way:

> The nature question decides whether in modern society it is possible to take a path of social evolution of practical reason which will allow us to block off practical unreason in interacting with nature. The nature issue is predestined to start a renewed ideologization of modern practical reason. For the social state of nature that has been achieved in modernity offers a concept of practical rationality that can do without morality. The 'cybernetic state of nature' looming on the horizon is based on a concept of practical rationality that reduces morality to the reproducibility of this state of nature.[38]

This, as will become apparent, is a relatively benign and rather restricted view of the ideological impact of technological reason upon 'nature', that is when it is compared with the declaration of the apparent redundancy and seemingly infinite plastic transformability of nature to be found in the literature of virtual and cyber-reality. The 'reproducibility' of the state of nature may have rather more dramatic implications than Eder

---

37 Mike Featherstone and Roger Burrows (eds.) *Cyberspace/Cyberbodies/Cyberpunk: Cultures of Technological Embodiment* (London: Sage, 1995); Roger Friedland and Deirdre Boden (eds.), *Now Here: Space, Time and Modernity* (Berkeley: University of California Press, 1994); Chris Hables Gray (ed.), *The Cyborg Handbook* (London: Routledge, 1995); Donna Jeanne Haraway, 'A Cyborg Manifesto: Science, Technology, and Socialist Feminism in the Late Twentieth Century', *Simians, Cyborgs, and Women: The Reinvention of Nature* (London: Free Association Books, 1991), pp. 149–81; Howard Rheingold, *Virtual Reality* (New York: Summit Books, 1991); Howard Rheingold, *The Virtual Community: Surfing the Internet* (London: Secker & Warburg, 1994).

38 Klaus Eder, *The Social Construction of Nature: A Sociology of Ecological Enlightenment* (London: Sage, 1996), p. 57.

is prepared to allow. The 'cybernetic state of nature' dislocates the secularisation paradigm in that it supersedes the materialist reduction of the religious to the secular by permitting an escape from biological determination, even as virtual reality would appear to dispose of the Kantian limits placed upon reason (*Vernunft*) and to refunctionalise both speculative thought and the unfettered imagination as experiential opportunities in a new market-place for notional spatialities of consciousness.

At the outset some basic clarifications are in order. Virtual reality and cyberspace have been defined in the following way by the science (or cyber-) fiction writer William Gibson, who defines cyberspace as 'a consensual hallucination . . . [People are] creating a world. It's not really a place. It's not really space. It's notional space.'[39] Such brief definitions are capable of, and would indeed require, massive expansion, but all we may say here briefly is that 'virtual reality' is an expanding sphere open for appropriation realised in both noetic artificial intelligence and physical prosthetic terms on a theoretical foundation laid by cybernetics, which was originally defined as the scientific theory of control and communication in the animal or machine. In terms of its own myth of origin, cybernetics is generally assumed to have originated with Norbert Wiener's neologism derived from the Greek *kubernetes* (steersman). The cyborg is an embodied adjunct of virtual reality and has been represented as 'postbiological humanity'.[40] The ethical and political implications are considerable when relatively painless reallocation in virtuality and the creation of virtual *Lebensraum* are regarded as possibilities.

Paradoxically, however, the discussion of the creation and extension of cyborgic and virtual reality is not driven simply by the actual experience of cybernetically induced virtuality, but also by certain texts which have attained the status of a formative 'Word' in networked communities dedicated to its representation. Thus, for example, 'Gibsonian space' is a construct derived from William Gibson's science-fiction novel *Neuromancer*.[41] This derivation has some similarity with Nowotny's treatment of 'times' as opportunity for the expansion of women's potential. In a rather remarkable way the socio-cultural theorisation of cybernetic possibilities is in the first instance a text-governed, rather than an experience-following, empirically induced community activity. Here it is possible to speak of a quasi-sectarian or quasi-cultic activity that prefigures the 'real' as it is

---

[39] Cheris Kramarae, 'A Backstage Critique of Virtual Reality', in Steven G. Jones (ed.), *CyberSociety: Computer-Mediated Communication and Community* (London: Sage, 1995), pp. 10–35.

[40] Featherstone and Burrows, *Cyberspace/Cyberbodies/Cyberpunk*, p. 4.

[41] William Gibson, *Neuromancer* (London: Victor Gollancz, 1984).

deconstructed and virtualised through technology. Gibson's foundational text and others have prefigured contemporary cultural transmutations and served as a conceptual bank from which much theory has subsequently drawn.[42] There are themes in Gibson's work which are clearly relevant to the present chapter. We now examine, albeit very briefly, a remarkable example which will allow us to add a further axis to those used to structure our understanding of the transmuting religious field.[43]

A close reading of key passages of *Neuromancer* reveals a theological *Doppelgänger* in which a redemptive drama of the flesh is played out. Gibson provides us with a virtual theatre in which the re-enactment of some of the primal myths of the West is staged. In *Neuromancer*, the nightmarish, gender-specific narcissisms of mind (a malleable, contested, identity-bearing commodity) and 'meat' (a Frankenstein-like corporeality) are countered by a dream-like regression, a partial decoding of lost memory, a recapitulatory *kenosis* of human pretension. In Gibson's work, this is not so much part of an overt quasi-political agenda as the expression of a complex nostalgia implicit in a retelling of the drama of fall and redemption. What the novelist Patrick White sought to achieve for the Australian outback in the novel *Voss*, Gibson attempts for virtual reality. In one of the most resonant and suggestive passages in *Neuromancer*, Gibson unfolds the life narrative of his burnt-out hero:

Case was twenty-four. At twenty-two, he'd been a cowboy, a hustler, one of the best in the Sprawl. He'd been trained by the best . . . He'd operated on an almost permanent adrenaline high, a by-product of youth and proficiency, jacked into a custom cyberspace deck that projected his disembodied consciousness into the consensual hallucination that was the matrix.

He stole from his employers . . . they were going to make sure he never worked again.

They damaged his system with a wartime Russian mycotoxin.
Strapped to a bed in a Memphis hotel, his talent burning out micron by micron, he hallucinated for thirty hours.

The damage was minute, subtle, and utterly effective.

For Case, who'd lived for the bodiless exaltation of cyberspace, it was the Fall. In the bars he'd frequented as a cowboy hotshot, the elite stance involved a certain relaxed contempt for the flesh. The body was meat. Case fell into the prison of his own flesh.[44]

[42] See George Robertson, Melinda Mash *et al.* (eds.), *Futurenatural: Nature, Science, Culture* (London: Routledge, 1996) and John Wood (ed.), *The Virtual Embodied* (London: Routledge, 1998).

[43] What follows here may be understood as a response to Sarah Coakley's introduction to her edited collection *Religion and the Body* (Cambridge: Cambridge University Press, 1999) as reviewed by R. H. Roberts in 'Religion and the Body: Comparative Perspectives', *Religion*, 30 (2000), 55–64.

[44] Gibson, *Neuromancer*, pp. 11–12.

On an immediate level, with its allusions to 'the Fall' into the 'prison of the flesh', this passage could be read in a quasi-gnostic sense, but this would be misleading. There are also hints of Samson, Prometheus and Christ. Yet, this imprisonment in the flesh does not lack irony, for the challenge to Case's hubris which begins with his 'Fall' into the limitations of the body presages the recovery of his humanity. Likewise, his (residually female) partner struggles with her feline cyborgic physical enhancement, yet in sexual communion the erotic union of two particular bodies is a moment of total reclamation:

> It was a place he'd known before; not everyone could take him there, and somehow he always managed to forget it. Something he'd found and lost so many times. It belonged, he knew – he remembered – as she pulled him down, to the meat, the flesh the cowboys mocked. It was a vast thing, beyond knowing, a sea of information coded in spiral and pheromone, infinite intricacy that only the body, in its strong blind way, could ever read.[45]

The act of intercourse amounts to an act of redemption paradoxically enacted through the recovery of the fleshly body and its limitations. This reversal challenges the unending demands for the extension of both physical and mental performance in the Gibsonian world of virtuality and cyborgic enhancement, where 'human nature' no longer exists other than as the point of departure for cyborgic accretion and processes of 'self'-improvement determined by low cunning and manipulation of a predatory global economy of body parts and cybernetic implants. 'Mind' and 'body' have capacities for permanent cyborgic transformation, a potential limited in principle only by the capacity of each subject to access his or her advancement on the basis of economic resources and crime. In Gibson's trans-temporal Panopticon, the struggle against total transparency is the battlefield on which the war for the privacy that secures identity is fought. *Neuromancer* is, at least in part, a narrative of redemption from the spiral of dehumanising self- and corporeal enhancement conjoined with the endless opportunities of virtuality and cyberspace. The truth lies in the flesh: the immanent mode of a limited form of self-transcendence in somatic self-appropriation involves a retreat (at first enforced as punishment) from the illusory grandeur of the mental and bodily realms of virtuality and the prosthesis into the benign, yet transfigured banality of an original, limited embodiment. Significantly, the recapture of the body, even of its limitations, is paralleled by similar developments in the recomposition of the religious field.

[45] *Ibid.*, pp. 284–5.

In Gibson's textual space, the past and present, original and artefact, co-exist in a haunting duplicity. The leading characters not only co-exist in each other's consciousness and ceaselessly strive to expand their limitations, but also strain to decipher each face for signs of real youth in the endless rebuilds of their 'meat'. Vat-cultivated and real flesh, cybernetic, narcotic and genetic implants and the warring mutual invasion of consciousness constitute an *imaginaire* that Gibson extrapolated from a then (1984) relatively limited technological actuality. *Neuromancer* helped launch a cloned culture of cybernetic and virtual expansion enacted in a series of films and a body of socio-cultural theory. Mutually so engorged, media and theory have exercised significant social agency as they help drive forward cultural change in a labile popular consciousness. Thus, for example, the destruction/reconstruction of the post-human in *The Terminator*,[46] Donna Haraway's f/emancipatory agenda,[47] and the appearance of a self-experimenting elite of prosthesophiliacs[48] all provide evidence of a consistent drive towards liberation from the imposition of any and all biological and socially constructed identities.[49] The current scenario provides examples of many developments that fall within the parameters of the Gibsonian *imaginaire*.

As Donna Haraway has maintained in the *Cyborg Manifesto*,[50] cyborg potential releases body and consciousness from all limitations, including any limitations imposed by gender identity. Writing as a woman, and as a feminist, Haraway can now exorcise any residual inheritance of patriarchal dominance. Like the feminist theologian Judith Plaskow, who has argued (against Reinhold Niebuhr) that for women, 'sin is the failure to take responsibility for self actualisation',[51] Haraway is free to exercise mythopoeic imagination in the creation of a regime of uncluttered female potentiation:

Race, gender, and capital require a cyborg theory of wholes and parts. There is no drive in cyborgs to produce total theory, but there is an intimate experience

---

[46] Jonathan Goldberg, 'Recalling Totalities: The Mirrored Stages of Arnold Schwarzenegger', in Gray, *The Cyborg Handbook*, pp. 233–54.

[47] Gray, *The Cyborg Handbook*, pp. xi–xx.

[48] Sandy Stone, 'Split Subjects, Not Atoms; or, How I fell in Love with My Prosthesis', in Gray, *The Cyborg Handbook*, pp. 393–406.

[49] See Judith Butler, 'The Subversion of Bodily Acts', *Gender Trouble: Feminism and the Subversion of Identity* (London: Routledge, 1990), ch. 3; Elizabeth Grosz, *Space, Time and Perversion: Essays on the Politics of Bodies* (London: Routledge, 1995), ch. 4; Lury, *Prosthetic Culture*, ch. 3.

[50] Haraway, 'Cyborg Manifesto'; Donna Jeanne Haraway, 'Cyborgs and Symbionts Living Together in the New World Order', in Gray, *The Cyborg Handbook*, pp. xi–xx.

[51] Judith Plaskow, *Sin, Sex and Grace: Women's Experience and the Theologies of Reinhold Niebuhr and Paul Tillich* (Washington, DC: University Press of America, 1980), p. 3.

of boundaries, their construction and deconstruction. There is a myth system waiting to become a political language to ground one way of looking at science and technology and challenging the informatics of domination – in order to act potently.[52]

The ecstatic reappropriation of body-transcending self-potentiation (as opposed to divinisation) is expressed in Haraway's remarkable utterance 'I'd rather be a cyborg than a goddess.'[53] This issues in a vision of the female emancipate, cyborgically enhanced and freed from biological identity-determination. Without embarrassment, or the neurotic depotentiation generated by a Feuerbach or a Freud that has drained male projections, Haraway's *Cyborg Manifesto* proclaims an increasingly pervasive image of the *Überweib*, the gender-transcending Superwoman emergent as the cyborgic ideal.

Unlike Gibson's tormented male hero Case, the equally tested and increasingly androgenous heroic warrior character Ripley, created by Sigourney Weaver in successive *Alien* films, provides a powerful and contrasting image of struggle. Looked at in terms of elective affinities within the vocabulary of images provided by the cultural inheritance upon which the creators of both sagas draw, Case enacts (as a male at the end of patriarchy) a *kenotic* (self-emptying) quasi-Christological descent from transpersonal potency into the vulnerability of the worn, limited body. By contrast and in inverse correspondence, Haraway's cyborg 'femancipate' climbs out of the body in a *plerotic* (self-fulfilling) ascent to power. Weaver's character Ripley acts out something akin to a warrior Christology in the performance of a representative role reminiscent of a *Christus Victor*, a battler for the innocent child against an insidious, nameless, relentless evil that resists all (male) efforts at its exclusion and subjugation.

Donna Haraway's sympathies lie within a continuing materialism, a this-worldly political agenda in which women exploit all means available to enhance their potency freed from the social construction that is projected upon them as 'nature'. But recently two male writers, Barrie Sharman and Phil Jundkins, have argued that virtual reality 'is the hope for the next century' and that it 'may indeed afford glimpses of heaven'.[54] Here virtual reality is seen to provide a specifically masculine refuge from environmental degradation and the involuntary *kenosis* of patriarchy

---

[52] Haraway, 'Cyborg Manifesto', p. 181.

[53] *Ibid.*

[54] Barrie Sharman and Phil Jundkins, *Glimpses of Heaven, Visions of Hell: Virtual Reality and its Implications* (London: Hodder & Stoughton, 1992), pp. 134ff.

executed through a scheme of male disempowerment imposed by women. This is evidence of a more alarming flight from responsibility. Yet the incipient polarity between 'femancipation' and what we might call 'demancipation' has, as we shall shortly see, intriguing points of correlation with current developments in the changing religious field.

GENDERED ULTIMACIES AND THE RELIGIOUS FIELD: THE CHTHONIC IMPERATIVE

In earlier sections of this chapter three lines of approach to the interaction of time as transmuted in the modern/postmodern problematic and in the recomposition of the contemporary religious field were opened up: the treatment of time in modern Western theology and religious thought; transformations in the understanding of time in modernity/postmodernity; and the emergent culture of virtual reality and the cyborg in the twentieth century. Taken together these form the basis of a multi-layered account of how time-change and the reappropriation of fragments of traditions interact in the transmutations of culture and value. The contemporary religious field is split between a noetic or quasi-gnostic tendency to resolve human identity into an inner self/God in the conscious cultivation of 'self-religion' on the one hand and, on the other, by a drive towards chthonic identification. This chthonic imperative is stated with uncompromising clarity by prominent Neo-Pagans like, for example, Monica Sjöö and Barbara Mohr, who derive all human social life and culture from the hearth around which the primeval women gathered.[55] For them, 'Human survival does indeed depend on a sacramental relation to nature.'[56] Original human identity was female: women were the bearers of culture until the 'fall' occasioned by the discovery and aggressive deployment of metal (above all iron) by men. With mythopoeic intensity Sjöö and Mohr elaborate a vision of primal female identity which, like that generated by Harraway, reflects contemporary gender politics all too readily. Thus woman as witch, the embodiment of the Goddess, emerges, a figure endowed with perfect politically correct attributes:

The original witch was undoubtedly black, bisexual, a warrior, a wise and strong woman, also a midwife, also a leader of her tribe . . . The nature of the Goddess

[55] Monica Sjöö and Barbara Mohr, *The Great Cosmic Mother: Rediscovering the Religion of the Earth* (San Francisco: Harper & Row, 1987; 2nd edn, 1991), p. 11.
[56] *Ibid.*, p. 80.

was in no way the pale, meek, and solely maternal one that has been associated with 'femininity' in patriarchal culture.[57]

As a woman activist and Pagan,[58] Monica Sjöö is prepared to make challenging discriminations between different strands of contemporary spirituality and religiosity. Indeed, in her passionate and sometimes eccentric cultural artifact, *New Age and Armageddon*, Sjöö condemns certain tendencies out of hand as world-injurious, even pernicious, and she cuts across the plethora of diversity in New Age beliefs and practices.[59] She erects a basic distinction between what I here designate the *chthonic* and *noetic* alternatives, which, in crude analytic terms, separate Paganism from New Age. The broad elective affinities of the two categories are extremely important. The associations and elective affinities between some main forms of Paganism (or Neo-Paganism) and earth-centred spiritual practices, environmental activism and the mythic and practical celebration of the pre-modern and (ultimately the matriarchal) prehistoric human condition are indicative. The predominant stress upon cyclic time within an aeonic conception of the evolution of the human condition conceived as having fallen from pre-metallic, matriarchal origins involves a conscious primitivism, but (as we have seen from Nowotny's analysis of the 'recovery of slowness') this is but one side of an emergent recomposition of the religious field.

The manifest assimilation, indeed the striking mutual empowerment of New Age practices and contemporary globalised (and thus simultaneity-seeking) capitalism in a cult of performativity (inseparable from time-acceleration), also falls within the parameters of Nowotny's account of the recent history of time and modernity/postmodernity. Regarding the slowing of time in order to gain possession of it, the Pagan might break with the practice of hyperperformativity through ritual intervention and departure into liminality, while Nowotny would advocate a review of time-management. Both the neo-primitivists and the postmodern theorists seek to recapture time, and thus value, from the invasive *totum simul* of a virtual reality empowered by global capitalism and realised by information technology in an interlinked constellation of possibilities largely controlled and exploited by men.

---

[57] *Ibid.*, p. 216.

[58] North American readers may be more familiar with the term 'Neo-Pagan'. European and British Pagans tend to assert (not uncontentiously) a historical continuity of indigenous practice and thus prefer the designation without prefix. See Ronald Hutton's contribution to Pearson, Roberts and Samuel, *Nature Religion Today*, ch. 7, 'The Discovery of the Modern Goddess'.

[59] Sjöö and Mohr, *Great Cosmic Mother*, ch. 1.

From the standpoint of main-line religious traditions, the quasi-theologisation of virtual reality and cyborg discourse presents itself as an illicit expropriation of conceptual territory. Through this appropriation, transcendence and the sublime become adjuncts of technology and the market. Resurgent (Neo-)Paganism proposes the re-enchantment of the earth: it purports to reinvest nature with intrinsic meaning.[60] On the mythological level and in the relevant ritual and cultural practices, the repeopling of the cosmos with divinities is doubtless intensely problematic, not least for those bred on the uncompromising purities of rationalism or monotheism. Yet infused through the interlinked recompositions of the religious and the cultural fields an epochal transition is taking place in the dimension of gender. In consequence, the whole evolving compact of secularised theism with patriarchal modernity as subsumed under the modes of rationality and instrumental reason associated with rational male hegemony is also called into question. These developments may now, I venture to suggest, be coming to assume the proportions of a paradigm shift from a masculinist and patriarchal to a feminist and matriarchal sensibility.[61] The two paradigms exist in parallel, comprising increasing areas of differentiated and contested space within the religious field.[62]

Thus main-line religion and the Abrahamic traditions are faced with two major alternative possibilities. The first is the continued decline of the patriarchal universalism of the 'grand narratives' (and correlative 'grand times') of the Jewish and Christian traditions. The second is an aggressive and particularistic alienation into the narratives and thus the 'times' of each brand of radical conservatism or 'fundamentalism'. The apocalypticism and the latent or actual violence and ecological catastrophism often characteristic of such forms of religious resurgence are evidence of deep alienation from a common time analogous to a global 'common good'. By contrast with the decline and convulsive reassertions of patriarchal religion, there is the dispersed option of a globalised, superficially differentiated market in spiritualities, represented under the rubric of New Age. There are affinities between New Age thus represented and both the understanding of time focused in a quasi-divine simultaneity of the virtual and Helga Nowotny's representation of the electronic and

---

[60] Pearson, Roberts and Samuel, *Nature Religion Today;* Graham Harvey, *Listening People, Speaking Earth: Contemporary Paganism* (London: C. Hurst & Co., 1997); Graham Harvey and Charlotte Hardman (eds.), *Paganism Today* (London: Thorsons, 1996).

[61] Vivianne Crowley, *Wicca: The Old Religion in the New Millennium* (London: Thorsons, 1996).

[62] See James R. Lewis (ed.), 'Christianity and Neo-Paganism', *Magical Religion and Modern Witchcraft* (New York: State University of New York Press, 1996), part v.

informational hyper-drive towards instantaneity. Standing in opposition to this are the regressive tendencies of the Pagan re-emergence.

There is an apparent dichotomy in the religious field between the world-alienative resurgent 'times' of the religion of patriarchy and global fundamentalisms and the quasi-theological *nunc stans* of New Age self-religion and its compact with capitalism and its relative ecological indifference. What possibilities might there be for a more benign configuration within a recomposing religious field? As *tertium quid*, an alternative third path might be the democratic and reflexive reappropriation of myth and ritual in the service of humankind and of a reconceptualisation of the divine in terms which incorporate female attributes. Here time might be remade, revalued through liminality and grace-acknowledging embodiment. This would be a religiosity of individual risk and communal enterprise, a distinctive response to the routinised, bureaucratised and faded charisma of much main-line religion. Such a vision cannot simply flow from fiction-driven theory within the ambit of the wilder shores of cultural studies, nor can it be confined to the dialectics of an isolated masculinity and the third nature of virtuality or the cyborg. It is, however, quite literally on the ground, in contact with the earth, where the incarnational *kenosis* of the linear time of the male God and the cyclic temporal *plerosis* of the Goddess might suggest the possibility of a mutual gendered reconciliation. Any such encounter of *animus* and *anima* would require a multiplicity of many-layered transvaluations, the beginnings of which are scarcely known, far less the ends. The 'times' of the God and the Goddess diverge: whose time is it that has now come? Where, then, is Time to be found?

Conclusion

CHAPTER 11

Identity as vocation: the prospect for religion

It now remains briefly to review in retrospect the contents of this book, and then to consider both what the prospect for religion might be and how reflection that persists in regarding the religious dimension as of central importance to an evolving human condition might evolve. The first part of this book began with an examination of Francis Fukuyama's assertion of the 'End of History' and then of the much-proclaimed assertion that 'capitalism has triumphed'. In effect, Fukuyama may be understood as the modern-day equivalent of a right-wing but non-theistic Hegelian who extends and transposes Hegel's equation of the real and the rational in the *Philosophie des Rechts* from the Prussian state to the global totality of 'liberal democratic capitalism'. We then traced out on the levels of global ideology, the Thatcherite revolution from above, the ingestion of spirituality into management training and consultancy, and the massified production of a skill-bearing 'product' in British universities, respectively, as a complex process of advanced capitalist 'normalisation' in which commodification now extends in virtually unbroken interconnection from the reconfiguration of globality down to each individual mind – or 'soul'. The 'normalisation' or mopping up operation that has taken place after the collapse of communist socialism has involved a cyclic process in which a discourse replete with key *topoi* or commonplaces inspired by resonant metaphors is proclaimed and then translated as 'vision' from metaphor into a managed and increasingly managerialised socio-cultural reality. This managerial modernity confronts humankind at every quarter, thus posing the question of how effectively the religious dimensions of tradition and experience may have moderated or critically impeded what now appears as a seemingly unassailable, even terminal transmogrification of the (post-)human condition. The emergence of new mutual synergies was detected; these were innovative elective affinities between religion (or quasi-religion) and social reality that are culturally located in the manipulation of the groundlessness of human beings in the matrix of modernity/postmodernity. Here identities proliferate that are little more than assemblages of semantic and semiotic fragments which can be bought, sold and exchanged like Cindy Sherman drapes in the 'contrived depthlessness' of postmodernity.[1] Fatefully, universities have become a key agent of facilitation in the brave new world in which the centralised production of identities and the consumerist dissipation of the market are in active conjunction.

The second part of this book took the reader into the realm of theology and power, and into the representations within the institutional tradition of the social and human sciences as applied to religion, in the hope of finding there some effective critique of the affinities and collusions examined earlier. Within, however, central strands of theological thought directed at specifying the identity of Anglican Christianity and locating the 'real power' of the Christian Gospel, we encountered the uncritical assimilation of managerial power and 'mission', and the problematic representation of managerialism as the restoration of the lost potency of the Gospel. Anglican theological tradition, the executive control of the Church and the Taylorised performance management of clergy in newly minted 'Quality circles', besides the wider response of earlier and contemporary theologians, provided examples of the continuing managerial normalisation within the 'empty shrine' or even the 'killing jar' of a managerialised Establishment. As after the Russian Revolution the Soviet constitution formally guaranteed the freedom of religion, as long as that religion remained confined within its own archaic and societally restricted sphere of residual influence, so, in addition, a postmodern Augustinian quasi-fundamentalist theology, so-called 'radical orthodoxy', now provides a refuge within which a quasi-Messianic elite hibernate until their eschatological 'moment' comes: meanwhile the world degrades. Here the emic anti-capitalist posture of this theology is all too similar to the strategy of Barthian theology earlier in the twentieth century; in etic terms such theology may be understood as a highly marketable cultural artifact that displays the splendour of the mind or minds that have created it, and offers to humankind an alienated Christian identity based upon the paradoxically ingestion and sublation of a nihilistic modernity. This issues in an impossible dilemma: opt for the Church (and its 'dogmatics' or 'radical orthodoxy') or slide away and sink into a heretical secularity.

---

[1] See David Harvey, *The Condition of Postmodernity: An Enquiry into the Origins of Cultural Change* (Oxford: Blackwell, 1989), pp. 58–9.

The third part of *Religion, Theology and the Human Sciences* assumes both the socio-cultural reconfiguration of religion and the evolution of theology during the period of epochal change examined in parts 1 and 2. In two successive chapters we examined in sequence the composition and recomposition of identities: first on the level of the expression of attempts to formulate the identity of 'Europe', and then, following this, in relation to globalisation and the global/local interface. The account of the 'souls of Europe' was written from the standpoint of a writer committed to the servicing and furtherance of a particular theological tradition facing a multiplicity of crises: this investigation was driven by a desire to find an *episteme*, a viable mode of operation from within, as it were, an ecclesial and academic establishment. The ethnographic study of the 1993 Chicago Parliament of the World's Religions that follows forms part of a long process of reflection which eventually enabled me to become convinced that questions about the human meanings of such ideas as 'religion', 'spirituality' and the 'sacred' or 'sublime' are existentially, epistemologically and ontologically prior to all commitments to 'tradition', even in the contemporary West.[2] In the last of these three chapters the argument was once again relocated, this time in the postmodern temporal problematic as presented by the prominent feminist theorist Helga Nowotny. Here it was possible to reconnect with the theology of the most prominent Protestant theologian of the twentieth century, Karl Barth, within the setting of the transformations of time. This closed another circle opened up and described within this collection of essays and papers.

As regards the future of religion and engaged reflection upon it, we may here recall the distant voice of Martin Luther heard in the words of the great sociologist Max Weber, who once wrote of science and politics as 'vocations' in a world undergoing rapid modernisation. The very term 'vocation', or *Beruf*, resonates with its theological ancestry in a way now seemingly remote from the mass experience of the late twentieth and early twenty-first centuries. In European, and in particular within a generic British culture, this sense of purpose and the possibility of finding and acting out such an individual life-trajectory or teleology have seemingly faded: each individual (other than a minute elite inhabiting the remaining redoubts of carefully preserved zones of privilege) is constructed as nothing more than a Humean bundle of competences, with or without

---

[2] Here I have in mind Geoffrey Samuel's seminal work on Tibetan Buddhism, *Civilized Shamans: Buddhism in Tibetan Societies* (Washington: Smithsonian Institution Press, 1993) and by the same author, *Mind, Body and Culture: Anthropology and the Biological Interface* (Cambridge: Cambridge University Press, 1990).

a market value. Each such conscious social atom seeks to locate, create and assert itself out of the mass of swirling fragments of meaning available, to a greater or lesser extent, to it. According to Jean-François Lyotard, the 'great voyages' are over: we have but to acquiesce and perform. The destruction of the idea and the reality of vocation and the voyage is consummated in a managerialised modernity, especially when this paradigm is welcomed into such public sacred space as remains. This is because the obedience required of an employee or operative is in principle total: there must, as Professors Gill and Burke put it, be no 'secret pockets' left for the spontaneous or the unexpected. The combination of ever more complete surveillance at the level of societal structures and the demand for utter transparency imposed upon the individual means that the quest for vocation degrades into a desperate craving for that intensity of experience and transient performative competence that masquerades as the human hypostasis. Under these conditions the ever-frustrated search for a viable, rooted identity has thus become the normal, rather than the exceptional, 'vocation' of our time.

Most contemporary human beings who subsist in the contexts considered in this book do not, of course, live in a vacuum: each stands amidst the massive forces which seek to mould and express forms of 'habitus' which may embody use- and enact exchange value, respectively. The education system has been fundamentally reconfigured in order to ensure that each social atom has a limited and degraded use-value which may be deployed in an ever-changing labour market: thus each individual needs to be fully aware at every moment of his or her imminent obsolescence and to act out of perpetual fear of being deprived of that minimal sense of being generated by performance. The so-called free market (including the entertainment industry) colonises and extracts from every conceivable (and newly conceived) dimension of the human and natural life-world that which may in turn be harnessed to exchange and surplus value. This is an immensely powerful and many-sided mechanism that consumes humankind; and once, as is increasingly the case, the managerial imperative elides the separation of powers and provides the hinge connecting both jaws of the machine, then resistance may seem futile. Under such conditions, associative and deliberative intermediate organisations, including main-line religions, may be greatly weakened unless they can find new resonance patterns, new elective affinities. The basic alternatives for religion in the face of modernity are familiar: secularising retreat to the margins, accommodation – or migration and transmutation.

In the case of the Church of England, accommodation as a response to secularisation has not so much taken the direction (as in the United States) of the religion of 'rational choice' in which failed economic aspiration becomes displaced maximisation as 'compensation', a position argued by Stark and Bainbridge,[3] but adopts the form of a nationalised and moderately differentiated 'service-provision' united by the enthusiastic absorption of managerialism at all levels. In Scotland, by relative contrast, the function of a national Church of Scotland has been at least in part that of the 'sacred marker' serving to intensify an ethnic and cultural specificity. The great Scottish poet Hugh MacDiarmid succinctly expressed this kind of function, and the difference, as he saw it, between English and Scottish 'cultures' in one of his less distinguished but nonetheless significant poems:

> The British are a frustrated people
> Victims of arrested development.
> Withered into cynics
> And spiritual valetudinarians,
> Their frustration due
> To a social environment
> Which has given them no general sense
> Of the facts of life,
> And no sense whatever
> Of its possibilities;
> Their English culture a mere simulacrum,
> Too partial and too provincial
> To fulfil the true function of culture
> The illumination of the particular
> In terms of the universal;
> Beside the strong vigour of daily life
> It is but an empty shadow.[4]

When MacDiarmid writes of the 'true function of culture' as 'the illumination of the particular in terms of the universal' he is doubtless reflecting the strongly Germanic background of his reading and intellectual interests (and his detestation of 'Englishness'), but his vision, expressed during an era of the progressive failure of main-line religion, is also 'religious' in a more anthropological sense. Like T. S. Eliot, MacDiarmid

---

[3] See Lawrence A. Young, *Rational Choice Theory and Religion: Summary and Assessment* (London: Routledge, 1997).

[4] Hugh MacDiarmid, *Hugh MacDiarmid: Complete Poems 1920–1976*, ed. Michael Grieve and W. R. Aitken, 2 vols. (London: Martin Brian and O'Keefe, 1978), vol. II, p. 938.

was aware of the destruction of identity under conditions of modernisation; both writers knew the 'wasteland' and focused upon both human futility and the lost grandeur of a benign attachment to land, language and place. The displacement of the connection of the particular and the universal into globalisation is intertwined with difficult and fascinating questions about the nature and cultural repositioning of transcendence. In the absence of adequate settings for the deep socialisation of national and universal reconnection in 'post-emotional society', special interest groups and new social movements often take on the character of complete life-worlds for those involved. Thus feminist reifications of the cyborg and the prosthesis as means of emancipation from social and biological construction, and male fantasy cultures of virtual reality in which pornography flourishes and a hysterical manhood decays into perverted displacement are contemporary instances of such quasi-cultic recreation and intensification of the *persona*.

Part of the collapse of socialisation can be associated with the disappearance of the ritual, experiential and mythic means of connecting the particular individual to the universals of cosmos, community – and even the family. If such connections are not built, as it were, from the bottom up, then they are likely to fail; such identities as emerge will not have what Vaclav Havel calls 'roots in the order of being'.[5] When Lady Thatcher made the dramatic claim on behalf of the Conservative programme of national revival that 'Economics are the method. The object is to change the soul',[6] she was prepared to make certain societal sacrifices in order to make possible the reversal of British economic decline. *Everything*, including the 'soul', had to be brought into conformity with that programme. We have seen how patterns of compliance did indeed emerge in which 'enterprise' was aggregated into an ever-expanding and routinised managerial modernity that now comprises both extremities, the global and the local, of the globalised world system. Managerialism is one dimension, but a critically important one, of the 'glocal' adhesive that attaches the core to peripheries, and facilitates the imposition of 'McDonaldised' life-worlds of 'efficiency', 'calculability', 'predictability' and 'control' upon the whole world itself.

If in societies and cultures where the 'performative absolute' reigns supreme and significant ideological challenge is thereby rendered redundant, then, in T. S. Eliot's terms, human life comes to lack that degree of mediated social friction necessary to the sustaining of its health and

---

5 Vaclav Havel, 'The Power of the Powerless', in Jan Vladislav (ed.), *Living in Truth* (London: Faber, 1987), p. 62.
6 Margaret Thatcher, *The Sunday Times*, 7 May 1988.

vitality. As we saw earlier, the forcible imposition of what Lord Conrad Russell called 'battery higher education' is a highly relevant case in point: the societal roles of the university as 'seat of the democratic intellect' and 'community of contested discourses' have been sacrificed to a reborn utilitarianism, in which humankind, and in particular young people, have become simply the means (or, as vice-chancellors prefer to put it, the 'raw material') to economic ends (the 'product'). Once main-line religion adopts this pattern of behaviour and not only fails to relate particular and universal effectively, but also to treat human beings within their own symbolic and affective domain as means to performative ends, then a theological and spiritual betrayal amounting to forms of treason is compounded.

A growing realisation underlies this book that the traditions that its author studied and served for a quarter-century in England, Germany and Scotland are fatally flawed in their present forms, and that the active collusions and unreflected elective affinities of these residual traditions render them incapable of self-generated inner reform. Because of a life-investment in gaining the competencies required to assist in the task of reform from within, much prolonged and painful resistance was experienced in reaching this difficult conclusion. As it happened, this decision was pre-empted: I underwent the sudden and complete dissolution of my hard-won identity. Thus a *habitus* consisting of loyalty to the university as community of critical truth-seekers, service given to managerialised and established or national churches in the belief that they might still afford transformatory sacred space, commitment to Christian theology as emancipatory discourse, reconstrual of 'divinity' as a creative interdisciplinary *episteme*, the role of the professor as academic leader rather than mere service provider and manager, critical reform of ancestral theological patriarchy, and so on, simply imploded and disintegrated. In future work I shall address this stripping of patriarchal identity – a veritable '*kenosis* of masculinity' – and the process of emergence from it.

In conclusion, let us explore a little more fully what 'identity as vocation' might mean today. The distinguished sociologist Zygmunt Bauman has contrasted two differing responses to the contemporary pressure to achieve identity experienced by individuals living in the matrix of modernity/postmodernity: the vagabond and the pilgrim.

The vagabond does not know how long he will stay where he is now, more often than not it will not be for him to decide when the stay will come to an end . . . What keeps him on the move is disillusionment with the last place of sojourn and the forever smouldering hope that the next place he has not visited yet, perhaps the place after next, may be free from the faults which repulsed him in the places he has already tasted . . . The vagabond is a pilgrim without a destination, a nomad without an itinerary.[7]

For Bauman, the predominant human type under postmodernising conditions is the 'vagabond' caught up in a serial squatting, unable to rest or put down roots. In the final analysis human beings may, however, choose to live either as 'vagabonds' or as 'pilgrims'. Victor and Edith Turner produced a magnificent compound definition of the meaning of the term 'pilgrimage' which bears repetition and merits a fuller exposition which we cannot enter into here:

Pilgrimage, then, has some of the attributes of liminality in passage rites: release from mundane structure; homogenization of status; simplicity of dress and behaviour; communitas; ordeal; reflection on the meaning of basic religious and cultural values; ritualized enactment of correspondences between religious paradigms and shared human experiences; emergence of the integral person from the multiple personae; movement from mundane centre to sacred periphery which suddenly, transiently, becomes central for the individual, an *axis mundi* of his faith; movement itself, symbol of communitas, which changes with time, as against stasis, which represents structure; individuality posed against the institutionalized milieu; and so forth. But since it is voluntary, not an obligatory social mechanism to mark the transition of an individual or group from one state or status to another within the mundane sphere, pilgrimage is perhaps best thought of as 'liminoid' or 'quasi-liminal', rather than 'liminal' in Van Gennep's full sense.[8]

As empowered moderns (and postmoderns) dare we be 'pilgrims' in Turner's sense of the word, that is responsible re-awakeners of ultimate identities, or as Zygmunt Bauman would have it, are we condemned to be destination-less, but perhaps better-rewarded nomadic 'vagabonds'? If, as I believe to be the case, much main-line institutionalised religion has in reality lost touch with the primal religious function, then what must now concern us is the investigation of those dimensions of human becoming and mutual existence that precede tradition. This leads us, as pilgrims, into the zone of the lost transcendental principles of societal renewal, the ritual *a priori*, an extra-territoriality explored, for example, in the last, posthumously published, work of the anthropologist Roy Rappaport.[9]

---

[7] Zygmunt Bauman, *Postmodern Ethics* (Oxford: Blackwell, 1993), p. 240.

[8] Victor Turner and Edith Turner, 'Introduction: Pilgrimage as Liminoid Phenomenon', *Image and Pilgrimage in Christian Culture: Anthropological Perspectives* (New York: Columbia University Press, 1978), pp. 34–5.

[9] Roy Rappaport, *Ritual and Religion in the Making of Humanity* (Cambridge: Cambridge University Press, 1999).

For anyone socialised both into the service of tradition as an erst-while theologian and into socio-scientifically aware research into religion (in Bauman's term as an 'interpreter'), yet who lacks the privileged security of ordained status (as a 'legislator'), there is much at stake: a continuing ascesis beyond the initial *kenosis* is required of him or her.[10]

At this juncture the words of the theatre director, the late Jerzy Grotowski are relevant. Without the security of tradition, the informed and engaged inquirer has to allow her or his subjectivity to become the inner laboratory in which experimentation is permitted and even encouraged as the adjunct of research. Grotowski argued that (and here I have taken the liberty of expanding the gendered narrowness of the original text):

The Performer, with a capital letter, is a man [or woman] of action. He [or she] is not a man [or woman] who plays another. He [or she] is a dancer, a priest, a warrior: he [or she] is outside aesthetic genres. Ritual is performance, an accomplished action, an act. Degenerated ritual is a spectacle. I don't want to discover something new but something forgotten . . . Essence interests me because in it nothing is sociological. It is what you did not receive from others, what did not come from outside, what is not learned . . . One access to the creative way consists of discovering in yourself an ancient corporeality to which you are bound by a strong ancestral relation . . . Starting from details you can discover in you somebody other – your grandfather, your mother. A photo, a memory of wrinkles, the distant echo of a color of the voice enable you to reconstruct a corporeality. First, the corporeality of somebody [or *something*] known, and then more and more distant, the corporeality of the unknown one, the ancestor. Is this corporeality literally as it was? Maybe not literally – but yet as it might have been. You arrive very far back, as if your memory awoke . . . as if you recall [the] Performer of the primal ritual . . . With the breakthrough – as in the return of an exile – one can touch something which is no longer linked to origins but – if I dare say to *the origin.*[11]

This may be a mangled translation of an already convoluted text, but it forcibly impels us into consideration of the new borderlands between ritual and performance, psychotherapy and spirituality, and reflexivity and tradition-making where the primal can be sought. If, on the one hand, as the anthropologist Charles Lindholm argues, main-line religion no longer meets basic human needs for communion, then 'charisma' may well take on dangerous and problematic forms. If, however, on the other hand, all charismatic action or shamanistic experience is represented

[10] Zygmunt Bauman, *Legislators and Interpreters: On Modernity, Post-Modernity and Intellectuals* (Cambridge: Polity, 1987).

[11] Jerzy Grotowski, *Workcenter of Jerzy Grotowski – Centro di Lavaro di Jerzy Grotowski* (Pontedera, Italy: Centro per la Sperimentazione e la Ricereca Teatrale, 1988), pp. 36–40.

as inevitably malign in its consequences, and treated as such, then the possibility of societal renewal through the ritual function and primal religiosity will die away. If this happens, then humankind will be perpetually condemned to what Stjepan Mestrovic describes as 'post-emotional society', in which primal human needs will never be met other than through control and consumption.

The mutual patterning of closure that is characteristic of both theology and social theory requires us to consider new ways of recollecting, envisioning and enacting the primal tasks of religion. The articulation in this book of the managerialist hegemony that has become, in the absence of effective challenge, a near caricature of itself is a restriction and blockage upon the legitimate pathways of human development, both individual and collective. Straightforward negation is not a sufficient response, for in increasingly complex societies sound and appropriate management is a necessity. When, however, managerialism stages an invasion and reconstitution of the neglected and etiolated springs of fundamental socialisation, then it should be challenged. To outflank this invasive hegemony is a more complex and difficult task. As we have argued earlier, albeit in passing, human existence has been divorced from rootedness in nature, and the way forward that suggests itself to me is through an interdisciplinary human ecology to which I intend to turn my attention in due course. The growing exhaustion of one complex paradigm, that of classical sociology, which to a significant degree came into existence in historical succession to theology and inherited its totalising explanatory ambitions, is now increasingly apparent. These forms of social construction merely compound human despair and add to a growing burden of pseudo-fundamental determinants. Enhanced reflexivity on its own is but a palliative; it fails adequately to reconnect the particulars of each human life and of attempted communities with the universals that underpin planetary homoeostasis and human security.

Unless and until religious traditions are judged in the light of their capacity to service primary human needs, they will remain both redundant or dangerous, or both. The critical scrutiny of the rediscovery and societal refunctioning of these primary processes now falls by default, albeit in part, into the lap of a disengaged, centrally directed academy now directed to the mass production of uniform conformity. Yet even as anthropologists have on occasion become the safe-keepers of ancient cultures and have resourced the recovery of the particular roots of being in the communities that they research, so truly serious students of religion are confronted by this loss of the primal and a corresponding need to regain the means of identity on their home territories. In societies and cultures which, in late modernity, have lost contact with their origins, have ceded active democracy to invasive managerial hegemony, have been seduced by postmodern, consumerist conceptions of the formation of identity, and which slide into ever deeper dysfunctionality, the discovery – or recreation – of these primal processes of renewal may prove impossible for all but a small and oppressed minority; but the obligation to try to discover them nonetheless remains.

The conclusions reached in this collection presuppose many issues, all of which deserve to be addressed more in informed and appropriate ways. The first step in all innovation, especially thinking within the managerial paradigm, is to step outside the box that circumscribes any given 'reality'. This book is a report; but it is also a provocation and a prelude. The resilient reader may now see a little better how a form of social construction has become so complete and all-comprehensive that it has attained the status of a, or *the*, societal transcendental in terms of which all other realities appear to subsist. Such totalisation, which has now grasped much main-line religion within its cold, fruitless embrace, closes off deeper sources for the renewal of the human condition. Once this happens, the mere words, made however strange, of theology must be judged in relation to the outcome of the investigation and reactivation of the 'deep ecology' of advanced modern societies. Intellectual perspectives, theoretical and methodological paradigms and the matrix of modernity/postmodernity are all intertwined. The decoding and eventual displacement of inadequate and dysfunctional societal transcendentals should, in the final analysis, be a, if not the, core goal of functional religion in our time. It is an individual and communal responsibility and a task to which traditions may in due course find their way back. This is where the true 'struggle for recognition' should take place.

In short, each sector of human life needs to pay the closest attention to the scrutiny and, if necessary, the protection and assertion of its intrinsic function and the correlative intrinsic values. This is no less true of theology than it is of religion and the university. The depth and extent of the betrayals are such that, as with the abuse of public transport, health-care and education – and of the physical environment itself – it may only be when catastrophe actually happens that the absence of responsibility and the neglect of due care will become apparent, and remedy be attempted. Let us hope that it is not too late to do so.

Bibliography

Abrams, M., D. Gerard and N. Timms (eds.), *Values and Social Change in Britain*, London: Macmillan, 1985.

Aganbegyan, Abel, *The Challenge: The Economics of Perestroika*, London: Hutchinson, 1988.

Anderson, Digby (ed.), *The Kindness that Kills: The Churches' Simplistic Response to Complex Social Issues*, London: SPCK, 1984.

Andresen, Karl (ed.), *Handbuch der Dogmen- und Theologiegeschichte*, 3 vols., Berlin: de Gruyter, 1985.

Archbishop of Canterbury's Commission on Urban Priority Areas, *Faith in the City: A Call for Action by Church and Nation*, London: Church House Publishing, 1985.

Arnott, Principal Struther, 'Six Centuries of Service – The Principal's Report', *University of St Andrews Annual Report 1992–3*.

Art. 'Europa', in *Literatur Lexikon*, Zurich: Kindler Verlag, 1964; 2nd edn, 1990, columns 2513–14.

Ash, Timothy Garton, *The Uses of Adversity*, Cambridge: Granta Books, 1989.

We the People: The Revolution of '89 Witnessed in Warsaw, Budapest, Berlin and Prague, Cambridge: Granta Books, 1990.

Bannet, Eve Tavor (1992), 'Marx, God and Praxis', in Philippa Berry and Andrew Wernick (eds.), *Shadow of Spirit: Postmodernism and Religion*, London: Routledge, 1992, pp. 122–34.

Barth, Karl, 'Hegel', *Protestant Theology in the Nineteenth Century*, London: SCM, 1972, pp. 384–421.

Bartlett, Robert, *The Making of Europe: Conquest, Colonization and Cultural Change*, London: Penguin, 1993.

Baudrillard, Jean, *Jean Baudrillard: Selected Writings*, ed. Mark Poster, Cambridge: Polity, 1988.

Symbolic Exchange and Death, London: Sage, 1993.

Bauman, Zygmunt, *Intimations of Postmodernity*, London: Routledge, 1992.

Legislators and Interpreters: On Modernity, Post-Modernity and Intellectuals, Cambridge: Polity, 1987.

Modernity and the Holocaust, Cambridge: Polity, 1989.

Postmodern Ethics, Oxford: Blackwell, 1993.

Beck, Ulrich, *Risk Society: Towards a New Modernity*, London: Sage, 1992.

Beckford, J., 'The Sociology of Religion 1945–1989', *Social Compass*, 37/1 (1990), 45–64.

Beckford, James, *Religion in Advanced Industrial Society*, London: Unwin Hyman, 1989.

Bell, Daniel, *The End of Ideology*, Cambridge, MA: Harvard University Press, 1960.

Bellah, R. N., 'Meaning and Modernization', *Beyond Belief*, Berkeley: California University Press, 1970, pp. 64–73.

'New Religious Consciousness and the Crisis in Modernity', in Charles Y. Glock and Robert N. Bellah (eds.), *The New Religious Consciousness*, Berkeley: California University Press, 1976, pp. 333–52.

Berger, Peter L., *The Capitalist Revolution: Fifty Propositions about Prosperity, Equality, and Liberty*, Aldershot: Wildwood House, 1987.

Facing up to Modernity: Excursions in Society, Politics, and Religion, New York: Basic Books, 1977.

Berman, Marshall, *All that is Solid melts into Air: The Experience of Modernity*, London: Verso, 1982.

Bernal, Martin, *Black Athena: The Afroasiatic Roots of Classical Civilization*, 2 vols., London: Free Association Press, 1987; 2nd edn, 1991.

Bernstein, Basil, 'A Socio-Linguistic Approach to Socialisation', in J. Gumperz and D. Hymes (eds.), *Directions in Socio-Linguistics*, New York: Holt, Rinehart & Winston, 1970.

Bernstein, R. J., *The New Constellation: The Ethical-Political Horizons of Modernity/Postmodernity*, Cambridge: Polity, 1991.

Berry, Philippa and Andrew Wernick (eds.), *Shadow of Spirit: Postmodernism and Religion*, London: Routledge, 1992.

Beveridge, Craig and Ronald Turnbull (eds.), *The Eclipse of Scottish Culture: Inferiorism and the Intellectuals*, Edinburgh, Polygon, 1989.

Beversluis, Joel (ed.), *A Source Book for the Community of Religions*, Chicago: Council for a Parliament of the World's Religions, 1993.

Beyer, Peter, *Religion and Globalization*, London: Sage, 1994.

Bloom, William (ed.), *The New Age: An Anthology of Essential Writings*, London: Rider, 1991.

Blumenberg, Hans, *Lebenszeit und Weltzeit*, Frankfurt: Suhrkamp, 1986.

The Legitimacy of the Modern Age, Cambridge, MA: MIT, 1983.

'Die Vorbereitung der Neuzeit', *Philosophische Rundschau*, 9 (1961), 81–133.

Bly, Robert, *Iron John: A Book About Men*, Shaftesbury: Element, 1990.

Boff, Leonardo, *Church, Charism and Power: Liberation Theology and the Institutional Church*, London: SCM, 1985.

Bohme, Joachim, *Das Seele und das Ich im homerishen Epos mit einem Anhang: Vergleich mit dem Glauben der Primitiven*, Leipzig, 1929.

Bonhoeffer, Dietrich, *Ethics*, London: SCM, 1955.

Letters and Papers from Prison, ed. E. Bethge, rev. edn, London: SCM, 1967

Sanctorum Communio: A Dogmatic Enquiry into the Sociology of the Church, London: Collins, 1963.

Bourdieu, Pierre, *Homo Academicus*, Cambridge: Polity, 1988.

Bourdieu, Pierre and Loïc J. D. Wacquant, *An Invitation to Reflexive Sociology*, Chicago: University of Chicago Press, 1992.

Bowker, John, *Licensed Insanities: Religion and Belief in God in the Contemporary World*, London: SCM, 1987.

    The Sense of God: Sociological, Anthropological and Psychological Approaches to the Origin of the Sense of God, Oxford: Clarendon Press, 1973.

Boyle, Nicholas, 'Understanding Thatcherism', *New Blackfriars*, 70 (1988), 306–18.

Brittain, Samuel, 'The Thatcher Government's Economic Policy', in D. Kavanagh and A. Seldon (eds.), *The Thatcher Effect*, Oxford: Clarendon Press, 1989, pp. 1–37.

Bruce, Steven (ed.), *Religion and Modernisation: Sociologists and Historians. Debate the Secularisation Thesis*, Oxford: Clarendon Press, 1992.

Butler, Judith, *Gender Trouble: Feminism and the Subversion of Identity*, London: Routledge, 1990.

Castles, Stephen, Heather Booth and Tina Wallace (eds.), *Here for Good: Western Europe's New Ethnic Minorities*, London: Pluto Press, 1984.

Caswell, Caroline P., *A Study of Thumos in Early Greek Epic, Supplements to MNEMOSYNE*, Leiden: E. J. Brill, 1990.

Cecchini, Paulo, Michel Continat and Alexis Jacquemar, *The European Challenge 1992: The Benefits of a Single Market?*, New York: Wildwood House, 1988.

Chadwick, Owen, *The Secularization of the European Mind in the Nineteenth Century*, Cambridge: Cambridge University Press, 1975; reprinted 1991.

Clegg, S. R., *Frameworks of Power*, London: Sage, 1989.

    Modern Organizations: Organization Studies in the Postmodern World, London: Sage, 1990.

    'Postmodern Management?', unpublished Inaugural Lecture, University of St Andrews, 11 March 1992.

Clegg, S. R. and C. Dunkerley, *Organization, Class and Control*, London: Routledge & Kegan Paul, 1980.

Clegg, S. R. and S. G. Redding (eds.), *Capitalism in Contrasting Cultures*, Berlin: de Gruyter, 1990.

Coakely, Sarah (ed.), *Religion and the Body*, Cambridge: Cambridge University Press, 1999.

Cockett, Richard, *Thinking the Unthinkable: Think-Tanks and the Economic Counter-Revolution, 1931–1983*, London: HarperCollins, 1995.

Congar, Yves M. J., *Lay People in the Church: A Study for a Theology of Laity*, London: Bloomsbury 1957.

Cooke, A. B. (ed.), *Margaret Thatcher: The Revival of Britain. Speeches on Home and European Affairs 1975–1988*, London: Aurum, 1989.

Cooper, Barry, *The End of History: An Essay on Modern Hegelianism*, Toronto: University of Toronto Press, 1984.

Cornford, F. M., *Microcosmographia Academica: Being a Guide for the Young Academic Politician*, Cambridge: Bowes & Bowes, 1908.

Cox, Harvey, *The Secular City: Secularization and Urbanization in Theological Perspective*, New York: Macmillan, 1965.

Crowley, Vivianne, *Wicca: The Old Religion in the New Millennium*, London: Thorsons, 1996.

Cumpsty, John S., *Religion as Belonging: A General Theory of Religion*, Lanham: University Press of America, 1991.

Dahrendorf, Lord Ralf, *Reflections on the Revolution in Europe*, London: Chatto & Windus, 1990.

David Cox (ed.), *The Walden Interviews*, London: LWT/Boxtree, 1990.

Davie, G. E., *The Crisis of the Democratic Intellect: The Problems of Generalism and Specialisation in Twentieth-Century Scotland*, Edinburgh: Polygon, 1986.

   The Democratic Intellect: Scotland and her Universities in the Nineteenth Century, Edinburgh: Edinburgh University Press, 1961.

Davie, Grace, 'Believing Without Belonging: Is This the Future of Religion in Britain?', CISR paper, Helsinki, 1989.

   Religion in Britain since 1945: Believing without Belonging, Oxford: Blackwell, 1994.

Dawisha, Karen, *Eastern Europe, Gorbachev and Reform*, Cambridge: Cambridge University Press, 1988.

Dawkins, Richard, *The Selfish Gene*, Oxford: Oxford University Press, 1989.

Dawson, Christopher, *The Making of Europe: An Introduction to the History of European Unity*, London: Sheed & Ward, 1932.

   Religion and Culture, Gifford Lectures, London: Sheed & Ward, 1948.

   Understanding Europe, London: Sheed & Ward, 1952.

Dilthey, Wilhelm, *Introduction to the Human Sciences: An Attempt to Lay the Foundation for the Study of Society and History*, Brighton: Harvester Wheatsheaf, 1989.

Dobbelaere, K. 'Church Involvement and Secularization: Making Sense of the European Case', in E. Barker, J. A. Beckford and K. Dobbelaere (eds.), *Secularization, Rationalism and Sectarianism*, Oxford: Clarendon Press, 1993.

Dray, W., *Perspectives on History*, London: Routledge & Kegan Paul, 1980.

Drucker, Peter F., *Post-Capitalist Society*, London: Butterworth-Heinemann, 1993.

Duchrow, U., *Global Economy: A Confessional Issue for the Churches?*, Geneva: WCC, 1987.

Dvornik, F., *The Photian Schism: History and Legends*, Cambridge: Cambridge University Press, 1948.

'Ecclesiology and the Culture of Management', *Modern Theology*, 9/4 (October 1993).

Eder, Klaus, *The Social Construction of Nature: A Sociology of Ecological Enlightenment*, London: Sage, 1996.

Edwards, John, *The Jews in Christian Europe*, London: Longmans, 1988.

Eliot, T. S., *The Idea of a Christian Society*, London, Faber, 1939.

   Notes Towards the Definition of Culture, London: Faber, 1948.

Enteman, W. F., *Managerialism: The Emergence of a New Ideology*, Madison: University of Wisconsin Press, 1993.

'The European Identity', *Bulletin of the European Communities*, 12/14 (December 1973), 118–22.

Ewing, K. D. and C. A. Gearty (eds.), *Freedom Under Thatcher: Civil Liberties in Modern Britain*, Oxford: Clarendon Press, 1990.

Farley, Edward, *Ecclesial Man: A Social Phenomenology of Faith and Reality*, Philadelphia: Fortress, 1975.

Ecclesial Reflection: An Anatomy of Theological Method, Philadelphia: Fortress, 1982.

Fastenrath, Elmer, *'In Vitam Aeternam': Grundzüge christlicher Eschatologie in der ersten Hälfte des 20. Jahrhunderts*, Erzabtei St Ottilien: Eos Verlag, 1982.

Featherstone, Mike (ed.), *Global Culture: Nationalism, Globalization and Modernity*, London: Sage, 1990.

Featherstone, Mike and Roger Burrows (eds.), *Cyberspace/Cyberbodies/Cyberpunk: Cultures of Technological Embodiment*, London: Sage, 1995.

Field, Frank, *Losing Out: The Emergence of Britain's Underclass*, Oxford: Blackwell, 1989.

Fields, E. 'Understanding Activist Fundamentalism: Capitalist Crisis and the "Colonization of the Lifeworld"', *Sociological Analysis*, 52/2 (1991), 175–90.

Flannery, Austin (ed.), 'Dogmatic Constitution on the Church, *Lumen Gentium*', in *Vatican Council II: The Conciliar and Post Conciliar Documents*, Leominster: Fowler Wright, 1975, pp. 350–426.

Foster, J., 'Nationality, Social Change and Class: Transformations of National Identity in Scotland', in David McCrone, Stephen Kendrick and Pat Shaw (eds.), *The Making of Scotland: Nation, Culture and Social Change*, Edinburgh: Edinburgh University Press/The British Sociological Association, 1989.

Foucault, Michel, *The Archeology of Knowledge*, London: Tavistock, 1972.

'Disciplinary Power and Subjection', in Steven Lukes (ed.), *Power*, Oxford: Blackwell, 1976.

The Order of Things: An Archeology of the Human Sciences, London: Tavistock, 1970.

Francis, E. D., 'Virtue, Folly, and Greek Etymology', in C. A. Rubino and C. W. Shelmerdine (eds.), *Approaches to Homer*, Austin, 1983, pp. 89–103.

Freidson, Eliot, *Professionalism Reborn: Theory, Prophecy, and Policy*, Cambridge: Polity, 1994.

Friedland, Roger and Deirdre Boden (eds.), *Now Here: Space, Time and Modernity*, Berkeley: University of California Press, 1994.

Fukuyama, Francis, *The End of History and the Last Man*, London: Hamish Hamilton, 1989.

'The End of History', *The National Interest*, 16/2 (1989), 3–18.

Trust: The Social Values and the Creation of Prosperity (London: Hamish Hamilton, 1995).

Gamble, A., *Britain in Decline: Economic Policy, Political Strategy and the British State*, London: Macmillan, 1981.

Gamm, Hans-Jochen, *Führung und Verführung: Pädogogik des National-Sozialismus*, Munich: List Bibliothek, 1990.

Gestrich, Christoff, *Neuzeitliches Denken und die Spaltung der dialektischen Theologie*, Tübingen: J. C. B. Mohr, 1977.

Gibson, William, *Neuromancer*, London: Victor Gollancz, 1984.

Giddens, Anthony, *The Consequences of Modernity*, Cambridge: Polity, 1990.
    Modernity and Self-Identity: Self and Society in the Late Modern Age, Cambridge: Polity, 1991.
    The Third Way, Cambridge: Polity, 1998.
    'Uprooted Signposts at Century's End', *The Times Higher Education Supplement*, 17 January 1992, 21–2.
Gill, Robin and Derek Burke, *Strategic Church Leadership*, London: SPCK, 1996.
Gorbachev, Mikhail, *Perestroika: New Thinking for Our Country and the World*, London: Collins, 1987.
Gore, Charles, *The Ministry of the Christian Church*, London: Longman, Green & Co., 1881.
Gray, Chris Hables (ed.), *The Cyborg Handbook*, London: Routledge, 1995.
Green, David G., *The New Right: The Counter-Revolution in Political, Economic and Social Thought*, Brighton, Harvester, 1987.
Habermas, Jürgen, *The Philosophical Discourse of Modernity: Twelve Lectures*, Cambridge: Polity, 1987.
Hague, Sir Douglas, *Beyond Universities: A New Republic of the Intellect*, London: Institute for Economic Affairs, 1989.
Hall, Stuart and Martin Jacques, *The Politics of Thatcherism*, London: Lawrence & Wishart, 1983.
Halsey, A. H., *The Decline of Donnish Dominion*, Oxford: Oxford University Press, 1988.
Handy, Charles, *The Age of Unreason*, London: Business Books, 1989.
Hanf, Theodor, 'The Sacred Marker: Religion, Communalism and Nationalism', *Social Compass*, 41/1 (1994), 9–20.
Haraway, Donna Jeanne, 'A Cyborg Manifesto: Science, Technology, and Socialist Feminism in the Late Twentieth Century', *Simians, Cyborgs, and Women: The Reinvention of Nature*, London: Free Association Books, 1991, pp. 149–81.
    'Cyborgs and Symbionts Living Together in the New World Order', in Chris Hables Gray (ed.), *The Cyborg Handbook*, London: Routledge, 1995, pp. xi–xx.
Harding, S. D. and D. Phillips, *Values in Europe: A Cross National Survey*, London: Macmillan, 1985.
Harvey, David, *The Condition of Postmodernity: An Enquiry into the Origins of Cultural Change*, Oxford: Blackwell, 1989.
Harvey, Graham, *Listening People, Speaking Earth: Contemporary Paganism*, London: C. Hurst & Co., 1997.
Harvey, Graham and Charlotte Hardman (eds.), *Paganism Today*, London: Thorsons, 1996.
Harvey-Jones, John, *Making it Happen*, London: Guild Publishing, 1987; London: Collins, 1988.
Harvie, Christopher, *Cultural Weapons: Scotland and Survival in a New Europe*, Edinburgh: Polygon, 1992.
Hatch, Edwin, *The Organisation of the Early Christian Churches*, London: Longmans, Green & Co., 1881.

Havel, Vaclav, 'The Power of the Powerless', in Jan Vladislav (ed.), *Living in Truth*, London: Faber, 1987, pp. 36–122.

Hays, Denys, *Europe: The Emergence of an Idea in History*, Edinburgh: Edinburgh University Press, 1968.

Heelas, Paul, 'Cults for Capitalism? Self Religions, Magic and the Empowerment of Business', in Peter Gee and John Fulton (eds.), *Religion and Power*, London: British Sociological Association, Sociology of Religion Study Group, 1991, pp. 27–41.

'God's Company: New Age Ethics and the Bank of Credit and Commerce International', *Religion Today*, 8/1 (1992), 1–4.

The New Age Movement: The Celebration of the Self and the Sacralization of Modernity, Oxford: Blackwell, 1996.

'The Sacralisation of the Self in New Age Capitalism', in N. Abercrombie and A. Ware (eds.), *Social Change in Contemporary Britain*, Cambridge: Polity, 1992, pp. 139–66.

Heelas, Paul, Scott Lash and Paul Morris (eds.), *Detraditionalization: Critical Reflections on Authority and Identity*, Oxford: Blackwell, 1996.

Heelas, Paul and Paul Morris (eds.), *The Values of the Enterprise Culture*, London: HarperCollins Academic, 1992.

Hegel, G. W. F., *Early Theological Writings*, tr. T. M. Knox, Philadelphia: University of Philadelphia Press, 1971.

The Phenomenology of Mind, tr. J. B. Baillie, London: Macmillan, 1910.

Hegel, G. W. F., *Phenomenology of Spirit*, tr. A. V. Miller, Oxford: Clarendon Press, 1977.

Heller, Agnes, *Can Modernity Survive?*, Cambridge: Polity, 1990.

Helps, A. (ed.), *Spengler Letters 1913–1936*, London: George Allen & Unwin, 1966.

Herrin, Judith, *The Formation of Christendom*, Oxford: Blackwell, 1987.

Higher Education: Meeting the Challenge, Cmnd 114, London: HMSO, April 1987.

Hobsbawm, E. J. and T. Ranger, *The Invention of Tradition*, Cambridge: Cambridge University Press, 1983.

Horkheimer, Max and T. W. Adorno, 'The Concept of Enlightenment', *Dialectic of Enlightenment*, London: Allen Lane, 1972, pp. 3–80.

Hubner, K., *Die Wahrheit des Mythos*, Munich: C. H. Beck, 1985.

Hughes, H. S., *Oswald Spengler: A Critical Estimate*, New York: Scribner, 1952.

Huntington, Samuel P., 'The Clash of Civilizations?', *Foreign Affairs*, 72 (1992), 22–49.

Husserl, Edmund, *The Crisis of the European Sciences and Transcendental Phenomenology: An Introduction to Phenomenological Philosophy*, Evanston: Northwestern University Press, 1970.

Huzinga, Johann, *Homo Ludens: A Study of the Play Element in Culture*, London: Routledge & Kegan Paul, 1949.

Jaeschke, Werner, *Die Suche nach den eschatologischen Würzeln der Geschichtsphilosophie: Eine historische Kritik der Säkulisierungthese*, Munich: Kaiser Verlag, 1976.

Jameson, Fredric, *The Political Unconscious: Narrative as Socially Symbolic Act*, London: Methuen, 1981.

The Prison-House of Language: A Critical Account of Structuralism and Russian Formalism, Princeton: Princeton University Press, 1972.

Jaspers, Karl, *Die Idee der deutschen Universität: Die fünf Grundschriften aus der Zeit ihrer Neubegrundung durch klassischen Idealismus und romantischen Realismus*, Darmstadt: H. Gentner, 1956.

Vom europäischen Geist: Vortrag gehalten bei den Rencontres internationales de Génève September 1946, Munich: Piper Verlag, 1947.

Jencks, Charles, *What is Post-Modernism?*, 4th rev. edn, London: Academy, 1989.

Jenkins, Peter, *Mrs Thatcher's Revolution: The Ending of the Socialist Era*, London: Pan, 1987.

Jessop, R., K. Bonnett, S. Bromley and T. Ling, *Thatcherism: A Tale of Two Nations*, London: Polity, 1988.

Laborem Exercens: Encyclical Letter of the Supreme Pontiff John Paul II on Human Work, London: Catholic Truth Society, 1981.

'The Ecological Crisis: A Common Responsibility', London: Catholic Truth Society, 1990.

'Cyril and Methodius', in *The Pope Teaches*, 4/1–3 (January–March 1981), London: Catholic Truth Society, 1981, pp. 15–18.

'Europe and the Faith', Address to the European Council of Bishops' Conferences, 11 October 1985, London: Catholic Truth Society, 1985.

John Paul II, Pope, *Centesimus Annus*, London: Catholic Truth Society, 1991.

Jones, R. Kenneth, 'Paradigm Shifts and Identity Theory: Alternation as a form of Identity Management', in Hans Mol (ed.), *Identity and Religion International: Cross-Cultural Approaches*, London: Sage, 1978, pp. 59–82.

Joseph, Keith and Jonathan Sumption, *Equality*, London: John Murray, 1979.

Kavanagh, D. and A. Seldon (eds.), *The Thatcher Effect*, Oxford: Clarendon Press, 1989.

Kavanagh, Dennis, *Thatcherism and British Politics: The End of Consensus*, Oxford: Oxford University Press, 1987.

Kay, John, 'Economics and Business', lecture delivered at the inauguration of the Centre for Research into Industry, Enterprise, Finance and the Firm (CRIEFF), University of St Andrews, 1992.

Keat, Russell and Nicholas Abercrombie (eds.), *Enterprise Culture*, London: Routledge, 1991.

Kedourie, Elie, *Perestroika in the Universities*, London: Institute of Economic Affairs, 1989.

Kennedy, Paul, *The Rise and Fall of the Great Powers*, London: Collins, 1989.

Kepel, Gilles, *The Revenge of God: The Resurgence of Islam, Christianity and Judaism in the Modern World*, Cambridge: Polity, 1994.

King, Anthony (ed.), *Culture, Globalization and the World System*, Binghampton, NY: State University of New York Press, 1989.

Klein, Julie Thompson, *Interdisciplinarity: History, Theory, and Practice*, Detroit: Wayne State University Press, 1990.

Kojève, Alexandre, *Introduction to the Reading of Hegel*, New York: Basic Books, 1969.

Kolakowski, Leszek, *Main Currents of Marxism*, 3 vols., Oxford: Clarendon Press, 1978.

Kramarae, Cheris, 'A Backstage Critique of Virtual Reality', in Steven G. Jones (ed.), *CyberSociety: Computer-Mediated Communication and Community*, London: Sage, 1995, pp. 10–35.

Kroker, Arthur and David Cook, *The Postmodern Scene: Excremental Culture and Hyper-Aesthetics*, New York: St Martin's Press, 1986.

Kuhn, Thomas S., *The Structure of Scientific Revolutions*, 2nd edn, Chicago: University of Chicago Press, 1970.

Küng, Hans, *Global Responsibility: In Search of a New World Ethic*, London: SCM, 1990.

Theology for the Third Millennium: An Ecumenical View, London: HarperCollins Academic, 1991.

Lane, David, *Soviet Society Under Perestroika*, London: Unwin Hyman, 1990.

Larry, Ray, 'The Protestant Ethic Debate', in R. J. Anderson, J. A. Hughes and W. W. Sharrock (eds.), *Classic Disputes in Sociology*, London: Allen & Unwin, 1987, pp. 97–125.

Lash, Scott, *Another Modernity: A Different Rationality* (Oxford: Blackwell, 2000).

Lash, Scott and Jonathan Friedman (eds.), *Modernity and Identity*, Oxford: Blackwell, 1992.

Lash, Scott, Andrew Quick and Richard Roberts (eds.), *Time and Value*, Oxford: Blackwell, 1998.

Lash, Scott and John Urry, *Economies of Signs and Space*, London: Sage, 1994.

The End of Organized Capitalism, Cambridge: Polity, 1987.

Lauer, Q., *Hegel's Concept of God*, Albany: State University of New York Press, 1982.

Lawson, Hilary, *Reflexivity: The Post-modern Predicament*, London: Hutchinson, 1985.

Lehmann, A. G., *The European Heritage: An Outline of Western Culture*, London: Phaidon, 1984.

Lewis, James R. (ed.), *Magical Religion and Modern Witchcraft*, New York: State University of New York Press, 1996.

Liddon, H. P., *The Divinity of Our Lord and Saviour Jesus Christ*, London: Longmans, Green & Co., 1867.

Lindholm, Charles, *Charisma*, Oxford: Blackwell, 1993.

Lortz, Joseph (ed.), *Europa und das Christentum*, Wiesbaden: Steiner, 1959.

Löwith, Karl, *Meaning in History*, Chicago: Chicago University Press, 1946.

Luhrmann, Tanya M., *Persuasions of the Witch's Craft: Ritual Magic in Contemporary England*, Oxford: Blackwell, 1989.

Lukes, Stephen, 'Power and Authority', in T. Bottomore and R. Nisbet (eds.), *History of Sociological Analysis*, London: Heinemann and New York: Basic Books, 1979, pp. 631–76.

Lury, Celia, *Prosthetic Culture: Photography, Memory and Identity*, London: Routledge, 1997.

Lyotard, Jean-François, *The Inhuman: Reflections on Time*, Cambridge: Polity, 1991.
The Postmodern Condition: A Report on Knowledge, 2nd edn, Manchester: Manchester University Press, 1984.

McCrone, David, *Understanding Scotland: The Sociology of a Stateless Nation*, London: Routledge, 1992.

McCrone, David, Stephen Kendrick and Pat Shaw (eds.), *The Making of Scotland: Nation, Culture and Social Change*, Edinburgh: Edinburgh University Press and The British Sociological Association, 1989.

MacDiarmid, Hugh, *Hugh MacDiarmid: Complete Poems 1920–1976*, ed. Michael Grieve and W. R. Aitken, 2 vols., London: Martin Brian & O'Keefe, 1978.

McIntosh, Alastair, *Soil and Soul*, London: Aurum Press, 2001.

MacIntyre, Alasdair, *Hegel: A Collection of Critical Essays*, Notre Dame: University of Notre Dame Press, 1976.
After Virtue: A Study in Moral Theory, London: Duckworth, 1981.
Three Rival Versions of Moral Enquiry: Encyclopaedia, Genealogy, and Tradition, London: Duckworth, 1990.

MacKinnon, Donald M., *God the Living and the True*, Westminster: Dacre Press, 1940.
Gore Memorial Lecture, 'Kenosis and Establishment', in *The Stripping of the Altars*, London: Collins, 1964, pp. 13–40.
'Theology as a Discipline in a Modern University', in Teodor Shanin (ed.), *The Rules of the Game: Cross-disciplinary Essays on Models in Scholarly Thought*, London: Tavistock Publications, 1972.

McLellan, D., *Karl Marx: An Introduction to his Life and Thought*, London: Macmillan, 1975.
Marxism and Religion: A Description and Assessment of the Marxist Critique of Religion, London: Macmillan, 1987.
Marx's 'Grundrisse', London: Macmillan, 1971.

MacNaghten, Phil and John Urry, *Contested Natures*, London: Sage, 1998.
'Towards a Sociology of Nature', *Sociology*, 29/2 (May 1995), 203–20.

Maffesoli, Michel, *The Time of the Tribes: The Decline of Individualism in Mass Societies*, London: Sage, 1994.

Major, Prime Minister John, *The Citizens' Charter: Raising the Standard*, London: HMSO, 1991.

Mann, M., *The Sources of Social Power: A History of Power: from the Beginning to AD 1760*, vol. I, Cambridge: Cambridge University Press, 1986.

Marcuse, H., *Studies in Critical Philosophy*, London: NLB, 1972.

Marquand, David, *The Unprincipled Society: New Demands and Old Politics*, London: Cape, 1988.

Martin, David, 'The Churches: Pink Bishops and the Iron Lady', in D. Kavanagh and A. Seldon (eds.), *The Thatcher Effect*, Oxford: Clarendon Press, 1989.

Martin, David, J. Orme-Mills and W. S. F. Pickering, *Sociology and Theology: Alliance or Conflict*, Brighton: Harvester-Wheatsheaf, 1980.

Martland, T. R., art. 'The Sublime', in Mircea Eliade (ed.), *Encyclopaedia of Religion*, 16 vols., New York: Macmillan, 1987, vol. XIII, pp. 97–9.

Marx, Karl, *Capital*, London: Swan & Sonnenschein, 1903.

'A Contribution to the Critique of Hegel's "Philosophy of Right": Introduction', in Joseph O'Malley (ed.), *Critique of Hegel's 'Philosophy of Right'*, Cambridge: Cambridge University Press, pp. 129–42.

Early Writings, tr. Rodney Livingstone and Gregor Benton, Harmondsworth: Penguin, 1974.

Grundrisse: Foundations of the Critique of Political Economy (Rough Draft), Harmondsworth: Penguin, 1973.

On Religion, Moscow: Progress Publishers, 1957.

Max Weber, *Die protestantische Ethik und der 'Geist' des Kapitalismus*, Hain Hanstein: Athenaum, 1993.

Mehl, Roger, *Das protestantische Europa*, Stuttgart: Fischer, 1959.

Mellor, Philip A. 'Reflexive Tradition: Anthony Giddens, High Modernity and the Contours of Contemporary Religiosity', *Religious Studies*, 29/1 (1993), 111–27.

Mellor, Philip A. and Chris Shilling, *Re-forming the Body: Religion, Community and Modernity*, London: Sage, 1997.

Mestrovic, S. G., *The Barbarian Temperament: Toward a Postmodern Critical Theory*, London: Sage, 1993.

Mestrovic, Stjepan G., *Postemotional Society*, London: Sage, 1997.

Mészáros, I., *Marx's Theory of Alienation*, London: Merlin Press, 1975.

Milbank, A. J., *Theology and Social Theory Beyond Secular Reason*, Oxford: Blackwell, 1989.

The Word Made Strange, Oxford: Blackwell, 1997.

Milliband, Ray, 'The Socialist Alternative', in Larry Diamond and Marc F. Plattner (eds.), *Capitalism, Socialism and Democracy Revisited*, Baltimore: The Johns Hopkins University Press, 1993.

Millward, Neil, *The New Industrial Relations? Based on the ED/ESRC/PSI/ACAS Surveys*, London: Policy Studies Institute Publications, 1994.

Mintzberg, Henry, *Mintzberg on Management Inside Our Strange World of Organizations*, New York: Free Press, 1989.

Mol, H., *Identity and the Sacred: A Sketch of a New Social-Scientific Theory of Religion*, Oxford: Blackwell, 1976.

Moltmann, Jürgen, *The Crucified God: The Cross of Christ as Foundation and Criticism of Christian Theology*, London: SCM, 1974.

Munford, P., 'Mrs Thatcher's Economic Reform Programme – Past, Present and Future', in R. Skidelsky (ed.), *Thatcherism*, London: Chatto & Windus, 1988, pp. 93–106.

Munro-Fauré, Lesley, Malcolm Munro-Fauré and Edward Bones, *Achieving Quality Standards: A Step-by-Step Guide to BS5750 and ISO9000*, London: Pitman, 1993.

Nairn, Tom, *Auld Enemies: Essays from the Nairn on Monday Column in* The Scotsman, Glasgow: Common Cause Declarations, 1992.

Newman, John Henry, *The Idea of a University*, New York: Chelsea House, 1983.

Nicoll, William and Trevor Salmon, *Understanding the European Communities*, London: Harvester Wheatsheaf, 1990.

Niebuhr, H. R., *The Social Sources of Denominationalism*, New York: Holt, 1929; reprinted New York: New American Library, 1975.

Norman, E. R., *Christianity and the World Order*, Oxford: Oxford University Press, 1979.

  Church and Society in England 1770–1970: A Historical Study, Oxford: Oxford University Press, 1976.

Northcott, Michael, *Identity and Decline in the Kirk*, Edinburgh: Centre for Theology and Public Issues, 1992.

Novak, Michael, *The Spirit of Democratic Capitalism*, London: Institute of Economic Affairs, 1982.

Nowotny, Helga, *Time: The Modern and Postmodern Experience*, Cambridge: Polity, 1994.

Onians, R. B., *The Origins of European Thought: About the Body, the Mind, the Soul, the World, Time and Fate*, Cambridge: Cambridge University Press, 1951.

Orwell, George, 'Appendix: The Principles of Newspeak', *Nineteen Eighty-four*, Harmondsworth: Penguin, 1949, pp. 241–51.

Osborne, John, *Luther*, London: Faber, 1961.

Overbeck, Henk, *Global Capitalism and National Decline: The Thatcher Decade in Perspective*, London: Unwin Hyman, 1990.

Ozment, Steven (ed.), *Culture and Belief in Europe, 1460–1600: An Anthology of Sources*, The Hague: Van Leeuwen, 1990.

Pattison, Stephen, *The Faith of the Managers: When Management Becomes Religion*, London: Cassell, 1997.

Pearson, Joanne, Richard Roberts and Geoffrey Samuel (eds.), *Nature Religion Today: Paganism in the Modern World*, Edinburgh: Edinburgh University Press, 1998.

Pelikan, J., *The Idea of the University: A Reexamination*, New Haven/London: Yale University Press, 1992.

Perkin, Harold, *The Rise of Professional Society: England since 1880*, London: Routledge, 1989.

Pfeffer, Karl-Heinz, 'Der Protestantismus in Europa: Dokumente', *Zeitschrift für internationale Zusammenarbeit*, 13 (1957), 171–4, 183–278.

Pirenne, Henri, *Mohammed and Charlemagne*, New York: W. W. Norton & Co., 1939.

Plaskow, Judith, *Sin, Sex and Grace: Women's Experience and the Theologies of Reinhold Niebuhr and Paul Tillich*, Washington, DC: University Press of America, 1980.

Plato, *The Dialogues of Plato*, tr. B. Jowett, 2 vols, Oxford: Oxford University Press, 1871.

  Plato's Republic: The Greek Text, tr. B. Jowett, Oxford: Clarendon Press, 1894.

Raban, Jonathan, *God, Man, and Mrs Thatcher*, London: Chatto & Windus, 1989.

Ramet, Pedro (ed.), *Religion and Nationalism in Soviet and East European Politics*, Charleston, NC: Duke University Press, 1989.

Rappaport, Roy, *Ritual and Religion in the Making of Humanity*, Cambridge: Cambridge University Press, 1999.

Raza, M. S., *Islam in Britain: Past, Present and Future*, Leicester: Volcano Press, 1991.

Rendtorff, Trutz, 'Universalität oder Kontextualität der Theologie: eine "europäische" Stellungnahme', *Zeitschrift für Theologie und Kirche*, 74 (1977), 238–54.

Rendtorff, Trutz (ed.), *Europa: Theologische Versüche einer Ortsbestimmung*, Gütersloh: Gerd Mohn, 1980.

Report of the Archbishop of Canterbury's Commission on Urban Priority Areas, *Faith in the City: A Call for Action by Church and Nation*, London: Church House Publishing, 1985.

Rheingold, Howard, *The Virtual Community: Surfing the Internet*, London: Secker & Warburg, 1994.

Riesebrodt, Martin, *Pious Passion: The Emergence of Modern Fundamentalism in the United States and Iran*, Berkeley: University of California Press, 1993.

Ritzer, George, *The McDonaldization of Society: An Investigation into the Changing Character of Contemporary Social Life*, Thousand Oaks: Pine Forge Press, 1993.

The McDonaldization Thesis: Explorations and Extensions, London: Sage, 1998.

Roberts, J. M., *The Triumph of the West*, London: BBC, 1985.

Roberts, R. H., 'The Bishop as Manager? – Some Observations on the Turnbull Report', in Andrew Walker and Lawrence Osborne (eds.), *Harmful Religion*, London: Mowbrays, 1998.

'The Chthonic Imperative: Gender, Religion and the Battle for the Earth', in Joanne Pearson, Richard Roberts and Geoffrey Samuel (eds.), *Nature Religion Today: Paganism in the Modern World*, Edinburgh: Edinburgh University Press, 1998, pp. 57–73.

'The Construals of "Europe": Religion, Theology and the Problematics of Modernity', in Paul Heelas (ed.), *Religion, Modernity and Postmodernity*, Oxford: Blackwell, 1998, pp. 186–217.

'The Dialectics of Globalized Spirituality: Some Further Observations', *Journal of Contemporary Religion*, 13/1 (1998), 65–71.

'Globalized Religion? The Parliament of the World's Religions (Chicago, 1993), in Theoretical Perspective', *Journal of Contemporary Religion*, 10 (1995), 121–37.

'Hegel and the "Synoptic Problem": Review Article of the New Translation of *The Lectures on the Philosophy of Religion*', *Journal of Theological Studies*, NS, 42/2 (1991), pp. 565–76.

Hope and its Hieroglyph: A Critical Decipherment of Ernst Bloch's 'Principle of Hope', Atlanta: Scholars Press, 1990.

'Identity and Belonging', in Theo van Willigenberg, Robert Heeger and Wibren van der Burg (eds.), *Nation, State, and the Coexistence of Different Communities*, Kampen: Kok Pharos Publishing House, 1995, pp. 25–56.

'Lord, Bondsman and Churchman: Integrity, Identity and Power in Anglicanism', in C. E. Gunton and D. W. Hardy (eds.), *On Being the Church*, Edinburgh: T. & T. Clark, 1989, pp. 156–224.

'Our Graduate Factories', *The Tablet*, 11 October 1997, pp. 1295–7.

art. 'Power', in Andrew Linzey (ed.), *The Routledge Encyclopaedia of Theology and Society*, London: Routledge, 1996, pp. 673–8.

'Power and Empowerment: New Age Managers and the Dialectics of Modernity/Postmodernity', *Religion Today*, 9/3 (1994), 3–13.

'The Reception of Hegel's Parable of Lord and Bondsman', *New Comparison*, 5 (1988), 23–9.

'Religion and the Body: Comparative Perspectives', *Religion*, 30 (2000), 55–64.

'Religion and Economic Life', in Neil J. Smelser and Paul M. Baltes (Editors-in-Chief), *International Encyclopedia of the Social and Behavioural Sciences*, Oxford: Elsevier, 2001.

'Religion and the "Enterprise Culture": The British Experience in the Thatcher Era (1979–1990)', *Social Compass*, 39/1 (1992), 15–33.

'The Spirit of Democratic Capitalism: A Critique of Michael Novak', in Jon Davies and David Green (eds.), *God and the Marketplace: Essays on the Morality of Wealth Creation*, London: Institute of Economic Affairs, 1993, pp. 64–81.

'Theological Rhetoric and Moral Passion in the light of MacKinnon's "Barth" ', in K. Surin (ed.), *Christ, Ethics and Tragedy: Pursuing the Thought of Donald MacKinnon*, Cambridge: Cambridge University Press, 1989, pp. 1–14.

'Theology and Social Science', in David Ford (ed.), *The Modern Theologians*, 2nd rev. edn, Oxford: Blackwell, 1996, pp. 700–19.

A Theology on its Way?: Essays on Karl Barth, Edinburgh: T. & T. Clark, 1992.

'Time, Virtuality and the Goddess', in Scott Lash, Andrew Quick and Richard Roberts (eds.), *Time and Value*, Oxford: Blackwell, 1998, pp. 112–29.

Roberts, R. H. (ed.), *Religion and the Transformations of Capitalism: Comparative Approaches*, London: Routledge, 1995.

Roberts, R. H. and J. M. M. Good (eds.), *The Recovery of Rhetoric: Persuasive Discourse and Disciplinarity in the Human Sciences*, Charlottesville, VA: University of Virginia Press, 1993.

Roberts, Wess, *The Management Secrets of Attila the Hun*, London: Bantam Press, 1989.

Robertson, George, Melinda Mash, Lisa Tickner, Tim Putnam, Jon Bird and Barry Curtis (eds.), *Futurenatural: Nature, Science, Culture*, London: Routledge, 1996.

Robertson, R., *Globalization: Social Theory and Global Culture*, London: Sage, 1992.

Robertson, Roland, 'After Nostalgia? Willful Nostalgia and the Phases of Globalization', in Bryan S. Turner (ed.), *Theories of Modernity and Postmodernity*, London: Sage, 1990, pp. 45–61.

Robertson, Roland and William R. Garrett, *Religion and Global Order*, New York: Paragon House Publishers, 1991.

Robey, David, *Structuralism: An Introduction*, Oxford: Oxford University Press, 1973.

Rodinson, Maxime, *Europe and the Mystique of Islam*, London: I. B. Taurus, 1988.

Rohde, Erwin, *Psyche: The Cult of Souls and Belief in Immortality among the Greeks*, London: Kegan Paul, 1925.

Rose, Nikolas, 'The Production of the Self', *Governing the Soul: The Shaping of the Private Self*, London: Routledge, 1991, ch. 10.

Rosenstock-Hüessy, Eugen, *Die Europäischen Revolutionen und der Charakter der Nationenen*, Stuttgart: W. Kohlhammer Verlag, 1931; reprinted 1951.

Roser, Hans, *Protestanten und Europa*, Munich: Claudius Verlag, 1979.

Roszak, Theodor, *Where the Wasteland Ends: Politics and Transcendence in Post-Industrial Society*, New York: Doubleday, 1972.

Roth, Michael S., *Knowing and History*, Ithaca, NY: Cornell University Press, 1988.

Rubenstein, Richard L. and John K. Roth, 'The Silence of God: Philosophical and Religious Reflection on the Holocaust', in Richard L. Rubenstein and John K. Roth (eds.), *Approaches to Auschwitz: The Legacy of the Holocaust*, London: SPCK, 1987, pp. 290–336.

Ruether, Rosemary Radford, *Faith and Fratricide: The Theological Roots of Anti-Semitism*, New York: Seabury Press, 1974.

Rupnik, J., *The Other Europe*, London: Weidenfeld & Nicolson, 1988.

Russell, Lord Conrad, *Academic Freedom*, London: Routledge, 1993.

Said, Edward, *Orientalism: Western Conceptions of the Orient*, Harmondsworth: Penguin, 1978; 2nd edn, 1991.

Samuel, Geoffrey, *Mind, Body and Culture: Anthropology and the Biological Interface*, Cambridge: Cambridge University Press, 1990.

    Civilized Shamans: Buddhism in Tibetan Societies, Washington: Smithsonian Institution Press, 1993.

Sauter, Gerhard, *Zukunft und Verheissung: Das Problem der Zukunft in der gegenwärtigen theologischen und philosophischen Diskussion*, Zurich/Stuttgart: Theologischer Verlag, 1965.

Schechner, Richard, *The Future of Ritual: Writings on Culture and Performance*, London: Routledge, 1993.

Schoef, Anne Wilson and Diane Fassel, *The Addictive Organisation*, New York: Harper & Row, 1988.

Schumpeter, J. A., *Capitalism, Socialism and Democracy*, New York: Harper & Row, 1940; reprinted 1975.

Schutz, A., *The Phenomenology of the Social World*, London: Heinemann Education Books, 1972.

Schwarz, Jurgen (ed.), *Katholische Kirche und Europa: Dokumente 1945–79*, Munich/Mainz: Kaiser Verlag, 1980.

Sedgwick, Peter, *The Enterprise Culture: A Challenging New Theology for the 1990s*, London: SPCK, 1992.

Seed, John, Joanna Macy, Pat Fleming and Arne Naess, *Thinking Like a Mountain Towards a Council of All Beings*, Philadelphia: New Society Publishers, 1988.

Sefton, Henry, 'The Church of Scotland and Scottish Nationhood', in S. Mews (ed.), *Religion and National Identity*, Oxford, Blackwell, 1982, pp. 549–56.

Segundo, J. L., *The Liberation of Theology*, Dublin: Gill & Macmillan, 1977.

Seldon, Arthur, *Capitalism*, Oxford: Blackwell, 1990.

Seldon, Raman, 'The Rhetoric of Enterprise', ch. 3 in R. Keat and N. Abercrombie (eds.), *Enterprise Culture*, London: Routledge, 1991.

Senge, Peter, *The Fifth Discipline: The Art and Practice of the Learning Organisation*, London: Random House Business Books, 1990.

Sharman, Barrie and Phil Jundkins, *Glimpses of Heaven, Visions of Hell: Virtual Reality and its Implications*, London: Hodder & Stoughton, 1992.

Sheppard, Bishop David, *Bias to the Poor*, London: Academic Press, 1980.

Shils, Edward, *Tradition*, London: Faber, 1981.

Sjöö, Monica and Barbara Mohr, *The Great Cosmic Mother: Rediscovering the Religion of the Earth*, San Franscisco: Harper & Row, 1987; 2nd edn, 1991.

Smart, Ninian, *The Religious Experience of Mankind*, London: Collins, 1969.

The World's Religions: Old Traditions and Modern Transformations, Cambridge: Cambridge University Press, 1989.

Smiles, Samuel, *Self Help, with Illustrations of Character and Conduct*, London: Murray, 1863.

Smith, Adam, *An Inquiry into the Nature and Causes of the Wealth of Nations*, New York: Random House, 1937.

The Theory of the Moral Sentiments, Oxford: Clarendon Press, 1976.

Smith, Anthony D., 'Towards Global Culture?', in M. Featherstone (ed.), *Global Culture: Nationalism, Globalization and Modernity*, London: Sage, 1990.

Smith, James A., *The Idea Brokers: Think Tanks and the Rise of the New Policy Elite*, New York: Free Press, 1991.

Snell, Bruno, *The Discovery of the Mind: The Greek Origins of European Thought*, Cambridge, MA: Harvard University Press, 1953.

Spengler, Oswald, *The Decline of the West: Form and Actuality*, London: Allen & Unwin, 1926.

Man and Technics, London: Murray, 1931.

Starhawk, *Dreaming the Dark: Magic, Sex and Politics*, London: Unwin 1990.

The Spiral Dance: A Rebirth of the Goddess, 2nd edn, San Francisco: Harper & Row, 1990.

Stark, Rodney and Laurence R. Iannaccone, 'A Supply-Side Reinterpretation of the "Secularization" of Europe', *Journal for the Scientific Study of Religion*, 33/3 (1994), 230–52.

Stark, Rodney and William Sims Bainbridge, *A Theory of Religion*, New York: Peter Lang, 1987.

Steinbuchel, Theodor, *Europa als Idee und geistige Verwirklichung*, Cologne, 1953.

Steiner, George, *In Bluebeard's Castle: Some Notes Towards the Re-definition of Culture*, T. S. Eliot Memorial Lectures, London: Faber, 1971.

Stepelevich, L. S., *The Young Hegelians: An Anthology*, Cambridge: Cambridge University Press, 1983.

Stone, Sandy, 'Split Subjects, Not Atoms; or, How I fell in Love with My Prosthesis', in Chris Hables Gray (ed.), *The Cyborg Handbook*, London: Routledge, 1995, pp. 393–406.

Storrar, William, *Scottish Identity: A Christian Vision*, Edinburgh: Hansel Press, 1990.

Swatos, W. H., Jr, *Religious Politics in Global and Comparative Perspective*, London: Greenwood Press, 1989.

Swatos, W. H., Jr (ed.), *A Future for Religion: New Paradigms for Social Analysis*, London: Sage, 1994.

Sykes, S. W., *The Identity of Christianity*, London: SPCK, 1984.

The Integrity of Anglicanism, London: Mowbrays, 1978.

'Sacrifice in the New Testament and Christian Theology', in M. F. C. Bourdillon and M. Fortes, *Sacrifice*, London: Academic Press, 1980, esp. pp. 8off.

'What is Anglican Theology?', *Theology*, 48 (1975).

Tawney, R. H., *Religion and the Rise of Capitalism: A Historical Study*, London: John Murray, 1926.

Taylor, Charles, *The Ethics of Authenticity*, Cambridge, MA: Harvard University Press, 1991.

Hegel, Cambridge: Cambridge University Press, 1975.

Multiculturalism and the Politics of Recognition, Princeton: Princeton University Press, 1992.

Sources of the Self: The Making of the Modern Identity, Cambridge: Cambridge University Press, 1989.

Taylor, F. W., *Principles of Scientific Management*, New York: Harper & Row, 1911.

Taylor, Frederick W., 'The Principles of Scientific Management', in *Scientific Management*, New York: Harper, 1947 (first published 1911). Also in Victor H. Vroom and Edward L. Deci (eds.), *Management and Motivation: Selected Readings*, Harmondsworth: Penguin, 1970; 2nd edn, 1992.

Taylor, Mark C., *Journeys to Selfhood, Hegel and Kierkegaard*, Berkeley: University of California Press, 1980.

Taylor, Ronald, *The Romantic Tradition in Germany: An Anthology*, London: Methuen, 1970.

Thomas, Terence, *The British: Their Religious Beliefs and Practices 1800–1986*, London: Routledge, 1988.

Thompson, E. P., *The Making of the English Working Class*, Harmondsworth: Penguin, 1968.

Thrift, Nigel, 'Soft Capitalism', unpublished lecture delivered at the Centre for the Study of Cultural Values, Lancaster University, June 1996.

Tiryakian, Edward A., 'Three Metacultures of Modernity: Christian, Gnostic and Chthonic', *Theory, Culture and Society*, 13/1 (1996), 99–118.

Todorov, Tzvetan, 'The Structural Analysis of Literature: The Tales of Henry James', in David Robey (ed.), *Structuralism: An Introduction*, Oxford: Oxford University Press, 1973.

Toews, J. E., *Hegelianism: The Path toward Dialectical Humanism*, Cambridge: Cambridge University Press, 1980.

Touraine, A., *The Post-Industrial Society: Tomorrow's Social History, Classes, Conflicts and Culture in the Programmed Society*, New York: Random House, 1971; London: Wildwood House, 1974.

The Self-Production of Society, Chicago/London: University of Chicago Press, 1977.

Towler, Robert, *The Fate of the Anglican Clergy*, London: Macmillan, 1979.

Troeltsch, E., *The Absoluteness of Christianity and the History of Religion*, London: SCM, 1972.

'Der Europäismus' and 'Das Problem einer objectiven Periodisierung', sections, 2 and 4 of 'Über den Aufbau der europäischen Kulturgeschichte' ch. 4 of *Das Logische Problem der Geschichtsphilosophie*, bk 1 of *Der Historismus und seine Probleme, Gesammelte Schriften*, vol. III, Tübingen: J. C. B. Mohr (Paul Siebeck), 1922; reprinted Darmstadt: Scientia Aalen, 1961.

'History', in James Hastings (ed.), *Encyclopaedia of Religion and Ethics*, Edinburgh: T. &. T. Clark, 1926.

Protestantism and Progress: A Historical Study of the Relation of Protestantism to the Modern World, London: Williams & Norgate, 1912.

The Social Teachings of the Christian Churches, 2 vols., London: Allen & Unwin, 1931.

Tuchman, Alan, 'The Yellow Brick Road: Total Quality Management and the Restructuring of Organizational Culture', *Organization Studies*, 15/5 (1994), 727–57.

Turner, Bryan S., *Theories of Modernity and Postmodernity*, London: Sage, 1990.

Turner, Victor, 'Myth and Symbol', in D. Sills (ed.), *International Encyclopaedia of the Social Sciences*, 18 vols., New York: Macmillan, 1968–79, vol. X, pp. 576–82.

'Ritual', in D. Sills (ed.), *International Encyclopaedia of the Social Sciences*, 18 vols., New York, Macmillan, vol. XIII (1968), 520–6.

Turner, Victor, *The Ritual Process*, New York: Aldine, 1969.

Turner, Victor and Edith Turner, Appendix A, 'Notes on Processual Analysis', *Image and Pilgrimage in Christian Culture: Anthropological Perspectives*, New York: Columbia University Press, 1978.

'Introduction: Pilgrimage as Liminoid Phenomenon', *Image and Pilgrimage in Christian Culture: Anthropological Perspectives*, New York: Columbia University Press, 1978.

Van Gennep, Arnold, *The Rites of Passage*, Chicago: University of Chicago Press, 1960.

Vattimo, Gianni, *The End of Modernity: Nihilism and Hermeneutics in Post-modern Culture*, Cambridge: Polity, 1988.

Volf, Miroslav, *Work in the Spirit: Toward a Theology of Work*, Oxford: Oxford University Press, 1991.

Wallace-Hadrill, J. M., *Bede's Europe*, Jarrow: St Paul's Rectory, 1962.

Wallerstein, I., 'Culture as the Ideological Battleground of the Modern World System', in M. Featherstone, *Global Culture: Nationalism, Globalization and Modernity*, London: Sage Publications, 1990, pp. 31–55.

Wallerstein, Immanuel, 'Typology of Crises in the World-system', *Review* of the Fernand Braudel Center, 11 (1988), 581–98.

Walz, Hans Hermann, *Der politische Auftrag des Protestantismus in Europa*, Tübingen: J. C. B. Mohr, 1955.

Ward, G., *Barth, Derrida and the Language of Theology*, Cambridge: Cambridge University Press, 1995.

Ward, Graham, 'Postmodern Theology', in David Ford (ed.), *The Modern Theologians*, Oxford: Blackwell, 1996.

Warnock, Mary, *Universities: Knowing Our Minds. What the Government should do about Higher Education*, London: Chatto & Windus, 1989.

Watt, W. Montgomery, *The Influence of Islam on Medieval Europe*, Edinburgh: Edinburgh University Press, 1972.

Weber, Max, *Economy and Society: An Outline of Interpretative Sociology*, 2 vols., Berkeley, CA: University of California Press, 1979.

The Protestant Ethic and the Spirit of Capitalism, ed. A. Giddens, London: Allen & Unwin, 1977.

'The Protestant Sects and the Spirit of Capitalism', in C. W. Mills and H. H. Gerth (eds.), *From Max Weber: Essays in Sociology*, New York: Oxford University Press, 1946, pp. 302–22.

Weidenfeld, Werner and Wolfgang, Wessels (eds.), *Die Identität Europas*, Bonn: Goldmann, 1981.

Whaling, Frank (ed.), *Contemporary Approaches to the Study of Religion*, 2 vols., Berlin: Mouton, 1984.

White, Hayden, *Metahistory: The Historical Imagination in the Nineteenth Century*, Baltimore: The Johns Hopkins University Press, 1973.

Wiener, M., *English Culture and the Decline of the Industrial Spirit 1850–1980*, Cambridge: Cambridge University Press, 1981.

Willaime, J. P., *Strasbourg, Jean-Paul II et l'Europe*, Paris: Cerf, 1991.

Williams, Rowan, 'Hegel and the Gods of Postmodernity', in Philippa Berry and Andrew Wernick (eds.), *Shadow of Spirit: Postmodernism and Religion*, London: Routledge, 1992, pp. 72–80.

Willigenburg, Theo Van, 'Reflections on Identity and Belonging', in Theo Van Willigenburg, Robert Heeger and Wibren van der Burg (eds.), *Nation, State and the Coexistence of Different Communities*, Kok Pharos: Kampen, 1995, pp. 207–19.

Wolf, Naomi, 'The Feminine Fear of Power', *Fire with Fire: The New Female Power and How it Will Change the 21st Century*, London: Chatto & Windus, 1993.

Wood, John (ed.), *The Virtual Embodied*, London: Routledge, 1998.

Working as One Body: The Report of the Archbishop's Commission on the Organisation of the Church of England, London: Church House Publishing, 1995.

Wright, A. D. (ed.), *The Counter-Reformation: Catholic Europe and the Non-Christian World*, London: Weidenfeld and Nicolson, 1982.

Wrong, H., *Power: Its Forms, Bases and Uses*, Oxford: Blackwell, 1979.

Young of Grafham, Lord, 'Enterprise Regained', speech at The Values of the Enterprise Culture Conference in September 1989 at Lancaster University, in Russell Keat and Nicholas Abercrombie (eds.), *Enterprise Culture*, London: Routledge, 1991, chs. 1 and 2.

 The Enterprise Years: A Businessman in the Cabinet, London: Headline, 1990.

Young, Hugo, *One of Us: A Biography of Margaret Thatcher*, London: Macmillan, 1989.

Young, Lawrence A., *Rational Choice Theory and Religion: Summary and Assessment*, London: Routledge, 1997.

Index